THIRTEEN PLAYS OF BHĀṢA

THIRTEEN PLAYS OF
BHĀSA

Translated into English by

A.C. WOOLNER

LAKSHMAN SARUP

2 Vols. Bound in One

MOTILAL BANARSIDASS PUBLISHERS
PRIVATE LIMITED • DELHI

2nd Reprint : Delhi, 2015
First Edition : 1930
Under Punjab University Oriental Publications, No. 13
First MLBD Reprint : Delhi, 1985

ISBN : 978-81-208-0908-6

MOTILAL BANARSIDASS
41 U.A. Bungalow Road, Jawahar Nagar, Delhi 110 007
8 Mahalaxmi Chamber, 22 Bhulabhai Desai Road, Mumbai 400 026
203 Royapettah High Road, Mylapore, Chennai 600 004
236, 9th Main III Block, Jayanagar, Bengaluru 560 011
8 Camac Street, Kolkata 700 017
Ashok Rajpath, Patna 800 004
Chowk, Varanasi 221 001

Printed in India

by RP Jain at NAB Printing Unit,
A-44, Naraina Industrial Area, Phase I, New Delhi–110028
and published by JP Jain for Motilal Banarsidass Publishers (P) Ltd,
41 U.A. Bungalow Road, Jawahar Nagar, Delhi-110007

PREFACE

THIS Translation is of thirteen Sanskrit plays discovered in South India by the late Paṇḍit Gaṇapati Śāstrī and edited by him in the Trivandrum Sanskrit Series.

Neither in the first MS. found, which contains twelve of the plays and portion of another, nor in other MSS. which contain single plays, is the author's name recorded.

Paṇḍit Gaṇapati Śāstrī attributed all thirteen plays to Bhāsa, a famous dramatist earlier than Kālidāsa. Some verses are ascribed to Bhāsa by medieval anthologies, but only ten with unanimity. We are told that he composed a Svapna-Vāsavadattam (his best play), and that in another play the device of the wooden elephant was used. Characteristic features of his work are described by Bāṇa, and other poets evidently held him in high estimation. One or two verses from his plays are quoted by writers on poetics. Otherwise the text of Bhāsa's numerous plays had completely disappeared.

The learned editor of the Trivandrum plays found that they contained a *Svapna-Vāsavadattam* (the best play in the collection), and, in the *Pratijñā-Yaugandharāyaṇam*, a scene dealing with the wooden elephant. He noticed also certain peculiarities in the technique of the plays which he regarded as signs of antiquity.

All these points confirmed him in the opinion that Bhāsa was the author.

At first this conclusion was generally accepted both in India and in the West.

Later on doubts were expressed. It was found that some of the special features which had been regarded as evidence of an early date (prior to Kālidāsa) were not peculiar to these plays. They occur with some modifications in other South Indian MSS. of plays as late as the seventh century.

The verses ascribed to Bhāsa by the anthologies do not occur in the Trivandrum plays.

Hence the sceptical school doubted whether any of this collection had been written by Bhāsa at all.

This is not the place to discuss the evidence, let alone the arguments, in detail. Nevertheless the question is not without interest even for the general reader. If we place the historical Bhāsa in the second or third century A.D., and if we can accept this collection of plays as the authentic work of Bhāsa, then we have a piece of evidence of great importance for the history of literature and the manner of life it reflects. If, however, these plays are to be regarded as compositions of the seventh century or later their importance is considerably reduced.

Now the problem may be approached along the lines of three hypotheses.

A. That all thirteen plays are the work of one writer, or at least of one period.

B. That they were written by different authors, perhaps at different periods.

C. That older material has been worked over, and to some extent worked up by a later hand.

A. Nearly all that has been written on the subject implies the first hypothesis. This is common to the most ardent supporters of the Bhāsa theory and to those who believe in the latest dates suggested. Dr. Sarup[1] has sought to link up eleven of the thirteen plays by their internal similarities. Now if this hypothesis be reasonable there is one important circumstance to be borne in mind. It can hardly be doubted by any one who has compared the two, line by line and word by word, that the *Daridra-Cārudattam* (incomplete as it is) is earlier than the *Mṛcchakaṭikam.*[2] Hence on this hypothesis all thirteen plays should be older than *The Little Clay Cart.*

Of course we do not know the date of *The Little Clay Cart,* but probably nobody will put it much later than the Gupta period.

[1] Introduction to *The Vision of Vāsavadattā.* The two plays without verbal resemblances are the *Dūtaghaṭotkacam* and the *Karṇabhāram,* both of them short. See also Dr. V. S. Sukthankar, *Studies in Bhāsa: IV. A concordance of the dramas,* Poona, 1923.

[2] Arguments stated by Dr. V. S. Sukthankar, *J.A.O.S.,* 42, p. 59, and by Dr. G. Morgenstierne. *Über das Verhältniss zwischen Cārudatta und Mṛcchakaṭikā,* Leipzig, 1921.

Plays that were older than *The Little Clay Cart* could hardly be contemporary with a farce like the *Matta-Vilāsa* of the seventh century.

B. If, in spite of certain external similarities and internal correspondences, we should assume a diversity of authorship, the claims of each play would have to be considered separately. *The Vision of Vāsavadattā* and *The Minister's Vows* would then have the strongest claims on the evidence.

The various similarities, however, would make it difficult to suppose the plays belonged to very different periods. So the evidence of the *Cārudatta* and *The Little Clay Cart* comes in again.

As a matter of fact few writers have adopted this hypothesis.

C. The third hypothesis is to a certain extent a variant of the first. It is implied in a limited form in what Dr. Sarup suggested about 'different recensions' in his Introduction to *The Vision of Vāsavadattā* (p. 28).

Something of the kind is suggested by Dr. F. W. Thomas in his article on the date of the *Svapna-Vāsavadattam*.[1] As defined above, however, this hypothesis contains the possibility of a much more extensive revision or rewriting than Dr. Sarup, for one, would be ready to admit.

On this hypothesis the problem becomes more complicated. It is no longer a matter of voting pro-Bhāsa or anti-Bhāsa once for all. It becomes a question of distinguishing the true Bhāsa from the pseudo-Bhāsa, not merely play by play, but scene by scene and even verse by verse. Along the lines of this hypothesis, we might explain some of the inconsistency of the Prākrit, mingling apparently old and more modern forms. Again, every reader must feel that some of the scenes are very inferior to the best, that some of the verses are flat and of inferior workmanship. *The Statue Play* has the one striking original scene that gives its name to the play. The later acts,

[1] *J. R. A. S.*, 1928, p. 877 and following. 'Minor changes are indeed probable', p. 899.

especially the sixth and seventh, are conventional and rather feeble. Have they not been added by a later hand?

If we ask why the *Cārudatta* was not completed by the later hand, the answer is that the existence of *The Little Clay Cart* made it unnecessary. Moreover it was customary in South India for an acting company to play incomplete plays or even single scenes, as modern schools and colleges often do. Dr. Sarup has a transcript of a MS. in old Malayalam character containing only one act (the third) of the *Pratijñā-Yaugandharāyaṇam*. If that is an old custom it might account for the preservation of isolated scenes from Bhāsa, which could be padded out or completed at a later date. It remains to see whether any linguistic indications coincide with the more subjective judgements of taste.

The translation has been made without prejudice regarding authenticity. One translator has been more sceptical than the other, but we have done our best for every act. The aim has been to represent all that is in the original (excepting a few repeated or redundant words), but to shake off the burden of the Sanskrit sentence just enough to make the dialogue and recited passages tolerable to the general reader.

No attempt has been made to render verses by verse, which would be apt to jingle, but only to suggest the difference between plain prose and recitative, between more dignified Sanskrit and colloquial or dialectic Prākrit.

'The best in this kind are but shadows.' We shall be content if our shadow be not too wooden to produce a momentary illusion.

A. C. W.
L. S.

LAHORE 1929.

NOTE

A MS. of Sanskrit play usually begins with a benedictory stanza called the Nāndī, followed by the stage direction *Nāndy-ante tataḥ praviśati sūtradhāraḥ* 'On the conclusion of the Nāndī then enters the Stage-manager'.

In these Trivandrum plays, as in a number of others in South India, this stage direction comes first, followed by a benedictory verse, which appears to be exactly what is ordinarily called a Nāndī.

Paṇḍit Gaṇapati Śāstrī argued that in these plays *Nāndī* must have had another meaning. Following him Dr. Sarup, in his translation of *The Vision of Vāsavadattā,* thought it referred to some kind of overture, and rendered it as 'flourish of trumpets'. Another explanation seems more likely. If the opening invocation of prayer was not originally fixed but could be varied on occasion, it would not necessarily be composed by the author, who could thus begin his draft of a play with the stock stage direction. When a special verse peculiar to the play was composed indicating the name of the play and of the characters, this would then be inserted in the play after that stage direction. Such verses might be composed at a later date, when rather tasteless paronomasia was more in fashion. Attached to plays of Plautus we find an acrostic prologue (even two of them) not supposed to be the work of Plautus. If, on the other hand, we regard the special verse as contemporary with the rest, we may regard it as a *Raṅgadvāra,* a benedictory verse composed by the author and recited after the *Nāndī* (*vide* H. R. Divekar, *Timing of Dramatic Representations in India, J.R.A.S.* October 1928, p. 894, and Keith, *Sanskrit Drama,* p. 340).

VOL. I

CONTENTS

PREFACE v

THE MINISTER'S VOWS (प्रतिज्ञायौगन्धरायणम्). 1

THE VISION OF VĀSAVADATTA (स्वप्नवासवदत्तम्) . . . 37

CĀRUDATTA IN POVERTY (दरिद्रचारुदत्तम्) 71

THE FIVE NIGHTS (पञ्चरात्रम्) 103

THE MIDDLE ONE (मध्यमव्यायोगः) 141

THE STATUE PLAY (प्रतिमानाटकम्) 155

VOL. II

THE EMBASSY (दूतवाक्यम्) 1

POTSHERD AS AN ENVOY (दूतघटोत्कचम्) 17

KARṆA'S TASK (कर्णभारम्) 31

THE BROKEN THIGHS (ऊरुभङ्गम्) 41

AVIMĀRAKA (अविमारकम्) 59

THE ADVENTURES OF THE BOY KṚISHṆA (बालचरितम्) 109

THE CONSECRATION (अभिषेकनाटकम्) 143

THE MINISTER'S VOWS

(*Pratijñā-Yaugandharāyaṇam*)

INTRODUCTION

MANY are the stories of Udayana the king of the Vatsas and his adventures in Ujjain. The capital of the Vatsas (also called Vaṃsas) was at Kauśāmbī, the modern Kosam, on the banks of the Jamna near Allahabad.[1]

In Buddha's days their king was called Udayana (Pali Udena). The stories of how he obtained his wives seem to reflect some ups and downs of that little kingdom between the powerful neighbours of Ujjain and Magadha.

Vāsavadattā, the first queen, represents an alliance with Ujjain and Padmāvatī, the second queen an alliance with Magadha. King Udayana, the hero of these tales, is represented as the perfection of chivalry, specially skilled in the management of elephants and of the lute. He captured the heart of Vāsavadattā, the Princess of Ujjain, by teaching her the lute. He carried her off on a stolen elephant. To do all this he must be in Ujjain. The story brings him there as a prisoner of war. But such a perfect hero could never be defeated in the ordinary way. He could only be captured by some trick. The ruse employed was that of the famous artificial elephant made to hold a hundred soldiers. This was made to look like a huge blue elephant and placed in a remote glade of the forest. King Udayana is induced to leave his army to hunt this wonderful elephant. Completely deceived in spite of his elephant lore, he is captured and taken to Ujjain.

Our play begins at a point where Udayana has set out, and his minister, Yaugandharāyaṇa, gets news of the trick which the king of Ujjain intends to use. The minister has sent for a man to take a message of warning to the king. A soldier Haṃsaka arrives and describes in a long dialogue with the minister how the king was captured and taken to Ujjain. The minister, full of remorse at the inadequacy of his precautions, makes a solemn vow that he will outwit the victorious king of Ujjain and restore Udayana to Kauśāmbī. (ACT I.)

Bhāsa's scene of the artificial elephant was criticized by Bhāmaha as incredible. Is this the scene so criticized?

[1] Long disputed, this identification has been finally established by R. B. Daya Ram.

The next act introduces us to a domestic scene in the palace at Ujjain. The old king cannot make up his mind about his daughter's marriage, and speaks of various suitors. 'Why these details?' says the queen. 'Give her to such a one that we may never rue the day.' 'Oh yes', replies the king, 'it is easy for you to say that now, and for me to listen to your reproaches afterwards.' As the king puts the question—'Which seems to thee most worthy?' a chamberlain bursts in with: 'The king of the Vatsas', and relates the capture of Udayana.

Here, as in the queen's mention of her daughter's latest craze to learn the lute, the audience gets hints of what is to come; a frequent feature of these plays.

The account of Udayana's capture and the orders given for his reception redound to his honour. The king begins to waver. (ACT II.)

In the third act the minister, Yaugandharāyaṇa, communicates his plot to his colleague, Rumaṇvān, and the jester of the Vatsa court. They meet in Ujjain disguised. The jester appears as a mendicant prattling about a bowl of sweets. To him come a Madman and then a Buddhist monk. The three forgather in a Fire Shrine, and we learn who they are. The plot is to infuriate a female elephant so that Udayana's assistance might be sought. He will then mount and ride away. Unfortunately the Vatsa king is enamoured of the Ujjain princess, and will never go without her. Yaugandharāyaṇa makes his second vow and swears his king shall take the maid as well. They break up their conference, the madman going out gibbering to the boys in the street. (ACT III.)

In an amusing interlude an intoxicated page, really a Vatsa spy, describes how he pawned the elephant Bhadrāvatī. Then he tells us of the capture of Yaugandharāyaṇa. 'What is this?' asks a soldier. 'All Kauśāmbī is here except the wall and the gatehouse.'

The captive minister converses with a minister of Ujjain. A chamberlain arrives with a present from the king of Ujjain and the news that their Majesties propose to make the best of things and celebrate the marriage by means of painted portraits. (ACT IV.)

Two of the principal characters in the story do not appear at all. We are told so much about the hero, Udayana, the king of the Vatsas, that it is almost with surprise we realize at the end of the play that we have never seen him. We seem to know him by his impulsive actions, his daring, his pride, and his readiness to fall in love, but all his words and whims have been reported by others. The author may well have felt that Udayana should not appear while he was in captivity. Vāsavadattā was still a girl not yet betrothed. We do not see her, but we are continually reminded of her existence and of her importance as a factor in the plot. There were several variant versions of the story, and it is not quite clear what is supposed to have happened between act ii and act iii or between act iii and act iv. Indeed, there seems to be some inconsistency. In act ii the conversation of the king and queen about their daughter seems to lead up to the well-known incident of the music lesson—in which Udayana, introduced behind a curtain as a teacher of the lute, is taunted by his pupil and lifts the curtain.

The queen says Vāsavadattā has gone to a lady-musician for a lesson on the lute. 'Whence this sudden desire for music?' asks the king. 'She saw another girl playing and wishes to learn herself.' 'That is just like a girl', grumbles the king. 'And there is something I was to tell you,' adds the queen; 'she would like a teacher, she says.' To which the king, 'What does she want a teacher for, just when she is about to be married? Her husband will teach her.' The audience must inevitably think of Udayana as the teacher and the husband.

Later on the chamberlain brings in Udayana's famous lute, and the king sends it to Vāsavadattā.

Then hearing of Udayana's wounds his heart softens towards his enemy. He orders that the captive is to be treated with every consideration. There should be no tactless talk.

Learning that he had been carried into the Middle Palace and placed near the peacocks' perches, he is dissatisfied, and commands that the wounded man be taken into the *maṇibhūmikā* to shield him from the sun.

By the end of the act he begins to feel some affection for his defeated adversary, whom we in the audience all know to be his future son-in-law.

Now in act iii a very different incident is used to introduce Vāsavadattā to Udayana, and we learn that the Vatsa king is in prison. 'His fetters clank as he bows before the gods' (iii. 4). But he still has (or has recovered) his lute. 'So by the very consent of his enemy he can come out of prison, grasping the lute, which shares his sorrows, and subdue the elephant.' Then we are told that the Princess Vāsavadattā went in an open palanquin to worship at a shrine opposite the prison gate. Udayana happened to be taking the air outside the prison gate with the permission of the superintendent. 'Then the palanquin was halted for the men to change shoulders, and he saw the princess as clearly as you like.' And then the prison was turned into a garden of delight and he was ready to play a comedy of passion.

'But surely', objects the minister, 'the king cannot have fallen in love with her?' 'Troubles, sir, comes in shoals', replies the jester, 'That is exactly what he has done.'

The music lesson is referred to in *The Vision of Vāsavadattā* in which Udayana speaks of his pupil. When did it take place? We can hardly place it before act iii, and suppose that the jester and the ministers knew nothing about it. Indeed, the usual account is that Yaugandharāyaṇa arranged it. We must suppose, then, that the music lessons were arranged between act iii and act iv. This would fit in as the means of carrying out the minister's second vow to carry off 'both the king and the long-eyed maid'. (III. 9.)

This involves postponing the departure of Udayana, which had been arranged for the following day. Also it involves a modification of the usual account of the music lesson as the occasion of the first meeting of the lovers.

Is it possible that act ii is by a different hand? The first act, or something like the first act, we know was written by Bhāsa as the main idea of it, and some details have been criticized. The third act is vigorous and original. Every one enjoys the Interlude, with the intoxicated page who pawned the elephant, and here we find the old verse common to the Arthaśāstra. The rest of the fourth act merely glorifies Yaugandharāyaṇa, and tells us that the king and queen have determined to celebrate the marriage between the Vatsa king and Vāsavadattā by means of painted portraits. (The painted portraits reoccur at the end of *The Vision of Vāsavadattā*.) For the stage act iv is slow with no dramatic movement or situation. It alludes to the music lesson (iv. 18) and to Mahāsena's kindness.

At the same time it must be admitted that the Court Scene is clever, and if it be by a second hand, that second hand was skilful, and reminds us of the delicate handling of several scenes in *The Vision of Vāsavadattā*.

Note. Dr. Sarup will not admit any inconsistency. He thinks acts iii and iv form a harmonious whole with act ii and give a logical development of the course of events in continuation of act ii. He admits that the playwright's version of the lover's first meeting differs from that of other writers, but no other version is given in this play. He thinks the music lesson came later, the famous lute having been restored to Udayana in the meantime, or at any rate in time to charm the elephant. The reversal of the sympathetic treatment of the captive king he would ascribe to the influence of the minister, Bharatarohaka.

Some inconsistency, of course, would not be necessarily fatal to authenticity.

DRAMATIS PERSONAE

(In order of appearance.)

Stage-manager, Actress — Only in the Prologue to introduce the play. The name of the Sūtra-dhāra 'holder of the strings' is derived from some form of puppet play.

In Kauśāmbī:

YAUGANDHARĀYAṆA, the principal minister of Udayana the Vatsa king.
Sālaka, the intended messenger not required.
Vijayā = Portress, stock name of a female doorkeeper.
Nirmuṇḍaka, 'Shaveling', servant in the minister's household.
Haṃsaka, 'Gosling' a soldier of Udayana's escort, returned.
Brahman.

In Ujjain:

Chamberlain of the Avantī Court. (Bādarāyaṇa.)
KING OF UJJAIN, Pradyota or Mahāsena.
Queen of Ujjain (Aṅgāravatī).
Jester (Vasantaka) of Kauśāmbī, disguised as a beggar.
Madman = Yaugandharāyaṇa in disguise.
Buddhist Monk = Rumaṇvān the other Vatsa minister.
Two soldiers (or servants).
Page (a Vatsa spy) who feigns intoxication.
Two servants.
Bharatarohaka, minister of Ujjain.

N.B. Two principals, Udayana, king of the Vatsas, and Vāsavadattā, princess of Ujjain, do not appear at all.

PROLOGUE

[*At the end of the Opening* [1] *enter the Stage-Manager.*]

Stage-Manager. May the son of Yugandhara [2] protect you, he that is styled the infant King, lord of a mighty host, of exceeding great vigour who, allied with his own energy, gave victory to Indra.[3] (1)

[*Walks about, looking towards the back of the stage.*]

Come here, good lady.

[*Enter an Actress.*]

Actress. Here I am, sir.

Manager. Come now, sing us something. After that, when the audience has been put into a good humour by your song, we will begin the performance. Why, good lady, what is this hesitation? Are not you going to sing?

Actress. I have had a dream, sir, this very day, that all is not well with my relatives, so I wish your honour would send a man to find out how my people are.

Manager. Very well,

A man will I send palpably fit for the purpose.

[*Voice behind the scene.*]

Sālaka, are you ready?

Manager. Just as Yaugandharāyaṇa
here is sending out his man. (2)

[*Exeunt ambo.*]

ACT I

[*The scene is in the Vatsa Palace at Kauśāmbī.*]

[*Enter Yaugandharāyaṇa with Sālaka.*]

Yaugandharāyaṇa. Sālaka, are you ready?

Sālaka. Quite ready, sir.

Yaugandharāyaṇa. You have a very long way to go.

Sālaka. The devotion with which I serve your honour will go still further.

Nāndī, see note, p. ix.

Skanda son of Śiva.

By paronomasia the verse introduces the names of Vāsavadattā, Mahāsena, Yaugandharāyana, and the King of the Vatsas.

Yaugandharāyaṇa. Ha! A strong man or a devoted man will go far. For,

A difficult task should be entrusted to devoted agents, or to a connoisseur of qualities held in esteem.
Whosesoever be the plan by which efficiency is purchased, success or failure depends on the dictates of fate. (3)

To-morrow the king is to leave the Bamboo Forest and pass through three of the densest woods to the Elephant Forest, and you must wait on him before he starts.

Sālaka. I suppose, sir, I shall be sent with a letter containing the gist of the business.

Yaugandharāyaṇa. Vijayā.[1]

[*Enter Vijayā.*]

Vijayā. Here I am, sir.

Yaugandharāyaṇa. Vijayā, hurry up that letter and the ribbon.[2]

Vijayā. Yes, sir. [*Exit.*]

Yaugandharāyaṇa. Have you ever been that way before?

Sālaka. No, but I have heard about it.

Yaugandharāyaṇa. That, too, is a sign of an intelligent man. Well, a report has reached us, that Pradyota means to hoodwink our king by setting up a blue elephant and masking its body with forest elephants. I only hope our master's judgement has not already been led astray. But oh, how fearful Pradyota must be of the king of the Vatsas! The inefficiency of his vast army is manifest. For,

A huge force he clearly has, but lacking in unity of action, a number of brave warriors there are therein, but no devotion.
So in the hour of battle he prefers to resort to a trick. For every army without devotion is no better than a wife that lacks the same.[3] (4)

[*Enter Vijayā.*]

Vijayā. Here is the letter. The queen-mother says the ribbon is being prepared quickly by all the married ladies.

Yaugandharāyaṇa. Vijayā, my compliments to her Majesty, and

[1] *Ovajjhai.* Comm. in sense of '*apavahati*' (= **ava-vahyati*) 'dispatches'; or *v. l. obajjhai* in sense of '*apabadhnāti*' (= **ava-badhyati*) 'restrains', so 'I am only waiting for the letter'.

[2] *Pratisarā.* 'Cord or ribbon worn as an amulet' M. W. It was prepared by ladies in the queen's suite. Its purpose is not clear. Was it to serve as a passport? Or as a protection against demons? It could hardly be the fastening of the letter, i. e. the strings on which the seal was stamped? Gaṇapati Śastrī quotes Keśava for the sense of a protective thread worn on the arm. Sukthankar agrees. It is still a custom to tie something as a charm on the arm of one departing on a journey.

[3] L. S. 'is as weak as a woman'.

would she let me have the ribbon whether it is prepared by all the married ladies, or is only a single one.

Vijayā. Very well, sir. [*Exit.*]

[*Enter Nirmuṇḍaka.*]

Nirmuṇḍaka. Your honour's health.

Yaugandharāyaṇa. How now, Nirmuṇḍaka?

Nirmuṇḍaka. Your honour, Haṃsaka is here, he has come from his Majesty.

Yaugandharāyaṇa. What, Haṃsaka, come alone? Sālaka, you can take a moment's rest. Either you will have to go doubly quick or else take your ease.

Sālaka. Very well, sir. [*Exit.*]

Yaugandharāyaṇa. Nirmuṇḍaka, bring in Haṃsaka.

Nirmuṇḍaka. Very good, sir. [*Exit.*]

Yaugandharāyaṇa. That Haṃsaka, who has never before left the king's side, should have come here alone fills me with apprehension. For,

Like a man who comes home from abroad, after leaving his kinsfolk in trouble, my mind is now on tenter-hooks. Shall I hear good news or bad? (5)

[*Enter Haṃsaka and Nirmuṇḍaka.*]

Nirmuṇḍaka. Come in, sir.

Haṃsaka. Where is his honour?

Nirmuṇḍaka. That's him standing there. Go up to him.

Haṃsaka. [*Approaching.*] Your honour's health.

Yaugandharāyaṇa. Haṃsaka, do not say the king has gone to the Elephant Forest.

Haṃsaka. Why, sir, the king went there yesterday.

Yaugandharāyaṇa. Alack! It's useless sending. We have been deceived. But is there any hope?[1] Or must our life end this very day?

Haṃsaka. The king still lives at least.

Yaugandharāyaṇa. 'Still lives'—that indicates a lesser calamity. My master must have been taken prisoner.

Haṃsaka. Yes, your honour's guessed right. The king's been taken.

Yaugandharāyaṇa. What, my royal master taken prisoner? Alas! alas! a mighty task has been accomplished by the good fortune of Pradyota. From this day on there is clear proof of the incapacity and disgrace of the ministers of the Vatsa king. Where is Rumaṇvān now, so wise in dealing with events before they happen? What has become of the cavalry? For,

This devoted cavalry recruited from good families, captivated

[1] L. S. 'countermeasure' *pratyāśā*.

by the friendship of the king—every trooper fit with exercise and versed in tactics—was it bought by the foe? or lost in a trackless jungle? Or was it all overwhelmed and destroyed in battle? (6)

Haṃsaka. If the king had been accompanied by the whole of his escort, this misfortune would not have happened.

Yaugandharāyaṇa. What! my master was not accompanied by the whole of his escort?

Haṃsaka. Hearken, your honour.

Yaugandharāyaṇa. You are tired with your journey. Sit down.

Haṃsaka. Very good, sir. [*Sits down.*] Hearken, your honour. One night just before dawn, a pleasant time for riding, the king crossed the River Narmadā by the sandy ford, and, leaving the ladies encamped in the Bamboo Forest, he set out for the Elephant Forest by a path fit for wild animals [1] with nothing but an umbrella and a force just sufficient to cope with a herd of elephants.

Yaugandharāyaṇa. Yes, and then?

Haṃsaka. When the sun had risen the space of an arrow-shot and we had gone so many leagues and were still a league away from the Madagandhīra Mountain, we sighted our herd of elephants, throwing up mud from a pond as uneven in appearance as stone-work half finished.[2]

Yaugandharāyaṇa. And what then?

Haṃsaka. While the troops were reconnoitring and the herd getting suspicious had formed up in a mass, a certain foot soldier, the author of all this trouble, came up to the king.

Yaugandharāyaṇa. Stay. Did he not say he had seen about a league from the place an elephant that was blue all over, except the nails and tusks, with its body covered by jasmine creepers and *sāl* trees?

Haṃsaka. What, your honour knew about that? Then the mischief has happened while we were awake.

Yaugandharāyaṇa. Ah, Haṃsaka, a man may be awake, but fate is stronger. Go on.

Haṃsaka. Then the king honoured the cruel fellow with a gift of a hundred gold pieces and said: 'It must be that sovereign elephant called Blue Lotus that I have read of in a treatise on elephants. Do you

[1] Reading *magga-maddaṇīe* for *magga-madaaṇīe*?

[2] The rounded slatey backs of the elephants splashed with wet mud resemble a wall of dark grey boulders being built. But L. S. following comm. prefers 'of terrifying appearance as if incompletely marked with red arsenic', i.e. taking *śilā* in the sense of *śilā-dhātu* and *nirmita* in the sense of *racita*.

attend carefully to this herd, while I go with my lute and bring in that other tusker.'

Yaugandharāyaṇa. What, then, was Rumaṇvān doing to neglect his master at that moment?

Haṃsaka. No, no! With all courtesy the minister tried to dissuade the king. 'Quite possibly you might capture even the elephants of the quarters, Airāvaṇa and the rest. But frontier districts being difficult to protect are always troublesome. People living on the frontier are shameless and devoid of good breeding. So let us leave this herd to the infantry only and all of us go together. Your Highness should not go alone.'

Yaugandharāyaṇa. Did Rumaṇvān say this to the king before the army? I wish I too could show such unspeakable devotion to my master. What happened then?

Haṃsaka. Then the king silenced the minister with an oath touching his life, got down from the elephant 'Dark Cloud' and mounted his horse Sundarapāṭala. Then the sun being less than half-way in its course, with only twenty soldiers, away he rode.

Yaugandharāyaṇa. To victory! Alack, in my zeal I am forgetting your previous story. Well, proceed.

Haṃsaka. Then after we had gone about double the distance, we sighted at a hundred bow-lengths that counterfeit of a divine elephant. Its blue colour was lost in the shadows of the *sāl* trees of the same hue, but it was revealed by the bright pair of tusks sticking out as it were from nothing.

Yaugandharāyaṇa. Say rather, Haṃsaka, it was our misery that you sighted. Well, go on.

Haṃsaka. Then the king dismounted from his horse and drew near with a salute to the deities and with his lute in his hand. Then there arose behind us a mighty uproar that seemed to be concerted with one purpose.

Yaugandharāyaṇa. An uproar, you say? Go on.

Haṃsaka. When we faced about to ascertain the cause of the uproar, that artificial elephant manned by warriors instead of elephant-men advanced towards us.[1]

Yaugandharāyaṇa. And then?

Haṃsaka. Then the king heartened the young noblemen, calling them by name and their family names. 'This is just one of Pradyota's tricks', says he.—'Follow me', he says; 'with valour will I now counter the enemy's move for all his unfair start', and with these words he rushed on the foe.

[1] *Mahāmātra-uttarāyudhīya-adhiṣṭhita.*

Yaugandharāyaṇa. Rushed on the foe? Nay, but he was right.

A high-minded hero relying on his courage, mortified at being deceived, and set in a narrow strait—what else could he do? (7)

Proceed.

Haṃsaka. Playing as it were with his horse Sundarapāṭala, who obeyed his slightest wish, he struck with even greater fury than he had intended, exerting himself to the utmost because the enemy was so much more numerous. Then when all his following was dead or wounded, with only myself to protect—no, no, to be protected by him, wearied with fighting the livelong day, fallen from his horse on account of buffets innumerable, at the dread hour of the darkening sun, the king swooned away.

Yaugandharāyaṇa. The king swooned away? What then?

Haṃsaka. Then to the best of their power they outraged the king, binding his person like a common fellow's with rough creepers, torn out recklessly from the nearest thicket.

Yaugandharāyaṇa. What, outraged the king?

Bonds were fixed on his arms in place of bracelets. Huge in the shoulder, those two arms with their expanding sinews are as thick as elephants trunks, while the hands thereof make the bow vibrate, endlessly fixing on arrows carried afar,[1] arms that are busy in homage to brahmans, arms that honour his friends with their embraces. (8)

At what time did the king recover consciousness?

Haṃsaka. Why, your honour, when the wretches had done with their insults.

Yaugandharāyaṇa. Thank heaven, though they assaulted his person they could not mar his glory. And then?

Haṃsaka. When they saw the king had come to, those wretches ran off in all directions, describing the valour of our royal master by crying 'He has slain my brother, he has slain my father, . . . and my son, and my mate —' and so forth.[2]

Yaugandharāyaṇa. What happened then?

Haṃsaka. Another strange thing. After urging one another on, one of them resolved to do a dreadful deed. Brutally he grasped the king's locks, dishevelled in the press of battle, and dragged his face to the south, then gripping the sword in his hand he took a run to give force to his onset and—

[1] ? *dūra-bharaṇāt.*

[2] This is mentioned by Bhāmaha.

Yaugandharāyaṇa. Stay a moment, Haṃsaka, that I may get my breath.

Haṃsaka. And at the pace he was going the brute stumbled where the ground was slippery with pools of blood, and fell down helpless, baulked of his fell design.

Yaugandharāyaṇa. Down he fell, the wretch. Yes,

When the Earth is not harried by foemen's chariots and is free from confusion of castes, herself protected she guards her lord in distress. **(9)**

Haṃsaka. Then there appeared on the scene one of Pradyota's ministers called Śālaṅkāyana, whom the king had stunned with a blow of his spear. He gave the order for no violence.

Yaugandharāyaṇa. Well?

Haṃsaka. Then he saluted the king, a rare courtesy at such a time, and had him freed of his fetters.

Yaugandharāyaṇa. My master released! Well done, Śālaṅkāyana! Distress can change even an enemy into a friend. Hamsaka, I feel somewhat relieved. And what did this excellent person do next?

Haṃsaka. The king was too badly wounded to ride, so this gentleman had him put in a litter, with many courteous expressions of sympathy, and took him to Ujjain.

Yaugandharāyaṇa. My master taken away!

This is the very disgrace we feared, this surpasses Pradyota's expectation. His very pride involves our king in misery. **(10)**

How shall the king look at him, whom erstwhile he ignored? Perfect in speech, how shall he listen to cowardly taunts? How shall he restrain his wrath made impotent by capture? A prisoner is humiliated be he well treated or insulted. **(11)**

[*Enter Portress.*]

Portress. Sir, here is the ribbon.

Yaugandharāyaṇa. These things are brought at a time when the destruction of our good fortune makes them useless, like the auspicious lustration of a charger, when the war is over. **(12)**

Portress. Here is the ribbon, sir.

Yaugandharāyaṇa. Put it away, Vijayā.

Portress. What am I to say to the queen-mother?

Yaugandharāyaṇa. Yes, Vijayā, there 's that.

Portress. What 's that?

Yaugandharāyaṇa. This.

Portress. Speak, sir, do speak out.

Yaugandharāyaṇa. Well, it cannot be suppressed. I shall inform her Majesty. Vijayā, steel your heart. [*Whispers.*] It 's like this . . .

Portress. Ah!

Yaugandharāyaṇa. Vijayā, your name forbids weakness.

Portress. So, I will go, unhappy.

Yaugandharāyaṇa. Do not tell her Majesty all at once, Vijayā, that the king has been taken prisoner. One must guard a mother's heart, so tender with affection.

Portress. How am I to tell her, then?

Yaugandharāyaṇa. Listen.

First discourse on the evils of war, suggesting dangers. When the meaning is doubtful, death suspected and grief at its height, then report the actual facts. (13)

Portress. I will manage it. [*Exit.*]

Yaugandharāyaṇa. Haṃsaka, why didn't you go with the king?

Haṃsaka. Sir, I was set on doing myself that honour, but I was charged by Śālaṅkāyana to go to Kauśāmbī and report the news.

Yaugandharāyaṇa. What was his intention, to reduce us to despair? Or is he ridding himself of the attendance of a devoted servant?

Haṃsaka. Very likely.

Yaugandharāyaṇa. By his arrogance he stands revealed, and in the success of all his undertakings he can rejoice. But did the king say nothing about me?

Haṃsaka. He did, your honour. As I took respectful farewell of the king, half-blind with unshed tears, seeming as if he had much to communicate, he said to me, 'Go and see Yaugandharāyaṇa.'

Yaugandharāyaṇa. Speak out freely, these are the words of the king.

Haṃsaka. 'Go and see Yaugandharāyaṇa.'

Yaugandharāyaṇa. Nay now, did he say nothing of all the ministers of the council, and only mention me?

Haṃsaka. That is so.

Yaugandharāyaṇa. If he sends you to me alone, it is because my precautions were inadequate, because I have not earned his salt, because I have made no return for the dignity bestowed upon me.

Haṃsaka. Very likely.

Yaugandharāyaṇa. The king shall see me another man.

Be it in the enemy's capital, in bondage or in the forest, be it in the next world, if destruction come upon him, he shall find me equally devoted.

I shall outwit that king who thinks himself the victor, and my lord, restored to his kingdom, shall praise the faithful servant at his side. **(14)**

[*Behind the Scene.*]

Woe, woe, the master taken.

Yaugandharāyaṇa. There are the women wailing to ease their grief as best they may, thereby proclaiming the incapacity of the ministers. **(15)**

[*Enter Portress.*]

Portress. The queen-mother, sir,—

Yaugandharāyaṇa. Yes ?

Portress. Says—

Yaugandharāyaṇa. What ?

Portress. 'To such a gallant king of the Vatsas, surrounded by his friends, this thing has happened. What can be done in the face of Fate ? So we must honour his friends and take heart. Now there is one man who is too wise to be despondent in difficulties, or lose heart before obstacles, who does not despair when he has been tricked, or abandon his life when he fails. That man I request, first as the friend of my Vatsa, and secondly as his minister, like another son, to restore my son to me.

Yaugandharāyaṇa. Ah, those are brave words from her Majesty, characteristic of the royal house. I reverence her for her esteem. Vijayā, some water.

Portress. Yes, sir. [*Exit and re-enters.*]
Here is water.

Yugandharāyaṇa. Give it me. [*Sips.*] Vijayā, what did her Majesty say ?

Portress. 'My son, restore my son to me.'

Yaugandharāyaṇa. What did the king say, Haṃsaka ?

Haṃsaka. 'Go and see Yaugandharāyaṇa.'

Yaugandharāyaṇa. Vijayā,

If I do not liberate the king, seized by the enemy's force, like the moon by Rāhu, my name is not Yaugandharāyaṇa. **(16)** [1]

Portress. So be it, your honour. [*Exit.*]

[*Enter Nirmuṇḍaka.*]

Nirmuṇḍaka. A strange thing, sir. A number of brahmans were bidden to a feast for the good of the king. Another brahman, dressed as a madman, saw them there and laughed aloud, saying: 'Eat freely, reverend gentlemen, eat to your hearts' content. Prosperity is

[1] This is the minister's first vow.

coming to this royal house.' And then right on the words he vanished.

Yaugandharāyaṇa. Is this true?

[*Enter a Brahman.*]

Brahman. These are the peculiar clothes that reverend brahman wore and left behind for some purpose of his own. It was the Blessed Dvaipāyana that came disguised in these clothes.

Yaugandharāyaṇa. So Dvaipāyana came here.

Brahman. Yes.

Yaugandharāyaṇa. Let us see those clothes.

Brahman. Here they are, sir.

Yaugandharāyaṇa. Why, now, I am transformed. Look you, sir, I feel as if I had reached the king's presence. These clothes have been left for my instruction.

This madman's guise, donned by the holy man, will cover me
and liberate the king. (17)

[*Enter Portress.*]

Portress. Your honour, the queen-mother says she wishes to see her son.

Yaugandharāyaṇa. At once, I come. Good sir, wait for me in the chapel.[1]

Brahman. Very well. [*Exit.*]

Yaugandharāyaṇa. Haṃsaka, now you may rest yourself.

Haṃsaka. Very well, sir. [*Exit.*]

Yaugandharāyaṇa. Lead the way, Vijayā.

Portress. As your honour wishes.

Yaugandharāyaṇa. Fire springs from wood which is rotated: the earth when dug yields water. Nothing is impossible for men of daring. All efforts starting on the right road come to fruition. (18)

[*Exeunt omnes.*]

END OF THE FIRST ACT.

[1] *Śāntigṛha.* A small room for the performance of propitiatory rites.

ACT II

INTERLUDE

[*The scene is in Ujjain, the capital of Avanti.*]

[*Enter the Chamberlain.*]

Chamberlain. Ābhīraka! Go, Ābhīraka, and take this message from Mahāsena to the keeper of the gate. 'The noble Jaivanti, preceptor of the king of Benares, has arrived to-day on an embassy. Let him be lodged in comfort without regard to the ordinary treatment of an envoy. Every effort must be made that he may enjoy the hospitality due to a guest.' Ah, so it goes on from day to day. Embassies are sent by royal houses of suitable rank to sue for the hand of the Princess, but Mahāsena refuses nobody and favours none. Now why is that? Surely it is Fate that is controlling the princess's marriage. For

It is manifest that our Monarch awaits an envoy from that king whose destined bride she is. Until that envoy comes, he knows, but disregards the qualities of other kings. (1)

Ah! the cowering of the attendants in this place shows the master is at hand. So here comes Mahāsena.

His sturdy arms are studded with sapphires, glistening like blades of *dūrvā* grass, and encircled with golden armlets; and he issues from this forest glade of golden palms like the God of War from a thicket of reeds.[1] (2)

[*Exit.*]

END OF THE INTERLUDE.

[*Enter the King of Ujjain with his retinue.*]

King. Kings reduced to servitude carry on their coronets the dust from my charger's hooves. Yet am I not content while the virtuous Vatsa king bows not his head, proud as he is of his elephant lore. (3)

Bādarāyaṇa!

[*Enter the Chamberlain.*]

Chamberlain. Greeting.

King. Is Jaivanti lodged?

Chamberlain. Yes, lodged and suitably entertained.

[1] Kārtikeya the God of War was said to have sprung from a thicket of reeds.

King. You have done well. Your zeal is ever for the glory of the royal house. An honourable reception is ordained for all arrivals. But every one I question about the marriage of the princess conceals his own opinion. [*Looking at the Chamberlain.*] I think you wish to speak, Bādarāyaṇa.

Chamberlain. It is nothing. An idea struck me about the marriage.

King. Come now, no concealment. This business concerns everybody. Speak out.

Chamberlain. Mahāsena, this is what I would say:

From day to day envoys are sent by royal houses of the proper rank to sue for the Princess' hand; but your Highness refuses nobody and favours none. Now why is that?

King. Bādarāyaṇa, this is how it is. I am so eager for the best qualities in the bridegroom, and so fond of Vāsavadattā, that I cannot make up my mind.

> For first of all I have set my mind on his coming from a noble house, and then he must have a tender heart, for this quality, though gentle, is powerful.
> Thirdly he must have beauty, no virtue indeed, but women dread its absence. Lastly he must be fierce and strong to protect his youthful bride. (4)

Chamberlain. All these virtues are not found in these days combined in one man, except in Mahāsena.

King. That is what makes me hesitate.

> To find a good mate for his girl, needs a father's greatest care.
> The rest depends on Fate. Contrariwise I have never seen it go. (5)

But the mothers always grieve when a daughter is given in marriage. So ask the queen to come here.

Chamberlain. As your Highness commands. [*Exit.*]

King. Ha! This embassy from the King of Benares reminds me of Śālaṅkāyana, who went to capture the Vatsa king. Another day and no news from the good brahman.

> Though our plan was based on his favourite sport, all his ministers are there to exert their zeal. (6)

[*Enter the Queen with her retinue.*]

Queen. Mahāsena, greeting.

King. Pray be seated.

Queen. As my lord commands. [*Sits down.*]

King. Where is Vāsavadattā?

Queen. She has gone to Uttarā, a lady-musician, for a lesson on the Nārada lute.

King. Whence this sudden desire for music?

Queen. She happened to see Kāñcanamālā playing on a lute and wished to learn herself.

King. That is just like a girl.

Queen. And there is something I was to tell you.

King. What is it?

Queen. She would like a teacher, she says.

King. What does she want a teacher for, just when she is about to be married? Her husband will teach her.

Queen. Oh! Has the time really come for my little girl to go?

King. Come now. You were always pestering me with, 'It must be arranged, it must be arranged.' So why are you distressed?

Queen. I am anxious for her betrothal. It is parting from her that pains me. But to whom is she betrothed?

King. We have not yet decided.

Queen. Not even yet?

King. A maid unwed is a source of shame, and when betrothed, of an anxious mind. Twixt love and duty mothers are in a sorry plight. (7)

Vāsavadattā is certainly of an age to attend her father-in-law. And to-day there has come another envoy, the noble Jaivanti, preceptor to the king of Benares. I am attracted by his reputation. [*Aside.*] She says not a word. But she is agitated and her eyes are filled with tears. How can she come to any conclusion? Well, I must tell her about it. [*Aloud.*] As suitors for alliance with us there are the kings . . .

Queen. Why these details? Give her to such a one that we may never rue the day.

King. Oh yes, it is easy for you to say that now, and for me to listen to your reproaches afterwards. This is a difficult matter, so do make your own choice, my queen. Listen,

Our ally of Magadha, Benares' king, the lords of Vaṅga, Surāshṭra, Mithilā, and Śūrasena, all of these attract me by their various qualities. Which seems to thee most worthy? (8)

[*Enter Chamberlain.*]

Chamberlain. The king of the Vatsas.

King. What is this, the king of the Vatsas?

Chamberlain. Pardon, Your Highness, pardon. In my haste to give you good tidings I forgot the proper procedure.

King. Good tidings, you say?

Queen. [*Rising.*] Long live the king.

King. [*Joyfully.*] Why would you miss the good news? Pray be seated.

Queen. As my lord commands. [*Sits down.*]

King. Rise and speak freely.

Chamberlain. [*Rising.*] The honourable minister Śālaṅkāyana has captured the king of the Vatsas.

King. [*Delighted.*] What did you say?

Chamberlain. [*Repeats.*] The honourable minister Śālaṅkāyana has captured the king of the Vatsas.

King. Udayana?

Chamberlain. Yes.

King. The son of Śatānīka?

Chamberlain. Certainly.

King. The grandson of Sahasrānīka?

Chamberlain. The same.

King. The lord of Kauśāmbī?

Chamberlain. Of course.

King. The expert musician?

Chamberlain. So they say.

King. Actually the Vatsa king?

Chamberlain. Why yes, the Vatsa king.

King. Then is Yaugandharāyaṇa dead?

Chamberlain. Not he, he is in Kauśāmbī.

King. Is he? Then I don't believe the Vatsa king is taken.

Chamberlain. Oh yes, believe me, your Highness.

King. Your tale of Udayana's capture passes my belief. As well say you lifted the Mandara mountain in the palm of your hand. His enemies recount his heroism in battles and Yaugandharāyaṇa's strategy resounds in our ears. (9)

Chamberlain. Pardon me, your Highness. I am an old brahman. I have never told your Highness a lie.

King. That is so. Who is this welcome messenger Śālaṅkāyana has sent?

Chamberlain. No messenger. The minister has come himself in the fastest chariot, with the Vatsa king before him.

King. Come himself? What joy! To-day let the army lay armour aside and rest in comfort. From to-day on princes will have no fear, and no need of secret espionage. The sum of it is—to-day I am myself.

Queen. The minister brought him here?

King. Yes.

Queen. Then we shall not affiance Vāsavadattā to any one at present.

King. This man is my enemy vanquished in battle. Bādarāyaṇa, where is Śālaṅkāyana?

Chamberlain. He is waiting at the Happy Gate.

King. Go and tell Bharatarohaka to receive the minister with the honours due to a prince and bring him in with the Vatsa king.

Chamberlain. As Your Highness commands.

King. Stay a moment.

Chamberlain. I am here.

King. None should be denied a sight of the Vatsa king.

My people have heard of his deeds, now let them see mine
enemy all fury within, like a lion captured for a sacrifice. (10)

Chamberlain. As your Highness commands.

Queen. We have known many occasions of rejoicing in this royal house, but I do not remember ever to have seen my lord so delighted.

King. Nor do I remember ever hearing such delightful news as the capture of the Vatsa king.

Queen. It really is the king of the Vatsas?

King. Why, of course!

Queen. I have heard of many royal houses sending to seek an alliance with us. This prince sent nobody.

King. My queen, he ignores my very name, not to speak of desiring an alliance by marriage.

Queen. Ignores? Is he a boy or a fool?

King. He may be a boy, he is no fool.

Queen. What makes him so haughty?

King. The Bharata dynasty, with its long roll of famous Royal Sages and its tradition of deep learning. He is proud of his hereditary knowledge of music. His youthful beauty makes him vain. His people's remarkable attachment makes him confident.

Queen. The very qualities one would desire in a son-in-law. By what perversity has his disability arisen?

King. My queen, would you lend your admiration to an unworthy object? Look you,

Like a fire started in a forest and burning the whole world
put together, the flames of my authority are quenched at this
man's boundary. (11)

[*Enter Chamberlain.*]

Chamberlain. Your Highness, greeting. Śālaṅkāyana has been honourably received as commanded. He has requested me to present to your

Highness this jewel of a lute, called Ghoshavatī. It used to be played by the Bharatas in the Vatsa Rāja's family. [*Shows the lute.*]

King. I accept it as an auspicious trophy of victory. [*Takes the lute.*] So this is the famous Ghoshavatī.

> Melodious to the ear with a natural harmony when the strings are pressed by finger-tips and set vibrating with a finger-nail, this lute perforce will tame the hearts of elephants like the magic art in the incantation of a sage. (12)

Ah! what joy it brings to use as one wills the treasures won in battle.

> My eldest son Gopālaka pursues the charms of polity, and Pālaka the younger shines in manly exercise, music he detests. (13)

So where would this lute be well-bestowed? Did you say, my queen, that Vāsavadattā had taken to the lute?

Queen. Yes.

King. Then give her this one.

Queen. If you give her a lute she will be wilder than ever for it.

King. Let her enjoy herself. It will be hard enough in her father-in-law's house. Bādarāyaṇa, where is the princess?

Chamberlain. She is with the minister.

King. And the ruler of the Vatsas?

Chamberlain. He was so tractable and had so many wounds on his feet and body, that he was carried into the Middle Palace on a litter.

King. I am sorry he has so many wounds. That is the fault of his undaunted valour. In these circumstances it would be too cruel to neglect him. Bādarāyaṇa, go and tell Bharatarohaka to attend to his wounds.

Chamberlain. As your Highness commands.

King. Nay, stay a moment.

Chamberlain. I wait.

King. Every significant gesture should be met with constant attention. His wishes should be inferred from his expression. There should be no talk about defeats or war, but a blessing uttered if he sneezes or anything like that. Compliments should be tactful.

Chamberlain. As your Highness commands.

[*Exit and re-enters.*]

Greeting, your Highness. The Vatsa king had his wounds dressed on the way. It is too soon, they say, for a second dressing. The noon-day sun is at its height.

King. Where is the proud warrior?

Chamberlain. Near the peacocks' perches.

King. Oh, fie! That's no place to shelter in. Bid them take him in to the inlaid room [1] to shield him from the sun.

Chamberlain. As your Highness commands. [*Exit and re-enters.*] Your Highness' commands have been carried out. The minister Bharatarokaha desires an interview.

King. Evidently he does not approve of kindness to the Vatsa king. It goes against his policy. I must talk him round.

Queen. Is the marriage settled?

King. No, not quite decided.

Queen. There is no hurry. My little girl is still a child.

King. As you please, Madam. You may withdraw now.

Queen. As my lord commands. [*Exit with retinue.*]

King. [*Thoughtfully.*] At first his arrogance made me his foe, and when he was brought in here I was barely neutral. But now that I hear of his exhaustion in battle, his sorry plight, his life in danger, I feel—nay, I know not what I feel. **(14)**

[*Exeunt ambo.*]

END OF THE SECOND ACT.

ACT III

[*In Ujjain. Secret meeting of the Jester and the two Ministers of Udayana in disguise.*]

[*Enter the Jester disguised as a beggar.*]

Jester. [*Gesticulating.*] Well now! I put my bowl of sweetmeats on the temple steps, then I counted the gold pieces of my donations and tied them up. Now I turn round and I can't see the bowl of sweets. [*Reflecting.*] That fellow who was hanging about, and I satisfied him with one sweetmeat—he has not followed me. The wall is too high for dogs to get in. The sweets were unbroken as they were cooked and would not attract passers by. Is it possible I ate them myself. If so I'll just bring them up again. Ha, ha! like an old hog's bladder I am bringing up nothing but wind. Or perhaps Śiva has annexed it thinking that what belongs to the Red Goddess [2] belongs to him. [*More gestures.*] Now this young celibate is misbehaving in several ways.

[1] *maṇibhūmikā*, lit. jewel room.

[2] *Kātyāyanī*. A name of Durgā, a wife of Śiva.

Well, I'll just have a look. Why this is my bowl of sweets set at Śiva's feet. Well, I'll take it back.

Give me, O Lord, give me my bowl of sweets. O Lord, thou art my thief. Why! my bowl is painted on the wall. I can't see properly because of the darkness of my distress. Well, I'll wipe it off. Ha! ha! well done, Mr. Painter, well done! The colours are so well laid on, that the more I rub, the clearer it becomes. Very good, I'll wash it off. Now where and oh! where is some water? Here we are, a beautiful tank of pure water. Now may Śiva, like myself, be disappointed of this bowl of sweetmeats.

[*Behind the scene.*]

Sweets, swee-eets—ahoy!

Jester. Curse it, here's a madman has grabbed my bowl of sweets, and laughing as he goes, comes running hither like a foaming stream of dirty rain water in the road. Stop, madman, stop, or I'll break your head with this wooden staff.

[*Enter the Madman.*]

Madman. Sweets, swee-eets, ahoy!

Jester. Good madman, bring me my bowl of sweets.

Madman. What, sweets? Where are they? Whose sweets? Are these sweets thrown away or tied up or eaten?

Jester. No, not eaten, and not thrown away.

Madman. Ah but my mouth waters—that's a sign for eating.

Jester. Good madman, bring me my bowl of sweetmeats. Don't set your heart on another man's goods and get yourself locked up.

Madman. Who, who will lock me up? The sweets protect me.

Dressed in a special way they are ready to give satisfaction.
Their price was paid in the king's palace. In the course of
time they have become rather soft at the moment. (1)

Jester. Good madman, bring me my bowl of sweets. With this provision I must go to my master's house.

Madman. With this provision I must go a hundred leagues.

Jester. What! are you Indra's elephant?

Madman. Ay, I am the elephant of Indra, only the king of the gods doesn't ride on my back, and I have heard say that Indra was bound with shackles. Then striking with lightning lashes that swallowed the showers of rain and rotating in a whirlwind he burst the clouds that bound him.

Jester. Oh, madman, wont you give it me? Or I shall shout for aid.

Madman. Shout away. Shout! scream! shout!

Jester. Help! help! sirs, an outrage!

Madman. I too will shout for aid. Indra is in bonds, sirs, Indra is in bonds!

Jester. Help! help! an outrage!

[*Voice behind the Scene.*]

Fear not, good brahman, do not fear.

Jester. [*Joyfully.*] When the moon rises all the stars are there. Brahman-hood is down in the world. It is a Buddhist monk with his good works that protects us.

[*Enter a Buddhist monk.*]

Monk. Fear not, good brahman, do not fear.
Who is there here? What's the matter? Why these shouts for help?

Jester. Dear me! This monk is playing the part of a gate-keeper. Good monk, O holy man, this madman has taken my bowl of sweetmeats and won't give it back.

Monk. Sweets! let me see them.

Madman. Have a look, have a look, mister Monk.

Monk. [*Spitting.*] Poh! Pst!

Jester. Oh, what bad luck I have! My sweets have reappeared in the madman's hands only to be spat on by this monk with his good works.

Monk. O reverend lunatic, return, return these sweetmeats, white as the foam of bubbling water, large and soft from many powderings, as sweet as mulled wine. Eat them not, lest they make you waste away.

Jester. Confound it, they have given me vintner's *laḍḍūs* for sweetmeats.

Monk. Return, reverend lunatic, return them, I say. If you don't return them, I shall curse you.

Madman. Gently, please, holy monk. Don't you go cursing me. Take them, do!

Monk. Reverend brahman, just see my power.

Jester. This madman sees the pious monk is about to curse him, and there he stands with my bowl of sweetmeats on the tips of his fingers trembling with fear. Good madman, give back my bowl of sweets.

Monk. Come, sir, come. With these sweets you shall give me a blessing.

Jester. Ha! ha! Give you a blessing with my own. It was I that accepted them as a gift at the hands of a householder. I will offer them to you too. May you be prosperous. This madman is going towards the Fire Shrine. It is midday. This place will be deserted even before noon. I shall just go and deposit the gold pieces of my donations in a house by the way. One man wants my cloth, another my money.

[*They all enter the Fire Shrine.*]

Yaugandharāyaṇa. Vasantaka! Is this shrine empty?

Jester. Yes, sir, quite empty.

Yaugandharāyaṇa. Then let us embrace.

Both. Good! [*They embrace.*]

Yaugandharāyaṇa. Well. Well. You have both shown equal efforts. Sit down. You too.

Both. Very well.

[*They all sit down.*]

Yaugandharāyaṇa. Vasantaka, have you seen the king?

Jester. Ay, sir, I have seen his Highness.

Yaugandharāyaṇa. Alas! There is no security at night. Now we must wait for the day.[1]

When the day is over, we look for the night: When the dawn is bright, we look forward to the day. Our satisfaction to see time ever passing, must see in troubles the advantages that are to come. (2)

Rumaṇvān. Well said. Though time is all alike, the night is full of obstructions. For

The night is a terror to foes who cannot succeed in their enterprises, or are unpopular in the world and find out their error in the morning. (3)

Yaugandharāyaṇa. Did you speak with the king?

Jester. Ay, sir, his Highness kept me a long while. To-day is the fourteenth day, and I attended him as he took his bath.

Yaugandharāyaṇa. Took his bath, you say?

Jester. Yes, his Highness has bathed.

Yaugandharāyaṇa. Did he worship the gods?

Jester. Ay, sir, with an obeisance only.

Yaugandharāyaṇa. It is excellent that the king has attained this state of convalescence. For

The joy drums were beaten as the noise of worship died away, when he had bathed and approached the deities: now by the power of Fate his fetters clank as he bows before the gods, worshipping on auspicious days. (4)

Rumaṇvān. Your efforts will soon enable the king to worship properly on the auspicious days.

Yaugandharāyaṇa. Vasantaka, go and see the king once more. And

[1] *atikrānta-yogakṣemā rātriḥ.* Verses 2 and 3 seem to be out of place here. They would have more point at the end of the scene where the company breaks up.

take him this message. To-morrow is the day to carry out that plan we discussed for our departure. The elephant Nalāgiri is to be infuriated in the regular old way with charms and herbs. We found a pretext for putting the herbs close to where he stands, takes his bath, has his feed, and lies down. Smoke is arranged for, to be started when the wind is the right way. To increase his rage the elephant opposite is in rut. A house near the stables, with nothing much in it, is to be set alight, for elephants, you know, are so fearful of fire. Conches and drums have been put in the temples to increase their terror. With all that din embodied in these devices to-morrow, Pradyota is sure to seek our master's aid. So by the very consent of his enemy he can come out of the prison, grasping the lute which shares his sorrows, and subdue the elephant. Then firmly seated on the back of Nalāgiri—

> He will put the tusker to such speed that the troops can follow his hindquarters in imagination only, and he will leave the Vindhyan forest behind before the lions have finished roaring. In one day he will know three states, in jail, in the wood, and in his own city. He will escape as he was caught, by an elephantine stratagem. (5)

Rumaṇvān. What are you thinking about, Vasantaka?

Jester. I am thinking that all your mighty efforts will be in vain.

Both Ministers. We do not see that.

Jester. I see it first, you will see it afterwards.

Yaugandharāyaṇa. Why should our plan fail?

Jester. Because of the wilfulness of the Vatsa king.

Yaugandharāyaṇa. How do you mean?

Jester. You listen to me.

Both Ministers. We are all attention.

Jester. When the eighth day of last dark fortnight was over, her Ladyship the princess Vāsavadattā, accompanied by her nurse, went to worship at the shrine of the holy Yakshiṇī, which is opposite the prison gate. As a young girl, whom all might see in innocence, she was in an open palanquin. They had to skirt the high road, which was flooded with water from a choked-up drain.

Yaugandharāyaṇa. Go on.

Jester. That very day the king was outside the prison gate with the permission of an officer named Śivaka, the superintendent of the jail.

Yaugandharāyaṇa. Well?

Jester. Then the palanquin was halted for the men to change shoulders, and he saw the princess as clearly as you like.

Yaugandharāyaṇa. What then?

Jester. What then? you ask. Why, the prison has turned into a garden of delight and he is ready to play a comedy of passion.

Yaugandharāyaṇa. But surely the king cannot have fallen in love with her?

Jester. Troubles, sir, come in shoals. That is exactly what he has done.

Yaugandharāyaṇa. Rumaṇvān, my friend, steel your heart. We shall become old men in this disguise.

Jester. And, sir, he said to me: 'Tell Yaugandharāyaṇa the plan as arranged does not please me. I am thinking of a particular insult to Pradyota at the very moment of my departure. Do not think I am blinded by passion: I am seeking redress for my humiliation.'

Yaugandharāyaṇa. Oho! What a speech for the mockery of his foes! What consummate assurance! How distressing for his friends! The king desires delights at the wrong time and place. Verily,

> The bare earth with a bed of straw made by his own hands can still make him proud. He can find sustinence for love in the jingle of the fetters on his feet. What prisoner would not be ripe for love, if the men told off to guard him addressed him as 'King'? (6)

Jester. Come, sir, our devotion is proved, we have done our manly best. Let us jolly well leave him and go home.

Yaugandharāyaṇa. Is this Vasantaka? Oh, Vasantaka, do not talk like that!

> Shall we abandon one that is smitten by woe and by love, who depends on his friends and cannot awake when he should? (7)

Jester. We shall go on like this till old age.

Yaugandharāyaṇa. That would be highly commendable.

Jester. It might be, if people knew about it.

Yaugandharāyaṇa. People are nothing to us. All our efforts are for our master's good.

Jester. Even he doesn't know.

Yaugandharāyaṇa. He will know in good time.

Jester. When will that good time come?

Yaugandharāyaṇa. When we succeed.

Jester. Then you must be able to take the king out of prison, and the princess out of the palace.

Rumaṇvān. There it is, you must see to it.

Yaugandharāyaṇa. Both! Very well, this is my second vow.

> If the king does not carry her off, like Subhadrā ravished by Arjuna, or a lotus plant by an elephant, my name is not Yaugandharāyaṇa. (8)

And again.

And I bear not away the one and the other, both the king and the long-eyed maid, I am not Yaugandharāyaṇa. (9)

[*Listening.*] Ah, some noise. See what it is.

Jester. Very well, Sir. [*Exit and re-enters.*] I can see people strolling about in crowds enjoying the evening air. What shall we do now?

Rumaṇvān. There are four doors to the Fire Shrine. Let us break up our meeting.

Yaugandharāyaṇa. No, no, not our meeting, let us break up the assembly of our foes. We must play our parts.

Both. So be it. [*Exeunt ambo.*]

Madman. Oho! the Demon is swallowing the moon. Let go, let go the moon, I say! If you don't, I'll smack you on the mouth and make you let go. Look, here is a mad horse running loose. Now he's at the cross-roads. I shall mount him and eat my alms. Here are the little masters. Beat me. No, don't you beat me. What do you say? dance a bit for you. Look, little masters, look. Oh, you little masters, beat me again with your sticks. Don't you beat me, or I will beat you.

[*Exit.*]

END OF THE THIRD ACT.

ACT IV

INTERLUDE

[*In Ujjain.*]

[*Enter a Soldier.*]

Soldier. The princess Vāsavadattā wishes to go bathing, and all this while I cannot find the page who attends her elephant, Bhadravati. Good Pushpadantaka, I cannot find the page-boy. What do you say? He has gone to the tavern and is drinking liquor. Well, you may go. [*Stepping round.*] Here is the liquor shop. I will just call him. Ho, page-boy! page-boy!

[*Voice behind the Scene.*]

Now who is this calling me on the high road, 'Page-boy! page-boy'!?

Soldier. Here comes the page, his eyes as red as China roses, full of liquor, laughing aloud and as drunk as drunk can be. I won't stand in his way. [*Stands aside.*]

[*Enter the Page as described.*]

Page. Now who is this calling me on the high road: 'Page-boy, page-boy!'? When I came out of the drinking-shop my father-in-law saw me, and full of wrath was he. Right into my mouth was popped a morsel of meat all seasoned with butter and pepper and salt, and a jug of good liquor as well. When the daughter-in-law is tight she falls love-sick, but the old woman raises the stick.

> Blessed are they that are drunken with wine, blessed are they that are anointed with wine, blessed are they that have bathed in wine, blessed are they that are scuppered in wine. (2)

Wretched are those rich fools who hear the misery of their son's wives and never try a cask of liquor. So I know whether there's a hell or not in the world of the dead.

Soldier. [*Approaching.*] Ho, page-boy, I have been looking for you for an age! The princess Vāsavadattā wishes to go bathing, and her elephant is not to be found. You are drunk, and loafing round here.

Page. Quite right. She is tight, that man is tight, I am tight, and thou art tight—every mortal thing is tight.

Soldier. Never mind about every mortal thing. What are you loafing about here for, and why have not you brought back Bhadrapīṭhikā?

Page. Hence wander I, here I drink, herewith I drink, don't be cross. What's to be done?

Soldier. Stop that irrelevant chatter. Bring the elephant at once.

Page. Let her come, let her come. The trouble is, I have pawned her hook.

Soldier. What do you want a hook for? Bhadravatī is so gentle by nature. Go and bring her at once.

Page. Let her come, let her come. The worst of it is, I have pawned her half-moon necklet.

Soldier. Bhadravatī could be bound with flowers, what does she want a half-moon necklet for? Bring her along at once.

Page. Let her come, let her come. Only, alack-a-day! I have pawned her bell.

Soldier. She wants to play about in the water, what do you want a bell for? Bring her at once.

Page. Let her come. Alack, but I have pawned her whip.

Soldier. What do you want a whip for? Bring her at once, I say.

Page. She shall come, but alack!

Soldier. Alack what?

Page. Alack, I've been and—

Soldier. You've been and —?

Page. Alack-a-day! why Bhadra—

Soldier. Bhadra—?

Page. Yes, alack! Bhadravatī.

Soldier. What about Bhadravatī?

Page. I've pawned her too.

Soldier. You are not to blame, but the tavern-keeper who takes a royal mount for liquor.

Page. Alas! I told him—don't lose the interest on your capital.

Soldier. Ha! there is some noise.

Page. Alack! I know, I know. Bhadravatī is breaking out of the tavern-keeper's house and running away.

Soldier. What do you say?

[*Voice in the air.*]

'His Majesty the King of the Vatsas has taken Vāsavadattā and departed.'

Page. [*Joyfully.*] May my master meet no obstacles!

Soldier. Now you may drink, and roam about as tipsy as you like.

Page. Ah, who is drunk with liquor or delight? Whose is this intoxication? We are the spies appointed each to our own place by Yaugandharāyaṇa. I will just give a signal to my friends. Here they are, running about like snakes that have just sloughed their skins. O, my friends, hearken to my words:

> May the man who fights not in return for his master's salt
> have no new vessel filled with water, consecrated with its coat
> of *darbha* grass, but go to Hell.[1] (3)

But where is the noble Yaugandharāyaṇa? Ah, here is his lordship.

> He has thrown aside his lunatic's disguise and donned many
> garments, swathing his head in a white turban; with a keen
> bright sword in his hand, while the left grasps a leather
> buckler embossed with gold, he looks like a lightning cloud
> with the edge of the moon just showing. (4)

Aha! a great fight has begun.

> Slaying tuskers with their drivers and troopers with their
> chargers, plunging for a while forcibly into the mighty host,
> now his arm is broken by a pestle blow from the tusk of a
> giant elephant, and he has lost his weapon, but even so he
> holds his ground facing the foe. (5)

Alas, he is taken, the noble Yaugandharāyaṇa.
I must be at his side. [*Exit.*]

[1] This verse occurs in the Kauṭilīya-Artha-śāstra, x. iii. 68.

Soldier. What is this? All Kauśāmbī is here except the wall and the gatehouse. Well, I will report this business to the ministers. [*Exit.*]

END OF THE INTERLUDE.

[*Enter two Servants.*]

Together. Out of the way, out of the way, sirs, out of the way!

First Fellow. Ugh! my throat is bursting but I can't shout loud enough.

Second Fellow. Curse it all, what with all this excitement over the abduction of the princess Vāsavadattā, I may yell, but nobody hears me. Curse it, what do you say, 'What's the reason for clearing the road?' Yaugandharāyaṇa has been taken prisoner. 'How was he taken?' say you? Well, listen to me. For a moment with nothing but his sword he checked the first onrush of the army. But his sword failed him, struck by the tip of the tusk of the elephant, Beautiful in Victory. Through the fault of his sword he was taken, by no fault in his valour.

First Fellow. I say, you'd better take care. There's all Kauśāmbī here except the wall and the gatehouse.

Together. Get down, your honour, do get down!

[*Enter Yaugandharāyaṇa, carried on a plank bed with his arms bound.*]

Yaugandharāyaṇa. Here I am.

Here am I, who rescued the Vatsa king from his enemies' hands. Though I was taken captive in the battle by the fault of my blade, I removed my master's trouble, so 'Victory!' say I, and enter the place with joy. (6)

It is an easy thing, Sir, for widowers to go and live in the forest. Affliction is pleasanter for those who have had their heart's desire. For those that have stored up merit, death brings no regret. For I,

Disregarding enmity, fear, and insult alike, have accomplished my work with my designs, by self-control and arrows, ending the glory of the foe and the disgrace of my friends. Thereby have I won victory, the king himself, and great renown. (7)

The Two Servants. Out of the way, out of the way, sirs, out of the way!

Yaugandharāyaṇa. No one wishing to see me should be driven aside.

Let the brave servants of the king gaze at me, brought to destruction by the force of my devotion to my king. This should strengthen or destroy the desire of those who pray in their hearts for the title of minister. (8)

Servants. Out of the way, out of the way. Have you never seen Yaugandharāyaṇa before?

Yaugandharāyaṇa. They have seen me before, but not like this.

Concealed in the guise of a madman running about in the streets my form is familiar, but now they will see my work. (9)

[*Enter the Soldier.*]

Soldier. Good news for you, sir. The Vatsa king has been captured.

Yaugandharāyaṇa. Impossible.

Freed long since from durance in the foeman's city, he has gained the forests on Bhadravatī and escaped. Will he fall into captivity now, while the leagues pass in the twinkling of an eye? (10)

Did you hear, good sir, how he was taken?

Soldier. Pursued and overtaken by the Mountain of Reeds.

Yaugandharāyaṇa. The elephant could do it, but he is not properly handled.

It is by training a rider can draw out the speed of a tusker. Who will ride him now the Vatsa king has left him? (11)

Soldier. Sir, the minister says, you are to be lodged in the arsenal. That place is guarded by our men.

Yaugandharāyaṇa. Oh, what a ridiculous order!

When watch and ward were needed on every side, after fastening in that fire, that we call the Vatsa king, then your ministers were fast asleep. Now the jewel is gone, why lock up the case? (12)

[*They walk round.*]

Soldier. Here is the arsenal. Pray enter, your honour.

[*Enter another Soldier.*]

Second Soldier. The minister's orders. Remove his fetters.

Yaugandharāyaṇa. Give me that relief. Bharatarohaka evidently wishes to see me. And I want to see him,

With his spirit depressed by my words, maddened by anger, defeated when my strategems were started and devoid of valid counter-schemes, ignorant of the good counsels in the Treatises, overcome by a greater intelligence, with his face down-cast from shame like a wrestler knocked out by a counter-stroke. (13)

[*Enter Bharatarohaka.*]

Bharatarohaka. Where is he, where is Yaugandharāyaṇa?

He carried out his duty by deception, it is painful to look at him, and how shall I upbraid him now that he is ruined for his master's sake? For a long time his work was hampered, but his plans were well directed. Like an angry snake that is overpowered, he kept raising his head. (14)

Soldier. Yaugandharāyaṇa is waiting for your honour in the arsenal.

Bharatarohaka. Very well.

Craftily outwitted in his ministry by the blue elephant, he is waiting now to reproach me with that hostile act. (15)

Soldier. Your honour, here is the minister.

Bharatarohaka. [*Approaching.*] Hail, Yaugandharāyaṇa.

Yaugandharāyaṇa. Hail.

Soldier. Ah! what a deep voice! The whole place is filled with his one word.

Bharatarohaka. [*Sitting down.*] The name 'Yaugandharāyaṇa' is familiar, sir, but not the person. I am glad to see you.

Yaugandharāyana. You are glad to see me, say you? Gaze at me.

My limbs you see are smeared with blood, in keeping with the usage of a warrior, but I am calm as Droṇa's son after he had slain the murderer of his father. (16)

Bharatarohaka. Ah! the self-esteem of one whose ruse with an elephant succeeded through trickery.

Yaugandharāyaṇa. Through trickery, say you? Now you may well say that.

What of that fraud with an elephant constructed under the *sāl* and *mallikā* trees, and our king lying bound on the ground with his arm for a pillow? And it is fraud, forsooth, if my king by his skill can charm a wild elephant with his lute! No blame to me if I follow your lead. (17)

Bharatarohaka. But, Yaugandharāyaṇa, to take the daughter of Mahāsena as a pupil and carry her off unplighted, without the fire as witness, was that robbery worthy of you?

Yaugandharāyaṇa. Nay, say not so. My master has married her.

Born in the Bharata house, the valiant Lord of the Vatsas, will he give a girl instruction and not the title of wife? (18)

Bharatarohaka. Then again Mahāsena has shown kindness to the Vatsa king. Why does n't he consider that?

Yaugandharāyaṇa. Nay, speak not thus.

If the Mountain of Reeds obeys his command he does but bide by the words of the skilled. So your master liberated mine to save his own skin and give life and glory to his friends. (19)

Bharatarohaka. If, as you say, he was only released to capture Nalāgiri, your master was not imprisoned afterwards.

Yaugandharāyaṇa. No, he sees to that from fear of being reproached with ingratitude.

Bharatarohaka. They say, sir, you are well known for your learning in the Law of States. What does the *śāstra* enjoin for enemies defeated in battle?

Yaugandharāyaṇa. Death.

Bharatarohaka. If the Vatsa king was deserving of death why did we treat him well?

Yaugandharāyaṇa. It was in consideration of the fact that he did not carry off your king himself.

Bharatarohaka. Your master thinks even that was possible?

Yaugandharāyaṇa. Of course.

Your king was in the hollow of his hand, yet my king in his virtue spared him. Unless one rides the lord of elephants the standard will not fall. **(20)**

Bharatarohaka. Very well, but in all these hostile acts against Mahāsena what was your idea with regard to Kauśāmbī?

Yaugandharāyaṇa. Oh, what an absurd question!

In spite of you all he has gone, why talk of future actions?
When a tree is uprooted, why toil to lop its branches? **(21)**

[*Enter a Chamberlain.*]

Chamberlain. [*Whispering.*] That's how it is.

Bharatarohaka. Speak out loud.

Chamberlain. 'Though many wiles were used, you did no wrong.
I have no quarrel with your qualities, pray accept the chalice.' **(22)**

That's the message.

Yaugandharāyaṇa. Ah me!

The houses I had fired still smoulder, so it is with the hearts of ministers. Here am I honoured, who should be punished, while the best honour for an offender is death. **(23)**

[*Lamentations are heard behind the scene.*]

Bharatarohaka. Ah!

What is this noise arising suddenly from the palace roof, like the screaming of ospreys[1] attacked by a falcon? **(24)**

Just find out what it is.

Chamberlain. As your honour commands. [*Exit and re-enters.*] Her Majesty, Aṅgāravatī, with her heart overwhelmed by grief, wished to throw herself down from the palace, but Mahāsena addressed her

[1] *Kurarī.* But would a falcon attack ospreys? Sarup suggests 'doves'. Another reading is *sārasānām*, 'cranes'.

with these words: 'Thy daughter has been married by the law of the warrior caste. Why now dost thou grieve on an occasion for rejoicing? So let us celebrate the ceremony of marriage between the Vatsa king and Vāsavadattā painted in a picture.' So now,

All of a sudden the women are performing the auspicious rite,
the proper order disordered by delight, and the things they use
for luck are wet with tears of joy. **(25)**

Yaugandharāyaṇa. So Mahāsena considers it an alliance by marriage. Then hand me the chalice.

Chamberlain. Pray accept it. [*Offers him the chalice.*]

Bharatarohaka. What further favour, sir, shall Mahāsena bestow on you?

Yaugandharāyaṇa. If Mahāsena is pleased with me, what else should I desire?

EPILOGUE

May the kine be without blemish[1] and, subduing the sovereignty of his foes, may our Lion King rule over this earth in its entirety!

[1] Sarup prefers 'May the regions be free from dust'. *Go* is sometimes used in the meaning of 'the earth'.

THE VISION OF VĀSAVADATTĀ

(*Svapna-Vāsavadattam*)

INTRODUCTION

After eloping with Vāsavadattā the Avanti princess, the Vatsa king, Udayana, began to neglect the affairs of his state. He had, as far as he could tell, made a bitter enemy of Pradyota-Mahāsena, king of Ujjain, by robbing him of his daughter. Some king or general named Āruṇi invaded the Vatsa kingdom.

In these straits the only remedy the Vatsa ministers could see was an alliance with the powerful state of Magadha, and the best way of effecting this was to marry their king to the Princess Padmāvatī, sister of Darśaka, the king of Magadha. The only obstacle was Udayana's devotion to Vāsavadattā.

So the minister, Yaugandharāyaṇa, concocts a plot, with the co-operation of the Queen Vāsavadattā herself. One day, while the king is away on a hunting expedition, the royal pavilion in a frontier village, Lāvāṇaka, is burnt down. A rumour is spread that Vāsavadattā and Yaugandharāyaṇa have both perished in the fire, whereas they have really slipped away to Magadha disguised as pilgrims.

In the first act the queen and minister are on their way, and passing by a forest hermitage, meet the retinue of the Magadhan princess, Padmāvatī. She has been to visit the queen-mother, Mahādevī. The princess, Padmāvatī, is to stay one night at the hermitage, and has it proclaimed that any one there may claim a boon. This is the minister's opportunity to put Vāsavadattā into the security of the Magadhan court. He pretends that she is his sister, and asks the princess to take her as a ward. His request is granted.

Then a student of theology wanders by and tells the story of the fire of Lāvāṇaka and of the king's great grief. When he leaves, it is evening and they all retire to the hermitage. (ACT I.)

In the next act we find Vāsavadattā at Magadha. The Princess Padmāvatī and her ladies are playing at ball in the palace garden. They talk of Udayana, and Vāsavadattā nearly gives herself away. Then a nurse enters and announces that Padmāvatī is betrothed to Udayana, and that the wedding must take place that very day.

'The more they hasten', says Vāsavadattā to herself, 'the deeper the gloom in my heart'. (ACT II.)

Vāsavadattā comes alone to the garden, while the preparations for the wedding are going on. But a maid comes with a request from the queen, and Vāsavadattā must needs plait the wedding garland for her husband's second marriage. (ACT III.)

The new queen, Padmāvatī, wanders in the garden with her train, including Vāsavadattā. King Udayana and his Jester come into the same garden. The ladies hide in a bower for Vāsavadattā's sake. The gentlemen sit down at the entrance, and the ladies cannot avoid overhearing their conversation. The king admits his heart is still bound to Vāsavadattā, and bursts into tears. Padmāvatī goes to comfort him, and he leaves to attend a court reception. (ACT IV.)

In an interlude we learn the young queen, Padmāvatī, is ill. Then Udayana goes to see her in the 'sea-room'. He finds the bed untouched, sits down to wait, and, musing on Vāsavadattā, falls asleep. Vāsavadattā, coming in the half-light to tend the young queen, takes Udayana's form to be Padmāvatī's. Resting on the bed, she finds it is her husband talking in his sleep, as he dreams of her. As she slips away, he wakes and catches a glimpse of her. Rushing after her, he runs against the door, and the Jester returning half persuades him it was all a dream. News comes that the other minister, Rumaṇvān, has brought a large army to defeat Āruṇi. (ACT V.)

The scene of the next act is Kauśāmbī. The Vatsa kingdom has been recovered. An interlude tells us that Udayana's grief has been renewed by the recovery of his lute. (It seems he must have dropped it on the banks of the Narmadā.) Then while the king mourns his lost love, messengers arrive from Ujjain to say that all is forgiven. Their majesties of Ujjain from the very first had intended Udayana to be their son-in-law, and they sent the painted portraits used as proxies in the wedding ceremony. Padmāvatī notices the resemblance of Vāsavadattā's picture to the 'Lady of Avantī' entrusted to her care.

Yaugandharāyaṇa in disguise comes to claim his 'sister'. All is revealed. The ministers are forgiven for their deceit, and the king decides to visit Ujjain, taking both the queens. (ACT VI.)

The general plot belongs to the old story.

The principal dramatic incident that gives its name to the play is the momentary vision of Vāsavadattā when Udayana wakes from a dream of her. (ACT V.)

The main feature of the play is the delicacy with which the feelings of Vāsavadattā are indicated.

DRAMATIS PERSONAE

(In order of appearance.)

Stage-manager, Sūtradhāra—in Prologue only.
Two guards in the retinue of Princess Padmāvatī.
YAUGANDHARĀYAṆA, Chief Minister of Udayana, king of the Vatsas.
VĀSAVADATTĀ, Princess of Ujjain, daughter of King Pradyota-Mahāsena, and the first Queen of Udayana, supposed to have been burnt alive and brought to Magadha in disguise as the Lady of Avantī.
Chamberlain } from Magadha with Princess Padmāvatī.
Maid }
PADMĀVATĪ, Princess of Magadha, sister of King Darśaka. In the last three acts the second queen of Udayana.
Lady hermit.
Student of theology.
Nurse of the princess of Magadha.
Second maid, of the princess of Magadha.
Jester (Vasantaka) of King Udayana.
UDAYANA, king of the Vatsas.
Padminikā } Maids in attendance on the princess of Magadha.
Madhukarikā }
Chamberlain of the Vatsa king at Kauśāmbī.
Vijayā, Portress at Kauśāmbī palace.
Raibhya, Chamberlain from the Avantī court at Ujjain.
Vasundharā, nurse of Vāsavadattā from Ujjain.

PROLOGUE

[*At the end of the Opening*[1] *enter the stage-manager.*]

Stage-manager. May the arms of Balarāma[2] protect thee, arms as fair as the young moon at its rising,[3] given their full vigour by wine,[4] full of Beauty[5] incarnate, and lovely as Spring. (1)

[*By paronomasia this verse introduces the names of Udayana, Vāsavadattā, Padmāvatī, and Vasantaka.*]

With these words, my lords and gentlemen, I have to announce to you . . . But what is that? I thought I heard a noise, just as I was to make my announcement. Well, I must see what it is.

[*Voice behind the scene.*]

Out of the way, there! Away, sirs, out of the way.

Stage-manager. So be it. I understand.

The devoted servitors of the King of Magadha, escorting their princess, are sternly driving aside everybody they meet in the Grove of Penance. (2) [*Exit.*]

END OF PROLOGUE.

ACT I

[*Forest road near a hermitage.*]

[*Enter two guards.*]

Guards. Out of the way! Away, sirs, out of the way!

[*Enter Yaugandharāyaṇa, disguised as a religious mendicant, and Vāsavadattā in the garb of a lady of Avantī.*]

Yaugandharāyaṇa. [*Listening.*] What? Even here are people driven aside? For,

These grave seniors, dwellers in the hermitage, content with woodland fruits and clad in bark, worthy of all respect, are being terrified.

Who is this insolent fellow, this lack-courtesy, made arrogant

[1] Nāndī, see note on p. ix.

[2] Bala, Baladeva, or Balarāma, the third Rāma and elder brother of Kṛishṇa. He was fair and a great lover of wine.

[3] Meaning 'at eventide', for the new moon rising is invisible, but this is an artificial stanza where *Udaya* 'rising' had to come in to give us *Udayana* the hero's name.

[4] This is an appropriate sense, though the construction is rather forced *āsava-datta-ā-balau*, i. e. *ā samantād*. The easier way 'with weakness given by liquor' is not appropriate to protecting arms.

[5] *Padmā*, the wife of *Vishṇu*, Goddess of Beauty.

by fickle fortune, who by his rough commands is turning a peaceful penance-grove into a village street? (3)

Vāsavadattā. Who is it, sir, that turns us aside?

Yaugandharāyaṇa. One who turns aside his own soul from righteousness.

Vāsavadattā. Nay, sir, that is not what I would say. Am I to be driven aside?

Yaugandharāyaṇa. Even the gods, lady, are rejected unawares.

Vāsavadattā. Ah! sir, fatigue is not so distressing as this humiliation.

Yaugandharāyaṇa. This is something your Highness has enjoyed and then given up. It should not trouble you. For,

Aforetime thou also didst obtain thy heart's desire;[1] with the victory of thy lord thou wilt once more attain an exalted state. The series of worldly fortunes revolves with the march of time like the spokes in a wheel. (4)

Guards. Out of the way, sirs, out of the way!

[*Enter the Chamberlain.*]

Chamberlain. No, Sambhashaka, no, you must not drive these people aside. Look you,

Bring no reproach on the King. Show no harshness to the inmates of a hermitage. These high-minded men make their home in the forest to escape from the brutalities of a town. (5)

Guards. Very well, sir. [*Exeunt.*]

Yaugandharāyaṇa. Why, he seems to be an enlightened person. [*To Vāsavadattā*] Come, child, let us approach him.

Vāsavadattā. As you please, sir.

Yaugandharāyaṇa. [*Approaching.*] Oh, sir, what is the reason of this hustling?

Chamberlain. Ah! good hermit.

Yaugandharāyaṇa. [*Aside.*] 'Hermit', of course, is an honourable form of address, but as I am not used to it, it does not please me.

Chamberlain. Hearken, good sir. Padmāvatī is here, sister to our great king, named by his parents Darśaka. She has been to visit the queen-mother, Mahādevī, who has made her home in a hermitage, and having taken leave of that noble lady, is on her way to Rājagṛiha. So to-day she is pleased to stay in this hermitage. Therefore,

You may fetch from the forest, at your sweet will, holy water, fuel, flowers, and sacred grass. The king's daughter is a friend of piety, she would not wish your pious duties to be hindered. Such is the tradition of her family. (6)

[1] 'You have already given your consent. This was the only course of action.' (L. S.)

Yaugandharāyaṇa. [*Aside.*] So this is the Padmāvatī, princess of Magadha, who, the soothsayers Pushpaka, Bhadraka, and others have predicted, is destined to become the consort of my royal master.

Aversion or respect arise from one's purpose. Because I am so eager to see her wedded to my master, I am inspired with great devotion. (7)

Vāsavadattā. [*Aside.*] Hearing that she is a princess, I too feel for her a sisterly affection.

[*Enter Padmāvatī with her retinue and a maid.*]

Maid. Come this way, please, princess. Here is the hermitage, be pleased to enter.

[*A lady-hermit is discovered, seated.*]

Lady-hermit. Princess, you are most welcome.

Vāsavadattā. [*Aside.*] This is the princess. Her beauty proclaims indeed her noble birth.

Padmāvatī. Reverend lady, I salute you.

Lady-hermit. Long may you live. Come in, my child, come in. A hermitage is indeed the guest's own home.

Padmāvatī. So it is, your reverence. I feel quite at home, and grateful to you for your kind words.

Vāsavadattā. [*Aside.*] Her words are as sweet as her looks.

Lady-hermit. [*To the maid.*] My good girl, has no king as yet sought the hand of your blessed sovereign's sister?

Maid. Yes, there is King Pradyota of Ujjain. He has sent an ambassador on behalf of his son.

Vāsavadattā. [*Aside.*] I am glad to hear it. And now she has become one of my own dear people.

Lady-hermit. Such loveliness well deserves this honour. We have heard that both are mighty royal families.

Padmāvatī. [*To the Chamberlain.*] Sir, have you found any hermits that will do us the favour of accepting our gifts? Distribute according to their heart's desire and demand, by proclamation, what any man would have.

Chamberlain. As your ladyship desires. Hearken, ye saintly men, dwelling in the hermitage, hearken to my words. Her Highness, the Princess of Magadha, is gratified by your cordial welcome, and invites you to accept her gifts that she may gain religious merit.

Who, then, needs a beggar's bowl? Who requires a robe? Some student whose studies are complete, according to the Rule, what fee would he have to offer his preceptor? The princess, devoted to those that delight in law, requests you as a favour to herself, whatever any one desires let him declare it, what shall be given to-day and to whom? (8)

Yaugandharāyaṇa. [*Aside.*] Ah, I see my opportunity. [*Aloud.*] Sir, I ask a boon.

Padmāvatī. Happily my visit to this penance-grove is fruitful.

Lady-hermit. Everybody in this hermitage is contented. This must be some stranger.

Chamberlain. Well, sir, what can we do for you?

Yaugandharāyaṇa. This is my sister. Her husband has gone abroad. My wish is that her Highness would take my sister under her protection for some time. For,

No need have I of wealth, or of worldly joys, or of fine raiment, nor have I donned the orange robe to gain a livelihood. The royal maid is wise and knoweth well the path of duty. She can well protect the virtue of my sister. (9)

Vāsavadattā. [*Aside.*] So! the noble Yaugandharāyaṇa is determined to leave me here. Be it so, he will not act without reflection.

Chamberlain. Lady! His expectation is great indeed. How can we consent? For,

Wealth it would be easy to give, or one's life, or the fruit of austerity. Anything else would be easy, but hard is the guarding of a pledge. (10)

Padmāvatī. My lord, after first making our proclamation—what would any one have?—it is improper to hesitate. Whatever he says, must be done.

Chamberlain. These words are worthy of your Highness.

Maid. Long live the princess, who keeps her word.

Lady-hermit. Long life to you, blessed lady!

Chamberlain. Very well, my lady. [*Approaching Yaugandharāyaṇa.*] Reverend sir, her Highness accepts the guardianship of your sister.

Yaugandharāyaṇa. I am much indebted to her Highness. [*To Vāsavadattā.*] My child! Approach her Highness.

Vāsavadattā. [*Aside.*] There is no escape. I will go, unfortunate that I am.

Padmāvatī. Yes, come hither. Now you belong to me.

Lady-hermit. She looks to me like the daughter of a king.

Maid. You are right, reverend mother. I, too, can see that she has known better days.

Yaugandharāyaṇa. [*Aside.*] Ah! half my task is ended. Things are turning out just as it was arranged with the other ministers. When my royal master is reinstalled and Vāsavadattā is restored to him, her

Highness, the Princess of Magadha, will be my surety for her. For, indeed,

> Those who first predicted our troubles, foretold that Padmāvatī was destined to become the consort of my king. On that prophecy I have relied in acting as I did, for fate does not transgress the words of well-tried oracles. (11)

[*Enter a Student of Theology.*]

Student. [*Looking upwards.*] It is midday and I am tired out. Where shall I take a rest? [*Turning about.*] Good, there must be a penance-grove nearby, because

> The deer are quietly grazing, free from fear, in a place where they feel safe. All the trees, tended with loving care, have their branches loaded with fruit and blossom. There is a great wealth of tawny kine, but no fields are tilled on any side. Undoubtedly it is a penance-grove, for this smoke arises from many an altar. (12)

I will go in. [*Entering.*] Hallo! This person is out of keeping with a hermitage. [*Looking in another direction.*] But there are also hermits. There is no harm in proceeding further. Oh! ladies!

Chamberlain. Come in, sir, with perfect freedom, sir. A hermitage is indeed common to all.

Vāsavadattā. How now!

Padmāvatī. Oho! this lady shuns the sight of strangers. Very well, I must take good care of my ward.

Chamberlain. Sir, we were here first. Please accept our hospitality to a guest.

Student. [*Drinks.*] Thank you. Now I am refreshed.

Yaugandharāyaṇa. Sir, whence have you come, whither are you going, and where is your abode?

Student. I will tell you, sir. I am from Rājagṛiha. In order to specialize in Vedic studies, I took up my abode in Lāvāṇaka; it's a village in the Vatsa country.

Vāsavadattā. [*Aside.*] Ah! Lāvāṇaka! At the mention of that name my anguish seems renewed.

Yaugandharāyaṇa. And have you completed your studies?

Student. No, not yet.

Yaugandharāyaṇa. If you have not finished your studies, why have you returned?

Student. A terrible catastrophe has happened there.

Yaugandharāyaṇa. What was that?

Student. There was a king there named Udayana.

Yaugandharāyaṇa. I have heard of his Highness. What about him?

Student. He was passionately enamoured of his queen, Vāsavadattā, a princess of Avantī.

Yaugandharāyaṇa. Quite possible. What then?

Student. When the king had gone out hunting the village took fire, and she was burnt alive.

Vāsavadattā. [*Aside.*] Untrue, untrue, I am living still, poor wretch!

Yaugandharāyaṇa. Well, go on.

Student. Then in attempting to rescue her a minister named Yaugandharāyaṇa fell into the flames himself.

Yaugandharāyaṇa. Did he really? Well, what then?

Student. Then the king came back, and when he heard the news he was distracted with grief at their separation, and wanted to end his life in that very fire. It was all the ministers could do to hold him back.

Vāsavadattā. [*Aside.*] Yes, I know my lord's tender feelings for me.

Yaugandharāyaṇa. And then?

Student. The king clasped to his breast the half-burnt ornaments that had adorned her person and fell down unconscious.

All. Alas!

Vāsavadattā. [*Aside.*] And now I hope the noble Yaugandharāyaṇa is satisfied.

Maid. Princess, this noble lady is in tears.

Padmāvatī. She must be very tender-hearted.

Yaugandharāyaṇa. Quite so, quite so. My sister is tender-hearted by nature. What happened then?

Student. Then, by degrees, he regained consciousness.

Padmāvatī. Thank goodness, he is alive. The words 'fell down unconscious' took my breath away.

Yaugandharāyaṇa. Well, proceed.

Student. Then the king suddenly got up, his body stained with dust from rolling on the ground, and burst into lamentation after lamentation. 'Oh! Vāsavadattā—Princess of Avantī—Alas, my beloved—my darling pupil—oh!' and so on and so on. In short,

> No love birds[1] so lament their loss, nor even those that are bereft of fairy brides.[2] Happy the woman who is thus loved by her lord: consumed by fire, but by reason of her husband's love not consumed by woe.[3] **(13)**

[1] Lit. Cakravāka birds, symbols of conjugal fidelity, supposed to be separated after every sunset.

[2] *strī-viśeṣaiḥ*, probably referring to Purūrava's lament for the Nymph Urvaśī.

[3] *adagdhā*, 'not burned'. [Immortalized. L. S.]

Yaugandharāyaṇa. But tell me, sir, was none of his ministers at pains to comfort him?

Student. Yes, there was a minister named Rumaṇvān who did his very best to console him.

> Like the king he will touch no food, his face is wasted by ceaseless weeping. Depressed by sorrow like his lord, he neglects the care of his person. Day and night he attends untiring on the king. Should the king suddenly depart this life, he also will expire. (14)

Vāsavadattā. [*Aside.*] Happily my lord is in good hands.

Yaugandharāyaṇa. [*Aside.*] What a heavy responsibility Rumaṇvān has to bear! For,

> My burden has been lightened, his toil is constant. Everything depends on him, on whom the king himself depends. (15)

[*Aloud.*] Well, sir, by this time is the king consoled?

Student. That I do not know.

The ministers left the village, taking with them—after great difficulty—the king, who was pouring out a piteous tale. 'Here it was that I laughed with her, here I talked with her, here I sat with her, here we fell out, and here I passed the night with her', and so forth. With the departure of the king the village became desolate like the sky when the moon and stars have set. Then I, too, came away.

Lady-hermit. He must indeed be a noble king who is praised like this even by a stranger.

Maid. What think you, princess, will he offer his hand to another woman?

Padmāvatī. [*Aside.*] My heart was asking that very question.

Student. Let me take leave of you. I must be going.

Both. Go, and fare you well.

Student. Thank you. [*Exit.*]

Yaugandharāyaṇa. Good. I too wish to go if her Highness permits.

Chamberlain. The holy hermit wishes to depart with your Highness's permission.

Padmāvatī. This gentleman's sister will feel lonely in his absence.

Yaugandharāyaṇa. She is in good hands, she will not repine.

[*To the chamberlain.*] Pray let me go.

Chamberlain. Very well, we shall meet again.

Yaugandharāyaṇa. I hope so. [*Exit.*]

Chamberlain. It is time now to go within.

Padmāvatī. Reverend lady, I salute you.

Lady-hermit. My child, may you get a husband as good as yourself.

Vāsavadattā. Reverend lady, I too salute you.

Lady-hermit. And you also, may you soon find your husband.

Vāsavadattā. I thank you.

Chamberlain. Come, please, this way. This way, my lady. For now,
The birds have returned to their nests. The hermits have plunged into the stream. Fires have been lit and are burning brightly, smoke is spreading in the penance-grove. The sun has dropped a long way down, gathering his rays together he turns his chariot and slowly descends on the summit of the western mountain. **(16)**

[*Exeunt omnes.*]

END OF THE FIRST ACT.

ACT II

INTERLUDE

[*Palace garden at Magadha.*]

[*Enter a Maid.*]

Maid. Kunjarikā, Kunjarikā! Where, O where is the Princess Padmāvatī?
What do you say? 'The princess is playing at ball near the jasmine bower.'[1] Very good, I shall go to her. [*Turning and looking around.*] Ah! here comes the princess playing with a ball. The jewels in her ears are turned upwards; the exertion has spangled her brow with tiny drops of perspiration, so that fatigue lends a charm to her face. I will go and meet her. [*Exit.*]

END OF THE INTERLUDE.

[*Enter Padmāvatī, playing with a ball, accompanied by her retinue and Vāsavadattā.*]

Vāsavadattā. Here is your ball, my dear.

Padmāvatī. Dear lady! Now that is enough.

Vāsavadattā. You have played over long with your ball, my dear. Your hands are quite red, they might belong to somebody else.[2]

Maid. Play on, princess, play on. Enjoy these charming days of girlhood while you may.

[1] She hears a voice off the stage.

[2] Suggesting the palms dyed for marriage.

Padmāvatī. What's in your thoughts, dear lady? I think you are laughing at me.

Vāsavadattā. No, no, my dear. You are looking more beautiful than ever to-day. I am getting a full view as it were of your pretty face.[1]

Padmāvatī. Away with you! Don't you make fun of me.

Vāsavadattā. Well, I am mute—O daughter-in-law elect of Mahāsena!

Padmāvatī. Who, pray, is this Mahāsena?

Vāsavadattā. There is a king of Ujjain, named Pradyota, who is called Mahāsena on account of the vast size of his army.

Maid. It is not with that king the princess wishes to be related.

Vāsavadattā. Whom does she want, then?

Maid. There is a king of the Vatsas named Udayana. It is of his virtues that the princess is enamoured.

Vāsavadattā. [*Aside.*] She wants my noble lord as her husband. [*Aloud.*] For what reason?

Maid. He is so tender-hearted—that's why.

Vāsavadattā. [*Aside.*] I know, I know. I, too, fell in love with him like that.

Maid. But, princess, suppose the king is ugly.

Vāsavadattā. No, no. He is very handsome.

Padmāvatī. How do you know that, dear lady?

Vāsavadattā. [*Aside.*] Partiality to my lord has made me transgress the bounds of propriety. What shall I do now? Yes, I see—[*Aloud.*] That is what everybody says in Ujjain, my dear.

Padmāvatī. Quite so. He is not, of course, inaccessible to the people of Ujjain, and beauty fascinates the hearts of all.

[*Enter a Nurse.*]

Nurse. Victory to the princess! Princess, you are betrothed.

Vāsavadattā. To whom, good lady?

Nurse. To Udayana, the king of the Vatsas.

Vāsavadattā. Is he in good health, that king?

Nurse. He arrived here quite well, and the princess is betrothed to him.

Vāsavadattā. Alack-a-day!

Nurse. Alack-a-day! Why, what's the matter?

Vāsavadattā. Oh, nothing. His grief was so great, and now he is indifferent.

Nurse. Madam, the hearts of great men are ruled by the Sacred Scriptures, and are therefore easy to console.

Vāsavadattā. Good lady, tell me, did he choose her himself?

Nurse. Oh, no. He came here on some other business, when our king

[1] There is a *double entendre.* Suggesting 'a husband's face'.

observed his nobility, wisdom, youth, and beauty, he offered her hand of his own accord.

Vāsavadattā. [*Aside.*] Just so. Thus my lord is without reproach.

[*Enter another Maid.*]

Second Maid. Make haste, madam. Our queen declares that the conjunction of stars is auspicious to-day, and the nuptial celebrations must take place this very day.

Vāsavadattā. [*Aside.*] The more they hasten, the deeper the gloom in my heart.

Nurse. Come, your Highness, come.

[*Exeunt omnes.*]

END OF THE SECOND ACT.

ACT III

[*Palace Garden.*]

[*Enter Vāsavadattā, deep in thought.*]

Vāsavadattā. I have left Padmāvatī in the ladies' court, with its festive wedding crowd of women, and have come here alone to this pleasure garden. Here I can give vent to the sorrow which fate has laid upon me. [*Walking about.*] Alas! I am undone. Even my noble lord now belongs to another woman. Let me sit down. [*Sits down.*] Blessed indeed is the Love-bird.[1] Parted from her mate she ceases to live. But I cannot escape from life. Miserable that I am, I live on in the hope of seeing him again.

[*Enter a Maid carrying flowers.*]

Maid. Where has the noble lady of Avantī gone? [*Turning and looking around.*] Ah, there she is, sitting on a stone bench under the *priyaṅgu* creeper. There she sits, wearing a graceful garment unadorned, her mind intent on distant thoughts, looking like a digit of the moon obscured by mist. I will go up to her. [*Approaching.*] Noble lady of Avantī, I have been seeking you for ever so long.

Vāsavadattā. What for?

Maid. What our queen says is this: 'The lady comes from a noble family, she is kind and skilful. So let her plait this wedding garland.'

Vāsavadattā. And for whom is it to be made?

Maid. For our princess.

Vāsavadattā. [*Aside.*] Must I do even this? The Gods are indeed cruel.

[1] *Lit.* Female Cakravāka, see note p. 45.

Maid. Madam, there is no time now to think of other things. The bridegroom is taking his bath in the inlaid room,[1] so please plait the garland quickly.

Vāsavadattā. [*Aside.*] I can think of nothing else. [*Aloud.*] My good girl, have you seen the bridegroom?

Maid. Yes, I have seen him. That was through affection for the princess and my own curiosity.

Vāsavadattā. What is he like?

Maid. Oh, madam, I tell you, I never saw any one like him.

Vāsavadattā. Well, tell me, tell me, my dear, is he handsome?

Maid. One might say the God of Love himself, without the bow and arrows.

Vāsavadattā. Thanks, that will do.

Maid. Why do you stop me?

Vāsavadattā. It is improper to listen to any one singing the praises of another woman's husband.

Maid. Then please finish the garland as quickly as you can.

Vāsavadattā. I shall do it at once. Give me the flowers.

Maid. Here they are. Please take them.

Vāsavadattā. [*Turns out the basket and examines the flowers.*] What is the name of this plant?

Maid. It is called 'Lords and Ladies'.[2]

Vāsavadattā. [*Aside.*] I must work in lots of this for myself and Padmāvatī. [*Aloud.*] What do you call this flower?

Maid. Oh, that is 'Old Wife's Bane'.[3]

Vāsavadattā. We needn't use that one.

Maid. Why not?

Vāsavadattā. His wife is dead, so it wouldn't be any use.

[*Enter another Maid.*]

Second Maid. Please make haste, madam. The ladies of living lords are conducting the bridegroom to the ladies' court.

Vāsavadattā. There, it's ready, I tell you. Take it.

First Maid. How beautiful! Madam, I must be off.

[*Exeunt the two maids.*]

Vāsavadattā. She is gone. Alas! All is over.
My noble lord is now another's. Heaven help me! I'll to bed; it may soothe my pain, if I can sleep. [*Exit.*]

END OF THE THIRD ACT.

[1] *Maṇi-bhūmi*, 'inlaid floor'.
[2] *Lit.* 'Antidote to widow-hood'.
[3] *Lit.* 'Co-wife's ruin.'

ACT IV

INTERLUDE

[*Palace at Magadha.*]

[*Enter the Jester.*]

Jester. [*Joyfully.*] Ha! ha! How good to see the delightful time of the auspicious and welcome marriage of His Highness the king of the Vatsas. Who could have known that after being hurled into such a whirlpool of misfortune, we should rise again to the surface. Now we live in palaces, we bathe in the tanks of the inner court, we eat dainty and delicious dishes of sweetmeats—in short, I feel myself to be in Paradise, except that there are no nymphs to keep me company. But there is one great drawback. I do not digest my food at all well. Even on the downiest couches I cannot sleep, for I seem to see the Wind and Blood disease circling round. Bah! there is no happiness in life, if you are full of ailments, or without a good breakfast.

[*Enter a Maid.*]

Maid. Wherever has the worthy Vasantaka got to? [*Turning and looking around.*] Why, here he is! [*Going up to him.*] Oh, Master Vasantaka, what a search I have had looking for you!

Jester. [*With a leer.*] And why were you searching for me, my dear?

Maid. Our queen says, 'hasn't the bridegroom finished his bath?'

Jester. Why does she want to know?

Maid. So that I may bring him a garland and unguents, of course.

Jester. His Highness has bathed. You may bring everything except food.

Maid. Why do you bar food?

Jester. Unfortunate that I am, like the rolling of cuckoo's eyes . . . my stomach is like that.

Maid. May you ever be as you are!

Jester. Off with you! I will go and attend on his Highness.

[*Exeunt ambo.*]

END OF INTERLUDE.

[*Palace garden.*]

[*Enter Padmāvatī with her retinue and Vāsavadattā dressed as a lady of Avantī.*]

Maid. What has brought your ladyship to this pleasure-garden?

Padmāvatī. My dear, I want to see if the *seoli* [1] clusters have flowered or not.

[1] *Seoli*, a modern form of *Śephālikā* = Nyctanthes Arbor Tristis—with a white and orange flower which falls in the morning.

Maid. Yes, princess, they have, with blossoms like pendants of pearls interset with coral.

Padmāvatī. If that is so, my dear, why do you delay?

Maid. Won't your ladyship sit on this stone bench for a moment while I gather some flowers?

Padmāvatī. Shall we sit here, dear lady?

Vāsavadattā. Let us do so.

[*Both sit down.*]

Maid. [*After gathering some flowers.*] Oh, look, princess, look! My hands are full of the *seoli* blossoms, with their half-way hose of *realgar*[1].

Padmāvatī. [*Looking at the flowers.*] See, lady, how brilliant are the colours of these flowers!

Vāsavadattā. Yes, how beautiful they are.

Maid. Princess, shall I pick any more?

Padmāvatī. No, no, my dear, no more.

Vāsavadattā. Why do you stop her, my dear?

Padmāvatī. If my noble lord should come here and see this abundance of blossom, I should be so honoured.

Vāsavadattā. Why, my dear, are you so much in love with your husband?

Padmāvatī. I don't know, lady, but when he is away from me I feel wretched.

Vāsavadattā. [*Aside.*] How difficult it is for me. Even she speaks in this strain.

Maid. How delicately the princess has told us that she loves her husband.

Padmāvatī. I have just one doubt.

Vāsavadattā. And what is that?

Padmāvatī. Was my noble lord as much to Vāsavadattā as he is to me?

Vāsavadattā. Nay, more.

Padmāvatī. How do you know?

Vāsavadattā. [*Aside.*] Ah! Partiality to my noble lord has made me transgress the bounds of propriety. I know what I will say. [*Aloud.*] Had her love been less, she would not have forsaken her own people.

Padmāvatī. Possibly not.

Maid. Princess, you might gently suggest to your husband, that you too would like to learn to play the lute.[2]

[1] The blossoms have orange stems, which are compared to puttees the colour of red arsenic.

[2] Udayana was a master player on the lute. When in captivity he gave lessons to the princess Vāsavadattā. See pp. 3, 4, 61.

Padmāvatī. I did speak to him about it.

Vāsavadattā. And what did he say?

Padmāvatī. He said nothing. He heaved a deep sigh, and became silent.

Vāsavadattā. What did that mean, do you think?

Padmāvatī. I think the memory of the noble Vāsavadattā's virtues came over him, but out of courtesy he restrained his tears in my presence.

Vāsavadattā. [*Aside.*] How happy I should be if that were true!

[*Enter the King and the Jester.*]

Jester. Aha! how pretty the garden looks with a thin sprinkling of *bandhujīva* flowers, fallen while they were being gathered. This way, my lord.

King. Very well, my dear Vasantaka, here I come.

Once in Ujjain, when the unimpeded vision of Avantī's princess brought me to that condition that you know of, the God of Love let fly at me with all his five arrows. Of those I still bear the pain in my heart, and now I am wounded again. If Cupid has only five arrows, what is this sixth dart he has discharged at me? (1)

Jester. Where has Lady Padmāvatī gone? Has she gone to the creeper-bower? Or perhaps to the stone seat called the 'Crest of the Hill', which is so strewn with *asana*[1] flowers that it looks as if it were covered with a tiger's skin. Or could she have entered the wood of the Seven-leaved Trees[2] with their powerful pungent scent? Or perhaps she has gone into the wooden pavilion with crowds of birds and beasts painted on the walls. [*Looking up.*] Oh, look, your Highness! Do you see this line of cranes advancing steadily along the clear autumn sky, as beautiful as the long white arms of the adored Baladeva?

King. Yes, comrade, I see it.

Now stretched in an even line, now wide apart; now soaring high, now sinking low, crooked in its twists and turns, as the group of Seven Ṛishis[3]. Bright as a serpent's belly just slipped from its slough, like a boundary line it cuts the sky in two. (2)

Maid. Look, princess, look at this flock of cranes advancing steadily in line, as delicately tinted as a garland of pink water-lilies. Oh! the King!

[1] *Asana* = Terminalia tomentosa M. W.

[2] *Saptacchada* = Alstonia scholaris M. W.

[3] The constellation of the Great Bear.

Padmāvatī. Ah! 'tis my noble lord. Lady, for your sake I shall avoid seeing my husband. So let us go into this bower of *mādhavī*[1] creepers.

Vāsavadattā. Very well.

[*They do so.*]

Jester. Lady Padmāvatī came here and went away again.

King. How do you know that?

Jester. Just look at these *seoli* clusters from which the flowers have been picked.

King. Oh, Vasantaka! What a gorgeous flower it is!

Vāsavadattā. [*Aside.*] That name 'Vasantaka' makes me feel as if I were at Ujjain again.

King. Let us sit down, Vasantaka, on this stone seat and wait for Padmāvatī.

Jester. Very well, sir. [*Sits down and gets up again.*] The heat of the scorching autumn sun is unbearable. So let us go into this bower of *mādhavī* creepers.

King. All right. Lead the way.

Jester. Very well. [*Both walk round.*]

Padmāvatī. The worthy Vasantaka is bent on spoiling everything. What shall we do now?

Maid. Princess, shall I keep his Highness away by shaking this hanging creeper swarming with black bees?

Padmāvatī. Yes, do.

[*Maid does so.*]

Jester. Help! help! Keep away, your Highness, keep away!

King. What is the matter?

Jester. I am being stung by these damnable bees.

King. No, no, do not do that. One should never frighten the bees. Look,

> Drowsy with drafts of honey, the bees are humming softly in the close embraces of their love-sick queens. Should our footsteps startle them, like us, they will be parted from their darlings. **(3)**

So let us stay here.

Jester. Very well.

[*Both sit down.*]

Maid. Princess, we are in truth made prisoners.

Padmāvatī. Happily it is my noble lord who sits there.

Vāsavadattā. [*Aside.*] I am glad to see my noble lord looking so well.

Maid. Princess, the lady's eyes are filled with tears.

[1] Gaertnera racemosa.

Vāsavadattā. The moringa pollen has got into my eyes because of the naughty bees, and made them water.

Padmāvatī. Quite so.

Jester. Well, now, there is nobody in this pleasure-garden. There is something I want to ask. May I ask you a question?

King. Yes, if you like.

Jester. Which do you love best, the lady Vāsavadattā that was, or Padmāvatī of to-day?

King. Now why do you put me in such a very difficult position?

Padmāvatī. Oh, my dear; what a difficult position for my noble lord!

Vāsavadattā. [*Aside.*] And for me, too, unfortunate that I am.

Jester. Now you must speak frankly. One is dead, the other is nowhere near.

King. No, my dear fellow, no, I am not going to say anything. You are a chatterer.

Padmāvatī. By so much he has said enough.

Jester. Oh, I swear truly, I won't tell a soul. My lips are sealed.[1]

King. No, my friend, I dare not speak.

Padmāvatī. How stupidly indiscreet he is. Even after that he cannot read his heart.

Jester. What, you won't tell me? If you don't, you shall not stir a single step from the stone seat. Your Highness is now my prisoner.

King. What, by force?

Jester. Yes, by force.

King. We shall see.

Jester. Forgive me, your Highness. I conjure you in the name of our friendship to tell me the truth.

King. No escape. Well listen,

Padmāvatī I much admire for her beauty, charm, and virtue,
and yet she has not won my heart still bound to Vāsavadattā. (4)

---

[1] *Lit.* 'See, I bite my tongue.'

Vāsavadattā. [*Aside.*] So may it ever be. This is my reward for all my suffering. My living here unknown is beginning to be delightful.

Maid. Oh, princess, his Highness is very discourteous.

Padmāvatī. My dear, don't say that. My noble lord is courteous indeed, for even now he remembers the virtues of the noble Vāsavadattā.

Vāsavadattā. My dear child, your words are worthy of your birth.

King. Well, I have spoken. Now you must tell me, which is your favourite: Vāsavadattā that was, or Padmāvatī of to-day?

Padmāvatī. My noble lord is mimicking Vasantaka.

Jester. What is the use of my chatter! I have the greatest admiration for both their ladyships.

King. Idiot. You made me tell, and now you are afraid to speak.

Jester. What, would you force me?

King. Why, yes, of course.

Jester. Then you will never hear it.

King. Forgive me, mighty brahman, speak of your own free will.

Jester. Now you shall hear. Lady Vāsavadattā I greatly admired. Lady Padmāvatī is young, beautiful, gentle, free from pride, gently spoken, and very courteous. But there is one other great virtue. Vāsavadattā used to come to me with delicious dishes, saying, 'Where has the good Vasantaka got to?'

Vāsavadattā [*Aside.*] Bravo, Vasantaka. You must remember this.

King. Very well, Vasantaka. I shall tell all this to Queen Vāsavadattā.

Jester. Alas, Vāsavadattā! Where is Vāsavadattā? She is dead long ago.

King. [*Sadly.*] It is true, Vāsavadattā is no more.

By your raillery you confused my mind, and by force of former usage those words slipped out. (5)

Padmāvatī. This was a delightful conversation, but now the wretch has spoiled it all.

Vāsavadattā. [*Aside.*] Well, well, I am consoled. How sweet it is to hear these words without being seen.

Jester. Be of good cheer, your Highness. Fate cannot be gainsaid. It is so, and that 's all about it.

King. My dear fellow, you do not understand my condition. For,

A deeply-rooted passion it is hard to abandon, by constant recollection the pain is renewed. This is the way of the world that the mind must cancel its debt with tears to gain tranquillity. (6)

Jester. His Highness's face is wet with tears. I will get some water to wash it.

Padmāvatī. Madam, my lord's face is hidden in a veil of tears. Let us slip away.

Vāsavadattā. Yes, let us go. Nay, you stay here. It is not right for you to go and leave your husband unhappy. I will go alone.

Maid. The lady is right. You should go to him, Princess.

Padmāvatī. What do you say? Shall I go?

Vāsavadattā. Yes, dear, do. [*Exit.*]

[*Enter the Jester.*]

Jester. [*With water in a lotus leaf.*] Why, here is Lady Padmāvatī.

Padmāvatī. What is it, my good Vasantaka?

Jester. This is that, that is this.

Padmāvatī. Speak out, sir, speak.

Jester. Lady, the pollen of the moringa flowers, carried by the wind, has got into his Highness's eyes, and his face is wet with tears. Please take him this water to wash his face.

Padmāvatī. [*Aside.*] Oho! like master, like man, how courteous he is. [*Approaching the king.*] Greeting, my lord. Here is some water for your face.

King. Eh, what, Padmāvatī? [*Aside to Jester.*] What 's this, Vasantaka?

Jester. It 's like this. [*Whispers in his ear.*]

King. Bravo, Vasantaka, bravo. [*Sipping water.*] Padmāvatī, pray be seated.

Padmāvatī. As my lord commands. [*Sits down.*]

King. Padmāvatī,

The motes of the moringa blossoms, agitated by the breeze, fair lady, have bathed my face in tears. (7)

[*Aside.*]

She 's but a girl and newly wed, should she learn the truth it would distress her. Courage she has, it is true, but women are by nature easily alarmed. (8)

Jester. This afternoon his Majesty the King of Magadha will, as usual, receive his friends, giving yourself the place of honour. Courtesy reciprocating courtesy engenders affection. So it is time for your Highness to make a move.

King. Yes, indeed. It is a good suggestion. [*Rises.*]

Men of eminent virtues are easily found in this world, as those whose hospitable treatment is unfailing, but it is difficult to find men who duly appreciate these qualities. (9)

[*Exeunt omnes.*]

END OF THE FOURTH ACT.

ACT V

[*At Magadha.*]

INTERLUDE

[*Enter Padminikā.*]

Padminikā. Madhukarikā, oh, Madhukarikā, come here quick.

[*Enter Madhukarikā.*]

Madhukarikā. Here I am, my dear, what do you want me to do?

Padminikā. Don't you know, my dear, that Princess Padmāvatī is ill with a bad headache?

Madhukarikā. Alas!

Padminikā. Run quick, my dear, and call Madam Avantikā. Only tell her the princess has a headache, and she will come of her own accord.

Madhukarikā. But, my dear, what good can she do?

Padminikā. Why, she will tell the princess pleasant stories and drive away the pain.

Madhukarikā. Very likely. Where have you made up the princess's bed?

Padminikā. It is spread in the sea-room.[1]

[1] *Samudra-gṛha.* Perhaps a room built out into a lake, or a room with jets of water.

Now you go. I shall look for the good Vasantaka, to inform his Highness.

Madhukarikā. Very well. [*Exit.*]

Padminikā. Now I will look for the good Vasantaka.

[*Enter the Jester.*]

Jester. The heart of the illustrious king of the Vatsas was depressed by separation from his queen, but now on this auspicious and extremely joyful occasion, fanned as it were by this marriage with Padmāvatī, it burns the more fiercely with the flame of the fire of love. [*Observing Padminikā.*] Hallo! here's Padminikā. Well, Padminikā, what's the news?

Padminikā. My good Vasantaka, don't you know that Princess Padmāvatī has a bad headache?

Jester. Truly, lady, I did not know.

Padminikā. Well, let his Highness know about it. Meanwhile, I will hurry up with the ointment for her forehead.

Jester. Where has Padmāvatī's bed been made up?

Padminikā. It is spread in the 'sea-room'.

Jester. Well, you had better be off. I will tell his Highness.

[*Exeunt ambo.*]

END OF THE INTERLUDE.

[*Enter the King.*]

King. Once again, with the lapse of time, I have taken up the burden of wedlock, but my thoughts fly back to Avantī's daughter, worthy daughter of a worthy sire; to her, whose slender frame was consumed by the fire at Lāvāṇaka, like a lotus-plant blasted by the frost. **(1)**

[*Enter the Jester.*]

Jester. Quick, your Highness, quick,

King. What is the matter?

Jester. Lady Padmāvatī has a bad headache.

King. Who told you?

Jester. Padminikā told me.

King. Alas!

Now that I have won another bride, endowed with grace and beauty, and possessed of all the virtues, my grief is somewhat dulled, yet after my experience of woe, still sick with the former pain, I anticipate the like for Padmāvatī. **(2)**

Where is Padmāvatī?

Jester. They put her bed in the sea-room.

King. Then show me the way.

Jester. Come this way, your Highness. [*Both walk round.*] This is the sea-room. Be pleased to enter.

King. You go in first.

Jester. Very well, sir. [*Enters.*] Help, help. Back, your Highness, stand back.

King. What is the matter?

Jester. Here's a snake wriggling on the floor. Its body is visible in the light of the lamp.

King. [*Entering, has a look round, and smiles.*]
Ha! the idiot thinks he sees a snake,

> For the dangling garland dropped from the portal arch, and lying stretched along the ground, thou dost suppose, poor fool, to be a serpent. Turned over by the light evening breeze it does move somewhat like a snake. (3)

Jester. [*Looking closely.*] Your Highness is right. It is not a snake. [*Entering and looking round.*] Lady Padmāvatī must have been here and gone away.

King. She cannot have come, comrade.

Jester. How do you know that?

King. What need of knowing? Look,

> The bed has not been pressed, it is as smooth as when made. There is no crinkle in the counterpane, the pillow is not rumpled nor stained with medicines for an aching head. There is no decoration to divert a patient's gaze. Those who are brought to bed by illness are not likely to leave it so soon. (4)

Jester. Then you might sit down on the bed for a while and wait for her ladyship.

King. Very well. [*Sits down.*] I feel dreadfully sleepy, old fellow. Tell me a story.

Jester. I will tell you a story, but your Highness must say 'Oh!' or something to show you are listening.

King. Very well.

Jester. There is a town called Ujjain. There there are most delightful swimming baths.

King. What, Ujjain did you say?

Jester. If you do not like this story, I will tell you another.

King. Comrade, it is not that I do not like it. But

> I remember the daughter of Avantī's king. At the moment of leaving she thought of her kinsfolk, and through affection

a tear welled up, which, after clinging to the corner of her eye, fell on my breast (5)

Moreover,

Time and again during her lessons she would fix her gaze on me and, dropping the quill, her hand would go on playing in the air. (6)

Jester. All right. I will tell you another.

There is a town called Brahmadatta, where there was a king named Kāmpilya.

King. What 's that? What did you say?

[*Jester repeats what he has just said.*]

King. Idiot! You should say King Brahmadatta and Kāmpilya City.

Jester. Is Brahmadatta the king and Kāmpilya the city?

King. Yes, that 's right.

Jester. Well, then, just wait a moment, while I get it pat. 'King Brahmadatta, Kāmpilya City.' [*Repeats this several times.*]

Now listen.

Why, his Highness is fast asleep. It is very chilly at this hour. I will go and fetch my cloak.[1] [*Exit.*]

[*Enter Vāsavadattā in Avantī dress and a Maid.*]

Maid. Come this way, lady. The princess is suffering from a severe headache.

Vāsavadattā. I am so sorry. Where has her bed been made up?

Maid. It is spread in the sea-room.

Vāsavadattā. Well, do you lead the way.

[*Both walk round.*]

Maid. This is the sea-room. Go in, madam, I will hurry up the ointments for her forehead. [*Exit.*]

Vāsavadattā. Oh, how cruel are the gods to me.

Padmāvatī, who was a source of comfort to my lord in the agony of his bereavement, has now fallen ill herself. I will go in. [*Entering and looking round.*] Ah! how careless the servants are. Padmāvatī is ill and they have left her alone with only a lamp to keep her company. So, she is asleep. I shall sit down. But if I sit elsewhere it might look as if I had but little love for her. So I shall sit on this same bed. [*Sits down.*] Why is it that now I am sitting beside her, my heart seems to thrill with joy? Happily her breathing is easy and regular. Her headache must have gone. And by leaving me one side of the bed she seems

[1] Or, 'blanket'?

to invite me to clasp her in my arms. I will lie by her side. [*Proceeds to lie down.*]

King. [*Talking in his sleep.*] O Vāsavadattā.

Vāsavadattā. [*Starting up.*] Ah! It is my lord and not Padmāvatī. Has he seen me? If so, the elaborate scheme of the noble Yaugandharāyaṇa will come to naught.

King. O daughter of Avantī's king.

Vāsavadattā. Happily my lord is only dreaming. There is no one about. I shall stay a little while and gladden my eyes and my heart.

King. Dear one, my darling pupil, answer me.

Vāsavadattā. I am speaking, my lord, I am speaking.

King. Are you displeased?

Vāsavadattā. Oh no! Oh no! Only very miserable.

King. If you are not displeased, why do you wear no jewels?

Vāsavadattā. What could be better than this?

King. Are you thinking of Viracikā?

Vāsavadattā. [*Angrily.*] O fie. Even here Viracikā!

King. Then I entreat forgiveness for Viracikā.

[*Stretches out his hands.*]

Vāsavadattā. I have stayed too long. Some one might see me. I will go. But first I will put back on the bed that hand of his hanging down. [*She does so and exit.*]

King. [*Rising suddenly.*] Stay! Vāsavadattā, stay! Alas!

Rushing out in my confusion, I struck against a panel of the door, and now I have no clear idea whether or no this was really my heart's desire. (7)

[*Enter the Jester.*]

Jester. Ah! Your Highness is awake.

King. Delightful news! Vāsavadattā is alive.

Jester. Oh, help us! What's this about Vāsavadattā? Why she died long ago.

King. Say not so, my friend,

As I lay sleeping on this couch she wakened me and disappeared. Rumaṇvān deceived me when he said she perished in the fire. (8)

Jester. Goodness gracious! but it's impossible, isn't it? I was talking about the swimming baths and you have been thinking of her ladyship, and you must have seen her in a dream.

King. So then it was only a dream.

If that was a dream, how glorious never to wake again, if this be illusion, long may that illusion last. (9)

Jester. There is a sylph dwelling in this city named Avantīsundarī. That 's what you must have seen, my dear fellow.

King. No, no.

At the end of my dream I awoke and saw her face; the eyes strangers to collyrium and the long unbraided locks were those of a lady guarding her virtue. (10)

Beside, see, comrade, see

This arm of mine was closely clasped by the agitated queen. Even now it has not ceased to thrill with joy though it felt her touch only in a dream. (11)

Jester. Come, now, no futile fancies. Come along, let us go to the ladies' court.

[*Enter the Chamberlain.*]

Chamberlain. Greeting to my noble lord.
King Darśaka, our sovereign lord, sends you these tidings: Rumaṇvān, the minister of your Highness, has arrived in the vicinity with a large force to attack Āruṇi. Likewise my own victorious army, elephants, cavalry, chariots, and infantry, is equipped and ready. Arise, therefore. Moreover,

Your foes are divided. Your subjects, devoted to you by reason of your virtues, have gained confidence. Arrangements are completed to protect your rear when you advance. Whatever is needed to crush the foe, I have provided. Forces have crossed the Ganges, the Vatsa kingdom is in the hollow of your hand. (12)

King. [*Rising.*] Very good. Now

I shall see that Āruṇi, adept in dreadful deeds and in the battlefield, surging like a mighty ocean with huge elephants and horses, with a lashing spray of arrows on the wing,—I will destroy him. (13)

END OF THE FIFTH ACT.

ACT VI

INTERLUDE

[*The Palace at Kauśāmbī.*]

[*Enter a Chamberlain.*]

Chamberlain. What ho, there! Who is on duty at the door of the golden arch?

[*Enter Portress.*]

Portress. Sir, it is I, Vijayā. What do you want me to do?

Chamberlain. Good woman, to take a message to Udayana, whose glory has increased by the capt re of the Vatsa kingdom. Tell him that a chamberlain of the Raibhya clan has come here from the court of Mahāsena. Also Vāsavadattā's nurse, named Vasundharā, sent by Queen Aṅgāravatī. They are both waiting at the gate.

Portress. Sir, this is not the place or time for a porter's message.

Chamberlain. Not the place or time—how's that?

Portress. Listen, sir. To-day some one in the sun-faced [1] palace was playing on the lute. When my lord heard it he said, 'I seem to hear the notes of Ghoshavatī' [2].

Chamberlain. And then?

Portress. Then somebody went and asked where he got that lute. He said he had found it lying in a thicket of reeds on the banks of the Narmadā. If it was any use, they could take it to the king. So they brought it, and my lord pressed it to his side and went off in a swoon. When he came to himself, with the tears running down his face, he said, 'Thou art found, Ghoshavatī, but her we cannot see'.
That, sir, is why the occasion is unsuitable.
How can I take your message?

Chamberlain. My good woman, you must really let him know, for this as it were hangs on to that.

Portress. I will let him know, sir. Why, here is my lord coming down from the sun-faced palace. I shall tell him here.

Chamberlain. Yes, do, good woman.

[*Exeunt.*]

END OF INTERLUDE.

[*Enter the King and the Jester.*]

King. Oh, my lute, whose notes are so sweet to the ear, after reposing in the lap of the queen and resting against her twin bosoms, how camest thou to dwell in that dreadful abode in the wilds, where flocks of birds have fouled thy strings? [3] (1)

How heartless art thou, Ghoshavatī, with no memory of thy unhappy mistress:

[1] Perhaps the palace or wing facing the sun.

[2] 'Sonorous', the name of his lute.

[3] Properly the 'neck' which was covered with the droppings of flocks of birds.

How she pressed thee to her side as she bore thee on her hip;
how when weary she tucked thee softly between her breasts;
how she bewailed the loss of me when we were parted; how
she smiled and chatted in the intervals of playing. (2)

Jester. Enough now, don't torment yourself beyond measure.

King. Say not so, dear friend.

My passion, for a long time dormant, has been awakened by
the lute, but the queen, who loved this lute, I cannot see. (3)

Vasantaka, have Ghoshavatī refitted with new strings by some skilful artist and bring it back to me at once.

Jester. As Your Highness commands.

[*Exit, taking the lute.*]

[*Enter Portress.*]

Portress. Greeting, my lord. There has arrived here from the court of Mahāsena a chamberlain of the Raibhya clan and also Vāsavadattā's nurse, Dame Vasundharā, sent by the Queen Aṅgāravatī. They are waiting at the entrance.

King. Then go and call Padmāvatī.

Portress. As my lord commands.

King. Can Mahāsena have learned this news so soon?

[*Enter Padmāvatī and the Portress.*]

Portress. This way, princess.

Padmāvatī. Greeting, my noble lord.

King. Padmāvatī, did they tell you? A chamberlain named Raibhya has come from Mahāsena with Dame Vasundharā, Vāsavadattā's nurse, from Queen Aṅgāravatī, and they are waiting outside.

Padmāvatī. My noble lord, I shall be glad to have good news of my relative's family.

King. It is worthy of you to speak of Vāsavadattā's relatives as your own. Padmāvatī, be seated. Now why do you not sit down?

Padmāvatī. My noble lord, would you have me seated at your side when you receive these people?

King. What harm is there in that?

Padmāvatī. That your lordship has married again may seem like indifference.

King. To hide my wife from the view of people who should see her would create a great scandal. So please be seated.

Padmāvatī. As my noble lord commands.

[*Sits down.*] My lord, I am rather uneasy as to what the dear parents will say.

King. Quite so, Padmāvatī.

My heart is full of misgivings as to what he will say. I stole away his daughter, and I have not kept her safe. Through fickle fortune I have greatly injured my fair name and I am afraid, like a son who has roused his father's wrath. (4)

Padmāvatī. Nothing can be preserved when its time has come.

Portress. The chamberlain and the nurse are waiting at the door.

King. Bring them in at once.

Portress. As my lord commands. [*Exit.*]

[*Enter the Chamberlain, the Nurse, and the Portress.*]

Chamberlain. To visit this kingdom, allied to ours by marriage ties, is a great joy, but when I remember the death of our princess I am filled with sorrow. O Destiny, was it not enough for thee that the kingdom should be seized by foes if the welfare of the queen remained? (5)

Portress. Here is my lord. Approach him, sir.

Chamberlain. [*Approaching the king.*] Greeting to your Highness.

Nurse. Greeting, your Highness.

King. [*Respectfully.*] Sir,

That king who regulates the rise and fall of royal dynasties on this earth, that king with whom I craved alliance, tell me, is he well? (6)

Chamberlain. Why, yes. Mahāsena is very well, and he would be informed of the health of everybody here.

King. [*Rising from his seat.*] What are the commands of Mahāsena.

Chamberlain. This is worthy of Vaidehī's son. Now pray be seated and listen to Mahāsena's message.

King. As Mahāsena commands. [*Sits down.*]

Chamberlain. 'Congratulations on the recovery of your kingdom seized by enemies, for,

There is no energy in those that are weak and faint-hearted—while the glory of kingship is enjoyed as a rule only by those that have energy.' (7)

King. Sir, it is all due to the might of Mahāsena.
For,

Aforetime when he had vanquished me he cherished me with his own sons. His daughter I stole away by force, but have not kept her safe. Now, learning of her decease, he shows me the same affection, for the king is the cause of my regaining the land of the Vatsas, my lawful subjects. (8)

Chamberlain. That is the message of Mahāsena.
The queen's message will be delivered by this lady.

King. Ah! tell me, nurse.

The holy goddess of the city, chief among the sixteen queens, my mother—so afflicted with grief at my departure—is she in good health? (9)

Nurse. The queen is well, and sends inquiries for the health of your lordship and all that are yours.

King. The health of all that are mine? Ah, nurse, what sort of health is that?

Nurse. Nay, now, my lord, do not torment yourself beyond measure.

Chamberlain. Compose yourself, my noble lord.

Though Mahāsena's daughter has passed away, she has not ceased to exist, while she is so mourned by her noble lord. But verily whom can any one protect in the hour of death? When the rope breaks, who can hold the pitcher? It is the same law for men and trees: now they grow, and anon they are cut down. (10)

King. Nay, sir, say not so.

Mahāsena's daughter was my pupil and my beloved queen. How could I forget her, even in births to come? (11)

Nurse. Thus saith the queen: 'Vāsavadattā has passed away. To me and to Mahāsena you are as dear as our Gopāla and Pālaka, for from the very first we intended you to be our son-in-law. That is why you were brought to Ujjain. Under the pretext of learning the lute we gave her to you, with no ritual fire as witness. In your impetuosity you carried her off without the celebration of the auspicious nuptial rites. So then we had portraits painted of you and of Vāsavadattā on a panel, and therewith celebrated the marriage. We send you the portraits,[1] and hope the sight of them will give you satisfaction.

King. Ah, how loving and how noble is the message of her Majesty!

Those words I hold more precious than the conquest of a hundred realms. For I am not forgotten in her love, in spite of all my transgressions. (12)

Padmāvatī. My lord, I would like to see the portrait of my eldest sister and salute her.

Nurse. Look, princess, look. [*Shows her the picture.*]

Padmāvatī. [*Aside.*] Why! It is very much like the Lady Avantikā. [*Aloud.*] My lord, is this a good likeness of her ladyship?

King. Likeness? No, I think it is herself. Oh, alas!

[1] The text gives but one picture-board for the two portraits. For the mock marriage and the action of this scene two separate pictures would be more convenient.

How could cruel calamity befall this charming loveliness?
How could fire ravage the sweetness of this face? (13)

Padmāvatī. By looking at my lord's portrait I can tell whether her ladyship's is a good likeness or not.

Nurse. See here, princess.

Padmāvatī. [*Looking.*] My lord's portrait is so good, I am sure her ladyship's must be a good likeness too.

King. My queen, ever since you looked at the picture I see you are delighted but perplexed. Why is that?

Padmāvatī. My noble lord, there is a lady living here who is exactly like this portrait.

King. What, of Vāsavadattā?

Padmāvatī. Yes.

King. Then send for her at once.

Padmāvatī. My noble lord, a certain brahman left her with me as a ward, before my marriage, saying that she was his sister. Her husband is away, and she shuns the sight of other men. So when you see her in my company you will know who it is.

King. If she be a brahman's sister, it is manifest she must be
another. Identity of form occurs in life as of very doubles. (14)

[*Enter Portress.*]

Portress. Greeting to my noble lord.
Here is a brahman from Ujjain who says he placed his sister as a ward in the hands of the princess. He wants to take her back, and he is waiting at the door.

King. Padmāvatī, is this the brahman you spoke of?

Padmāvatī. It must be.

King. Let the brahman be introduced at once with the formalities proper to the inner court.

Portress. As my lord commands. [*Exit.*]

King. Padmāvatī, do you bring the lady.

Padmāvatī. As my noble lord commands. [*Exit.*]

[*Enter Yaugandharāyaṇa and the Portress.*]

Yaugandharāyaṇa. Ah! [*Aside.*]
Though it was in the king's interest that I concealed the Queen
Consort, though I can see that what I've done is to his benefit,
yet even when my work is done my heart misgives me as to
what my royal master will say. (15)

Portress. Here is my lord. Approach him, sir.

Yaugandharāyaṇa. Greeting to your Highness, greeting!

King. I seem to have heard that voice before.

Sir Brahman, did you leave your sister as a ward in the hands of Padmāvatī?

Yaugandharāyaṇa. Certainly I did.

King. Then let his sister come here at once without delay.

Portress. As my lord commands. [*Exit.*]

[*Enter Padmāvatī, Avantikā, and Portress.*]

Padmāvatī. Come, lady. I have pleasant news for you.

Avantikā. What is it?

Padmāvatī. Your brother has come.

Avantikā. Happily he still remembers me.

Padmāvatī. [*Approaching.*] Greeting, my noble lord. Here is my ward.

King. Make a formal restitution, Padmāvatī. A deposit should be returned in the presence of witnesses. The worthy Raibhya here and this good lady will act as recorders.

Padmāvatī. Now, sir, resume your charge of this lady.

Nurse. [*Looking closely at Avantikā.*] Oh, but this is the princess Vāsavadattā.

King. What, Mahāsena's daughter? Oh, my queen, go into the ladies' court with Padmāvatī.

Yaugandharāyaṇa. No, no, she must not go in there. This lady, I tell you, is my sister.

King. What are you saying? This is the daughter of Mahāsena.

Yaugandharāyaṇa. O king,

> Born in the Bharata clan, you are self-controlled, enlightened, and pure. To take her by force were unworthy of you, a model of kingly duty. (16)

King. Very well, but let us just see this similarity of form. Draw the curtain aside.[1]

Yaugandharāyaṇa. Greeting to my royal master.

Vāsavadattā. Greeting to my noble lord.

King. Heavens! This is Yaugandharāyaṇa, and this Mahāsena's daughter.

> This time is it true, or do I see the vision again? I saw her before just like this, but was deceived. (17)

Yaugandharāyaṇa. Sire, by concealing the queen I am guilty of a grave offence. Please, pardon me, my royal master.

[*Falls at his feet.*]

[1] Perhaps idiomatic—'unveil'. It is difficult to see how the minister and Vāsavadattā could be behind a curtain. A transverse curtain would not help us. See Keith, *Sanskrit Drama*, p. 113.

King. [*Raising him.*] You are certainly Yaugandharāyaṇa.

By feigning madness, by battles and by plans worked out according to the codes of polity—you, by your exertions, raised me up when I was sinking. (18)

Yaugandharāyaṇa. I do but follow the fortunes of my royal master.

Padmāvatī. So then this is her Majesty the Queen. Lady, in treating you as a companion, I have unwillingly transgressed the bounds of propriety. I bow my head and beg your forgiveness.

Vāsavadattā. Rise, rise, happy lady of a living lord, rise, I say. If anything offends it is your suppliant form.[1]

Padmāvatī. I thank you!

King. Tell me, my dear Yaugandharāyaṇa, what was your object in concealing the queen?

Yaugandharāyaṇa. My one idea was to save Kauśāmbī.

King. What was your reason for putting her in the hands of Padmāvatī as a ward?

Yaugandharāyaṇa. The soothsayers, Pushpaka and Bhadraka, had predicted that she was destined to become your queen.

King. Did Rumaṇvān know of this?

Yaugandharāyaṇa. Sire, they all knew.

King. Oho! what a rogue he is—Rumaṇvān!

Yaugandharāyaṇa. Sire, let the worthy Raibhya and this good lady return this very day to announce the news of the safety of the queen.

King. No, no. We will all go together, taking Queen Padmāvatī.

Yaugandharāyaṇa. As your Majesty commands.

EPILOGUE.

This earth, that extends to the ocean, with the Himālaya and Vindhya mountains as ear-drops—may our Lion King rule over her, marked with the symbol of a single sovereign sway. (19)

[1] Reading doubtful.

CĀRUDATTA IN POVERTY

(*Daridra-Cārudattam*)

INTRODUCTION

THERE lived in Ujjain an opulent young merchant named Cārudatta. He was so charitable, so liberal in offerings to the gods and in gifts to his friends, that all his wealth was dissipated. Then it happened that he became enamoured of a beautiful young courtesan of the refined, affectionate type familiar in the literature of the East from Greece to Japan. Vasantasenā, the courtesan, had fallen in love with the young merchant.

The play opens with a prologue in which the stage-manager speaks Prakrit and goes out to invite a poor brahman to share a meal. This introduces Maitreya, the Jester boon-companion of the hero Cārudatta. From him, and from his dialogue with Cārudatta, we hear much of the woes of poverty.

Outside the house the Courtesan is chased by the villain, that is by the King's brother-in-law, and an attendant Parasite. She gives them the slip in the dark. The Hero sends out the Jester and a maid for some religious observance. The Courtesan enters the Hero's house and is mistaken for the maid. Having shaken off the libertines in the street, the Jester returns. The Courtesan is discovered, and, claiming protection, leaves her jewels in the Hero's care. She is escorted home by the Jester. (ACT I.)

The Courtesan discusses her beloved with her maid and then with the Shampooer, who rushes in to escape a creditor. He has been in Cārudatta's service, so Vasantasenā befriends him. A page rushes in with a story of a rogue elephant and of Cārudatta's kindness. They catch a glimpse of Cārudatta from the parapet. (ACT II.)

The Hero and the Jester have been to a concert and are returning late. The Courtesan's jewels are made over to the Jester. He and his master sleep. Sajjalaka, an expert burglar, cuts an artistic hole in the wall and goes off with the jewels, which the sleepy Jester thought he was handing over to Cārudatta. When the theft is discovered, his wife sacrifices her pearl necklace, worth a lakh, to compensate the owner. (ACT III.)

It appears that Sajjalaka, the enterprising burglar, is in love with Vasantasenā's maid, Madanikā, and needed money to buy the young woman out. He comes to the Courtesan's house and confesses his crime to the Maid. She recognizes the jewellery and tells him to give it to her mistress in the merchant's name. In the meantime the Jester arrives with the pearl necklace. After he has gone, Sajjalaka brings in the Courtesan's own jewellery, pretending to bring it from Cārudatta.

Vasantasenā loads her maid with jewellery and packs her off to marry her burglar. The Courtesan is preparing to visit Cārudatta, in spite of a threatening storm, in order to return the necklace, when the play suddenly ends. (ACT IV.)

What we have here is obviously a fragment, not a complete play in itself. *The Little Clay Cart* completes the story up to the reprieve of Cārudatta, who has been condemned to death for the murder of Vasantasenā. The later play has more literary polish, including an elaborate description in Prakrit of Vasantasenā's palace, but the dramatic force seems to come from the earlier play. How much in the later scenes of *The Little Clay Cart* is due to the second hand (said to be King Śūdraka) we can hardly guess. The way in which *The Little Clay Cart* is based on an older play is a warning of how we may be deceived by what appears to be uniform original work.

DRAMATIS PERSONAE

(In order of appearance.)

Stage-manager } in Prologue.
Actress }

JESTER, Maitreya, friend of Cārudatta.
HERO, Cārudatta, the impoverished merchant of Ujjain.
Śakāra, the king's brother-in-law, a libertine pursuing Vasantasenā, the villain of the play. (Saṃsthāna.)
Parasite, attendant on Śakāra.
Radanikā, maidservant in Cārudatta's house.
COURTESAN, Vasantasenā, in love with Cārudatta.
Maid, Madanikā, in Vasantasenā's house.
Shampooer, formerly in Cārudatta's service.
Page in Vasantasenā's household. (Karṇapūra.)
Vardhamānavaka, servant in Cārudatta's house.
Sajjalaka, burglar who marries Madanikā.
Brahman lady, wife of Cārudatta.
Second maid, in Vasantasenā's house, Vicchittikā.
Third maid, in Vasantasenā's house, Caturikā.

PROLOGUE

At the end of the opening[1] *enter the Stage-manager.*

Stage-manager. I left my house so early in the morning that my eyes are rolling with hunger like two water drops on a lotus leaf. [*Turning round.*] I will just go home and see whether or no there is a meal ready. [*Turning about.*] Here is my house. I will go in. [*Enters and looks round.*] The ground has been blackened by turning round iron pots. There is a scent like the savoury smell of grease, and as a good omen the attendants are running to and fro. Is there then a meal ready? Or does hunger make me think the whole world is made of rice? Well, I will call my wife. Madam, will you come here a moment?

Actress. Here I am, sir. It is a good thing that you have come.

Manager. My dear, is there any breakfast in the house?

Actress. There is.

Manager. Long life to you, and may you ever be the giver of good food!

Actress. Why, sir, I have been waiting for you.

Manager. Ah, my dear, is there what I want?

Actress. There is.

Manager. So may the gods bless you. What is there, my dear?

Actress. There is melted butter, sugar, curds, and rice.

Manager. All this in our house?

Actress. No, no, in the market.

Manager. Oh, you wicked woman, so may your own hopes be cut off, and you shall come to naught. I am like a wisp of grass[2] tossed up by a fierce wind so high from the hill top and then let fall again.

Actress. Don't be alarmed. Just wait a little while. Everything will be ready. I have got it, never fear. You must assist me, sir, in my fast to-day.

Manager. What is this fast of yours, ma'am?

Actress. It 's the fast to get a handsome husband.

Manager. In your next life, I presume?

Actress. Quite so.

Manager. That 's all right then. But who gave you the idea of this fast?

Actress. This servant of ours, Cūrṇagoṣṭha.

Manager. Well done, Cūrṇagoṣṭha, well done.

[1] Nāndī, see note p. ix.

[2] *Varaṇḍī.*

Actress. If you approve, sir, I should like to invite some brahman worthy of our company.

Manager. A most pious suggestion. In that way I shall get a good breakfast. Very well, do you go in, ma'am, and I will find a brahman worthy of our company.

Actress. As you bid, sir. [*Exit.*]

Manager. Now where can I get a poor brahman? [*Looking around.*] Ah! here comes the noble Maitreya, Cārudatta's friend. I will invite him. [*Stepping round.*] Sir, I invite you to take a meal at my house. Do not despise me and my invitation because I am poor. There will be everything good to eat. There's melted butter, sugar, curds, rice, everything. Moreover, there will be a fee, in gold pieces.

[*Voice behind the Scene.*]

'You must invite somebody else. I am not free.'

Manager. Deign to enjoy, good sir, this exquisite rice offered with great respect. Well prepared with butter and sugar and curds, it is flavoured with scented curry and spice. (1)

END OF PROLOGUE.

ACT I

[*Outside Cārudatta's house and later inside.*]

[*Enter the Jester.*]

Jester. You must invite somebody else. I am not free. I am not free, I tell you. What do you say? There will be an ample meal? Yes, I know. But one doesn't eat the stone of the very sweetest mango, because it doesn't suit one. Now why do you keep on trying to coax me? I tell you I am engaged. What do you say—'there will be a fee, in gold coins'? I decline it—in words, but cling to it in my mind. Alas! oh, misery! I, too, am looking for the invitations of others. I used to pass my days in Cārudatta's house chewing the cud of savoury sweetmeats, like a bull at the cross-ways stuffed up to the gullet. I used to sit like a painter amid his numerous pans of paint, surrounded by countless dishes of various kinds, ready throughout the twenty-four hours, seasoned with asafoetida, and in between whiles there were drinks, fragrant for gargling, produced at the lift of an eyebrow. And now that same I, because the noble Cārudatta is poor, must live like the pigeons, running elsewhere for my food before I come to his house.
And there's another wonderful thing. My belly understands the change

in affairs. It is satisfied with quite a little. It will take a good weight of rice if it is offered. What is not offered it does not demand or expect. Of course it is not I that am not content with such a state of affairs.

The noble Cārudatta is at his devotions,[1] so I have got him a garland and a garment of air. Now let me attend at his side. [*Stepping and looking around.*] Here is the noble Cārudatta, beautiful but pitiful like the moon at dawn. He is coming this way worshipping the household deities according to his means. I will go up to him. [*Exit.*]

[*Enter the Hero offering oblations, the Jester, and a Maid-servant with a basket* [2] *in her hands.*]

Hero. [*Sighing deeply.*] Oh! poverty is a living death to a high-minded man. For,

On this threshold of my house, where swans and flocks of cranes enjoyed the flower of libations, there sprouts the corn of old libations, and my handful of seed falls mumbled by the mouths of worms. (**2**)

Jester. Do not torment yourself too much. The young days of a house are like those of a man, subject to vicissitudes of circumstance. The ruin of your wealth, by charity from sea to sea, lends a charm to your present poverty like that of the moon loosing all its light in the dark fortnight.

Hero. Nay, I do not grieve for a fortune lost. But the ruin of a man with a sense of virtue and of sentiment seems to me very pitiful. For,

Prosperity after a season of woe is glorious like the sight of a lamp to one lost in the dark, but he who comes to poverty after prosperity lives in his body but is as good as dead. (3)

Jester. Ah, comrade. Where has it all gone, such heaps and heaps of wealth, the choicest from mart and sea?

Hero. [*Sighing.*] Gone, my friend, the same way as my luck. Look you,

My money has been used up on the needs of my friends. I remember none that was refused. This spirit has paid the price of confidence, but cannot perish. (4)

[*Shows his grief.*]

Jester. Are you grieving for wealth and prosperity?

Hero. In truth my trouble does not come from the loss of riches, for they can come again with a turn of fortune. This it is tor-

[1] *Saṭṭhīkida-devakayyassa*, 'one who has performed the religious duties (pertaining) to the sixth'. Sukthankar, *Studies in Bhāsa*, vi. J. B. B. R. A. S. I., p. 110. Mṛcch has *siddhī-kida* (*deva-kajjassa*).

[2] *Cāngerikā.*

ments me, now that I have lost my wealth, my friends become indifferent to a man that's merely good. (5)

Again,

If a man be poor his kinsmen reck nothing of his words. His magnanimity becomes ridiculous. The beauty of a moon of virtue is dimmed. Without enmity friends are estranged. Calamities abound. The evil deeds that others do are put upon his head. (6)

Jester. These damnable business affairs are running away from the house like herd boys scared by gnats. You are troubled now by the loss of your wealth. But it will sprout up again like the shoots of an old clump of reeds in the spring. So do not be so depressed.

Hero. Why should I be depressed, comrade? Am I poor, whose wife will follow my fortunes, whose good friend, thou, wilt share my joys and woes? And what is lacking with the indigent, I have not lost my magnanimity. (7)

[*Enter a Courtesan in flurry pursued by the Parasite and Śakāra.*]

Śakāra. Stop, Vasantasenā, stop I say.

Why are you going away, running away, racing away as you stumble? Oh, please now, I won't slay you. Do stop. My body, indeed, is scorched with love like a bit of leather fallen on red-hot coals. (8)

Parasite. Vasantasenā,

Why dost thou flee in terror like a gazelle frightened by a tiger's pursuit? Why transform thy delicate grace to hustle thy feet so skilled in teaching the dance?

Why should thine eyes dart sidelong glances tremulous with fright? (9)

Śakāra. Ah, doctor, this Vasantasenā's off.

Closely chased by us two lads like a jackal by a couple of hounds, with the merry jingling of her anklets and girdle, she's stolen my heart with the pericardium. (10)

Parasite. Vasantasenā,

Taking step after step by the hundred, why dost thou glide away like a female snake overwhelmed with the fear of the lord of birds? When I run at full speed I am like unto the wind. Dost thou think then I cannot catch thee? (11)

Courtesan. Pallavaka! Pallavaka! Parabhṛitikā! Parabhṛitikā! Madhukaraka! Śārikā! Alas. I have lost all my servants, so I must just take care of myself by myself.

Śakāra. Shout away. Shout for the sprout, the cuckoo, the bee, and the starling; the whole month of Spring.[1] Who in the world will protect you?

Like Vishṇu am I, the lord of the corpse bazaar, or Janamejaya, Kuntī's son. I shall catch thee with my hand in thy hair and carry thee off as Duḥśāsana did to Sītā.[2] (12)

Parasite. Vasantasenā, put me down as a man whose heart is entirely innocent of fear. Look you,

The murk of night is familiar to me from the blackness of my character.

Again and again have I passed through side-alleys shady with unending darkness. Though I should not say this before a young woman, go and ask the policemen in the market-place, who have escaped being murdered? (13)

Courtesan. Now I am in a pretty pass. Will these men who vaunt their own qualities abstain from evil deeds?

Parasite. Lady, kindly comply with our request. Look you,

It is a cause of wrath when a civil request is refused. When such as I are full of wrath what is it they cannot do? Thou art wooed by this powerful hand, made longer by my sword. Save me, save thyself from the horror of a maiden's murder. (14)

Courtesan. Even his wooing is most alarming.

Śakāra. Vasantasenā, the doctor is quite right.

The suit of such a mighty man is rare and you should make much of it. Look you, my wench,

Right sharp is the sword, blue as the peacock's neck. I'll cut off thy head or else I'll slay thee. Have done with enraging men like us. When a man's dead he lives no more. (15)

Courtesan. Good sir, I am but a courtesan who gets her living by the virtuous entertainment of the scions of nobility.

Parasite. Yes, that's why we're after you.

Courtesan. Good sir, what can you want from a little woman like me, her person or her jewellery?

Parasite. Who would strip a creeper of its flowers?

Have done—with your jewellery.

Courtesan. Well, then there is no need to worry.

Śakāra. Vasantasenā. You must love me, I am a prince.

Courtesan. Rest in peace.

[1] Play on the names of Vasantasenā's servants.

[2] Mythology muddled, somewhat like 'Apollo Lord of Hades, Romulus son of Helen'. Something similar in *The Little Clay Cart*.

Śakāra. Listen to that, doctor. She thinks I need a rest.

Parasite. [*Aside.*] The fool doesn't see she 's cursing him. She means he 'll be dead, and he thinks she means 'tired'. Besides,

Gesticulating with all his limbs, he utters rubbish devoid of sense. His movements are uncouth, his speech is debased. A new incarnation of a beast in human form. (16)

[*Aloud.*] Vasantasenā, what is this you are saying to my face? This is contrary to the ways of your house. Mind you,

The dwelling of a courtesan must be reckoned the friend of all the youth. Remember thou art like the flowering tree that grows beside the road. Thy body is a chattel to be bought at a price, so serve the man you love, fair lady, and serve the man you hate. (17)

Courtesan. The nobility appreciate my devotion.

Śakāra. Doctor, here is a lane full of the deepest gloom. Don't let her slip away down there. Ever since the Love God's festival she 's been sweet on a lad called Cārudatta, a poor merchant's son, firm only in her eyes. This is the side-door of his house.

Courtesan. [*Delighted. Aside.*] This is his house. Fortunately I have been brought near my beloved by the persecution of my enemies. Good, I'll do it! [*Slips away.*]

Śakāra. [*Looking round.*] Eh, doctor, she 's lost, the baggage is lost, I say.

Parasite. What do you mean by 'lost'? Search her out, search her out!

Śakāra. She 's nowhere to be seen, doctor.

Parasite. Confound it all, we have been cheated. Vasantasenā, I know now where you are.

Albeit thou art not visible in the evening dusk, like a lightning flash confined in the belly of a cloud, thy jingling ornaments will betray thee and thy perfume wafted by the breeze. (18)

[*The Courtesan removes her garland and throws off her ornaments.*]

Parasite. Ah! This darkness is plaguey thick. For now,

Darkness anoints my limbs, the sky it seems is raining lamp-black; my sight is useless, like service rendered to a rascal. (19)

Moreover,

As a ready shelter and as a source of dangers, darkness is the equal of a deep forest. Both are protected by the dark, what causes terror and the terrified. (20)

Again,

My eyes are staring wide to see, but all at once are completely wrapped in darkness; open though they are, they seem to be closed by the gloom. (21)

Courtesan. Oh, the side-door seems to be by the end of the wall. The gloom of disappointment makes the darkness thicker. So I shall wait here. [*Does so.*]

Hero. Maitreya, go and make oblation to the mothers in the square.

Jester. I have no faith. Let somebody else go.

Hero. What do you mean?

Jester. My intellect is like the reflection in a mirror, right for left and left for right.

Hero. Idiot! One must worship according to one's means. The feeling of devotion satisfies the deities. So go along.

Jester. How can I go all alone?

Hero. Radanikā, accompany this gentleman.

Radanikā. As you order, sir.

Jester. I will bring the lamp, lady.

Hero.[1] As you think best, very well.

Jester. [*Taking the lamp.*] Open the side-door, Radanikā.

Radanikā. [*Opening the door.*] There you are.

[*Courtesan puts out the lamp with the end of her robe.*]

Jester. Oh, damn!

Hero. What's the matter, comrade?

Jester. I was going out, and when the door was opened a filthy gust of wind came in from the street and put out the lamp in my hand.

Hero. Tut! What a fool you are.

Jester. It was only a small mistake. Radanikā, go and wait for me in the square. I'll come in a moment with a lamp from the inner room.

Maid. Very well, sir. [*Steps round.*]

Courtesan. Good, the door is open, so I can enter. This is no time to hesitate about the proprieties. I shall go in. [*Goes inside and waits.*]

Parasite. [*Looking round, aside.*] Here is a woman who has come out of the house and is coming this way. Good. I'll palm her off on this swine.

[*Aloud.*] Here is a smell that reeks of the perfume of a scented bath.

Śakāra. Ay, doctor, I can hear the smell with my own ears, but I can't see properly, my nostrils are so full of fog.

Parasite. Stop, stop. Where are you going. [*Catches the maid.*]

[*The maid falls to the ground in fright.*]

Śakāra. Catch her, doctor, catch her.

[1] Should be the maid, Radanikā.

Parasite. In the pride of her youth she spurned the scions of nobility. Now she is dragged along by her tresses that should be dressed with flowers. (22)

Śakāra. Have you caught her, doctor?

Parasite. Why, yes. I caught her by following the scent.

Śakāra. I'll cut her bloody head off and then I'll kill her.

Parasite. Catch hold of her then.

Śakāra. [*Catching hold of the maid.*]

Now I've got the wench by the head, by the hair, by the locks, and by the tresses. Now you may coo, or squeak, or scream to God, to the Lord, or to the Almighty. (23)

[*Drags the maid violently along.*]

Maid. Gentlemen! What are you going to do?

Śakāra. I say, doctor, I can tell from her voice this is not Vasantasenā.

Parasite. Don't let her go. Of course it's Vasantasenā.

She's been on the stage and she is trained in the arts, so she's clever at changing her voice. So do not release her. (24)

[*Enter the Jester with a lamp.*]

Jester. I have managed to bring the lamp, but it is difficult to keep it in. There's a cool breeze blowing down the street, and every step I take shakes up the oil in the bowl into waves.

Maid. [*Kicking Śakāra and screaming.*] Oh, sir! Maitreya! Is this an insult or simply insolence?

Jester. None of that, now, none of that.

[*Sees that the Parasite and Śakāra have swords, hesitates and stops.*]

Parasite. Ah! this is Maitreya, the noble Cārudatta's comrade. This, then, is not Vasantasenā. Great brahman, we have not acted thus through overweening pride, but owing to a mistaken identity. Look you, sir,

We were in pursuit of a certain lady, mistress of her youth, who denies us. She has eluded us. We mistook this lady for the same, hence this breach of good behaviour. (25)

Śakāra. Drat it! This is a maidservant of that fellow Cārudatta, the son of a miserable merchant. This is not Vasantasenā. Bravo, Vasantasenā! The doctor was deceived by its being dark in between. And I was deceived by the tricky slippery wench. Anyhow, it's a bad business.

Jester. Nay now, this is not right.

Parasite. Great brahman, lo, I fold my hands, which is the essence of entreaty.

Jester. Very well. You're not to blame. It's I that am to blame for letting you wheedle me.

Śakāra. I say, doctor, you seem mightily afraid of that fellow Cārudatta, the son of a miserable merchant.

Parasite. Truly, I am afraid of him.

Śakāra. Why, doctor, why?

Parasite. Because of his virtues. Look you,

He is beggared by the suits of men like me.
There is none but has been adorned by his riches. He is like a great tank dried up in summer, but it dried up after quenching men's thirst. **(26)**

Great brahman, please don't tell the merchant's son about this business.

[*Exit Parasite.*]

Śakāra. Mārisha, my lad, take a message from me to that fellow Cārudatta, son of a miserable merchant—'the king's brother-in-law, Saṃsthāna, salutes you with his turbaned head and says, "An actress, named Vasantasenā, daughter of a courtesan of the gold caste, being taken in arrest by two of us, has entered your house with a lot of gold ornaments. She must be handed over to-morrow. Otherwise there will be serious trouble between us." And Mārisha, my lad, you can go on to say. "Otherwise, you son of a slave, I'll crack your skull-cap like a garlic root in the beak of a turtle-dove; otherwise, I'll chew up your head like a ripe apple caught between two doors.'

Jester. Oh, you will, will you? [*Frightens the Śakāra with the lamp.*]

Śakāra. [*Looking all round.*] Where's the doctor? He's gone. Hi! doctor! [*Exit Śakāra.*]

Jester. Let us report to the noble Cārudatta that the oblation has been offered to the deities. Put away resentment from your heart, my good girl. Don't say anything about this affair indoors.

Maid. I shall be mum, sir.[1]

Jester. Come, let us go.

[*Both step around.*]

Hero. Has the oblation been offered to the deities, my good girl?

Courtesan. [*Aside.*] He mistakes me for his maid. Never mind, I am saved.

Hero. The evening is inclined to be windy. So take this mantle.

Courtesan. [*Taking the mantle, joyfully.*] This garment has a scent of perfume, that shows he is not quite indifferent to the vanities of youth.

Hero. Radanikā, you had better go into the inner room.

[1] Lit. 'I am Radanikā', i. e. all teeth (and no tongue).

Courtesan. [*Aside.*] Not I. I have no right to enter there.

Hero. Well, why don't you go in?

Courtesan. What am I to say now?

Hero. Why are you loitering, Radanikā?

[*Enter Radanikā and the Jester.*]

Radanikā. My good master, here I am.

Hero. Who, then, is this lady?

In ignorance I ventured to press my garment on her. She shines like a digit of the moon enclosed in autumn clouds. (27)

Courtesan. [*Aside.*] There he is, his beauty lit up by the lamp, for whose sake I inhabit this body, kept together only by sighs.

Jester. Cārudatta, the king's brother-in-law, Saṃsthāna, salutes you with his turbaned head and says, 'An actress named Vasantasenā, daughter of a courtesan, being taken in arrest by two of us, has entered your house with a lot of gold ornaments. She must be handed over to-morrow.'

Courtesan. [*Aside.*] He calls it 'taken in arrest', does he? Well, this is my opportunity. [*Aloud.*] Sir, I throw myself on your protection.

Hero. Don't be afraid, don't be afraid. Is this Vasantasenā?

Jester. Oh, yes, this is Vasantasenā. [*Aside to Cārudatta.*] This is the Vasantasenā, whom your eyes have extolled ever since the Love God's festival, who is exalted by your love-sick heart. So look at her.

Hero. I can see her, comrade.

Love has come to me, when the mass of my wealth has left me.
It must subside in my own breast like a coward's wrath. (28)

Courtesan. I have done wrong, sir, to enter boldly, uninvited. I bow my head, and ask your pardon.

Hero. If so, I also am to blame for treating you unawares like a servant, and I ask your pardon.

Jester. Oh, these two are worrying each other like a pair of ill-trained bullocks pulling a cart in opposite directions. Whose pardon shall I ask? I know, Radanikā's. Radanikā, I beseech your ladyship to pardon me.

Hero. I am no longer independent, lady. What place is there for affection?

Courtesan. [*Aside.*] Sweet indeed, what we would like would be. But it wouldn't do to stay here on our first meeting, especially as I came here of my own accord. I know what. [*Aloud.*] If, sir, I am pardoned, will you let me leave my ornaments here? Wicked men follow me because of my jewellery. And I would like to go to my house, sir, under your protection.

Hero. Her suggestion is quite reasonable. Maitreya, take the jewels.

Jester. Nay, I have no faith.

Hero. Take them, idiot.

Jester. As you command. Bring them over, lady.

[*Courtesan takes off her jewellery and hands it over.*]

Jester. [*Taking them.*] Radanikā, take this golden jewellery and keep it on the sixth and seventh. I'll keep them on the eighth, which is a holiday.

Radanikā. [*Laughing.*] The young master will have a rest from his studies, so you will have some spare time. Hand them over, sir.

Hero. Ho, without there! bring a lantern.

Jester. There's no oil in the lantern, as there is no affection in a courtesan.

Hero. Well, there is no need of a lantern. [*Gazing out.*] The moon has risen, the common lamp for all the world. So,

> Here rises the moon, pale yellow like soft dates, the light of the highway, the escort of young ladies. The white beams fall amid the dense darkness like streams of milk on dried-up mire. (29)

Lady, now you can go on the king's highway. My friend, follow this lady.

Jester. As you command. Come, lady.

[*Exeunt omnes.*]

END OF THE FIRST ACT.

ACT II

[*Vasantasenā's house.*]

[*Enter the Courtesan and a Maidservant.*]

Courtesan. And what then?

Maid. But I said nothing. Why do you ask, 'What then'?

Courtesan. Did I say anything, my dear?

Maid. Mistress dear, it's love, not curiosity, asks the question, What are you thinking about?

Courtesan. What would you guess, my dear?

Maid. I believe that contrary to the needs of her profession my mistress is in love with some one.

Courtesan. You have guessed right. Your perception is unerring. That's what's the matter with me.

Maid. I see my mistress has made her toilet without her jewellery. The Lord of Love is the unsung festival of the young.

Courtesan. Silly girl, what can you feel for my beloved?

Maid. Mistress dear, I want to ask, is he some prince as charming as he's grand?

Courtesan. I wish to love, not to serve.

Maid. Well, then, is it some young brahman fascinating with his deep learning?

Courtesan. Do the highly respected ever relax their self-control? I should have to reverence him.

Maid. Is it a visitor, some merchant's son?

Courtesan. Lunatic! What woman in love could endure the disappearance of her hopes?

Maid. Can't I hear, then, who has possessed your heart?

Courtesan. Didn't you go to the Love God's festival?

Maid. Yes, I did.

Courtesan. Then why do you talk as if you knew nothing about it?

Maid. Oh, tell me, mistress dear, tell me, tell me!

Courtesan. Listen, my dear. It's the young merchant, Cārudatta.

Maid. Who protected you when you sought shelter?

Courtesan. The very same.

Maid. Unfortunately—he is poor.

Courtesan. That's why I am in love with him. A courtesan attached to a very poor man earns no reproach.

Maid. My dear mistress, do the bees settle on a mango when the flowers have fallen?

Courtesan. That's so, my dear, they settle—and that's why they are called[1] bees.

Maid. What if he doesn't come? The loss of his wealth might make him shy of frequenting a courtesan's house.

Courtesan. But it is I that am in love with him.

Maid. If you think so much of him, why don't you go to him?

Courtesan. I don't say I won't go. But I am putting it off, because if I went all of a sudden and he couldn't give me a present, I mightn't be able to see him again.

Maid. Ah, then that was why you left your jewellery in his house.

Courtesan. Quite so.

[*Enter a Shampooer, in great haste.*]

[1] *Pucchianti*, Mṛcch has *vuccanti*.

Shampooer. Lady, I seek your protection.

Courtesan. Come, calm yourself.

Maid. Oh, but who is this fellow?

Courtesan. Silly girl, does one question one who seeks protection?

Maid. All the same, he might be a violent person.

Courtesan. Silly girl, the virtuous must always be protected.

Shampooer. Lady, I forgot my manners through terror, not from impudence. You know, lady, those who are scared, harried, in an accident, or easily put about, may readily offend.

Courtesan. Never mind, sir, be at your ease. I am only a courtesan.

Shampooer. By birth only, not by character.

Courtesan. Yes, my dear.

Maid. Mistress would like to know what frightened you.

Shampooer. A dun, lady.

Courtesan. If that is so, give the gentleman a seat.

Maid. Very well. [*Offers a seat.*]

Courtesan. Sit down, sir.

Shampooer. [*Aside.*] She's so polite about it, I suppose I must. [*Sits down.*]

Courtesan. One moment, my dear. [*Whispers.*]

Maid. Oh, my mistress, really? Sir, my mistress would like to set you on the road free of embarrassments. What is due, and to whom?

Shampooer. Listen, lady.

Courtesan. I am all attention.

Shampooer. I was born in Pāṭaliputra. By origin I am a trader, but owing to the vicissitudes of fortune I now follow the profession of a shampooer.

Courtesan. So you are a shampooer. You have learned a very delicate art.

Shampooer. I learned it as an art. Now it is my livelihood.

Courtesan. Your words point to a bitter experience. Well, what then?

Shampooer. Why, mistress, as I'd heard about it from travellers and was keen on meeting distinguished people, I've come here to Ujjain.

Courtesan. Well?

Shampooer. When I got here, I fell in with a certain young merchant.

Courtesan. What was he like?

Shampooer. A fine figure of a man, dignified, but not arrogant, charming but not conscious of his charm, clever but kindly, able but very polite, generally esteemed, calm and collected but easy to please. Generous without boasting of it, he always remembered even trifling obligations but forgot all the wrongs done to him. In short good mistress, one could not describe the quarter of the virtues of this noble youth in the longest summer day. To sum it up, he is so kind he treats his body as if it were a trust.

Courtesan. [*Aside to her Maid.*] My dear, who can it be, that imitates the virtues of the noble Cārudatta?

Maid. I am curious to hear who it is that adorns Ujjain with his virtues.

Courtesan. Well, go on.

Shampooer. Then, being completely won by his qualities, I forgot my wife and became one of his attendants.

Courtesan. Isn't he poor?

Shampooer. How could you tell that, lady, without being told?

Courtesan. It is difficult to find wealth and merit together. Go on.

Maid. What 's the gentleman's name?

Shampooer. Cārudatta.

Courtesan. I thought as much. Well, what then?

Shampooer. Then, on account of his scanty means, he dismissed his attendants and, relieved of the burden of a household, he is living in the merchant's house with nothing left but his character. My master asked me to find another employer. I thought I could never find another jewel of a man like him. Nor would I sully this hand by shampooing common men after touching his tender charming exquisite body. So I was filled with disgust for the world, but to keep my blasted body going I became a professional gambler.

[*The Courtesan looks at her Maid with tears of joy.*]

Maid. Well then?

Shampooer. Then one day I lost ten pieces of gold to a man from whom I had won for several days.

Courtesan. Yes?

Shampooer. Then to-day, when I happened to be near the street of pretty ladies, I ran across the man. It was from fear of him I came in here. So now your ladyship knows all about it.

Courtesan. [*Aside.*] Alack-a-day! It is sad to think how the birds are scattered on the destruction of the sheltering tree. [*Aloud.*] And so you have come to us. Go, girl, and send that man away.

Maid. Very well. [*Exit.*]

Courtesan. You need not worry, sir, about the money. You may regard it as a present from the noble Cārudatta.

[*Enter the Maid.*]

Maid. I sent the man away, mistress. He went away quite satisfied.

Shampooer. I am much obliged to you.

Courtesan. Good sir, you may go, and give us the pleasure of seeing you again.

Shampooer. I am disgusted with the world, and shall renounce it this very day. But if this art of mine were entrusted to your humble servant I should be very grateful to your ladyship.

Courtesan. It would be better to attend on him for whose sake you learned this art.

Shampooer. [*Aside.*] A clever way of declining my services. For who will spoil a favour by accepting a return for it? [*Aloud.*] Lady, I take my leave.

Courtesan. Good-bye, sir, till we meet again.

Shampooer. Amen to that, lady. [*Exit.*]

Courtesan. Hullo. What noise is that?

[*Enter a Page.*]

Page. Vicchittikā, where is the mistress?

Courtesan. What's the matter, boy?

Page. Oh, I am so disappointed that my mistress did not see Karṇapūra's valiant deed. If only she had seen, leaning forward from the casement with bosom bowed . . .

Courtesan. Feather-headed people are easily amazed. What is the cause of your excitement?

Page. Oh, mistress, listen. The sacred elephant, Bhadrakapota, was returning at great speed from a bath, making the high road fragrant with his flowing ichor. And in the street, crowded with innumerable people, he made for an ascetic, who was conspicuous by the red colour of his robe.

Courtesan. Oh, yes, go on.

Page. Then the elephant caught hold of the ascetic by the feet, hauled him up and knocked him about with his trunk. So there he lay between the two tusks. And the people cried, 'Alas, alas, he is torn in pieces, alas, alas, he is killed!' Then I released him, driving away the elephant with blows of my fist.

Courtesan. I am glad of that—go on.

Page. Then everybody said, 'Bravo, boy, well done', but nobody wanted to give me anything. Then, mistress, some young nobleman looked down where ornaments are usually worn and felt with his fingers, but finding nothing, he sighed deeply and reviled his fate. Then he sent me this mantle by an attendant, saying it was all he had.

Courtesan. Who is this that emulates the virtues of Cārudatta?

Maid. I, too, am very curious to know who it can be.

Courtesan. It must be a very good man.

Maid. Well, ask him.

Courtesan. Ah, my dear, partiality for one man kills all other qualities.

Maid. Do you know his name, dear boy?

Page. No, I don't know.

Courtesan. You were very thoughtless.

Maid. Well, then, what did you say to him?

Page. I do know this—the gentleman is not at all proud.

Courtesan. Come, let us have a look at him.

Page. Look, mistress, here he comes.

Courtesan. [*Looking from the parapet.*] My dear, why it is the selfsame Cārudatta. He has nothing but his sacred thread for an upper garment. Let us look at him before he is too far away.

[*Exeunt omnes.*]

END OF THE SECOND ACT.

ACT III

[*Street. Then Hero's house and a room in it.*]

[*Enter the Hero and the Jester.*]

Hero. Ah! comrade. The lute is a jewel, though not from the sea.[1] For,

> Like a friend, it is in tune with a lover's heart, a discourse of purest tone on the objects of his passion. A delightful companion where the torments of love are nothing but play, but a real rival to the ladies who delay their delights. (1)

Jester. What's the time, my friend? The street is deserted as if by proclamation. Even the dogs have gone to sleep. But we get no sleep at all. There's another funny thing. I don't enjoy the cursed lute. I wish its strings would snap in the thickest place.

Hero. But, comrade, the master's[2] singing to-day was extremely sweet. Didn't you enjoy that?

Jester. That's why I didn't enjoy it. Too much sweet stuff is indigestible.

Hero. Besides, his voice was beautifully clear.

> Melodious, sweet at the highest pitch and equally clear, full of feeling but free from flourishes. But why praise him in

[1] All jewels like pearls were supposed to come from the sea.

[2] Bhāva-Sabala. Professor Variegato.

various ways, quoting this and that—were he behind a wall, I should think it was a woman. (2)

Jester. You may praise him if you like. But as for me, I don't care for a man singing nor a woman reading. A man singing cuts a sorry figure like a priest garlanded with red flowers. And a woman reading is as ghastly as a cow with a slit nose.

Hero. My friend, midnight is upon us.

The streets are wrapped in darkness. Traffic has stopped, and Ujjain seems fast asleep. For,

That eight-day moon gives place to darkness and sets, as when a woodland elephant plunges into water, the curved end of his tusk is gradually submerged. (3)

Jester. You 're quite right. The darkness gets its chance when the moon disappears and seems to steal down from the roof.

Hero. [*Stepping about.*] Here is our house.

Vardhamānavaka! Vardhamānavaka!

Jester. Vardhamānavaka! Vardhamānavaka, open the door.

[*Enter a Servant.*]

Servant. Hullo, it 's the noble Maitreya.

Hero. Vardhamānavaka!

Servant. Oh, the master! Sir, I salute you.

Hero. Bring water to wash our feet.

Servant. [*Stepping round.*] Here is the foot-water. [*Washes the Hero's feet.*]

Jester. Vardharmānavaka, wash my feet too.

Servant. When your feet are well washed you'll go rolling on the ground. Pour away the water. Nay bring them here, I'll wash 'em. [*Indicates the washing of the Jester's feet.*]

Jester. The scoundrel has not only washed my feet, but my face too.

Hero. Comrade.

Sleep descends upon mine eyes and from my brow creeps over me, unseen, elusive, like old age, that waxes greater as it saps a mortal's strength. (4)

Let us sleep, Maitreya.

[*Exit Servant.*]

[*Enter the Maid with a casket of jewels in her hands.*]

Maid. Master Maitreya, wake up, do.

Jester. What is it, lady?

Maid. I was to look after this gold box on the sixth and seventh. To-day is the eighth.

Hero. Is this the property of Vasantasenā?

Maid. Yes. Oh, tell him, Master, he must take it.

Hero. Take it, Maitreya.

Jester. Why don't you send this jewellery into the inner apartments?

Hero. Idiot! Somebody in the house must not see jewellery worn by outsiders.

Jester. No way out of it. Bring it here. I'll take it. It's sure to be stolen by thieves.

[*Maid gives it to him and exit.*]

Jester. I say. Why did you give your mantle to the courtesan's servant?

Hero. From sympathy.

Jester. What, sympathy even for that creature?

Hero. Nay, my friend, speak not so.

Jester. I have to roll on the ground like a pack donkey.

Hero. I am sleepy. Be quiet.

Jester. Sleep well and wake refreshed. Well. I'll go to sleep too.

[*Both sleep.*]

[*Enter Sajjalaka.*]

Sajjalaka. Here I am,

I have made a road for my work by strength and skill in my art, an entrance easy for the body's girth. In I glide like a snake that sloughs his worn-out skin by rubbing his sides as he creeps along the ground. (5)

Ha! I have come in here by cutting a hole in the garden wall. Now I must get into the inner rooms.

[*Thinks anxiously.*] Ah!

Let the wiseacres call it low, this business when folks are asleep, for the shame of cheating those that are trustful comes from daring, not from cruelty. Independence though of ill report is better far than the folded hands of servility. This was the road that was taken of old by Drona's son when he slew the sleeping kings. (6)

[*Reflects.*] As for a merchant greedy and rich, despising honest folk, ruthless in his business, if I get hold of his house, my mind is not overpowered with remorse. (7)

So let things wag. What doesn't the Love God drive us into? I must get to work. Ah!

Now where is the spot where the bricks have been loosened by running water and can be breached without a sound? Where can a yawning cavity be easily made in the wall to show the interior? Where is the mansion decayed, rotten with saltpetre and thinned by falling bricks? Which way can I avoid the sight of women and crown my efforts with success? (8)

[*Steps round.*] This is the operation called quartering the site. The presence of moisture shows this foundation to be the best in the house. It is here I shall make room for an entrance. Now what kind of breach should I make?

Lion's stride or full-orbed moon? The jaws of a pike or semi-circular? Tiger's maw or triangular? Like a stool or like an elephant's mouth? How should we amaze the votaries of our art? (9)

So be it, I'll carve the 'lion's stride'.

Jester. I say. You're awake, aren't you?

Hero. What is it?

Jester. I can't sleep any more than a Buddhist monk that's made an assignation with a servant girl. My left eye is throbbing. I believe I can see a thief cutting a hole in the wall. If this is what it feels like to have wealth, I would be a poor man by caste.

Hero. Tut! What a fool you are, longing for poverty.

Sajjalaka. Now what shall I use to measure the breach?

This will do, sacred thread by day and measuring line by night.

To-night I pierce the walls of this house leaving them smooth after the cutting and touching them once with the burglar's drone.[1]

To-morrow the neighbours will foregather with long and gloomy faces to discuss my errors and the skill of my work. (10)

Praise be to the Lord of Thieves. Praise to the Gods that go by night. [*Makes the breach.*] Ha! ha! 'tis done. Let's go in. [*Enters.*] Oh, there's a lamp burning. I must be off. Nay now, I am Sajjalaka,

A cat to leap, a wolf to slink away, a snake to glide, a hawk to sight a mouse; like sleep to weigh the strength of slumberers. Illusion's self in donning disguise of form or hue, goddess of speech in the lingos of the land, a light by night, in danger darkness, like the wind on land, like a boat on water. (11)

[*Looking all round.*] As a stranger, I know nothing of the extent of this man's affluence. I came in relying simply on the appearance of the mansion. But now I don't see anything special in the way of furniture. Is he but a poor man after all? Or does he keep what's

[1] Low-toned instrument to ascertain if all are asleep.

worth seeing hidden away and out of use? Yet the mansion is nobly planned. He must have squandered his wealth on pleasure.

So, though short of funds, he keeps the house, when it's time
to sell, because it is his birth-place and he loves it dearly.[1] (12)

Well we must see. Or rather a gentleman no better off than myself should not be troubled. I will go.

Jester. Oh, take this golden casket.

Sajjalaka. Eh, what? 'Golden casket' says he? Had he seen me, when he spoke? Or through lack of self-control was he talking in his sleep? We must have a look. [*Takes a look at him.*] He is really asleep. For,

His breathing is regular and steady and comes at even intervals.
His body is stretched out with joints relaxed, too long for the
bed. His eyes are firmly closed, not rolling beneath the lids.
Nor could he bear to face the lamp, if he were feigning
sleep. (13)

Now where is it? Ah, now it is visible in the light of the lamp wrapped in a piece of an old cloak. He has got his arms round it. The moment has come. Here I have some moths. I let one loose to extinguish the lamp. [*Lets one loose from a bee-box.*] Ah he's down and the lamp's out.

Jester. Damn it, now the lamp's gone out. I shall be robbed. Ho, Cārudatta, do take this golden jewellery. I can't sleep for fright, like a trader who's got off the right road. I'll curse you with a brahman's curse if you don't take it.

Sajjalaka. No need of imprecations, I will take it. [*Takes it.*]

Jester. [*After handing it over.*] Now I shall sleep soundly like a trader who has sold all his wares.

Sajjalaka. Sleep sound, great brahman. [*Reflects.*] Ah! ought I to take what a brahman gives me in confidence?

A curse on poverty. Young blood has no remorse. For I
blame this cruel deed and do it. (14)

[*A drum is beaten behind the scene.*]

Sajjalaka. [*Listens.*] Ah! It is dawn. I must be off at once.

[*Exit Sajjalaka.*]

[*Enter a Maidservant.*]

Maid. [*Shouting.*] Master Maitreya. A thief has been and cut a hole in the orchard door and got into the house.

Jester. [*Getting up in a hurry.*] What do you say, girl?

[*Maid repeats what she said before.*]

[1] *Nīlasneha*, affection constant as (the colour of) indigo.

Jester. Cut a hole in the thief? And the breach came in?

Maid. Drat the man. The thief cut the hole and got into the house.

Jester. Come and show me.

Maid. [*Stepping round.*] There.

Jester. Damn it all, the rascally dog got in all right.
Come lady, I will break the pleasant news to Cārudatta.

[*Both return to Cārudatta.*]

Cārudatta. I've got some pleasant news for you.

Hero. [*Waking.*] What is this pleasant news for me? Has Vasantasenā come?

Jester. No, not a lady, but a gentleman.[1]

Hero. What does he mean, Radanikā?

Maid. Oh, Sir, a thief has cut a hole in our orchard door and got into the house.

Hero. A burglar got in?

Jester. Ah, my friend, you are always saying 'Maitreya is a fool, Maitreya is a blockhead'. But I did well to entrust that golden casket to your hands.

Hero. You gave it to me?

Jester. Why, of course!

Hero. At what time?

Jester. At midnight.

Hero. At midnight you say? You really gave it to me?

Jester. Yes, Cārudatta, I gave it to you while you were awake.

Hero. [*Aside.*] Alas! the golden casket has been stolen.

Jester. Now you had better give it back to me.

Hero. [*Aside.*] Who will credit the truth? Every one will suspect
me. For in all crimes powerless poverty is suspect. (15)

[*Enter a Brahman lady.*]

Lady. Radanikā! Radanikā! Come here. She doesn't hear. I must knock on the door. [*Does so.*]

Maid. Oh, a knock on the door. My mistress calls me.
[*Stepping round.*] Here I am, mistress.

Lady. They are not wounded or killed? My husband or Master Maitreya?

Maid. They are both all right. But that person's jewellery has been stolen by a burglar.

Lady. What do you say? Stolen by a burglar?

Maid. Yes.

Lady. What recompense can we give that person? Nay, I will give

[1] Not *Vasantasenā* (fem.) but *Vasantasena* (masc.)

this. [*Puts her hands to her ears.*] Alas! only palm leaf. Old habit is mocking me. Now what shall I do? [*Reflects.*] Yes, I know. There is the pearl necklace worth a lakh that I have from my family. My lord is so munificent, he will give that instead. Good, that's what I'll do. [*Exit.*]

Jester. With bowed head I entreat your pardon for this fault due to the dark. Now you can give it back to me.[1]

Hero. What, are you pressing me now?

Thou knowest my character day by day, yet thou hast misgivings. How much more so one that lives by the arts, learned in deceits? **(16)**

[*Remains in grief.*]

Jester. I believe, wretched fellow that I am, that I handed it to the burglar.

[*Enter the Brahman Lady.*]

Lady. Radanikā, call Master Maitreya here.

Maid. Master Maitreya, the mistress calls you.

Jester. What me, lady?

Maid. Yes.

Jester. Here I come. [*Approaches.*]

Lady. Master Maitreya, accept this donation.

Jester. This costly present is not in keeping with our circumstances. Why does this come to me?

Lady. Why on the sixth day I observe a fast. I desire the blessing of a brahman propitiated by the best of my possessions; that's why it comes to you.

Jester. But to-day is the eighth.

Lady. My neglect is due to thoughtlessness. The rite is completed to-day.

Jester. This gift is so lavish it savours of compassion. [*Aside to the Maid.*] What shall I do, Radanikā?

Maid. [*Aside to him.*] My mistress gives it to you to free the master from debt, because she thinks he must be worried about what to give that person. So you'd better take it.

Lady. Pearls grow in water and it was difficult to meet you, so my duty slipped by. Please accept. [*Gives the necklace.*]

Jester. [*Taking the necklace.*] May all be well. But there are tears in your eyes.

Lady. The temple smoke has made my eyes water.

Jester. The noble Cārudatta will curse you, if that is untrue.

[1] *paḍicchadu.* ? read *paacchadu.*

Lady. Alas! [*Exit.*]

Jester. She has gone without betraying her grief in words, but her tears make it plain. [*Going up to the Hero.*] Well, here it is.

Hero. What is it?

Jester. The result of marrying a lady of your own rank.

Hero. What, my wife takes pity on me?

Jester. As you see.

Hero. Fie on me! To-day I am crushed indeed.

> So reduced am I by loss of wealth, the man is rescued by a woman's help. The man in fact is but a woman, and the woman is the man. (17)

Jester. Her ladyship entreats you from her heart, I entreat you with my bowed head. Please accept it.

Hero. Very well. [*Takes the pearls.*] Comrade, take this pearl necklace to Vasantasenā.

> My desire that found its pleasure in my wealth now pays unseemly court to women's treasures, loitering behind both pride and duty. What 's family pride if a man is a pauper? (18)

Jester. Alack-a-day! here's a necklace worth a lakh to replace a trumpery golden casket.

Hero. Nay, comrade, say not so.

> She trusted us in making this deposit. Give her this present as the price of her great confidence. (19)

[*Exeunt omnes.*]

END OF THE THIRD ACT.

ACT IV

[*Enter Vasantasenā in love and a Maid with a portrait-panel holding paint-box, and brushes in her hand.*]

Courtesan. Look, my good girl. Is it like him?

Maid. My dear mistress, that 's just how he looked, that prince among men, when I saw him from a distance—with my eyes respectfully cast down—in the confusion of the struggle with the elephant.

Courtesan. 'None so sly as those that serve a courtesan.' You fulfill the proverb and are telling fibs.

Maid. What 's that? 'Every servant of a courtesan is sincere'? Look you, my Mistress, *nimbu* trees do grow in a *campaka*[1] garden. I am

[1] *Michelia champaka,* with yellow flowers.

delighted that it is so very like. In very truth it does him honour, I mean the God of Love.

Courtesan. My good girl, I do not allow my friends to make a mock of me.

Maid. That is right. Courtesans, they say, find rival wives in their own girl friends.

[*Enter another Maid with her hands full of ornaments.*]

Second Maid. Is my mistress well?

Courtesan. You are welcome, my good girl.

Second Maid. Mistress mine, your mamma sends this message. 'The blue lotus carriage has returned and just come into the gateway. So be quick with your finery and come with your veil.' Here are the ornaments, put them on.

Courtesan. Will the noble Cārudatta grace us with a visit?

Second Maid. No, the man who sent the ornaments is Saṃsthāna the king's brother-in law.

Courtesan. Away with you, insolent creature!

Second Maid. Forgive me, mistress mine, forgive me, I was only giving the message. [*Falls at her feet.*]

Courtesan. Get up, get up, 'tis the evil message I am displeased with, not with you.

Second Maid. What am I to say to your mamma?

Courtesan. Tell her that I will put on my finery if I am to meet the noble Cārudatta.

Second Maid. Very well. [*Exit.*]

[*Enter Sajjalaka.*]

Sajjalaka. By night I did a famous wrong, overcoming sleep and darkling fear. But with the rising of the sun my valour grows gradually fainter like the moon in daylight, and I am frightened. (1)

Fortunately my work was finished before dawn. I have just done this to compensate Vasantasenā for her lady's-maid Madanikā. [*Steps around.*]

This is Vasantasenā's house. I will go in. [*Enters.*] Now is Madanikā in the inner rooms? Why yes, in the morning these people always stick to the inner rooms. So that's where she must be. I will call her. Madanikā! Madanikā!

Maid. [*Listening.*] That sounds like Sajjalaka's voice. My mistress is busy. So I will slip out. [*Coming out to Sajjalaka.*] Here I am.

Sajjalaka. Come here.

Maid. Why do you look so apprehensive?

Sajjalaka. Not at all, I want to tell you something.

Courtesan. My good girl, put this picture on my bed. [*Looking around.*] Where has the silly girl gone? Well, she can't have gone far. I'll have a look for her. [*Steps round and looks about.*] Oho, there she is, talking to some man, fairly drinking him up with most loving glances. I think it must be the man who wants me to let her go by purchase.

Sajjalaka. I will tell you a secret.

Courtesan. It is wrong to listen to other people's secrets, I will go.

Sajjalaka. Will Vasantasenā— [*Stops in the middle.*]

Courtesan. So I am the subject of this story. Very well, I shall listen. [*Comes back and waits.*]

Sajjalaka. Will she set you free for a compensation?

Courtesan. That is he. Good, I shall listen.

Maid. Sajjalaka, my mistress was the first to suggest setting me free.

Sajjalaka. Then offer her this and say,

These ornaments are fashioned as if to fit thee. Show them not abroad, but wear them for love of me. (2)

Maid. Let me see them.

Sajjalaka. Take them. [*Shows them.*]

Maid. I seem to have seen this jewellery before.

Courtesan. It looks like mine.

Maid. Tell me, tell me, how did you get them?

Sajjalaka. Through love of you I did a violent deed.

Both Women. Oh, a man of violence!

Maid. [*Aside.*] Indeed it is hers. This fellow's face is troubled because of his cruel deed.[1] [*Aloud.*] Alas, for my sake you have imperilled both your life and your character.

Sajjalaka. Nonsense! Fortune[2] dwells with daring.

Maid. You are an ignoramus. For who, forsooth, will sell his body[2] for his life? But in whose house did you commit this breach of confidence?

Sajjalaka. As I heard in the morning, there was a merchant's son living in the Bankers' Square called Cārudatta.

Both Women. Oh dear! oh dear!

Sajjalaka. Gracious!

All thy limbs are drooping in distress, thine eyes dilated in alarm. Thou art trembling like a wounded deer and quivering with compassion. (3)

Maid. Tell me truly, when you were robbing the merchant's house

[1] Reading *didī imassa.*

[2] Play on *Śrīr* and *Śarīra.*

did you kill a young man of the house, or wound him with your weapon?

Courtesan. Good, she has asked exactly what I wanted to ask myself.

Sajjalaka. Madanikā! Hadn't I done enough, that I should commit a second crime? No, I neither killed nor wounded anybody.

Maid. Is that true, Sajjalaka?

Sajjalaka. Quite true.

Maid. Good for you, Sajjalaka. My heart rejoices.[1]

Sajjalaka. Your heart rejoices? What is the meaning of that? So, Madanikā,

I, that am sprung from forbears contented with their lot,
commit a crime, because my heart is bound with love of thee;
I keep this frame together torn by passion—and thou pretendest
I am thy friend but goest to another. (4)

Maid. Listen to me, Sajjalaka. This jewellery belongs to my mistress. [*Whispers.*] It was like this . . . .

Sajjalaka. So,

Tormented by the summer heat and seeking shade I have
returned to the selfsame branch that I stripped erstwhile of all
its leaves in ignorance. (5)

Courtesan. I think he is repenting that he did the crime.[2]

Sajjalaka. That being so, what am I to do, Madanikā?

Maid. Return them where they were. My mistress will not put them on.

Sajjalaka. But if the gentleman should be angry and hand me over to the police as a thief, what shall I do then?

Maid. Don't be afraid. He is a gentleman, and will be conciliated by your good qualities.

Courtesan. Well said, my dear, you are beyond reproach. That speech of yours does you honour.

Sajjalaka. I can't go there, absolutely.

Maid. There's another way.

Courtesan. These are the tricks of the trade.

Sajjalaka. What's the other way?

Maid. Could the merchant or my lady recognize you?

Sajjalaka. No, not at all.

Maid. Well then, present this jewellery to my lady in the merchant's name. In this way you will be quite safe, that noble man will be free from anxiety, and I shall not be worried. Otherwise, if my lady is cheated again, I shall be back in slavery.

Sajjalaka. Madanikā, I agree.

[1] *Piam me.* 'I am glad' or 'My darling'.

[2] Reading defective?

Courtesan. Good, I will go and wait inside. [*Does so.*]

Maid. Come along, Sajjalaka. Wait for me in the Love God's temple. I will tell my lady as soon as I get a chance.

Sajjalaka. Splendid! [*Exit.*]

[*Enter another Maid.*]

Second Maid. Good luck, my lady. A brahman has come from a merchant's house to see you.

Courtesan. [*Respectfully.*] Go, show him in at once.

Second Maid. Very well. Come in, sir.

[*Enter the Jester.*]

Jester. [*Looking all' round.*] Oho, she's got a magnificent mansion, this courtesan. Visitors from various towns are busy reading. Various delicacies are being prepared. People are playing on lutes. Goldsmiths are carefully setting every kind of jewellery.

Second Maid. Here is my lady, sir. Go up to her.

Jester. [*Coming forward.*] Good health to your ladyship.

Courtesan. You are welcome, sir. Come, girl, a seat for the gentleman and water for his feet.

Jester. [*Aside.*] She can bring everything except food.

Maid. As my lady commands. [*Gives him a seat and water for his feet.*] Sit down, sir.

Jester. [*Sitting down.*] Please take a seat, lady. I have come to say something.

Courtesan. [*Sitting down.*] I am all attention.

Jester. What is the value of those ornaments?

Courtesan. Why do you ask me that, sir?

Jester. Listen, Lady. You deposited your jewellery with Cārudatta because you relied on his virtue, and he's lost it gambling.

Courtesan. Gambling? Quite so. Well?

Jester. So will your ladyship please accept this pearl necklace in payment for the jewellery?

Courtesan. [*Aside.*] Alack, what it is to be a courtesan! He thinks me greedy. If I do not take it, it will be the same trouble over again. Give it here, sir.

Jester. Here it is; take it, ma'am.

Courtesan. [*Taking hold of it.*] Please report that I accept it.

Jester. [*Aside.*] Not a word of polite refusal. [*Aloud.*] Very well. [*Hands it over and exit.*]

Courtesan. Bravo, Cārudatta, bravo! Though your fortune has changed you have saved your pride from a fall.

[*Enter Madanikā.*]

Madanikā. Oh, my lady, there's a man come from the house of a merchant's son and wants to see you.

Courtesan. Have I seen him before or is he a new comer?

Madanikā. No, lady, I think he is a dependent of that one.

Courtesan. Go, bring him in.

Madanikā. Very well. [*Exit.*]

Courtesan. Oh, what a delightful day!

[*Enter Madanikā with Sajjalaka.*]

Sajjalaka. 'Tis an ill thing an uneasy conscience.

If a man walks briskly by and looks at me, if he comes up quickly in confusion or stands still, my mind suspects them all alike; for a man's own guilt makes him apprehensive. (6)

Madanikā. Here is my lady. Go up to her.

Sajjalaka. [*Approaching.*] All happiness to your ladyship.

Courtesan. You are welcome, sir. My dear, give the gentleman a seat.

Sajjalaka. Nay, let be. Here is a seat. I have some very pressing business.

Courtesan. Very well. Speak out, sir.

Sajjalaka. I come from the noble Cārudatta with this message. He finds it difficult to take care of the jewellery entrusted to him because the house is unkempt through lack of use[1] and the family is away. So would you kindly take it back.

Courtesan. Come, sir, give it back to Cārudatta.

Sajjalaka. Lady, I am not going.

Courtesan. I know what it is, you have stolen that jewellery with violence from his house. You should respect his virtues, sir.

Sajjalaka. [*Aside.*] How did she find me out?

Courtesan. Ho there, a carriage for the gentleman!

Madanikā. I hear the sound of wheels. The carriage must have come.

Courtesan. [*Leading Madanikā with the jewellery.*] Into the carriage, sir, with your lady.

Madanikā. Mistress dear, what do you mean?

Courtesan. Restraining him with warning words you have now become his lawful wife. Take her, sir. [*Takes hold of Madanikā and pushes her towards him.*]

Sajjalaka. [*Aside.*] Ah, when can I requite her kindness? But may all harm be averted.

The man who looks for recompense does but gain calamity. May destruction fall on those that hate them, either him or the lady. (7)

[1] *Asambhoga-malinatayā.*

[*Exit Sajjalaka with Madanikā.*]

Courtesan. Caturikā!

[*Enter Caturikā.*]

Caturikā. Here, my lady.

Courtesan. Look, girl, I was wide awake but had a dream like this.

Caturikā. I am glad. That 's just the play they call the Ambrosial Act.

Courtesan. Come, let us take this jewellery to Cārudatta.

Caturikā. As you will, my lady. But that storm is coming up, the escort of trysting ladies.

Courtesan. Little wretch, don't delay me.

Caturikā. Come, dear mistress, come along.

[*Exeunt.*]

END OF ACT IV.

THE FIVE NIGHTS

(*Pañcarātram*)

INTRODUCTION

THE Five Nights takes us into the world of Epic story. This is one of the seven of our plays which are based on the Mahābhārata. These, of course, were written for audiences familiar with the stories of the Great Epic. A reader or an audience without a knowledge of the stories used, and of the main characters figuring in the epic, will not thoroughly appreciate these plays. Nevertheless, there are dramatic scenes which are striking in themselves.

The plot of The Five Nights is based on the Fourth Book of the Mahābhārata called Virāṭa-parvan. In the thirteenth year of their exile the Pāṇḍavas enter the palace of Virāṭa, king of the Matsyas, in various disguises, Yudhishṭhira, the eldest, as a brahman skilled in dice, Bhīmasena as a cook and pugilist, and Arjuna, the great bowman, as an effeminate creature of no sex in particular to teach dancing to the princesses. These are the three sons of Kuntī. The twin sons of Mādrī, Nakula (Mongoose), and Sahadeva, also obtained posts to look after the horses and the cows. Draupadī, the wife of the Pāṇḍavas, is employed by the queen as a coiffeuse. (SECTION LII. *Pāṇḍava-praveśa-parvan.*)

Senāpati Kīcaka, one of the *sūtas*,[1] commander-in-chief and a brother of the queen, molests Draupadī. She is protected by an invisible giant. Bhīma avenges the insult by taking Draupadī's place at a pretended rendezvous in the dancing hall, and throttling Kīcaka. He mutilates the corpse and shows it to Draupadī. Her cries attract the guard. Kīcaka's kinsmen want to burn Draupadī with the corpse. The king is afraid of the *sūtas* and agrees. Bhīma plucks up a palm-tree and destroys 105 *sūtas*. The remainder take to flight. The citizens are afraid of the supernatural protectors of Draupadī, and the king agrees to deport the coiffeuse, who is allowed to stay another thirteen days. (SECTION LIV. *Kīcaka-vadha-parvan.*)

The Kurus learn of the death of the Kīcakas, and at the suggestion of the king of Trigarta decide to raid the cattle of the Matsyas. The force from Trigarta attacks from the south-east. Virāṭa's cowherd reports the loss of 100,000 cows. The Matsyas arm and attack the

[1] A *sūta* could be groom, equerry, herald, or bard.

raiders. Four Pāṇḍavas go with them. There is a bitter battle which lasts all day and goes on by moonlight. The king of Trigarta captures the king of the Matsyas, but Bhīma rescues him and brings Suśarman, king of Trigarta, in bonds to Yudhishṭhira, who grants him his life and lets him go free.

Then the Kurus, attacking from the north, raid the Matsya cattle. The overseer of the herdsmen hurries into the city and, the army being absent, asks Prince Uttara to snatch their booty from the Kurus. The prince says he would go if he had a good charioteer. Bṛihannalā, the effeminate dancing-teacher, really Arjuna in disguise, is recommended and accepted by the prince. Out they drive, but near the cemetery by the *śamī* tree the young prince sights the Kuru host and takes alarm. He jumps out of the chariot and runs away, followed by the dancing-teacher.

The Kurus laugh, but guess that the charioteer is Arjuna. Then Arjuna gives the reins to the prince, undertakes the fighting himself and gets his own weapons from off the *śamī* tree. Arjuna reveals himself to the prince, and arms himself for the battle. There is a long, complicated struggle. Bhīshma, the veteran warrior, sends Duryodhana, the eldest of the Kaurava princes, towards Hastināpura[1] with part of the army and the stolen cattle. Arjuna forces the cattle back and performs prodigies of valour. The whole Kuru army is put to flight. Arjuna takes the cattle. The two return to the *śamī* tree and hide the weapons. Arjuna charges Uttara to take the credit of the fighting and not to give him away. The herdsmen are sent on ahead with the same story. King Virāṭa provides his son, Uttara, with a triumphal reception. He plays dice with Kaṅka (Yudhishṭhira in disguise), who gives the credit of the victory to Bṛihannalā, the dancing-teacher, whereupon the king throws the dice in his face and makes his nose bleed. Kṛishṇā catches the blood in a jar. Uttara and Bṛihannalā are announced, but Yudhishṭhira whispers to the doorkeeper to admit only Uttara, so that Arjuna should not see that he had been hurt. Uttara enters and asks his father to conciliate 'Kaṅka'. Then Bṛihannalā enters and Virāṭa praises Uttara. Uttara tells the true facts about the battle, but substitutes for Arjuna 'a son of the gods' who has disappeared. (SECTION LV. *Goharaṇa-parvan.*)

On the third day after the battle the Pāṇḍavas took their seat on the throne. King Virāṭa was enraged, but Arjuna reveals to him Yudhishṭhira and his other brothers. Uttara supports him and relates Arjuna's deeds. Virāṭa makes his peace with the Pāṇḍavas and offers

[1] Fifty-seven miles north-west of Delhi.

his daughter to Arjuna, who asks that she may be wedded to his son Abhimanyu. The Pāṇḍavas settle in Upaplavya, a Matsya town. There they are joined by many kings and Kṛishṇa. Abhimanyu's wedding is celebrated with great pomp. (SECTION LVI. *Vaivāhika-parvan.*)

This Fourth Book contains over two thousand verses. It will be seen how the story is simplified in our drama and details in the epic freely handled.

For any readers not familiar with the Mahābhārata story, it may be well to explain the importance of the thirteenth year. There had been a great gambling match at Hastināpura. The unscrupulous Śakuni, representing Duryodhana the principal Kuru, played with loaded dice against the virtuous Yudhishṭhira, the eldest of the Pāṇḍavas. The Pāṇḍava lost everything; property, money, kingdom, brothers, wife, and finally himself. The victorious Duryodhana insulted Draupadī, the wife of the Pāṇḍavas. Bloodshed was averted by a pact imposed by the elders of the family. For twelve years the Pāṇḍavas were banished to the jungles. During one more year, the thirteenth, they were to live so completely hidden that the Kurus and their spies could not find them—if they succeeded, half the kingdom was to be restored to them—if they failed, they were to be banished for twelve more years.

So they determined to send away their retinue and to take service in a palace, where they were unknown. All went well till the year was nearly over, when the unfortunate infatuation of the commander-in-chief for the little hairdresser led to such violent action on the part of Bhīma, the pugilist in the kitchen. Draupadī wished to stay another fortnight as then the thirteenth year would be over.

The Kurus meanwhile got no news of the Pāṇḍavas but heard of the slaughter of the Kīcakas and thought this an excellent opportunity to raid the Matsyas' cattle.

Thus we have the dramatic situation of the Pāṇḍavas in hiding forced into battle with the Kurus and their allies. We, the audience know who they are, but if they are discovered by the Kurus, or by their spies, among the Matsyas, before the year is out, they are undone and trickery is triumphant for another dozen years. The play begins with a description of the sacrifice performed for the Kuru king given us by three brahmans speaking in turn. Duryodhana is congratulated by all his friends. He is very affable and wishes to give his old preceptor Droṇa a present. He promises to give him anything in his power and swears it over water. Then Droṇa asks, 'Share thine inheritance with the homeless Pāndavas, who for these twelve years have found no refuge. This is the reward I beg of you'. Śakuni objects. There is an altercation. Duryodhana does not wish to break his solemn promise but is willing to get out of it by any quibble. So he accepts Śakuni's suggestion. If tidings of the Pāṇḍavas are brought to him within *five days*[1] he will present them with half the kingdom. News comes of the slaughter of the Kīcakas. Bhīshma recognizes the handiwork of Bhīma, and on his advice Droṇa accepts the condition of the five days. Bhīshma professes a private feud with Virāṭa and proposes a cattle raid. They all agree. (ACT I.)

In the next act the interlude shows us the herds of Virāṭa being raided by the Kurus. News is brought to the king, who wishes to go and fight. He sends 'Bhagavān' the brahman, called Kaṅka in the epic, who is really Yudhishṭhira in disguise. Then he sends for his chariot, to learn Prince Uttara has already taken it. The story of the defeat of the Kurus by the young prince and his strange charioteer is brought in by messengers. Arjuna, disguised as Bṛihannalā, is brought in to give further details of battle. Then we learn that Abhimanyu, Arjuna's son, who was with the Kurus, has been captured by the scullion (really Bhīma). Bṛihannalā is sent to bring him in. Abhimanyu does not recognize his father or his uncles. Then Uttara reveals who they are. Virāṭa offers his daughter, and Arjuna accepts her for his son. (ACT II.)

The Kurus learn that Abhimanyu has been captured. Bhīshma guesses it was Bhīma who captured him, and then they suspect the work of Arjuna in the archery ascribed to Uttara. While they are discussing this, an arrow is brought in marked with Arjuna's name.

Uttara brings a message from Yudhishṭhira inviting all the Kurus to the wedding of Uttara and Abhimanyu. Droṇa claims the fulfilment of the promise as the five days have not ended. Duryodhana agrees, and Droṇa expresses his delight. 'Oh joy! Now we are all content in the union of the mighty houses. May our Lion-King rule over all this earth.'

This verse ends the play and serves as the Bharata-vākyam, epilogue or final benediction. (ACT III.)

It will be obvious that our dramatist has taken enormous liberties with the epic story. Indeed, by working in a happy ending at this point he has excluded every reason for the great battle which is the central point of the Mahābhārata. In his treatment of the Virāṭa-

[1] Hence the name of the play Five Nights, i.e. five days. Compare 'fortnight' for fourteen-night = fourteen days and the obsolete 'sennight' for seven-night = a week.

parvan itself he has omitted a great deal, modified several particulars, and invented much of his own. Only three of the Pāṇḍavas are mentioned, nothing is said of Nakula and Sahadeva. The slaughter of the Kīcakas is not explained. Duryodhana's sacrifice is invented, so is the capture of Abhimanyu. Trigarta's attack is suppressed so that the original reason for Uttara's action is removed. The old King Virāṭa may be slow to act, but there is really no time for Uttara to have found his charioteer. Nor was there any reason for it. It has to be explained as a joke. Regarded as a story, the version in this play is far inferior to that of the epic. It may be noted that all the rougher aspects of the old story have been smoothed away—e. g. Kīcaka's brutality to Draupadī and Yudhishṭhira's bleeding nose. Moreover, Duryodhana is represented in a more favourable light. Śakuni is the only villain and has replaced Karṇa of the original. Karṇa in the play is generous and inclined to peace, in the epic he is haughty, insolent, jealous of the Pāṇḍavas, and particularly hostile to Arjuna.

It has sometimes been said that Bhāsa is closer to the epic feeling than later poets. This play lends no support to that view. The characters of the epic story are treated here with a respect and delicacy that are no signs of antiquity. The atmosphere is one of piety and polite courtesy. The merit of the play lies in its skill in telling of a battle indirectly and in the enjoyment of the audience who can see through the disguises. The situation in which the young Abhimanyu cannot recognize his father and uncle, who taunt him, must have been specially pleasing to the poet who invented it, and to his audience.

The last verse suggests that the play may have been written for some special occasion on the ending of a feud in some royal family, but as to this, of course, we are completely in the dark.

DRAMATIS PERSONAE

(In order of appearance.)

Stage-manager, in Prologue only.

Three Brahmans, in Prelude of Act I.

Bhīshma, son of Śāṁtanu, old warrior who guides the Kurus.

DROṆA, the old preceptor of the Kuru and of the Pāṇḍava princes.

DURYODHANA, eldest of the Kuru princes, sons of Dhṛitarāshṭra.

Karṇa, King of Aṅga, elder half-brother of the Pāṇḍavas, being a son of Kuntī.

Śakuni, brother of Queen Gāndhārī, maternal uncle of the Kuru princes, Prince of Gāndhāra.

Servant of the Kurus.

Messenger.

King Bhūriśravas of the Deccan, King Bhīshmaka, King Vasubhadra, and Sahadeva son of Jarāsandha do not speak. (Nor does Abhimanyu in Act I.)

Old Cowherd.

Gomitraka, younger cowherd.

Other Cowherds.

Soldier, Jayasena.

Chamberlain of Virāṭa's palace.

King Virāṭa (of the Matsyas).

Servant of Virāṭa.

BHAGAVĀN, Yudhishṭhira (epic Kaṅka, a dicer).

Attendant of Virāṭa.

Charioteer of Virāṭa.

BṚIHANNALĀ, Arjuna, the great archer.

BHĪMA or BHĪMASENA, the powerful Pāṇḍu, disguised as a scullion pugilist. (Epic Ballava.)

Abhimanyu, Arjuna's son.

Uttara, Virāṭa's son.

Charioteer of the Kurus.

The rather intricate relationships of the Pāṇḍavas and Kauravas are not essential to the story of the play, but the following table may be of use in indicating to which generation each of them belongs.

14th from Kuru:	Śaṁtanu m. (1) Satyavatī	—Vicitravīrya m. Ambikā and Ambālikā but no issue			
	(2) Gaṅgā	—BHĪSHMA			
	Parāśara with Satyavatī	—VYĀSA with			
		(1) Ambikā half-brother's widow	— DHṚITARĀSHṬRA blind m. Gāndhāri, sister of Śakuni	*Duryodhina* + 99 brothers	
		(2) Ambālikā half-brother's widow	— PĀṆḌU m. (1) Kuntī, a Yādava (mother of Karṇa)	*Yudhishṭhira*, *Bhīma*, *Arjuna* m. Subhadrā	Abhimanyu m. Uttarā d. of Virāṭa
			(2) Mādrī	Nakula, Sahadeva	
		(3) Slave girl	— Vidura the Wise		

PROLOGUE

[*At the end of the Opening*[1] *enter the Stage-manager.*]

Stage-manager. May the Resplendent One[2] protect you, that cloud harbinger upon the earth of the bright and terrible. Pilot of the lord of birds,[3] he is hard to combat, grimly steadfast in battle, but takes the higher path intent on sacrifice. **(1)**

[*By paronomasia this verse introduces the names of Droṇa, Arjunā, Bhīma, Karṇa, Śakuni, Duryodhana, Bhīshma, Yudhishṭhira, Uttara, and Abhimanyu.*]

[*Turning round.*] With these words, my lords and gentlemen, I have to announce to you— But what is that? I thought I heard a noise, just as I was to make my announcement. Well, I must see what it is.

[*Voice behind the scene.*]

Ah, how magnificent is the sacrifice of the Kurus' king!

Stage-manager. So be it; I understand.

Duryodhana, the Kurus' king, performs a sacrifice, attended through affection by the vassal kings with all their courts. **(2)**

[*Exit.*]

END OF PROLOGUE.

ACT I

PRELUDE

[*Enter three Brahmans.*]

All together. Ah, how magnificent is the sacrifice of the Kurus' king!

First Brahman. All the land seems flowering with Kāsa from the fragments of the feasting of the priests. All these lines of trees lose the fragrance of their blossom in the oblation fumes. Tigers are as tame as deer, and the lions in the hills too quiet to attack.[4] By the consecration of the king for the rite, the whole world, it seems, is consecrated. **(3)**

[1] Nāndī, see note, p. ix.

[2] Virāj identified with Purusha, Prajāpati, &c., and later with Vishṇu: here with Kṛishṇa.

[3] Garuḍa.

[4] Comm. suggests also, 'not retaliating when beaten'.

Second Brahman. 'Tis true,

Fire at the head[1] of the greater deities is satisfied with oblations, the chief of the twice-born content with treasures. Full-fed are the flocks of birds and herds of kine, all men in the world are content. At present this world is altogether full of joy, eloquent of the king's good qualities. So by his virtues all the universe has become an abode for the gods. (4)

Third Brahman. Here are noble brahmans,

Honoured for their lore profound, their feet are chafed by the diadems[2] of kings. Even in old age they continue austerities with faces brave from study. Priests that are feeble with advance of age lay crooked hands on their pupils' shoulders and so advance with a staff like aged elephants, on three legs. (5)

Together. Ho there, you acolytes, acolytes! The ritual lustration is not complete, you must not let the fire go free.

First Brahman. Alas, you see how careless the lads are.

The ground is bright with its sacrificial post illumined as with an arm of gold. The sacred fire suffers not the common fire beside it as a twice-born man shrinks from a churl. The surface of the altar is but slightly scorched in its circle of green *kuśa* grass. The smoke is making for the east bamboos[3] like an elephant for a lotus plant in blossom. (6)

Second Brahman. 'Tis even so,

The priests remove the holy fire fearful of the common flame, like a kinsman kept from contact with his kin in a house that has transgressed the moral law. (7)

Third Brahman. Look you on the other side,

The barrow full of butter is ablaze though sprinkled with water, as a woman bereft of her child, though drenched in tears, burns with the love of her babe.[4] (8)

First Brahman. 'Tis true,

Leaping up where the *kuśa* grass is dry to burn the emperor's sacrificial cart, the fire is gradually dwarfed where the grass is dark and green. Now blown about by the breeze it flames around and in its course it gains the wheel, and forming a circle round the rim mimics the sun. (9)

Second Brahman. Look you, here is another thing.

[1] Comm. 'the mouth'.
[2] Or 'silk of the turbans'.
[3] Front portion of the sacrificial shed.
[4] A tasteless play on words. The woman sizzles through her tears like the sacrificial cart full of clarified butter.

Five snakes at once, frightened by the fire, are issuing from holes at an ant-hill's base, like the five senses at once from the body of one that has just died. (10)

Third Brahman. Again look you,

Birds that nested in the hollows of that tree now burning with the sacrificial fire in the wind have flown out like the breath of life. (11)

First Brahman. 'Tis even so,

The forest with its flowering trees is destroyed through one dry trunk, as a family through one wicked member. (12)

Second Brahman. These bamboos moving in the wind as they are burned by the sacred fire rise and fall like the fortunes of mortal men. (13)

Third Brahman. Well said.

The tree is entangled in the dry creeper clinging to its trunk, as a good man is destroyed by a woman's fault. (14)

First Brahman. Look you again,

After feasting on this forest, to its heart's content, on trees and shrubs and bushes, the fire has run along the *kuśa* grass down to the stream to rinse its lips and fingers. (15)

Second Brahman. The very same

Fire with its flying robe of grass goes from tree to tree, and the scorched plantains fall as if they were over-ripe. That palm tree in front with its great ring of honeyed hives, burnt for a long time at its root, falls like Kudra's axe. (16)

Third Brahman. Ah, now the holy fire dies down like a good man's anger.

The force of the fire is ended from the lack of fuel like the munificence of a noble man when his wealth is exhausted. (17)

First Brahman. The flames are licking the ritual ladle, the bowls, the firesticks, and grass as a man brought low by vice drinks up his own clothing. (18)

Second Brahman. This Flame of the Forest with boughs overhanging the stream dips one leafy hand in the breeze to make the last libation for the trees that lost their lives in the forest fire. (19)

Third Brahman. Come then, let us also perform the proper ablutions.

The other two. 'Tis well.

[*They all dip their hands in the water.*]

First Brahman. Ah, hither comes this very way his Majesty,[1] Duryodhana, the Kuru king, preceded by Bhīshma and Droṇa and followed by a galaxy of all the kings. And here

The citizens with sweet speech and opportune, to wit—'Feed with sacrifices, and win the earth with valour. Lay wrath aside and be merciful to thy own people', do homage—really to the sons of Pāṇḍu. **(20)**

Come then, we too will wait on the Kuru king.

The other two. Very good.

All together. Victory to the king!

[*Exeunt omnes.*]

END OF THE PRELUDE.

[*Enter Bhīshma and Droṇa.*]

Droṇa. My thanks at least are due to Duryodhana for upholding the law. For

A pupil's fault comes home to the teacher, passing by kin and ignoring friends; for no blame lies with father or mother if they hand over the child to a preceptor at an early age. **(21)**

Bhīshma. Here is Duryodhana,

Reaching his eminence by winning wealth he has drained the dregs of infamy through his love of strife. Now at long last, honouring the sacred law, a vessel of good works, this very man shines in a new guise. **(22)**

[*Enter Duryodhana, Karṇa, and Śakuni.*]

Duryodhana. My mind is confident, my preceptor fully satisfied. The world is reassured. My virtue is established and infamy departed. Only the dead, they say, can gain heaven, but that is false; heaven is not invisible, but bears its manifold fruit here in this world of ours. **(23)**

Karṇa. Son of Gāndhāri! your action was but just to lavish wealth justly acquired. For

The prosperity of warriors depends on their arrows. Who hoards for his sons is deceived. Pouring his treasure into the laps of the priests, a king should give his sons for all their patrimony nothing but a bow. **(24)**

Śakuni. The Aṅga king speaks truly, purified of guilt by ablutions in the Ganges.

[1] Reading *atrabhavān*.

Ikshvāku and other ancient heroes[1] possessed great treasures and mighty kingdoms. Their bodies have perished, but by their sacrifices they survive. (25)

All together. Gāndhāri's son! Congratulations on the successful termination of the sacrifice.

Duryodhana. I thank you. My teacher, I salute you.

Droṇa. Come, come, my son, this is not the proper order.

Duryodhana. What is the order, then?

Droṇa. Do you not see?

This man that is a god in human form, should receive the first obeisance. I cannot approve your salutation if Bhīshma is passed over. (26)

Bhīshma. No, say not so. In many ways am I inferior to you.

I was born from a mother, thou from thyself alone. My livelihood depends on arms, thine on their denial. Thou art a brahman, we are born of a warrior's house. Thou art the preceptor, and we thy pupils' pupils. (27)

Droṇa. Great-souled men cannot praise themselves. Come then, my son, salute me.

Duryodhana. Preceptor, I salute you.

Droṇa Come hither, my son. May you attain fatigue in such ritual ablutions.

Duryodhana. I thank you. Grandfather, I salute you.

Bhīshma. Come to me, my grandson, may your spirit ever be as tranquil.

Duryodhana. I thank you. Uncle, I salute you.

Śakuni. My child.

Having thus completed all the rites with guerdons to the priests and having subdued all the kings, mayest thou assemble them like Jarāsandha in a coronation ceremony. (28)

Droṇa. Ah! Even while pronouncing a benediction Śakuni excites his ambition. Alas! This young warrior prince is fond of strife.

Duryodhana. Karṇa, my friend, having saluted all my elders in due order, I may now enjoy your friendly confidence.

Karṇa. Gāndhāri's son!

Ritual vows have made thy body thin, yet thou canst endure my violence, let me embrace thee tightly. Till I have made my loving greeting, I will not trouble thee within, but I am scared of this solemn title 'Royal Sage'.[2] (29)

[1] Lit. Ikshvāku, Śayyāti, Yayāti, Rāma, Māndhātṛi, Nābhāga, Nṛiga, and Ambarīsha.

[2] Newly gained by the king on account of his sumptuous sacrifice.

Duryodhana. I hope you will always feel the same.

Droṇa. Duryodhana, my son, this is King Bhīsmaka, a favourite of mighty Indra, come to honour you.

Duryodhana. Welcome, noble prince. I salute you.

Bhīshma. Grandson, this is King Bhūriśravas, the iron bolt of the Deccan's gateway. He desires to offer his congratulations.

Duryodhana. Welcome, noble prince.

Droṇa. King Vasubhadra, wishing to honour your sacrifice, has sent Abhimanyu with his felicitations.

Śakuni. Duryodhana, my child, here is Sahadeva, the son of Jarāsandha, to salute you.

Duryodhana. Come hither, boy. May you grow up a hero like your father.

All together. This gathering of all the kings congratulates you.

Duryodhana. I thank you all. But if all the kings have gathered here, why has Virāṭa not appeared?

Śakuni. I have sent a messenger. I think he is on the way.

Duryodhana. Now, my preceptor, my teacher of the sacred lore as well as of the bow, be pleased to accept a teacher's fee.

Droṇa. A fee? Well, be it so. There is something for which I will petition.

Duryodhana. How, shall a teacher make petition?

Bhīshma. Why, what do you need?

> When he has quaffed the *soma* in his youth, when he is attended by an umbrella of state, and attains renown, what wealth remains, what reward, what special thing, wherein a brahman, teacher of warriors, can be poor? **(30)**

Duryodhana. Command me, what do you desire? What can I do for you?

Droṇa. My son, Duryodhana, I will tell you.

Duryodhana. Why now do you hesitate?

> Dearer to thee than life, I have gained from thee my training. My valour is established and I rank with heroes. Speak out freely, what thou wouldst have. What can I give? While the mace rests in my hand, all is thine. **(31)**

Droṇa. My son, I will tell you, but the torrent of my tears impedes me.

All together. What! Is the preceptor shedding tears?

Bhīshma. Duryodhana, my grandson, you have had all your trouble in vain.

Duryodhana. Ho, without there!

[*Enter Servant.*]

Servant. To the great king, victory.

Duryodhana. Bring me water.

Servant. As the great king commands. [*Exit and re-enters.*] Victory to the great king! Here is water.

Duryodhana. Bring it here. [*Takes the bowl.*] My teacher, prithee cleanse thy cheeks stained by falling tears.

Droṇa. Very well. But the cleansing stream shall be the fulfilment of my heart's desire.

Duryodhana. Alack!

If thou thinkest of my erstwhile duplicity and doubtest of my giving, stretch out thy hand, hardened with hundreds of arrows. Lo, this water is a guarantor of gifts. **(32)**

Droṇa. Ah, now my heart is confident. Hearken, my son.

Share thine inheritance with the homeless Pāṇḍavas, who for these twelve years have found no refuge. This is the reward I beg of you. **(33)**

Śakuni. [*Excitedly.*] Nay, not so.

Is it worthy of thee, this religious fraud, broaching thyself the question of the sacrifice to cozen thy pupil initiated by thyself and trusting thee as his teacher? **(34)**

Droṇa. Religious fraud? Speak not thus, Śakuni, with the arrogance of Gandhāra. Dishonourable yourself, you think every one else is the same.

Is it fraud if I bid him to restore his cousins their sire's domain? Is it better to give what is asked, or for them to take it by force? **(35)**

All. What? By force?

Bhīshma. Grandson! At the moment we are concerned only with the final purification. Do not listen to Śakuni, who is an enemy in the guise of a friend. Look you, my child,

If Pāṇḍu's sons with the daughter of King Drupada roam over the earth dishevelled with desert dust, if thou art averse from them and they adverse to thee, all this comes from the harsh conceit of Śakuni. **(36)**

Duryodhana. It may be so, but one question I will put to you, my teacher.

Droṇa. Speak out, my son.

Duryodhana. At first, when in the gambling hall in the open court they were stripped of realm and pride, why did they restrain their wrath if they were capable of force? **(37)**

Droṇa. That you should ask Yudhishṭhira, who with his devotion to the dice was cheated by a pretence of fair play.

'Twas he checked Bhīma just as he was measuring the pillars of the halls. Had he been allowed one movement, Śakuni would not chide us now. (38)

Bhīshma. One thing is proposed, another comes about. Good preceptor, the important thing is our purpose, not the quarrel.

Droṇa. No cringing, let us rather have the quarrel.

Bhīshma. Be calm, preceptor! Look you, my grandson,

They are powerless, miserable, and destitute. Humbly they seek conciliation with thee. Thou art the eldest and thou hast their affection. Wilt thou sustain them in thy household, or shall they remain with beasts? (39)

Śakuni. Let them remain, let them remain.

Karṇa. Good, my teacher, be not impatient. Duryodhana in sooth,

Is wroth when given bitter counsel, however wise, nor can he brook the praising of the pre-eminence of better men. Have a care now of your pupil's performance almost come to completion. He should be guided gently like an elephant with many faults. (40)

Droṇa. Karṇa, my child, glorious is the dignity of a brahman.[1] You have reminded me in time. Lo, I will follow your suggestion. Duryodhana, my son, am I your teacher?

Bhīshma. Now he has started on the right track. Conciliation is the only remedy for the ill-behaved.

Duryodhana. Not only my teacher, but the lord of all my house.

Droṇa. That is worthy of you. So, my son,

If thou art deceived by me that is no fault of thine; or if I trouble thee, be that for thy gain. Mutual dissensions in great houses are reconciled by the weighty words of law. (41)

Duryodhana. And so I wish to take counsel.

Droṇa. With whom will you take counsel, my son?

With Bhīshma or with Karṇa? With what king?[2] With Jayadratha the ruler of Sindh? Or perhaps with Droṇa's son, with Vidura, with thy father or thy mother? Speak, my son, with whom? (42)

Duryodhana. No, no, with my uncle.

Droṇa. With Śakuni? Alas, our task is hopeless.

Duryodhana. Come hither, uncle, and you too, dear Karṇa.

[1] Or, brahmanhood is passionate. Comm.

[2] Reading *nṛpeṇa*.

Droṇa. [*Aside.*] So be it. I know what I will do. [*Aloud.*] Come along, my child, king of Gāndhāra.

Śakuni. Here I am.

Droṇa. My child,

Old age is prone to anger, forgive my childish indiscretion.
Let my embrace be peacemaker for my sharp words. (43)

Bhīshma. [*Aside.*] Here is the preceptor, through affection for his pupil, beseeching Śakuni, and he, though he be conciliated, does not forego his crookedness. (44)

Śakuni. [*Aside.*] Ha, ha, the teacher is a rogue, he is coaxing me to get his own way.

[*All step round and sit down.*]

Duryodhana. Uncle, what is your opinion about giving half the kingdom to the Pāṇḍavas?

Śakuni. It should not be given—that is my opinion.

Duryodhana. Yet my mother's brother might well say it should be given.

Śakuni. If the realm is to be given,[1] why do you ask our advice? Go on, give it all away.

Duryodhana. You say nothing, my dear king of the Aṅgas.

Karṇa. Now what shall I say?

The brotherly goodness that Rāma has enjoyed and himself maintained I would not oppose. Pardon or no pardon, that is for thee to decide. We assist thee in times of battle. (45)

Duryodhana. My uncle, think of some wretched country hard to live in and beset by a powerful foe, where the Pāṇḍavas might dwell.

Śakuni. Nay, beware.

My answer is, the empty air. What foe more powerful than Arjuna? Yet corn will grow in salty soil if Yudhishṭhira be king. (46)

Duryodhana. But now,

I have poured the water in the hollow of my teacher's palm, as the elders of the house heard me declare what is binding on this earth.
Impolitic it may be, or deception, anything you like, O king, but I intend to make that promise[2] true. (47)

Śakuni. So you wish to avoid breaking your word?

Duryodhana. Why, yes.

Śakuni. Then come this way a moment. [*Going up to Droṇa.*] Good teacher, his Majesty the king of the Kurus gives you this answer.

Droṇa. My dear Prince of Gāndhāra, pray tell me.

[1] *Yadi* with loc. absol. [2] Lit. 'water'.

Śakuni. If tidings of the Pāṇḍavas are brought[1] to him within five days, he will present them with half his kingdom. So now you may bring them home.

Droṇa. Nay, say not so.

Intent on trickery you would have me bring them in five days, though none has seen them for twelve years. In plain words the boon is not granted. (48)

Bhīshma. Grandson, no tricks in duty! In this matter I also approve. Look you, my boy,

Do thou share with the Pāṇḍavas, be it in one year or a hundred. Make thy promise true, my hero, for the Kurus ever keep their word. (49)

Duryodhana. That is my decision.

Droṇa. [*Aside.*] Eagerness for my purpose makes me wish to-day that I resembled Hanumān, who leapt across the flood and brought back news of the vanished Sītā. (50)

Now whence in the world can I bring tidings of the Pāṇḍavas?

[*Enter a Servant.*]

Servant. To the great king, victory! The messenger has returned from Virāṭa city.

All. Bring him in at once.

Servant. As you command.

[*Exit.*] [*Enter the Messenger.*]

Messenger. To the great king, greeting!

All. Has the lord of Virāṭa arrived?

Messenger. He is in mourning and cannot come.

All. Why is he in mourning?

Messenger. Let his Majesty hear. Closely related to him were the hundred brothers of the Bamboo clan,[2] and,

One night they were slain by one unknown with his naked hands, for all the corpses seem to have been slaughtered without a weapon. (51)

All. What? Slaughtered without a weapon?

Bhīshma. Without a weapon? [*Aside to Droṇa.*] Good teacher, agree to the five days.

Droṇa. [*Aside to Bhīshma.*] Why?

Bhīshma. [*Aside.*] It is quite evident this was the sport of Bhīma with the mighty arms. His wrath against a hundred brothers here has borne fruit in another hundred. (52)

Droṇa. How do you know?

[1] *Yadi* with future participle. [2] Kīcaka.

Bhīshma. How, Paṇḍit? If calves wander on the river banks,
frisking as young things do, will the old bulls fail to recognize
the marks of their horns? **(53)**

Droṇa. 'Old bulls' you say? Good, the thing is done. [*Aloud.*] Duryodhana, my son, I agree to the five days.

Duryodhana. Very well. Five days let it be.

Droṇa. Hearken, all you kings here present to attend this sacrifice. His Majesty the king of the Kurus, Duryodhana—nay, not he, but he together with his uncle on his mother's side, will surely present the Pāṇḍavas with half the kingdom if news of them is brought within five days. Is it not so, my son?

Duryodhana. Exactly.

Droṇa. Reflect on that a second time and a third.

Śakuni. I shall know when the time is over.

Droṇa. What say you, Bhīshma?[1]

Bhīshma. [*Aside.*] If the preceptor's joy outstep his self-control
and becomes too plain, I fear he may be cheated by Duryodhana,
who is now deceived. **(54)**

[*Aloud.*] Duryodhana, my grandson, I have a secret feud with Virāṭa. That is why he did not attend your sacrifice. So let us raid his cattle.

Droṇa. [*Aside to Bhīshma.*] Oh, Bhīshma! His Highness the Lord of the Virāṭas is a dear pupil of mine. Why would you raid his cattle?

Bhīshma. [*Aside to Droṇa.*] Honest-hearted brahman!
Deafened by the din of chariots the Pāṇḍavas will be enraged.
They are possessed of gratitude, so our success lies in the
cattle-raid. **(55)**

[*Enter Servant.*]

Servant. To the great king, victory! The chariots are ready for the state entry into the city.

Duryodhana. With the selfsame chariots let us at once go lift his
kine. The mace that was at rest throughout the sacrifice shall
come to my hand again. **(56)**

Droṇa. So let my people bring my car.

Śakuni. Bring my elephant.

Karṇa. Hither bring my chariot yoked with steeds full eager for their burden.

Bhīshma. My heart hastens to go to the Virāṭa's city, hasten hither with my bow.

[1] Lit. Son of the Ganges.

All. Let the bow be and do thou stay here. We will do thy bidding.

Droṇa. Duryodhana, my son, we two old men desire to see your valour in the battle.

Duryodhana. As you please.

Droṇa. Dear Lord of Gāndhāra, in this raid do you go in the leading chariot.

Śakuni. Good! An excellent suggestion.

[*Exeunt omnes.*]

END OF THE FIRST ACT.

ACT II

[*The scene is laid in the Virāṭa country.*]

INTERLUDE

[*Enter an old Cowherd.*]

Old Cowherd. May my kine never lack for calves. May our young women never be widows. May our King Virāṭa be the lord of all the earth under one umbrella. The great King Virāṭa is going to give away cows at his birthday festival, that is why the herd was to come into this paddock outside the city, with all the cowherd lads and lasses in holiday attire and merry mood. I will find the eldest among them and see about it.[1] [*Looking round.*] Now why is that crow perched on that dead tree, rubbing his beak on a withered branch and croaking hoarsely, with his face to the sun? Peace be on us, and peace be on the herd. I will just find the leader and call out the lads and lasses. [*Steps around.*] Hello, Gomitraka, Gomitraka!

[*Enter Gomitraka.*]

Gomitraka. Good day to you, grandpa![2]

Old Cowherd. Peace be on us, and peace be on the herd. Gomitraka, the great King Virāṭa is going to give away cows at his birthday festival, that's why the herd was to come into this paddock outside the city, and all the lads and lasses in holiday attire and merry mood. Call them out, Gomitraka.

Gomitraka. As you will, grandpa. Ho, Gorakshiṇikā! Ghṛitapiṇḍa,

[1] Comm. takes *dāva* with preceding sentence and renders jjeṣṭaṃ by *jjaiṣṭhyaṃ* = having attained seniority, leadership among them. L. S. 'I shall go and honour the best among them.'

[2] Lit. 'uncle', i.e. mother's brother; affectionate term for old man.

Svāmini, Vṛishabhadatta, Kumbhadatta, Mahishadatta, come here at once.[1]

[*They all enter.*]

All together. Good day to you, grandpa!

Old Cowherd. Peace be on us, and peace be on the herd, and the lads and lasses too. The great King Virāṭa is going to give away cows at his birthday festival, that 's why the herd was to come into this paddock outside the city. Meantime let us be singing and dancing.

All together. As grandpa bids. [*They all dance.*]

Old Cowherd. Hee, hee! Well danced, well sung! Now I am going to dance. [*Dances.*]

All. Oh, grandpa, you've raised a mighty dust.

Old Cowherd. Not only dust, but a din of conches and drums.

All. Oh, grandpa, the sun is nearly gone, with its circle veiled in dust pale as the light of the morning moon.

Gomitraka. Look, grandpa, these people on horse-carts, with umbrellas as white as lumps of curd, are driving all through the camp, the thieves.

Old Cowherd. Oho, a flight of arrows! Lads and lasses, quick, into the huts.

All. Right you are, grandpa. [*Exeunt.*]

Old Cowherd. Ha! stop them, strike away, seize them, seize them! We will report this matter to the great King Virāṭa.

[*Exit.*]

END OF THE INTERLUDE.

[*Enter a Soldier.*]

Soldier. Ho there! take word, take word to the great king, Lord of Virāṭa—for those cows are being lifted by the sons of Dhṛitarāshṭra, concealing their valour with the works of rogues.

> This herd is pitiable in its agitation, with scampering calves and lines of frightened cows, while the bulls' faces show terror of what they see. All around the air is rent with bellows of distress. (1)

[*Behind the scenes.*]

By the sons of Dhṛitarāshṭra?

Soldier. Yes, sir.

[*Enter Chamberlain.*]

Chamberlain. It is likely enough of men malicious to their brothers. For,

[1] Names suggesting the herdsman's life: 'Cow-keeper, Butterball, &c.'

Clad in mail, with arrow-guards bound on arm and hand, they ride, elate with valour, on well-furnished chariots, with long-bows strung and weapons drawn, and their feud with the king they avenge on cows. (2)

Jayasena! His Majesty is intent on his birthday ceremonies, so your announcement would be most untimely. It would make him very angry. So I will tell him at the end of this auspicious day.

Soldier. But, Sir, this matter is very urgent. Do inform him at once.

Chamberlain. Well, it shall be done.

[*Exeunt.*]

[*Enter the King.*]

King. Out upon it! My cows are being stolen, with their calves rushing round in alarm through dread of the chariots' roar. And all the while my own right arm,[1] with its massive shoulder, is jingling with bracelets and wet with sandal paste, shamelessly feasting on dainties. (3)

Jayasena! Jayasena!

[*Enter a Soldier.*]

Soldier. Victory to the great king!

King. Oh, drop your 'great king'. My knighthood is in the mud. Tell me the details of the battle.

Soldier. Great king! Unpleasant news is not worth telling in detail. This is the gist of it.

The limbs of the kine made all one hue by the chariot's dust are lined in black and blue by the blows of the lash.[2] (4)

King. Then,

Swiftly bring my bow and make my chariot ready. Who loves me may follow of his own free will. A struggle for the cattle in the van of the fight cannot be futile. Though death ensue, there will be glory, and if we release them the law is upheld. (5)

Soldier. As your Majesty commands. [*Exit.*]

King. Now why, I wonder, does Duryodhana show this hostility to me? Because I did not go to his sacrifice? How could I attend? The destruction of the Bamboo brethren involved us in exceeding grief. Or perhaps it is because I secretly favour the Pāṇḍavas. In any case, I must fight. Now Bhagavān knows Duryodhana's character, for he lived a long while in Hastināpura. Though

[1] Lit. 'hand'.

[2] Lit. 'the distinctions of various colours appear in the blows of the lash.'

Willingly he will not tell me Duryodhana's faults, yet when need be, a man with a purpose asks and asks without tiring. (6)

Ho, without there!

[*Enter a Servant.*]

Servant. To the great king, victory!

King. Just call Bhagavān, will you?

Servant. As Your Majesty commands. [*Exit.*]

[*Enter Bhagavān.*]

Bhagavān. [*Looking all round.*] Ah! what is this?

Mighty elephants are being harnessed. The captains of the horse are clad in mail. Chariots are yoked, and soldiers tighten up their belts. Seeing all this preparation I feel unwonted apprehension. I am resolute, but my brothers are more changeable. (7)

[*Approaching.*] Greeting to you, sir.

King. Bhagavān, Virāṭa salutes you.

Bhagavān. Bless you.

King. I thank you, Bhagavān. Here is a seat. Pray sit down.

Bhagavān. Thanks. [*Sits down.*] O king,

Why is this activity toward? Is your Majesty unsatisfied? Is it to subdue the arrogant, or to rescue the oppressed? (8)

King. Bhagavān, I have been insulted by the lifting of my cattle.

Bhagavān. By whom?[1]

King. By the sons of Dhṛitarāshṭra.

Bhagavān. By the sons of Dhṛitarāshṭra? [*Aside.*] Alas, it is unfortunate.

In this world community of descent moves the hearts of the wise, for when my quarrelsome kin do wrong, in truth it seems as though I had done wrong myself. (9)

King. Bhagavān! On what now are you pondering?

Bhagavān. Nay, nothing. I am sorry for them.

King. From this day on they will be humble. Though Yudhishṭhira can forgive them, I shall not.

Bhagavān. Quite so. [*Aside.*]

Now is all commendable, a couch of leaves upon the ground, the loss of my realm, Draupadī put to shame and living in disguises—for my clemency is recognized. (10)

[*Enter an Attendant.*]

Attendant. To the great king, victory!

King. What is Duryodhana doing now?

[1] Reading *Kena* for *Kena karaṇena*, why?

Attendant. Not only Duryodhana, but the kings of the earth, have come, all of them.

Droṇa, Bhīshma, Jayadrathra, Śalya, and the Aṅga king, with Śakuni and Kṛipa. No need of arrows, we are beaten by their very standards with streamers oscillating with the jolting of their cars. **(11)**

King. [*Rising and folding his hands.*] What? Has the royal Bhīshma also come?

Bhagavān. [*Aside.*] Good. Although insulted he does not transgress the rules of etiquette. Ha!

Why now has the noblest elder of the Kurus come? I suspect he would remind me that our promise is fulfilled. **(12)**

King. Ho, without there!

[*Enter a Servant.*]

Servant. To the great king, victory!

King. Call my charioteer.

Servant. As the great king commands. [*Exit.*]

[*Enter the Charioteer.*]

Charioteer. Long live the king!

King. Swiftly bring my chariot, a noble battle-guest has come.

Bhīshma shall have all the arrows he desires; to defeat him is beyond my hopes. **(13)**

Charioteer. As the king commands. Long live Your Majesty!

The chariot which thou art wont to use to break the foeman's ranks, Prince Uttara has taken it to manifest his skill with a car. **(14)**

King. What! has the prince gone out?

Bhagavān. O king, keep back the prince, call him back.

His youth makes him keen on the battle, recking nought of good or bad. There is no fire of battle that does not burn when one is close. It is from no disrespect I tell thee the dangers of battle. **(15)**

King. Then get another chariot ready at once.

Charioteer. As the king commands.

King. Nay, come here a moment.

Charioteer. Your Majesty, I am here.

King. Now how comes it thou didst not drive the prince's car?

Did he dismiss thee? Art thou not the royal charioteer? **(16)**

Charioteer. Be not wroth, Your Majesty. I prepared the car and was in attendance according to my duty of charioteer. But the prince,

Be it for a jest or on account of skill in driving, passed me by and appointed as his driver—the girlish Bṛihannalā.[1] (17)

King. What! Bṛihannalā?

Bhagavān. O king, be not alarmed.

If Brihannalā has gone with him mounting the car, overcast by the dust which its own wheel raises, that car will be victorious without the aid of arrows, instantly vanquishing the foes by the roaring of its fellies. (18)

King. Then quickly get ready another chariot.

Charioteer. As your Majesty commands. [*Exit.*]

[*Enter a Soldier.*]

Soldier. The prince's chariot is smashed!

King. What! Smashed, do you say?

Bhagavān. How now, smashed?

Soldier. Will the great king deign to hear?

Numerous foes, expert in war, cut off the horses' path, and the car, making for a thicket, was shattered in front of the burial ground. (19)

Bhagavān. [*Aside.*] Ah, that's where we hid Arjuna's bow.[2] [*Aloud.*] O king,

There is some reason for that, the car before the burial ground. The ground whereon the sons of Dhṛitarāshṭra stand will soon become a cemetery. (20)

King. Bhagavān, your cool talk out of season makes me angry.

Bhagavān. Do not be angry. I have never told you what was false.

King. Yes, that is so. [*To Soldier.*] Go and bring more news.

Soldier. As the great king commands. [*Exit.*]

King. What is this thundering noise, started all of a sudden, that seems to shake the earth, like the curving flood of a river? (21)

Find out what it is.

[*Enter the Soldier.*]

Soldier. To the great king, victory! From the burial ground, after breathing his horses a while, the prince——

Bhagavān. May he not make my words untrue.

King. What did the prince do?

Soldier. He made the dark-blue elephants tawny by shooting arrows by the hundred. There is not a steed or warrior but his body bears a hundred arrows. The best chariots are clogged

[1] Masculine or feminine. 'A Lofty Reed', a name adopted by Arjuna disguised as a hermaphrodite.

[2] Gāṇḍīva, the bow of Arjuna.

with arrows, and with arrows pinned around. The roads are hidden by showers of arrows, and the bow pours forth a gruesome stream of darts. (**22**)

Bhagavān. [*Aside.*] That is the work of the quiver inexhaustible, whereby in the Khāṇḍava wood shafts were sped as numerous as Indra's drops of rain. (**23**)

King. Then what is the state of the enemy now?

Soldier. I have not seen for myself, but the scouts report—

Droṇa recognized the twang of the bow and has retired. Bhīshma saw an arrow in his standard. 'Enough', said he, and strikes no more. Karṇa is overwhelmed with arrows, and the other kings are crying, 'What can it be?' And in the alarm there is only one who, by reason of his youth, makes no account of danger, and that is Abhimanyu.[1] (**24**)

Bhagavān. What! has Abhimanyu come? O king,

If Subhadrā's son is in the fight, the fiery lustre of two royal houses, send another charioteer, for in front of him Bṛihannalā will hesitate.[2] (**25**)

King. Nay, say not so,

If he has driven back Bhīshma, whose mail was not pierced by even Rāma's[3] arrows, and Droṇa, who has spells for weapons, and Karṇa with Jayadratha, and all the other kings, will he not overpower Saubhadra with his arrows? Is he afraid of the father's reputation? Moreover, in company he will protect youth like his own, and worthy of companionship. (**26**)

Soldier. The prince's chariot,

When held in, moves in a curve, and when he lets it go, races ahead. When it draws near it does not dash in, and will not charge another car. Getting quite near, it whirls around and slips away. His chariot seems to give a lesson in the proper arts of driving. (**27**)

King. Go, bring the latest news.

Soldier. As the great king commands. [*Exit and re-enters.*] To the great king, victory! Victory to the Lord of Virāṭa! I bring your Majesty pleasant news. The cattle raid is defeated. The sons of Dhṛitarāshṭra have been put to flight.

Bhagavān. You have been fortunate.

[1] The son of Arjuna.

[2] Yudhishṭhira disguised as a brahman knows that Bṛihannalā is really Abhimanyu's father, Arjuna. The king does not.

[3] Paraśu-Rāma, the Rāma of the Axe, son of Jamadagni.

King. Nay, this success is due to you. Where is the prince now?

Soldier. The prince is preparing a report of the gallant deeds of warriors whose heroism he witnessed.

King. Ah, he is engaged in a commendable task.

For when a warrior is wounded in an honourable action an honour coming hard upon the event removes his pain. **(28)**

And where is Bṛihannalā?

Soldier. Gone into the ladies' quarters to tell the joyful news.

King. Send for Bṛihannalā.

Soldier. As the great king commands. [*Exit.*]

[*Enter Bṛihannalā.*]

Bṛihannalā. [*Looking round thoughtfully.*] I had to strain my strength a while in stringing the Gāṇḍīva bow. In handling the arrows my fist was awkward and unsteady. There was no dexterity where the arrow-guard is fixed, and suppleness had gone. Made languid by this woman's guise, by practice I soon became myself again. **(29)**

For I,

Did ply the bow, with this disguise shaming me midst fighting men, but that expedition was soon so rained upon with arrows that the dust sank quickly stained with blood. **(30)**

Ha!

Though I have won back the kine, and have gained a victory for the king, my heart does not feel a victor's joy. For I failed to seize Duryodhana in the forefront of the fray,[1] nor brought him bound this very day into the city of Virāṭa. **(31)**

Decked out in this finery which the princess gave me as a token of her pleasure, I feel ashamed to face the king.[2] And so I will see the Lord of Virāṭa. [*Steps round looking about.*] Why, here is the noble Yudhishṭhira.

So young and yet so fond of the holiest penance-forests, a king of men who leads a brahman's life. Though he has lost his kingdom his glory is increased. Though he does not wield a sovereign's sceptre he bears the triple staff of an ascetic.[3] **(32)**

[*Approaching.*] Bhagavān! Greeting, my salutations, my respects!

Bhagavān. Bless you.

Bṛihannalā. Hail, my lord!

[1] Duḥśāsana 'of hard commands' for Duryodhana.

[2] Yudhishṭhira.

[3] Made of three bamboos, symbolizing control of thought, word, and deed.

King. How one is formed does not matter, nor what is one's family. High and low alike shine by their deeds. This very shape that erstwhile was despised, has now gained great respect. **(33)**

Brihannalā! Tired as you are, I shall tire you further. Tell me the details of the battle.

Bṛihannalā. Listen, my lord—

King. Nay, it was a vigorous action. It should be told in Sanskrit.

Bṛihannalā. Great king, deign to hearken.

[*Enter a Soldier.*]

Soldier. Great king, victory!

King. Thy joy seems excessive. Speak. Why art thou excited?

Soldier. Good news beyond belief. Abhimanyu has been taken. **(34)**

Bṛihannalā. What, taken? [*Aside.*]

I weighed the strength of our host to-day and reckoned it up. And this very day I saw him in the fight. There is none to match him on this side. Who could it be, now the Bamboo brothers are slain? **(35)**

Bhagavān. What can it mean, Bṛihannalā?

Bṛihannalā. Bhagavān, I cannot guess his vanquisher. He is strong and excellently trained. Perhaps he met with this disgrace through the misfortune of his sire. **(36)**

King. But how was he taken?

Soldier. Fearlessly he went up to the car and lifted him out with his two arms.

King. Who did?

Soldier. That very man the king appointed scullion in the kitchen. **(37)**

Bṛihannalā. [*Aside.*] So he was embraced by the noble Bhīma, not taken prisoner after all.

Even at a distance I was delighted at the sight of him, but a son's affection was enjoyed by one who could act more openly. **(38)**

King. Well then, let Abhimanyu be well received and admitted to our presence.

Bhagavān. O king, people may think this honouring of Abhimanyu, a ruler of the Yādavas and Pāṇḍavas, is due to fear. Disdain would be more appropriate.

King. The son of Yādavī does not deserve disdain. For,

He is the son of Yudhishṭhira, of the same age as our son. We claim hereditary kinship with Drupada, and thus he is our grandson. He may soon be a son-in-law as well, for we are the father of a maid unwed.[1] As a guest he would be worthy of respect, and the Pāṇḍavas with their great qualities we admire. **(39)**

Bhagavān. That is so. But we must guard against what may be said.

King. Well, who shall present him?

Bhagavān. Let Bṛihannalā do so.

King. Bṛihannalā, do you present Abhimanyu.

Bṛihannalā. As your Majesty commands. [*Aside.*] I have been given as a duty what I have long desired. [*Exit.*]

Bhagavān [*Aside.*] Now he may go and see his son in private, see him and embrace him closely. His tears of joy may flow freely. For in my presence he would be shy about his son. **(40)**

King. Regard the prince's heroism.

Kings like Bhīshma are defeated. Subhadrā's son is taken prisoner. To-day, in short, Uttara has indeed conquered the whole earth. **(41)**

[*Enter Bhīmasena.*]

Bhīma. When the house of lac was ablaze I carried out my brothers and my mother clinging to my arms. From the chariot I lifted out one youth, Subhadrā's son. The exertion on the first occasion and that of to-day I think were equal. **(42)**

[*Enter Abhimanyu and Bṛihannalā.*]

Abhimanyu. Ah, I wonder who he is.

His chest is broad, his waist fined down to slenderness. His shoulders are erect and steady, his thighs huge and buttocks lean. He has carried me here with one arm, but, greatly stronger, he has hurt me not at all. **(43)**

Bṛihannalā. This way, prince.

Abhimanyu. Oh, but who is this other?

Adorned with lady's ornaments that suit him ill, he is like an elephant bull tricked out in the trappings of his mate. He seems small in this disguise, but his energy shows him great. He resembles Shiva masquerading as his spouse.[2]

Bṛihannalā. [*Aside to Bhīma.*] What have you done, my noble brother, in bringing him here?

He is disgraced as being defeated in his first fight, Subhadrā will grieve being parted from her darling son. Then Kṛishṇa will be angered to hear of his reverse. Well! no need of

[1] Uttarā, affianced to Abhimanyu at the end of the act.
[2] Umā.

many words, thou hast shamefully misused the brute force of thy arms. (45)

Bhīma. Arjuna!

Bṛihannalā. What do you say? This is the son of Arjuna.

Bhīma. [*Aside to Bṛihannalā.*] I recognize the drawbacks of his capture, but who could endure to leave his own son in the hands of foes? Methought that Draupadī should see him, for she is sunk in woe ever longing for her children, that is why I brought him. (46)

Bṛihannalā. [*Aside to Bhīma.*] Noble brother, I have a great yearning to talk with him. Make him speak.

Bhīma. Very well. Abhimanyu!

Abhimanyu. 'Abhimanyu' indeed!

Bhīma. He is angry with me. Do you speak to him.

Bṛihannalā. Abhimanyu!

Abhimanyu. How now? Am I 'Abhimanyu' to you?

Do low-caste people address the scions of the warrior race by their names? Is this the etiquette of this place? Or is this an insult for my capture? (47)

Bṛihannalā. Abhimanyu! Is thy mother well?

Abhimanyu. What! You speak of my mother?

Art thou my King of Righteousness, or Bhīmasena or Arjuna, that thou boardest me like a father, and askest me news of ladies in my house? (48)

Bṛihannalā. And, Abhimanyu, Keśava the son of Devakī, is he also well?

Abhimanyu. What, even him you call by name? Yes, of course. He must be well if he be associated with you.

[*Both look at each other.*]

Abhimanyu. Are you two making a mock of me?

Bṛihannalā. No, not at all.

Granted Arjuna is his father and Janārdana his uncle, it is proper for a youngster fully armed to be worsted in the battle. (49)

Abhimanyu. Enough of this idle chatter.

My own praises I may not sing. In our family it is not seemly. Do but see the arrows in the slain. You will find no other name. (50)

Bṛihannalā. [*Aside to Bhīma.*] What he says is true enough. In the whole array of chariots, cavalry, fierce elephants, and foot, there was none he left unwounded, so dexterous was his archery. I should have been hit myself if I had not turned aside the car. (51)

[*Aloud.*] That is mere bragging. Why were you taken prisoner by a foot soldier?

Abhimanyu. Unarmed he came at me, and so was I captured. For who would strike a man that has laid down his arms, if he remembered Arjuna was his father? (52)

Bhīma. [*Aside.*] Blessed indeed is Arjuna who himself has witnessed both his son's pride in his father and his prowess in the conflict. (53)

King. Hasten hither Abhimanyu.

Bṛihannalā. This way, prince, this way. Here is the king. Go up to him.

Abhimanyu. Ah! Whose king?

Bṛihannalā. No, no, no. He is sitting with a brahman.

Abhimanyu. With a brahman? [*Approaching.*] Reverend sir, I salute you.

Bhagavān. Come hither, child.

Mayest thou attain the qualities combined in one, thy father, heroism and perseverance, modesty and kindness, and compassion for his own people, together with victory in archery and prowess in war. And of the other four do thou attain whatever is of good report. (54)

Abhimanyu. I thank you.

King. Come here, my son. Why do you not greet me? Oho! How arrogant is this warrior stripling. Well, I shall humble his pride. Who took him prisoner?

Bhīma. Great king, I did.

Abhimanyu. 'Unarmed' you should add.

Bhīma. Heaven forfend!

My own two arms plump with sturdy shoulders, that is my weapon. Those are the things to fight with, weaklings use the bow. (55)

Abhimanyu. Say not so, sirrah!

Are you my middle uncle, whose arm is like a host, whose valour needs no artifice? Those words were suitable for him. (56)

Bhagavān. My son, who is this middle one?

Abhimanyu. Listen. Nay, I will not make a retort to a brahman. It were well if some one else would speak.

King. Very well, reply to me. Who is this middle one, my son?

Abhimanu. Listen. It is he

Who made a halter for Jarāsandha with an arm about his neck, and by that irresistible act cheated Kṛishṇa of his claim thereto. (57)

King. Thy haughty words will not anger me, thy anger gives me pleasure. What can I say without offence. 'How are you?' or 'you may go?' (58)

Abhimanyu. If you would show me a favour,

Treat me as a captive should be treated, with fetters on my feet. I was carried here, only Bhīma's arms shall carry me away. (59)

[*Enter Uttara.*]

Uttara. This false praise irks me, though they show devotion in their lying words. Extolled about this battle I must accept their compliments, but at heart I am ashamed. (60)

[*Approaching.*] Bhagavān, I salute you.

Bhagavān. Bless you!

Uttara. Daddy! I salute you.

King. Come to me, my son. Long may you live. Have you honoured the brave warriors who did their duty in the battle?

Uttara. I have. Now do you honour him who deserves it most.

King. Who is that, my son?

Uttara. His Highness here, Dhanañjaya.[1]

King. What? Dhanañjaya?

Uttara. Why, yes. This noble prince

Took his bow and quivers twain with shafts unending and from the cemetery he defeated Bhīshma and the other kings and protected me. (61)

King. Is this so?

Bṛihannalā. By your grace, great king,

By reason of his youth he is confused, strikes blows but knows it not. Having done it all himself he fancies it the work of another. (62)

Uttara. You can remove your doubt. I shall only say,

Here is the hidden scar on his forearm inflicted by the Gāṇḍīva's string, a scar that after a dozen years is still discoloured. (64)

Bṛihannalā. This scar of mine was made by removing bracelets.

Pressure has changed the colour and it comes just in the place of an arrow-guard. (64)

King. Just let me see.

[1] 'Winning wealth', a name of Arjuna.

Bṛihannalā. If I am Arjuna, of the Bharata clan, whose limbs were licked by Kudra's darts, then 'tis evident, this is Bhīmasena and this is King Yudhishṭhira. (65)

King. Yudhishṭhira! Bhīma! Arjuna![1] Could you not trust me? Very well, when the right time comes. Bṛihannalā, go into the inner apartments.

Bṛihannalā. As your Majesty commands.

Bhagavān. No, Arjuna; you must not enter. Our promise is fulfilled.

Arjuna. As my noble brother bids.

King. By the residence of the Pāṇḍavas, heroes true to their troth and keepers of their word, my house is cleansed of stain. (66)

Abhimanyu. Then here are my respected kinsmen.[2] That's why They were not wroth when I insulted them but laughed and taunted back. Bravo! the cattle raid that has brought me to see my kin. (67)

[*To Bhīmasena.*] O uncle,

It was from ignorance I did not salute thee before. Pray forgive this error in thy son. (68)

Bhīma. Come here, my son. May you be as brave as your father.

Abhimanyu. Thank you.

Bhīma. Now, my son, salute your father.

Abhimanyu. Oh, daddy, I salute you.

Arjuna. Come to my arms, my son! [*Embraces him.*]

This clasping of my own son's body in my arms gladdening my heart, was banished for thirteen years but has now returned to me. (69)

Now, my son, you should salute the Lord of the Virāṭas.

Abhimanyu. My salutations.

King. Come here, dear child.

Mayest thou attain the patience of Yudhishṭhira, Bhīma's might, and the skill of Arjuna. Mayest thou attain the beauty of Mādrī's sons,[3] with the wisdom and the glory of Kṛishṇa, the Beloved of the World. (70)

[*Aside.*] But this intimacy with my daughter[4] troubles me. What shall I do? Good, I have it. Ho, without there!

[*Enter servant.*]

Servant. To the great king, victory.

King. Bring me some water.

[1] Dharmarāja, Vṛikodara, Dhanaṃjaya.

[2] Lit. fathers.

[3] Nakula, and Sahadeva, younger Pāṇḍavas.

[4] Uttarā. Arjuna disguised as Bṛihannalā has been living in the inner rooms.

Servant. As the great king commands. [*Exit and re-enter.*] Here is the water.

King. [*Taking it.*] Arjuna! As a guerdon for the defeat of the cattle raid do thou accept my daughter, Uttarā.

Bhagavān. So are our heads bowed down.

Arjuna. [*Aside.*] He weighs my virtue. [*Aloud.*] O king,

All the ladies of thy household are dear to me and honoured like my mother. Uttarā, whom thou offerest to me, I accept, to wed my son. **(71)**

Yudhishṭhira. So we hold up our heads again.

King. Now he is established in the noble needs of warlike heroes, who erstwhile performed the proper duties of an inmate of the inner palace. **(72)**

To-day the stars are auspicious. So the marriage shall take place this very day.

Yudhishṭhira. Very well, so be it. Let us send Uttara to grandfather.[1]

King. As you suggest. Come Yudhishṭhira, Bhīma, and Arjuna, come. In this joyful mood let us go in to the inner palace.

All. Good!

[*Exeunt omnes.*]

END OF THE SECOND ACT.

ACT III

[*Enter a Charioteer.*]

Charioteer. Ho, there, take word, take word to the warriors led by Droṇa, the preceptor of all warriors!

Casting aside all terror born of Kṛishṇa's disc, disregarding the long-lost Pāṇḍavas, they have captured Abhimanyu, nor could the Kuru bowmen protect him. Shame be on them! **(1)**

[*Enter Bhīshma and Droṇa.*]

Droṇa. Tell me, charioteer, tell me,

Who has carried off my pupil's son, so skilled in battle? Who is fain to fight against my superhuman shafts? Tell me the essence of the man, his weapons and strength, and I will send him messengers of mighty power. **(2)**

[1] Bhīshma, grand-uncle of the Pāṇḍavas, leader of the Kuru army.

Bhīshma. Tell me, tell me, charioteer.

Unused as he was to the dangers in a retreat of broken men he kept up the fight by his youthful force. Who was it then, trained to capture elephants, could capture him like a baby when the herd has passed? (3)

[*Enter Duryodhana, Karṇa, and Śakuni.*]

Duryodhana. Charioteer, tell me, who has carried off Abhimanyu? I myself will set him free. For

I began the family dissension with his kin, so in this the wise will lay the blame on me. Moreover, I hold him for my son, and afterwards of the Pāṇḍavas. And though there be a feud in the family the children are not to blame. (4)

Karṇa. Your words are very gracious and appropriate, Gāndhārī's son. Not, I trust, from fear of thy people's wrath, nor because he is a boy. Abhimanyu has met with this disaster in the forefront of the fight on thy behalf. We failed to guard him; let us throw away our bows and don the robes of bark.[1] (5)

Śakuni. Subhadrā's son has many protectors. We may consider him as released already.

The King of Virāṭa himself will set him free when he learns he is the son of Arjuna. This very day he will release him remembering Dāmodara[2], unconquered in the field of battle. Or he will let him go through fear of Kṛishṇa's brother, who smashed the demon Pendulous brandishing a ploughshare in his rage. Nay, mighty Bhīma will bring him here after slaughtering those powerful foes. (6)

Droṇa. Speak out, O charioteer! How was he taken?

Was his chariot overturned? Were his horses out of hand? Did the ground give way beneath the wheels? Was the quiver short of arrows? Didst thou fail him? Was the bow made useless by the snapping of the string? These are the accidents of battle that come by fate on those that fight in cars. Or perhaps the foemen dragged him off with a flight of arrows. Yet is he a master of the art. (7)

Charioteer. Venerable sir, he is the science of archery incarnate. Does your reverence not know him?

'Twas none of the faults thou hast retailed, and he the mighty warrior was one great stream of arrows; my car was like the blazing ring of a whirling firebrand. A foot-soldier came up and captured him. (8)

[1] Of ascetics in the forest.

[2] Kṛishṇa, Abhimanyu's uncle.

All. What? A foot-soldier?

Droṇa. What sort of foot-soldier was that?

Charioteer. Shall I describe his appearance or his prowess?

Bhīshma. Women are described by their appearance, men by their prowess. So tell us of his prowess.

Charioteer. Venerable sir!

Duryodhana. What boots this praise of some one with phrases puffed with pride. Say what you will, I have no fear, though his speed be like the wind's. **(9)**

Charioteer. Deign to hear, your Majesty.

Surpassing the horses in speed he laid his hand upon the car, and, though the steeds had their necks outstretched, the car stood motionless. **(10)**

Bhīshma. Then we may lay aside our arms.

All. Why so?

Bhīshma. If the car was brought to a standstill by one arm, we must suppose it in the grip of Bhīmasena. For once before on foot he defeated Jayadratha who was carrying off King Drupada's daughter. **(11)**

Droṇa. Bhīshma is right. I taught him from a boy and know his pace. For in the archery school

He would draw to the ear and let fly his shaft, and when I said he had moved his head, went swift as a bolt and caught the arrow ere it reached the mark. **(12)**

Śakuni. What nonsense you are talking! I will put you one question. Is there no other strong man in the world? You attribute everything to your favourites. Do you all regard the Pāṇḍavas as pervading the whole earth? **(13)**

Bhīshma. King of Gāndhāra, it is only an inference.

We all ride to battle on our chariots equipped with swords and bows. Only two have ever gone into the fray with their own bare arms as weapons, Balarāma and Bhīmasena. **(14)**

Śakuni. All of us, without love of daring, were suddenly defeated by one man, and some will say that Uttara, that very man, was Arjuna himself. **(15)**

Droṇa. Oh, King of Gāndhāra, have you any doubt in this?

Could Uttara draw in battle a bow that hisses with a flight of rainless thunderbolts? Could Uttara's shafts make the sunshine vanish? Or cause the momentary setting of the sun? **(16)**

Bhīshma. Gāndhārī's son, it is plain enough. Surely you know,

By the words his arrow-feathers spell on the tip of the bowstring's tongue. Arjuna drew the bow and sends a message for our ears. **(17)**

[*Enter a Charioteer.*]

Charioteer. Venerable sir, greeting. It were well to make peace.

Bhīshma. Why?

Charioteer. It had been fitting to make peace before, when an arrow fell upon the standard, for this arrow has some one's name written on its end. **(18)**

Bhīshma. Bring it here. [*Charioteer hands over the arrow.*]

Bhīshma. [*Takes the arrow and examines it.*] My child, Gāndhāra, my eyes are dim with age. Read me the word on this arrow.

Śakuni. [*Takes the arrow and reads.*] Arjuna's. [*Throws the arrow down. It falls at Droṇa's feet.*]

Droṇa. [*Picking up the arrow.*]

Come, come, my son.

This arrow was shot by my pupil to salute Bhīshma. It has now fallen on the ground at my feet to salute me as well in my turn. **(19)**

Śakuni. Nay, not so. Shall we have faith in the evidence of an arrow? Any warrior there may be named Arjuna, he may well have shot this dart. Moreover, something written by Uttara should be brought to light. **(20)**

Duryodhana. If any falsehood is abroad that I may surrender them the realm, then half the realm I will not give over till I have seen Yudhishṭhira. **(21)**

[*Enter Servant.*]

Servant. To the great king, victory. A messenger has arrived from the Virāṭa city.

Duryodhana. Let him enter.

Servant. As your Majesty commands. [*Exit.*]

[*Enter Uttara.*]

Uttara. The journey is short, I let out my steeds to their utmost speed, yet was my chariot delayed on the way; all round were so many tuskers slain by Kaunteya's shafts, my horses could hardly move, the ground was so uneven. **(22)**

[*Comes forward with folded hands.*]

Preceptor, grandsire, and all this assembly of kings, I salute you.

All. Long may you live.

Droṇa. What is the message of his Highness of Virāṭa?

Uttara. I have not come from him.

Droṇa. Then who has sent you?

Uttara. His Majesty, Yudhishṭhira.

Droṇa. What saith the King of Righteousness?

Uttara. Hearken.

Uttarā is given in marriage to my son. I invite this assembly of kings. Shall it be with you or over here? Or where shall the wedding take place? **(23)**

Śakuni. Over there, over there.

Droṇa. This business brought us here, the five days have not ended. The gift vouchsafed with solemn rite should now be rightfully presented. **(24)**

Duryodhana. Very well, I grant the Pāṇḍavas the realm they had before. For if troth be dead all men are done; as troth stands firm, so do they. **(25)**

Droṇa. Oh joy! now are we all content in the union of the mighty houses. May our lion-king rule over all this earth!

[*Exeunt omnes.*]

FINIS.

THE MIDDLE ONE

(*Madhyama-vyāyoga*)

INTRODUCTION

This one-act play is founded on an incident in the Mahābhārata, which is in the nature of a fairy tale. In the ninth section of the first book we hear of the demon or giant Hiḍimba. As the Pāṇḍavas are flying through the forest this giant smells humans and sends his sister, with the feminine form of the same non-aryan name, to bring them in. The ogress Hiḍimbā finds Bhīma keeping watch, falls in love with him, and assumes the form of a lovely maiden, but he resists her advances. Then the ogre comes along, and, finding his sister in conversation with Bhīma, threatens to kill her also. After a long argument Bhīma fights the giant and kills him. He has a mind to kill the sister Hiḍimbā also, but allows himself to be won over and marries her instead. After some time she gives birth to the demon giant Ghaṭotkaca ('Potsherd') and then leaves Bhīma with his consent. (*IX. Hiḍimba-vadha-parvan.*) That is all the Great Epic tells us. We hear no more of the ogress, though her semi-human son appears in battle and is finally killed by Karṇa. Our dramatist imagines a situation when Bhīma should come across this semi-demon son of his and naturally not recognize him. The motif of a father meeting and sometimes fighting his own son unawares is familiar. That a hero should find a son in such a monster seems original.

The play introduces an old brahman with his wife and three sons pursued by Potsherd (Ghaṭotkaca), whose mother, Hiḍimbā, has ordered him to find her a human for her breakfast. There is no escape. The Pāṇḍava hermitage is believed to be near by, but the Pāṇḍavas are away. Even if the middle one (i.e. the second) Bhīma has remained to guard the settlement, he would be roaming far for exercise. Each member of the brahman family claims to be the victim. The second son, the middle one, gets his way. He is allowed to go and quench his thirst in a forest pool. The demon is impatient and demands the name of the victim. He is told he is the middle one. That serves him as a name and he shouts for 'Middle one'.

Bhīma passing by, hears a voice shouting 'Middle one' and thinks it is calling him. The demon is puzzled by the appearance of another 'middle one'. This emphasis on *Madhyama* 'middle one' explains the name of the play, *Madhyama-vyāyoga*. (A *Vyāyoga* is a one-act play on a military or heroic episode without any love interest.) Then there is the scene between father and son, who do not know each other. The demon son wrestles and uses magic all in vain. Then he runs to fetch his mother, Hiḍimbā the giantess. Bhīma recognizes her. She tells him Ghaṭotkaca is his son. The old brahman and his family are allowed to go in peace.

DRAMATIS PERSONAE

(In order of appearance.)

Stage-manager, in Prologue.
Old man, the brahman Keśavadāsa.
Wife.
First Son.
Second Son, the 'middle one'.
Third Son.
Ghaṭotkaca ('Potsherd'), son of Bhīma and Hiḍimbā.
Bhīma or Bhīmasena, the second Pāṇḍava, called here the 'middle one', i.e. considering only the three sons of Kuntī.
Hiḍimbā, the giantess sister of the slain Hiḍimba, married to Bhīma and mother of Ghaṭotkaca.

PROLOGUE

[*At the end of the Opening,*[1] *enter the Stage-manager.*]

Stage-manager. May Hari's foot protect you—a torment for the hearts of demons' dames—lotus-blue like a burnished blade.
His foot, upraised to overstep the triple world, which gleams like a bridge of beryl in the ocean of the sky. (1)

With these words, my lords and gentlemen, I have to announce to you ... But what is that? I thought I heard a noise, just as I was to make my announcement. Well, I must see what it is.

[*Voice behind the scene.*]

Oh, father, who, pray, is this?

Stage-manager. So be it—I understand.
By his speech[2] this is evidently a brahman. He is terrified by some dauntless evil creature. (2)

[*Behind the scenes.*]

Oh, father, who, pray, is this?

Stage-manager. Ah! Now I understand. This must be the son of the Middle Pāṇḍava, an ogre, sprung like fire from the firestick his mother Hiḍimbā, and a terror to brahmans that have done him no harm. Oh! how very sad is the plight of this brahman with his wife and children.

Here indeed,

This is an aged brahman and his wife, with their weary children round them, followed by a monster of the night.
He is distraught like a bull with his cow and frightened calf pursued by a tiger. (3)

[*Exit.*]

END OF PROLOGUE.

ACT I

[*Enter the old man Keśavadāsa with his wife and three sons, and after them Ghaṭotkaca.*]

Old Man. Oh! who, indeed, is this,
With hair streaming like the morning rays, with long yellow eyes blazing in their frowning sockets, with necklet of gold,

[1] Nāndī, see p. ix.

[2] Lit. by his uttering the word—*bhoḥ*.

looking like a lightning cloud, the very image of the Destroyer at the annihilation of an Age? (4)

First Son. Oh! father, who ever is this?

With eyes like a pair of planets, with his broad and muscular chest, with locks of golden brown and garments of yellow silk, black as a mass of darkness with white protruding teeth, he resembles a storm[1] cloud half concealing the digit of the moon. (5)

Second Son. Who is it? Oh,

That stands shining there, with teeth like the tusks of an elephant calf, with a snout as long as a plough, with arms like the trunk of a lordly tusker, with the hue of a dark blue cloud lit up like a fire of burnt offering, dire as the wrath of Śiva destroying the Triple City?[2] (6)

Third Son. Oh! father, who, pray, is this that troubles us?

A thunderbolt on lofty mountains, a falcon among all the birds, a lion on herds of deer, Death in a human form. (7)

Wife. My lord! who is this that afflicts us?

Ghaṭotkaca. Ho, Brahman, stay,

Why dost thou flee, thy fortitude destroyed by fear of me; devoid of ability to protect thy frightened wife and sons? like a harried snake and its mate gliding swiftly with the fire of its wrath fanned by the wind from the tips of Garuḍa's wings? (8)

Ho, Brahman, do not go . . .

Old Man. Do not be afraid, my dear. Fear not, my sons, fear not. His speech is kindly.

Ghaṭotkaca. Ah me! I know that always everywhere the best among the twice-born are most worthy of honour on the earth. This is a foul deed I must do to-day, but it is by my mother's behest, and that removes all hesitation. (9)

Old Man. My dear, don't you remember what the reverend Jalaklinna said—'This forest is haunted by demons; you must proceed with caution.' That very danger has befallen us.

Wife. Then why do you seem so indifferent?

Old Man. What can I do, unfortunate that I am?

Wife. Why, let us call for help.

First Son. But, mother, to whom can we call?

This wood is desolate, the horizon blocked by numerous trees

[1] Lit. 'new'.

[2] Tripura, 'triple citadel', three Asura fortresses of gold, silver, and iron burned by Śiva.

dark as masses of shade, and the depths thereof are full of birds and beasts, a place where only hermits would wish to dwell. (10)

Old Man. Do not be afraid, my dear, that mention of a place where hermits would wish to dwell has almost removed my apprehension. Not far from here, I think, must be the Pāṇḍavas' hermitage. Now the Pāṇḍavas

are fond of battle and kind to those who seek their protection: men of mighty deeds, taking sides with the oppressed. They have the power to inflict proper punishment on such perpetrators of frightful deeds. (11)

First Son. But, father, the Pāṇḍavas are away, I think.

Old Man. How do you know, my son?

First Son. I heard from a brahman who had been to that hermitage, they had gone to the great sage Dhaumya's to assist at the sacrifice called 'One Hundred Vessels'.

Old Man. Alas! we are lost.

First Son. But they didn't all go, father. The middle one was set to look after the hermitage.

Old Man. If that is so, it is as good as having all the Pāṇḍavas at hand.

First Son. At this moment he also, I fear, has gone some distance away taking exercise.

Old Man. Alas! we have no hope. Nay, my son, I will supplicate him.

First Son. You may spare your pains.

Old Man. Entreaty, my son, is a council of despair.

First Son. Very well, let us see. Ho, fellow, will you let us go?

Ghaṭotkaca. You may go—on one condition.

Old Man. What condition?

Ghaṭotkaca. My worthy mother commanded me, saying, go into the forest, my son, and find me a human and bring him to me for my breakfast. And then I came across you.

With your virtuous spouse and two of your sons you may go free, but taking thought of faults and merits one son you must surrender. (12)

Old Man. Out on you, vile demon. Am I not a brahman?

A venerable brahman, learned in the scriptures, how could I obtain salvation if I gave my virtuous son to a cannibal? (13)

Ghaṭotkaca. O best of twice-born men! And you yield not one son to my demand, in a trice you will be destroyed with all your family as well. (14)

Old Man. Good wife, this is my decision.

This body of mine, decrepit with age, has fulfilled its function: this body purified by sacraments I will offer as a burnt oblation to this demon that I may save my sons. (15)

Wife. Nay, nay, my lord. A true wife exists for her husband only. This body has borne its fruit. I will save my lord and family.

Ghaṭotkaca. Oh, no, my worthy mother does not want a woman. You must withdraw.

Old Man. I will come with you.

Ghaṭotkaca. Hm! you are old, away with you.

First Son. Oh, father, I wish to say something.

Old Man. Speak out, my son.

First Son. I would fain preserve my parents' lives with my own, prithee let me go to save the family. (16)

Second Son. Say not so, good brother.

In the home and in the world the eldest is the best, best beloved of his parents, so it is I that will go, mindful of duty to my seniors. (17)

Third Son. Not so, my brothers.

An elder brother is like a sire, as theologians have declared, so I am the one to save my seniors' lives. (18)

First Son. No, boy, no!

When a father is in trouble the eldest son assists him, so it is I that will go to save my parents' lives. (19)

Old Man. The eldest is the most desired, I cannot give him up.

Wife. As my lord wants the eldest, so I want the youngest.

Second Son. Unwanted by my parents, who cares for me?

Ghaṭotkaca. I am content. Come quickly.

Second Son. Blessed am I that with my own life have protected the lives of my elders. From the great love of kin comes the desire for death that is rare indeed. (20)

Ghaṭotkaca. How this brahman lad dotes on his relations!

Second Son. Father, I salute you.

Old Man. Come here, my son.

Devoted to thy elders thou hast rescued them with thine own life; mayst thou obtain the world divine that those with soul unsanctified may hardly gain. (21)

Second Son. I thank you. Mother, I salute you.

Wife. My child, farewell.

Second Son. Thank you. Brother, I salute you.

First Son. Come, boy, come.

Embrace me closely, as thou art embraced by the brightest virtues. Thy fame shall embrace the whole world. **(22)**

Second Son. Thank you.

Third Son. Brother, I salute you.

Second Son. Good-bye.

Third Son. Thank you.

Second Son. Ho! fellow, I have a word to say.

Ghaṭotkaca. Say on, but quickly.

Second Son. In this forest ride I see there is a pool. There would I allay my thirst before departing for the other world.

Ghaṭotkaca. Stout-hearted! Go, but come quickly; the time for my mother's meal is passing.

Second Son. Father, here I go. [*Exit.*]

Old Man. Alas! alas! we are robbed. Oh! we are robbed.

Three splendid peaks there were in the range of my posterity. The breaking of the middle peak torments my heart exceedingly. **(23)**

Alas! my son. What, gone?

A youth as fair as youth itself, thy mind devoted to self-control and study of the scriptures, art thou to perish like a tree that has blossomed and is smashed by the tusks of a mighty elephant? **(24)**

Ghaṭotkaca. The brahman lad is tarrying. The time for my mother's meal is passing. Well, what shall I do about it? Good, I know. Brahman, call your son.

Old Man. Ough! Your words are more than devilish.

Ghaṭotkaca. Why, he is angry! Forgive me, I pray. It is the fault of my nature. But what is the name of your son?

Old Man. That, too, you cannot hear from me.

Ghaṭotkaca. Of course not. Ho! brahman boy, what is the name of your brother?

First Son. The ascetic unfortunate middle one.

Ghaṭotkaca. 'Middle One' is a good name for him. I shall call him myself. Ho there! Middle One, Middle One, come here at once!

[*Enter Bhīmasena.*]

Bhīma. Ah, whose voice is this?

Loudly this voice resounds in this close-packed forest dense with trees and resonant with the notes of innumerable birds, and it thrills my heart so mightily it resembles the voice of Dhanañjaya. **(25)**

Ghaṭotkaca. The brahman lad is tarrying. My mother's meal-time is passing by. What am I to do? I know; I must shout at the top of my voice. Ho there! Middle One, come here at once!

Bhīma. Ah, who is in this wood interrupting my exercise by shouting after me, 'Middle One, Middle One'? Well, we will just see. [*Steps and looks round.*] Oh here's a handsome fellow—

Lion-faced and lion-jawed, with eyes like sparkling wine, his voice is soft though deep. Eyebrows brown, with a falcon nose and the jaws of an elephant king, he has long and flowing hair. Broad-chested but slender-waisted as a thunderbolt, he stalks like a tusker bull. Arms long and shoulders stout, endowed with enormous strength, he is clearly the son of some world-hero born of a demon dame. **(26)**

Ghaṭotkaca. He still tarries and the time is passing. I must call him again as loud as I can.[1] Middlemost, Middlemost, come here at once!

Bhīma. Well, here I am.

Ghaṭotkaca. This is not the brahman lad. Oh, but this fellow is handsome!

With arms like golden palm-trees, in the waist thin, with sides as smooth as Garuḍa's wings, he is like a lion. He might be Vishñu, his eyes like petals of a lotus blooming wide. He attracts my eves like a kinsman visitor. **(27)**

Ho! Middle One. I am shouting for you.

Bhīma. But I am here.

Ghaṭotkaca, What? Are you also Middle One?

Bhīma. Nay, none else.

Middlemost am I of the invulnerable and mighty. Born of the middle world, good sir, and of my brethren I am the middle one. **(28)**

Ghaṭotkaca. It must be so.

Bhīma Moreover,

Of the five elements the middle one and middlemost of kings, I am middlemost in the world and in all affairs. **(29)**

Old Man. He declares that he is middlemost, so he must be the middle Pāṇḍava, come here to save us as if arisen from the Pride of Death. **(30)**

[*Enter Second Son.*]

Second Son. Sipping the bright drops on the lotus leaves of this pool, that none may get in the other world, I have myself made libation to myself. **(31)**

[*Approaching.*] Ho, fellow, here I am.

[1] Compressed to avoid the third repetition.

Ghaṭotkaca. So you have come at last, you Middle One. This way, then.

Old Man. [*Going up to Bhīma.*] Oh, Middle One! Rescue a brahman family.

Bhīma. Have no fear. I the middle one salute you.

Old Man. May you live for ever like the very air.[1]

Bhīma. I thank you. What, sir, has alarmed you?

Old Man. Hearken. I am a brahman, Keśavadāsa by name, a resident of the village Yūpa in Kuru-jaṅgala, where Yudishṭhira, king of the Kurus, used to reign. I belong to the Māṭhara clan and am a priest of the Kalpa school. Now I have an uncle Yajñabandhu, who lives in a village Udyāmaka in the north and belongs to the Kuśika clan. I set out with my wife to attend the initiation of his son.

Bhīma. I wish you a safe journey. What then?

Old Man. Why, then

> There comes this demon, with limbs as black as a storm of rain, with eyes as large as lotus leaves, with the sportive gait of the lord of beasts, with ghastly projecting teeth—oh! he wants to slay me with my wife and sons, as if he feared nobody in the world, right in the face of men like you. **(32)**

Bhīma. So, he has barred a brahman's path. Well, I will restrain him. Ho, fellow, stop! stand, I say.

Ghaṭotkaca. Here I am.

Bhīma. Why are you molesting this brahman?

> The old priest is like the moon, bright with the beauty of his wife, with the constellations of his sons around him, and thou art come like the demon Rāhu[2] to devour him. **(33)**

Ghaṭotkaca. Why, yes. I am Rāhu.

Bhīma. Ah,

> Pray release this brahman, most excellent, with wife and sons, for he has performed his duty and should not be smitten for any offence. **(34)**

Ghaṭotkaca. I shall not let him go.

Bhīma. [*Aside.*] Whose son can he be?

> Ah, who can it be, this thief of all my brothers' qualities? His youthful haughtiness puts me in mind of Subhadrā's son.[3] **(35)**

[*Aloud.*] Come, my man, set him free.

Ghaṭotkaca. He shall not go free.

[1] A play on *dīrghāyus* 'long-lived' and Vāyur 'wind'.

[2] Rāhu the devouring demon of eclipses.

[3] Abhimanyu.

Though my sire should sternly bid me to release him, yet would I not obey, for he is seized by the orders of my mother. (36)

Bhīma. [*Aside.*] What, the orders of his mother? The poor good fellow shows his filial obedience.

A mother is for humans the deity of deities. By honouring our mother's command we have come to this condition. (37)

[*Aloud.*] Well, my man, let me put you a question.

Ghaṭotkaca. Ask it quickly.

Bhīma. What is the name of your mother?

Ghaṭotkaca. You shall hear. The demon dame Hiḍimbā,

And she, happy lady, has for her lord the great-souled Pāṇḍava, the light of the Kuru race, as the sky has the full moon. (38)

Bhīma. [*Aside.*] So, then, this is Hiḍimbā's son. He may well be proud.

His form, his courage, and his strength are like his sire's, but what heart has he, devoid of pity for our subjects? (39)

[*Aloud.*] Come now, you must set him free.

Ghaṭotkaca. Nay, I will not.

Bhīma. Brahman, take thy son. I will go with this fellow myself.

Second Son. No, no, you must not.

Already have I resigned my life for the sake of my elders' lives. Thou art young, beautiful, and virtuous. Thou must remain on the surface of the earth. (40)

Bhīma. Noble youth, say not so. I am born of the warrior race. Most worthy of honour is a brahman. So I wish to redeem the body of a brahman with my own.

Ghaṭotkaca. So he is a warrior. That is why he is so haughty. Well, I will kill this one and take him away. Who will prevent me?

Bhīma. I will.

Ghaṭotkaca. You will?

Bhīma. Certainly.

Ghaṭotkaca. Then come yourself.

Bhīma. You may be very brave and strong, but I will not follow you. Take me by force, if you can.

Ghaṭotkaca. Don't you know who I am?

Bhīma. Yes. I know you are my son.

Ghaṭotkaca. What do you mean by calling me your son?

Bhīma. How angry he is. Forgive me, I pray. Warriors address all their subjects as sons. And so I used the word.

Ghaṭotkaca. You use the weapon of a coward.

Bhīma. By the truth I swear, I know not what fear is. I would fain learn of it from you. What is it like? Tell me, good sir, and when I know the good and bad of it I can decide accordingly. (**41**)

Ghaṭotkaca. I will teach you what fear is. Take a weapon.

Bhīma. A weapon? I have this one.

Ghaṭotkaca. How do you mean?

Bhīma. Like a pillar of gold, delighting in the capture of foes, this my own right arm is a weapon worthy of myself. (**42**)

Ghaṭotkaca. This is like my father Bhīmasena.

Bhīma. Who is this Bhīma?

Tell me, good sir, whom does thy sire resemble? Śiva the Creator, Kṛishṇa, Indra the Mighty, or the God of Death? (**43**)

Ghaṭotkaca. All of them.

Bhīma. Oh, fie on you, that is untrue.

Ghaṭotkaca. What? 'Untrue' says he? He insults my father. Well, I will pull up this thick tree to strike him. [*Does so.*] Why, I cannot kill him with this. What shall I do? Good. I will tear off this mountain peak to smite him.

This rocky peak I'll hurl to take thy life on its way.

Bhīma. Though full of rage a woodland elephant should not assail a tiger in the forest. (**44**)

Ghaṭotkaca. [*Striking.*] Why, even with this I cannot kill him. What shall I do? I know;

Bhīma's son am I, grandson of the Lord of the Sky. Stand now well prepared, none is my match in wrestling. (**45**)

[*They both wrestle.*]

Ghaṭotkaca. [*Holding Bhīma fast.*] Gripped in my arms like a tusker in strong chains canst thou master my strength and escape? (**46**)

Bhīma. [*Aside.*] What, has he caught me? Ha! Suyodhana, your opponent gains in strength. Take care! [*Aloud.*] Ho, fellow, on your guard!

Ghaṭotkaca. I'm on my guard all right.

Bhīma. [*Shaking himself free.*] Abandon thy pride in thy strength, my hero, thy mettle is gauged. The wrestling bout was no distress to me.[1] (**47**)

Ghaṭotkaca. Even so I cannot kill him. What now? Yes, I have it. There is the magic noose I had by mother's favour. I will bind him

[1] Wrongly numbered 46 in the text.

with that and lead him away. Where is there some water? Ho, mountain, I prithee, water! Ha! here it streams. [*Takes a sip and recites a charm.*] My man,

Bound with a magic bond, helpless thou shalt not move.
Bound by cords thou art as bright as Indra's banner at a festival. (**48**) [*Binds him by magic.*]

Bhīma. So I am bound by a magic noose. What shall I do now? There is a charm for releasing magic bonds that I learned by Śiva's favour. That will I recite. But where is there water? Good, oh brahman boy, bring me water in your gourd.

Old Man. Here is water.

[*Bhīmasena sips the water, recites the charm, and dissolves the magic.*]

Ghaṭotkaca. Ah, the noose fails. What to do? That's it. Remember, man, your former promise.

Bhīma. Promise? Now I remember. Lead on.

[*Both step around.*]

Old Man. What shall we do, my sons? There goes Bhīma.[1] Subduing this shining demon of dreadful form endowed with terrible courage and strength of arms, he shakes him off, and strides quietly on like a bull playfully tossing off raindrops in a moment. (**49**)

Ghaṭotkaca. Stay here—I will tell my mother you have come.

Bhīma. Very well. Go on.

Ghaṭotkaca. [*Going forward.*] Mother, it is I, Ghaṭotkaca, that calls, saluting you. I have brought you a man for your meal that you have been wanting so long.

[*Enter Hiḍimbā.*]

Hiḍimbā. Live long, my child. What sort of a man have you brought?

Ghaṭotkaca. He is a man by his speech, lady, not by his valour.

Hiḍimbā. What, a brahman?

Ghaṭotkaca. No, not a brahman.

Hiḍimbā. Then an elder?

Ghaṭotkaca. He is not old.

Hiḍimbā. A boy?

Ghaṭotkaca. Not a boy.

Hiḍimbā. If so, let me have a look at him.

[*Both step around.*]

Hiḍimbā. Is this the man you have brought?

Ghaṭotkaca. What is he, lady?

Hiḍimbā. You lunatic, he is a deity.

[1] 'Wolf-bellied', an epithet of Bhīma.

Ghaṭotkaca. Oh! whose deity

Hiḍimbā. Yours and mine.

Ghaṭotkaca. What proof is there of that?

Hiḍimbā. This is the proof. Victory to my lord!

Bhīma. [*Looking round.*] Who is this? Ah, the queen Hidimbā.

When we had lost our kingdom and wandered in the deepest glade, thou didst allay my torment, noble lady, with thy clemency inborn. (50)

What is this, Hiḍimbā?

Hiḍimbā. [*Whispers.*] That's how it was, my lord.

Bhīma. By birth, of the demons, not by behaviour.

Hiḍimbā. Come, madcap, salute your father.

Ghaṭotkaca. Dear father, I salute you. I am Ghaṭotkaca, the fire to burn the forest of Dhṛitarāshṭra's sons. Pray forgive your son's rashness.

Bhīma. Come to my arms, my son. Your indiscretion was delightful. [*Embraces him.*] That is what a father's heart would wish for in his son, a forest fire to burn the Dhritarāshtra kin. My son, may you be of matchless strength and prowess.

Ghaṭotkaca. I thank you.

Old Man. So this is Ghaṭotkaca, Bhīmasena's son.

Bhīma. My son, salute the reverend Keśavadāsa.

Ghaṭotkaca. Reverend sir, I salute you.

Old Man. May you win virtue and renown like your father's.

Ghaṭotkaca. I thank you.

Old Man. Bhīma, you have saved my family, and raised your own to honour. Now let us depart.

Bhīma. Thanks to you all, this has ended well. Our hermitage is not far. Rest there before you go. (51)

Old Man. By giving us our lives you have shown us hospitality. So now let us take our leave.

Bhīma. Fare you well with your household. We shall meet again.

Old Man. Yes, I shall make a point of it.

[*Exit Keśavadāsa with his wife and sons.*]

Bhīma. Hiḍimbā! come, and you my son, Ghaṭotkaca.

We will see the reverend Keśavadāsa as far as the gate of the hermitage.

As the ocean dominates the rivers, and fire controls oblations: as the mind is master of the senses—so is our Lord Vishṇu the Blessed.

[*Exeunt omnes.*]

FINIS.

THE STATUE PLAY

(*Pratimā-nāṭakam.*)

INTRODUCTION

THE story of the Statue Play is based upon that of the Rāmāyaṇa, beginning with the abandonment of the consecration of Rāma at the demand of Kaikeyī, the mother of Bharata, and ending fourteen years later with the return of Rāma to Ayodhyā.

In a play of seven acts only a few of the episodes in the epic can be employed. The most striking scene in the play is the return of Bharata to Ayodhyā, and his learning of his father's death by seeing his statue in the sculpture gallery. This scene gives the play its name, and seems to have been invented by the author.

In the First Act we hear that all the preparations are being made for the consecration of Prince Rāma by Daśaratha, the old king, his father. One of Sītā's maids brings in a bark dress from the theatre, and Sītā tries it on. We, the audience, know well enough that this is an omen of the long exile in the forest. Then Rāma comes with the news that the consecration has been set aside. The Chamberlain blames Kaikeyī, but Rāma will hear nothing against her. Lakshmaṇa comes in raging, but Rāma soothes him. Then Lakshmaṇa tells him he has 'to dwell an exile in the forests for fourteen years'. Sītā and Lakshmaṇa insist on going with him. (ACT I.)

The Second Act portrays the grief of the old king, supported by the two queens, Kausalyā and Sumitrā, the mothers of Rāma and Lakshmaṇa. Sumantra brings word of Rāma's departure with wife and brother. The king swoons and finally expires. (ACT II.)

The Third Act gives us the statue gallery. Bharata, the son of Kaikeyī, who has been staying with an uncle, returns to Ayodhyā knowing nothing of the news. His charioteer, however, knows what has happened. 'Although we know, we cannot tell him, for "Who will relate the triple bane, his father's death, his mother's lust of power, and the exile of his elder brother?"' Waiting for an auspicious moment to enter the town he goes into what looks like a temple, but proves to be a sculpture gallery. He is impressed by the statues—learns that they represent warriors of the Ikshvāku clan, namely, Dilīpa, Raghu, and Aja, the last being his own grandfather. Looking at Daśaratha's statue, he is troubled, and guessing the truth, seeks to avoid it. The keeper insists on telling him. Just then the three queens come to visit the gallery, and find Bharata there. He upbraids his own mother. She says she will explain at the proper time and place. He pays little heed to that and determines at once to go off to the forest and find Rāma and Lakshmaṇa. (ACT III.)

Bharata visits the exiles. Rāma refuses to return, and Bharata accepts the kingdom as a trust for fourteen years, but asks for Rāma's sandals that he may set them on the throne. So Bharata returns again to Ayodhyā. (ACT IV.)

Rāma converses with Sītā about the rites to be performed in his father's memory. Rāvaṇa, the demon king of Laṅkā, disguised as an ascetic, professes a wide knowledge of the sacred lore, and talks to Rāma about some wonderful deer in the Himālayas, whose flesh would satisfy the royal shade. Rāma is ready to go to the Himālayas to find the deer with golden sides. Rāvaṇa produces by magic an illusion of such a deer, and Rāma runs off to chase it. Rāvaṇa abducts Sītā, slaying the vulture Jaṭāyu. (ACT V.)

In an Interlude two old ascetics describe the fight between Rāvaṇa and the vulture Jaṭāyu. The scene then shifts to Ayodhyā. Sumantra, who had been sent to visit the exiles, returns to Bharata with the news that Rāvaṇa has abducted Sītā. Once again he reproaches Kaikeyī his mother. Then he is told how a curse had been laid on the king his father, that he should perish through grief for his son. That was the real cause of Rāma's exile, not lust of power. 'But fourteen years?' asks Bharata, 'what did you mean by that?' 'Oh, my child', the queen replies, 'it was fourteen *days* I meant to say, but in the confusion of my mind the fourteen years slipped out.' Bharata is satisfied, makes his peace with Queen Kaikeyī, and sets out to vanquish Rāvaṇa. (ACT VI.)

Rāma has slain Rāvaṇa, and is returning with Sītā. They stay at the hermitage whence Sītā was abducted. Bharata arrives with the queens and a large army—also the priests to consecrate Rāma. Rāma enters, newly consecrated, and the play ends in a chorus of congratulations. (ACT VII.)

Our dramatist has taken considerable liberties with the epic story. In the Rāmāyaṇa Bharata gets no news of Sītā's abduction, nor does he set out to vanquish Rāvaṇa; Rāma is assisted in that struggle not by an army from Oude, but by the apes and bears.

DRAMATIS PERSONAE

(In order of appearance.)

Stage-manager } in the Prologue only.
Actress }
Portress, Vijayā.
Chamberlain of Ayodhyā court. (Bālāki.)
Avadātikā, one of Sītā's maids of honour.
SĪTĀ, wife of Rāma, daughter of Janaka, king of Mithilā. (Hence 'Maithilī, Lady of Mithilā'.)
Maid, another of Sītā's retinue.
Second Maid, another of Sītā's retinue (Nandanikā).
RĀMA, the heir apparent, son of King Daśaratha and Queen Kausalyā.
LAKSHMAṆA, brother of Rāma, son of King Daśaratha and Queen Sumitrā.
Maid from the tiring room.
KING DAŚARATHA of Ayodhyā.
Kausalyā, chief queen of Daśaratha, mother of Rāma.
Sumitrā, second queen, mother of Lakshmaṇa.
Sumantra, minister of Daśaratha.
Sudhākāra, keeper of the Statue Gallery.
Attendant of Ayodhyā court.
BHARATA, son of King Daśaratha and Queen Kaikeyī.
Soldier of Ayodhyā.
Kaikeyī, queen, mother of Bharata.
Charioteer of Bharata.
Female ascetic.
Rāvaṇa, the demon king of Laṅkā.
Two old ascetics.
Nandilaka, servant in the hermitage.
Śatrughna, twin brother of Lakshmaṇa.

PROLOGUE

[*After the Opening*[1] *enter the Stage-manager.*]

Manager. May the Fortune of the Furrow guard us, he that is pleased with lovely verses, charming with his beauteous neck, and every auspicious mark; the supporter whose soul inspireth awe, matchless foe of him that made the goddess cry, may he protect us in every birth.[2] (1)

[*By paronomasia this verse introduces the names of Sītā, Sumantra, Sugrīva, Lakshmaṇa, Rāvaṇa, Vibhīshaṇa, and Bharata, and alludes to Pratimā in the name of the play.*]

[*Looking off behind the scene—towards the living-room.*]

Madam, come here.

[*Enter an Actress.*]

Actress. Here I am, sir.

Manager. Now, madam, sing us something about this autumn season.

Actress. Very well, sir. [*Sings.*]

Manager. This is the season when,

The swan takes her delight wandering on the banks of sand clad in grassy silks—

[*Voice behind the scene.*]

Sir, sir!

Manager. [*Listening.*] Good! I understand.

Bustling with joy like a portress in the royal palace. (2)

[*Exeunt ambo.*]

END OF PROLOGUE.

ACT I

[*Enter Portress.*]

Portress. Oh, sir, which of the Chamberlains is at hand?

[*Enter Chamberlain.*]

Chamberlain. Here I am, lady. What am I to do?

Portress. Why, sir, 'tis the command of the great king Daśaratha—warrior unmatched in the wars of gods and demons—to bring swiftly all the requisites for consecration suitable for the conferment of the dignity of sovereignty on Prince Rāma.

[1] Nāndī, see p. ix.

[2] Sugrīva and Vibhīshaṇa do not appear.

Chamberlain. His Majesty's commands have been already carried out. Look you,

The umbrella with the fan, joy-drums and sacred chair are ready. The golden vessels filled with holy water are set in place with blossoms and sacrificial grass. The Pushya car is yoked. The citizens and the ministers are assembled. Near the altar stands the ornament of all the ceremony, the blessed Vasishṭha. (3)

Portress. If that is so, it is well done.

Chamberlain. Ah!

Now that the protector of the world will consecrate that moon on earth, that we call Rāma, his subjects have all that they desire. (4)

Portress. Come now, hurry up, sir.

Chamberlain. Why, lady, see how I am hurrying. [*Exit.*]

Portress. [*Stepping and looking around.*] Sambhavaka! Good Sambhavaka! Do you take a message from the king and with all courtesy hurry up the high-priest. [*Moves to another place.*] Sārasikā! Sārasikā! Go to the concert-hall and tell the actresses to be ready with a performance appropriate to the occasion. Meanwhile I will go and report to the king that everything has been done. [*Exit.*]

[*Enter Avadātikā with a dress made of bark.*]

Avadātikā. Oh, what it is to be wicked! If I tremble like this while making off with a bark dress for a joke, what must it be with one who steals another's property through greed? I want to have a good laugh, but I can't laugh alone.

[*Enter Sītā with her train.*]

Sītā. My dear, Avadātikā has a startled look. What is the matter?

Maid. Servants are always ready for mischief. Princess, she must have been up to something.

Sītā. No, no, she looks as if she wanted to laugh.

Avadātikā. [*Approaching.*] Princess, all happiness! No, Princess, I haven't done anything wrong.

Sītā. Who asked you whether you had? What have you got in your left hand, Avadātikā?

Avadātikā. A birch dress, Princess.

Sītā. A birch dress? From whom did you get it?

Avadātikā. Listen, Princess. The Lady Revā, the mistress of the tiring-room, had finished her work on the stage, and we asked her for one shoot of the *aśoka* tree. But she wouldn't give it. So I thought one ill turn deserves another, and I took this dress.

Sītā. That was wrong of you. Go and take it back.

Avadātikā. But, Princess, I only took it for fun.

Sītā. Silly girl, that way a fault grows worse. Go and return it at once.

Avadātikā. As your Highness commands. [*She is about to go.*]

Sītā. Come here a moment.

Avadātikā. Here I am, Princess.

Sītā. My dear, how would it suit me, do you think?

Avadātikā. Princess, beauty looks well in everything. Try it on, your Highness.

Sītā. Bring it here. [*Takes the dress and puts it on.*] Look dear, does it suit me?

Avadātikā. It suits you beautifully. The bark seems turned to gold.

Sītā. But you, my dear, say nothing.

Maid. I have no need of words. These thrills of delight speak for me.[1] [*Shows her arm.*]

Sītā. Bring a mirror, my dear.

Maid. As Your Highness commands. [*Exit, and returns.*] Here, Princess, is a looking-glass.

Sītā. [*Looking at the maid's face.*] Never mind the looking-glass. You look as if you wanted to say something.

Maid. Princess, I heard Master Bālāki the chamberlain keep saying, 'The consecration! the consecration!'

Sītā. Somebody is to become lord of the realm.

[*Enter another Maid.*]

Second Maid. Good news, Princess, good news!

Sītā. What are you keeping back?

Second Maid. Why, the prince is to be consecrated.

Sītā. Is his father well?

Second Maid. His Majesty will consecrate the prince himself.

Sītā. If so, the news is doubly good. Give me a long and close embrace.

Second Maid. Oh, Princess, like that? [*Embraces her.*]

[*Sītā takes off her ornaments and gives them to the maids.*]

Second Maid. Princess, the joy-drums.

Sītā. Yes.

Second Maid. The drums were beaten in one place, but now they are silent.

Sītā. Perhaps the consecration is interrupted. Many things happen in courts.

[1] Lit. 'These delighted hairs.'

Second Maid. They tell me, Princess, that when the king has anointed the prince, he will go away to a forest.

Sītā. If that is so, the consecration water must wash away our tears.[1]

[*Enter Rāma.*]

Rāma. Ha! my friends.

A roll was beaten on the drums, the elders were in readiness, I was on the sacred chair, and shoulder-high the vessel whose water was to trickle over a face down-cast. The king summoned me and sent me away. The people are amazed at my patience, but is it a marvel, if a son obeys the words of his own father? (5)

When the king dismissed me saying, 'Now you can rest, my son', my mind breathed a sigh of relief as if a weight was removed. Happily I am still the same Rāma, and the king is king. Now I will go and see the princess of Mithilā.

Avadātikā. Oh, princess, here comes the prince, and you have not taken off the bark dress.

Rāma. Lady of Mithilā, how is it with you?

Sītā. Oh, it is my lord. Victory to my lord!

Rāma. My lady, be seated. [*Sits down.*]

Sītā. As my lord commands. [*Sits down.*]

Avadātikā. Princess, that is the prince's ordinary dress. It seems it is n't true.

Sītā. Such a man does not say what is false, but many things can happen in a court.

Rāma. What are you saying, dear lady of Mithilā?

Sītā. Nay, it is nothing; this girl was talking about a consecration.

Rāma. I can understand your curiosity. There was a consecration. Listen. To-day I was summoned by the king in the presence of the Preceptor, Ministers, and citizens. The king placed me on his knee as he used to do, when I was a child. He called me by my mother's name most lovingly. Then comprising all the realm of Kosala in one gesture he said: 'Rāma, my son, do thou accept the kingdom.'

Sītā. What did my lord say then?

Rāma. What do you think I said, Lady of Mithilā?

Sītā. I think you fell at the king's feet without a word, but sighing deeply.

Rāma. You have guessed well. Rarely are couples born with natures so alike. For thereupon I fell at his feet.

[1] Lit. 'It is not consecration water, but face-water.'

My father's tears above and mine below rained upon my head and my father's feet. (6)

Sītā. And then?

Rāma. Then as I was deaf to his entreaties, he conjured me by his own life, so near the ills of age.

Sītā. Well?

Rāma. Then—

At the consecration, while Lakshmaṇa and Śatrughna held the sacred vessels, and the king, still weeping, was holding the umbrella—Mantharā came suddenly and whispered something in the royal ear, and lo, I am not the king. (7)

Sītā. I am glad. His Majesty is king and my lord is my own dear lord.

Rāma. Lady of Mithilā, why have you taken off your ornaments?

Sitā I am not wearing them now.[1]

Rāma. Nay, it cannot be long you have discarded them.

The edges of thine ears are bent by snatching off their jewellery. Thy palms are pale from the slipping of thy bangles. These little hollows on thy limbs pressed down by the weight of ornaments have not come level yet. (8)

Sītā. My lord's words have the power of making what is unreal seem true.

Rāma. So then, put on your jewellery. I will hold the mirror. [*Does so and looks closely.*] Stay,

In the mirror I seem to see a dress of bark. Or are these rays of the sun? Thy laughter tells me. Is this a game, or the desire for penance? (9)

What is it, Avadātikā?

Avadātikā. Why, my lord, she put it on from curiosity to see if it suited her or not.

Rāma. Why now, Lady of Mithilā, do you wear the dress of the old men of my clan?[2] I like it.[3] Bring it here.

Sītā. No, no, don't say that. It 's unlucky.

Rāma. Why do you stop me, lady?

Sītā. Just when my lord's consecration has been broken off. It seems to me unlucky.

Rāma. Raise not wrath thyself, especially in jest—for half my body was already in it, when thou didst put it on. (10)

[1] Lit. 'I am not adorned.'

[2] Ikshvākus.

[3] 'Have you no love for me', Sarup.

[*Voice behind the scene.*]

Woe, woe, to the king!

Sītā. What 's that, my lord?

Rāma. [*Listening.*]

If this be the extravagant wailing of men and women, it shows that Fate has smitten us at the roots to manifest his power. (11)

Find out quickly. What is that noise?

[*Enter Chamberlain.*]

Chamberlain. Protection, prince, protection!

Rāma. Who, Sir, needs protection?

Chamberlain. The king.

Rāma. The king? Then say, sir, that the whole earth, in one form compact, needs guarding. But whence comes this trouble?

Chamberlain. From his own kin.

Rāma. From his own kin? Alas, there is no remedy.

The foemen strikes the body, while the kinsman strikes the heart. Who will shame me with the name of kin? (12)

Chamberlain. The Queen Kaikeyī?

Rāma. What, Mother? This then is a quality fated from the past.

Chamberlain. How so?

Rāma. Listen. Her husband is a second Indra, in me she has a son. What fruit can she desire that she should do an act unworthy? (13)

Chamberlain. My prince, do not attribute your own sincerity to the infatuated minds of women. Why, it was at her request that your consecration was put off.

Rāma. There are advantages, sir, in that.

Chamberlain. How so?

Rāma. Listen.

The king has been deterred from retiring to the forest. I am still a minor and subject of the king as before. The people are not troubled with the question of a new ruler. Moreover, my brothers are not deprived of their enjoyments. (14)

Chamberlain. But she came uninvited and asked that Bharata be anointed king. Was that not greed?

Rāma. From your partiality to me, sir, you overlook the truth. For,

If she demands for her son a kingdom stipulated in her dower, is the greed hers? Or ours, if we robbed a brother of his realm? (15)

Chamberlain. But—

Rāma. Henceforth I wish to hear no further charge against my mother. Tell me what has happened to the king.

Chamberlain. Then after that,

Mute with grief the king dismissed me with his hand. I count it something of a blessing he went off in a swoon. **(16)**

Rāma. What! He fainted away?

[*Voice behind the scene.*]

What, what, lost his senses, you say?
If thou canst not brook the king being out of his wits, seize thy bow and have no compassion.

Rāma. [*Listening and looking in front of him.*]

Who has so moved the immovable Lakshmaṇa, an ocean of patience? With him enraged I seem to see a host of hundreds before me. **(17)**

[*Then enter Lakshmaṇa with bow and arrows in his hands.*]

Lakshmaṇa. [*Angrily.*] What, what? Lost his senses you say?

If thou canst not brook the king being out of his wits, seize thy bow and have no compassion. Every one that is gentle and mild with his king is pushed on one side. And thou likest it not, do thou leave me alone. My mind is fixed to rid the world of young women, for we have been cheated. **(18)**

Sītā. Sumitrā's son has siezed his bow, when he should weep. Such violence is unheard of.

Rāma. What does all this mean, Lakshmaṇa?

Lakshmaṇa. What! you ask me what it all means?

The inherited realm has been raped, the ruler has his seat of sorrow on the ground. Now do you doubt that mercy equals cowardice? **(19)**

Rāma. Oh, Sumitrā's son! Has my loss of the kingdom caused this excitement? Alas! you are unwise.

If Bharata be the king, or I, 'tis all the same. If thou hast a pride in thy bow, then protect the king. **(20)**

Lakshmaṇa. I cannot hold in my anger. Well, well, I will go. [*Walks away.*]

Rāma. This scowl of Lakshmaṇa's clinging to the creases of his brow, as though it fain would burn the Triple World, stays fixed like Fate itself. **(21)**

Lakshmaṇa! One moment.

Lakshmaṇa. I am waiting, sir.

Rāma. I spoke that way to steady you. Now speak out.

Shall I bend my bow on my sire if he keeps not troth with

me? Shall I let fly an arrow at my mother if she take my wealth? Shall I slay my younger brother Bharata who has no part in these troubles? Of these three crimes which will satisfy thy wrath? (22)

Lakshmaṇa. [*In tears.*] Alas, you reproach me before you understand. I care nothing about the realm for which there is such mighty moiling. But thou hast to dwell an exile in the forests for fourteen years. (23)

Rāma. That's why his Majesty fainted. Alas, that shows weakness in a ruler. Lady of Mithilā,

Bring me that dress of bark, this girl's lucky gift. I must practice virtue unattained by other kings, not even essayed. (24)

Sītā. Take it, my lord.

Rāma. Lady of Mithilā, what is your intention?

Sītā. Why, I will practise virtue with you.

Rāma. But I must go alone.

Sītā. That is why I must go with you.

Rāma. It means dwelling in the forest.

Sītā. That will be my palace.

Rāma. But you have your duties, to attend upon my parents,

Sītā. As for them, may the gods forgive me.[1]

Rāma. Lakshmaṇa, dissuade her.

Lakshmaṇa. I dare not dissuade her ladyship from an opportunity so laudable.

Moonlight follows the moon even in eclipse. When the forest tree falls the creeper lies on the ground. The lord of elephants is not deserted by his mate though bogged in the mire. Let her make her pilgrimage practising virtue, for husbands are as gods to women. (25)

[*Enter Maid.*]

Maid. Princess, greeting! The Lady Revā, mistress of the tiring room, humbly reports that Avadātikā broke into the concert hall and carried off a bark dress. This is another one unworn, which may be made use of.

Rāma. Bring it here, good maid. The princess is satisfied. It is I that need one.

Maid. Pray take it. [*Hands over the garment and exit.*]

[*Rāma takes it and puts it on.*]

Lakshmaṇa. Forgive me, noble brother.

Of decorations, jewels, and garlands ever hast thou given me

[1] Lit. 'An obeisance is made to the gods.'

half, but thou hast put on all the bark thyself: for the bark it seems thou art selfish. (26)

Rāma. Oh, Maithilī, dissuade him.

Sītā. Yes, let me, Lakshmaṇa.

Lakshmaṇa. Lady!

Fain wouldst thou wait on the footsteps of my elder brother all alone. Thine shall be the right foot and the left shall be mine. (27)

Sītā. Give him half, my lord. He is in such distress.

Rāma. Lakshmaṇa! Listen. A dress of bark

Is armour for the battle of penance. It is the iron to guide the elephant of self control. Take it then, a curb for the prancing senses and charioteer of virtue. (28)

Lakshmaṇa. I thank you. [*Takes the bark and puts it on.*]

Rāma. The king's highway is all beset by citizens who have heard the news. Please send them away.

Lakshmaṇa. Noble brother, I will go in front. Way there! make way!

Rāma. Lady, take off your veil.

Sītā. As my lord commands. [*Takes it off.*]

Rāma. Good citizens, hearken to my words.

Gaze freely on this my spouse while your faces stream with tears. For women may be looked at without offence at sacrifice or wedding, in calamity or in the forest. (29)

[*Enter Chamberlain.*]

Chamberlain. Prince, you must not, must not, go. For his Majesty

Has heard of your going to the forest, attended by your lady and by Lakshmaṇa determined by kindly brotherhood. He got up from the ground, his limbs all smeared with dust, and is coming hither like an ancient tusker from the wilds. [30]

Lakshmaṇa. Noble brother,

Those who dwell in forests clad in coats of bark need see nobody.

Rāma. The king shall see our palaces after we've departed. (31)

[*Exeunt omnes.*]

END OF THE FIRST ACT.

ACT II

INTERLUDE

[*Enter Chamberlain.*]

Chamberlain. Ho! Watchers at the gates! Each at your station be vigilant.

[*Enter Portress.*]

Portress. What 's the matter, sir?

Chamberlain. Why, the king is set on keeping his word and unable to turn Rāma from going to the forest. His heart is burnt by the fiery pain of separation from his son. Lamenting mightily like a madman he is lying in the fountain chamber.[1]

Like Meru moving close on the dissolution of an aeon, like an ocean of untold depths approaching desiccation, like the sinking sun seen only by his disc, so the king: his limbs and wits unravelled by his woe. (1)

Portress. Dear, dear! Is the king like that?

Chamberlain. Madam! begone.

Portress. Very well, sir. [*Exit.*]

Chamberlain. [*Looking all round.*] Alas! Since the day that Rāma went, Ayodhyā seems deserted. For,

Lordly elephants are off their feed, the chargers stand without a neigh, tears in their eyes. The city folk, with greybeards, babes, and women, have no thought of food or talk. With mournful faces they cry aloud and gaze the way that Rāma goes with wife and brother. (2)

Meanwhile I must attend upon the king. [*Steps around and looks off.*] Ah, here is the king attended by the great queen and Sumitrā. They have composed themselves after mastering even the overwhelming grief that comes from being separated from their sons. It is a painful situation. The poor king

Gets up to fall, gets up again lamenting loudly, again and again, and gazes out the way that Rāma went. (3)

[*Exit.*]

END OF THE INTERLUDE.

[*Enter the king as described and the two queens.*]

King. Alas, my child! Rāma! Delight of the eyes of all the worlds.

Oh, Lakshmaṇa, my child! Whose every limb bears auspicious

[1] *Samudragṛhaka*, cf. *Vision of Vāsavadattā*, 'sea-room'.

marks. Oh, virtuous lady of Mithilā with heart devoted to thy lord! Alas, alas, they have gone. Gone, woe is me, to the forest. My own children. (4)

Oh, how strange it is that I should yearn to see Lakshmaṇa who lost all love for his father in his love for his brother. Oh, daughter Vaidehī,

Even Rāma abandons me, Lakshmaṇa reproaches me. Wilt even thou abandon me a vessel of infamy for all the world? (5)

Rāma, my son! Lakshmaṇa, my child! Daughter mine from Videha, answer me, my babies.

Alas, all is silent. None will answer me.

Son of Kausalyā, where are you?

True to thy word, with wrath subdued, unselfish and beloved of the world, so apt to serve thine elders—vouchsafe to me an answer. (6)

Oh, where is he? Where is that Rāma who delights the eyes and hearts of all the people. Where is he? So obedient to his elders. So kindly to those in distress, despising sovereignty as a trifle. My son, Rāma! If you desert your old father what boots the practice of senseless virtue? Woe is me. Alas—

Like the sun Rāma has gone, Lakshmaṇa has followed him as the day follows the sun. Sītā has disappeared like a shadow when sun and day are gone. (7)

[*Looking up above.*] Ah! Wretched fate.

Why didst thou not establish three decrees: myself to have no children; Rāma to be the son of another monarch and Kaikeyī . . . a tigress in the jungle? (8)

Kausalyā. [*Weeping.*] Peace now, Majesty, do not torment yourself beyond measure and lose all control. You are bound to see them both, and the princess, when the period is ended.

King. Oh! Who art thou?

Kausalyā. She that bare that son unloved.

King. What, art thou Kausalyā, mother of Rāma, the delight of the eyes and hearts of all mankind?

Kausalyā. Majesty! I am that unlucky woman.

King. Kausalyā! Thou art great indeed, for thou hast carried Rāma in thy womb.

While I have lost my wits and have no strength either to bear or to restrain this grief, boundless and unbearable like a flame. (9)

[*Looking at Sumitrā.*] Who is this other?

Kausalyā. Majesty! Dear Lakshmaṇa— [*Breaks off.*]

King. [*Springing up.*] Where is he? Where is Lakshmaṇa? I cannot see him. Woe is me.

[*The two queens rise hurriedly and hold up the king.*]

Kausalyā. Majesty! I was saying—dear Lakshmaṇa's mother, Sumitrā.

King. Oh, Sumitrā!

Thy son is a good son, for in the forest day and night he follows Rāma, best of the Raghu clan, like a shadow. (10)

[*Enter Chamberlain.*]

Chamberlain. To the king, greeting. The noble Sumantra has arrived.

King. [*Springing up in delight.*] With Rāma?

Chamberlain. No, with a chariot.

King. What? Only with a chariot? [*Falls down in a swoon.*]

Both queens. Take heart, your Majesty, take heart! [*They massage his limbs.*]

Chamberlain. Alack! Fate is inexorable. So even such great ones incur such dire calamity! Take heart, your Majesty, take heart!

King. [*Recovering somewhat.*] Bālāki, has Sumantra come back all alone?

Chamberlain. Why yes, your Majesty.

King. Alas! alas!

If the chariot has come back empty, my heart is broken. Now has Death sent the chariot to fetch Dasaratha. (11)

So bring him in at once.

Chamberlain. As your Majesty commands. [*Exit.*]

King. Blessed indeed are the breezes in the forest that circle round the lakes touching Rāma at their ease as he wanders in the wood. (12)

[*Enter Sumantra.*]

Sumantra. [*Looking all round sorrowfully.*]

These servants leave their duties, blinded by tears welling up through love for Rāma. Oppressed by care, their bodies burning with sorrow, they reproach the monarch as he screams his lamentations. (13)

[*Approaching.*] Great king—greeting.

King. Brother Sumantra.

Where is my first-born, Rāma?

No, no, I said not that aright.

Where, dear child, is Rāma thy eldest son? And where is that daughter of the Videhas so absolutely devoted to her spouse? Where is Sumitrā's son devoted to his elders? What do they say of me, their wretched father on the point of death? What

do they say of one that has brought a deluge of sorrow to all
my people? (14)

Sumantra. I beseech your Majesty, do not utter so inauspicious words. Ere long you shall see them.

King. You are right. My words were out of place. It was not a proper question to ask of anchorites. So tell me then, Is all well with the penance of those anchorites? And wandering at will through the forests is the lady of Videha not distressed?

Sumitrā. Did she say anything for us and the king, Sumantra? Child as she is, all dressed up in bark, sharing the pilgrimage of her lord, she is no child in her conduct.

Sumantra. They all send your Majesty word—

King. No, no. Let me hear it with names of each, an elixir for my ears and medicine for the trouble in my heart.

Sumantra. As the king commands. Rāma, long life to him.

King. Rāma! Yes, here 's Rāma. The very sound of his name brings him close to me. Go on.

Sumantra. Lakshmaṇa—long life to him.

King. Here 's Lakshmaṇa. And then?

Sumantra. Janaka's daughter, Sītā, long may she live, . . .

King. Here is Sītā. Rāma, Lashmaṇa, and Sītā, but that is not the proper order.

Sumantra. What order then?

King. Rāma, Sītā, and Lakshmaṇa.

Let the maid of Mithilā stand betwixt those two. The forests
are full of dangers, so shall she be well protected. (15)

Sumantra. As the king commands. Rāma, long life to him.

King. Here is Rāma.

Sumantra. Janaka's daughter, Sītā, long life to her.

King. Here is Sītā.

Sumantra. And Lakshmaṇa, long may he live.

King. Here is Lakshmaṇa. Rāma, Sītā, Lakshmaṇa, embrace me, my children!

If I may just touch Rāma once again, or even see him, I think
I may live like a dead man revived by ambrosia. (16)

Sumantra. At Śṛiṅgabera they got out of the chariot and stood looking towards Ayodhyā. Bowing low they were about to send your Majesty a message.

Long they pondered something they would say, and their lips
trembled with the words, but their throats were paralysed with
tears and they went off into the forest without a word. (17)

King. What? Went off without a word. [*Goes off in a deeper swoon than before.*]

Sumantra. [*Anxiously.*] Bālāki, tell the ministers the king is in a hopeless state.

Chamberlain. Very well. [*Exit.*]

The two Queens. Take heart, your Majesty, take heart!

King. [*Recovering slightly.*]

Touch my arm, Kausalyā, I cannot see thee with mine eyes. My wits have wandered after Rāma, and are not yet returned. (**18**)

Oh Rāma, my son. Ever had I set my heart on the thought

That enthroning thee I should bless my people with a noble king, and bidding thee bestow equal fortune on thy brothers. I would pass hence to a forest grove, and now, alas! Kaikeyī has changed all that in a single second. (**19**)

Sumantra, take word to Kaikeyī—

Rāma has gone. Be thou content—I am on the point of death. Send swiftly for our son. Let the error bear its fruit. (**20**)

Sumantra. As the king commands.

King. [*Looking upwards.*] Ah! Here come the shades of my ancestors to comfort my burning heart for news of Rāma. Whom have we here?

[*Enter the Chamberlain.*]

Chamberlain. Victory to the king!

King. Some water.

Chamberlain. As the king commands. [*Exit and re-enters.*] Majesty, here is water.

King. [*Sips and looks off.*]

Here is Dilīpa, friend of the Lord of Immortals, here is the majestic Raghu, this is my father Aja. Why have you come? It is time for me to dwell there with you. (**21**)

Rāma, Sītā, Lakshmaṇa, I am passing hence to the spirits of my ancestors. Great spirits, here I come!

[*Expires in a swoon.*]

[*Chamberlain throws a cloth over him.*]

All. Woe, woe, the king!

[*Exeunt omnes.*]

[END OF THE SECOND ACT.]

ACT III

INTERLUDE

[*Enter Sudhākāra.*]

Sudhākāra. [*Cleaning up.*] Well, now I have done what master Sambhavaka told me. I'll just have a nap. [*Goes to sleep.*]

[*Enter Attendant.*]

Attendant. [*Going up to the servant and striking him.*] Ah, you rascal! Why are n't you working? [*Strikes him again.*]

Sudhākāra. [*Waking up.*] Beat me, that 's right!

Attendant. If I do beat you, what will you do?

Sudhākāra. Unluckily I don't have a thousand arms like Arjuna.

Attendant. What do you want a thousand arms for?

Sudhākāra. To kill you.

Attendant. Oh, you rascal! Now I'll thrash you to death. [*Strikes him repeatedly.*]

Sudhākāra. [*Blubbering.*] May I know, master, what is my fault?

Attendant. What, no fault of yours I suppose! Didn't I tell you all the harem ladies were coming here to-day, with the queen at their head? . . . coming here to this portrait gallery to see the statue of King Daśaratha, who went to heaven with a broken heart, because Prince Rāma lost the succession? Now what have you done about it?

Sudhākāra. Why look, master. I've cleaned out the pigeons' nests from the room inside. I've marked the walls with five-finger prints of beautiful sandal. I have decorated the doors by hanging up wreaths of flowers. I have strewn fresh sand. What then haven't I done?

Attendant. If that 's so, go in peace. I will just let the Minister know everything is ready.

[*Exeunt ambo.*]

END OF THE INTERLUDE.

[*Enter Bharata in a chariot, and a charioteer.*]

Bharata. [*Eagerly.*] Driver, I have lived so long with my uncle, that I have no news. They say the king is very ill. Tell me then,

What disease afflicts my sire?

Charioteer. A great affliction of the heart.

Bharata. What do the physicians say?

Charioteer. Nay, the doctors are helpless in this case.

Bharata. Does he take his food and sleep?

Charioteer. He lies on the earth tasting nothing.

Bharata. Is there any hope?

Charioteer. Only destiny.

Bharata. My heart throbs; speed the car. (1)

Charioteer. As the prince commands! [*Accelerates the chariot.*]

Bharata. [*Acting the speed of the chariot.*] Ah, how swift the chariot moves! Those

Trees appear to race towards us, so swiftly is their range reduced by the motion of the chariot. The ground runs down into the hollow betwixt the wheels like an agitated stream. The single spokes cannot be seen for the speed, only solid circles. The dust raised by the steeds flies in front but cannot follow behind.[1] (2)

Charioteer. Prince, we must be nearing Ayodhyā, there is more moisture from the trees.[2]

Bharata. How my mind hurries ahead eager to see my kinsmen.

My head is bowed at my father's feet, lovingly, methinks, he raises me, my brethren hasten up to me, the mothers' tears bedew me. 'How well he looks! how tall and strong he's grown!' so say the servants complimenting me. I see it all, my jests, my dress, my talk with Lakshmaṇa. (3)

Charioteer. [*Aside.*] Alas. How sad that the prince should enter Ayodhyā ignorant of the king's death and nursing hopeless expectations of the future. Although we know, we cannot tell him, for

Who will relate the triple bane, his father's death, his mother's lust of power, and the exile of his elder brother? (4)

[*Enter a soldier.*]

Soldier. Highness, greeting.

Bharata. Ah, good fellow, has Śatrughna come to meet me?

Soldier. The prince is on his way. But the preceptors say—

Bharata. What do they say?

Soldier. There is still half an hour in the regency of the Pleiades. After that you may enter Ayodhyā as Rohiṇī[3] arrives.

Bharata. Very well. I have never disobeyed a preceptor's words. You may go.

Soldier. As the prince commands. [*Exit.*]

Bharata. Where shall I spend the time? Yes, I see; I will rest awhile

[1] L. S. prefers 'does not fall in front but only falls behind'.

[2] *Sopasnehatayā vṛkṣānām.* L. S. thinks it means 'Beautiful trees being well-arranged'.

[3] Ninth lunar asterism.

in that temple which I see through the trees. That will serve the double purpose, worship and repose. And it is the proper custom to sit a moment before entering a town, so stop the chariot.

Charioteer. As the prince commands. [*Stops the chariot.*]

Bharata. [*Dismounting from the chariot.*] Charioteer, rest the horses in a quiet spot.

Charioteer. As the prince commands.

Bharata. [*Taking a few steps and looking round.*] Oblations are indicated by the fried grains and the flowers strewn by a pious hand. The walls are marked with five-finger prints of sandal. The doors are festooned with garlands. There is fresh sand on the ground. Is it something special at the turn of the moon, or daily piety? To what deity can the place belong? I see no external sign, neither weapon nor banner. Well, I will go in and find out. [*Entering and looking round.*] What exquisite carving in these sculptures! How lifelike they are. Though these statues represent deities they look just like men. Is this a glorification of the four deities? Nay, be they what they may, they delight my heart.

> If they be deities it is right to bow the head, only a churl would worship them without a verse of praise. **(5)**

[*Enter the Keeper.*]

Keeper. Hullo! Who is this that has gone into the gallery while I was engaged on my own affairs, after finishing my official duties? He strongly resembles the statues. Well, I will go in and find out.

[*Enters the gallery.*]

Bharata. Salutation.

Keeper. No, no, do not worship them.

Bharata. Oh, sir, say not so!

> Is there something you should tell me? Why is this special prohibition maintained? Is it tyranny of rules? **(6)**

Keeper. Those are not the reasons why I forbade you, but I would not have a brahman worship, thinking they were gods. For they are of the warrior caste.

Bharata. So! Warriors, you say? Then what are their names?

Keeper. Sons of Ikshvāku.

Bharata. [*Joyfully.*] Sons of Ikshvāku! So these are the rulers of Ayodhyā.

> These are they that rallied with the Gods at the destruction of the Demon city. These are they that by their good deeds pass to Indra's realm with the subjects of the country and the town. These are they that hold the whole world won by

the might of their arms. These are they that Death so long sought an excuse for not removing. (7)

Oh, what a great privilege chance has given me! Tell me, who is this noble king?

Keeper. This is Dilīpa, who kindled the lamp of sacred law, and founded the rite of universal conquest that bestows all jewels.

Bharata. Salutations to the devotee of *dharma*. And who is this great king?

Keeper. This is Raghu, at whose rising and sleeping many thousands of brahmans chanted auspicious hymns.

Bharata. Ah, death is powerful indeed to over-pass that protection. Salutation to him that enriched the brahmans with the fruits of sovereignty. And who is this?

Keeper. That is Aja, who gave up the burden of his realm from grief at separation from his beloved and soothed his sorrow in the purifications of constant rites.

Bharata. Salutations to him of such praiseworthy penance. [*Looks at Daśaratha's statue and becomes troubled.*] My mind is confused with awe. I have not grasped it clearly. Tell me who is this?

Keeper. This is Dilīpa.

Bharata. The great grandfather of the king. Proceed.

Keeper. The royal Raghu.

Bharata. The grandfather of the king. Yes?

Keeper. The royal Aja.

Bharata. The father of my dear father. What? Once more.

Keeper. This is Dilīpa, this Raghu, and this Aja.

Bharata. Good sir, one question. Do they put up statues of living kings?

Keeper. Oh no, only of the dead.

Bharata. Then I bid you farewell.

Keeper. Stay. Why dost thou not question me of this other statue, that of Daśaratha, who yielded up both life and realm as a bridal fee? (8)

Bharata. Alas, my father. [*Falls down in a swoon and then recovers.*]

Oh, my heart, be thou content with the truth of thy suspicions. Learn now of my sire's decease and for a moment be thou calm. If this base term 'a bridal fee' touches me and it be true, then this my body must be cleansed—with fire. (9)

Noble sir,

Keeper. 'Noble sir'? that is the greeting used by princes of the royal blood. Can you be Bharata, Kaikeyī's son?

Bharata. Why yes, I am Bharata, the son of Daśaratha—not of Kaikeyī.

Keeper. Then excuse me if I leave you.

Bharata. Stay. Tell me the rest.

Keeper. No escape! Then listen. King Daśaratha is no more. Why Rāma went away to the forests with Sītā and Lakshmaṇa, I do not know.

Bharata. What do you say? My noble brother gone to the forest?

[*Goes off in a deeper swoon.*]

Keeper. Oh prince, take heart, be brave!

Bharata. [*Reviving.*]

I find Ayodhyā is a wilderness abandoned by my father and my brothers, as a man tormented by thirst hastens to a stream and finds it all dried up. **(10)**

Noble sir, it will brace my mind to hear the tale in full. So tell me all, concealing nothing.

Keeper. Hearken then. The king was about to consecrate Rāma when your mother said—

Bharata. Hold.

She said, 'Remember the bridal forfeit and let my son be king' Then encouraged by his patience she addressed my elder brother, 'Go thou, my son, to the forest'. When he saw him dressed in bark the king came to an unhappy end. And all the blame the people justly cast on me. **(11)** [*Faints away.*]

[*Voice behind the scene.*]

Out of the way, sirs, out of the way!

Keeper. [*Looking behind.*] Ah!

Here come the queens, just in time, as the prince has swooned. For the touch of a mother's hand is like a handful of water to the parched. **(12)**

[*Enter the queens and Sumantra.*]

Sumantra. This way, ladies.

This is that statue-gallery of our king, the height whereof surpasses palaces. Here may travellers resort, without obeisance, without the guidance of custodians. **(13)**

[*Enters and looks round.*]

Oh, ladies, do not enter.

For here lies one like the king in his youthful days.

Keeper. Mistake him not, but take him, for this is Bharata. **(14)** [*Exit.*]

Queens. [*Approaching hastily.*] Oh, Bharata, my child.

Bharata. [*Reviving somewhat.*] Noble sir.

Sumantra. Victory to the Ki— [*Breaks off sadly.*] Ah, how like the voice. It sounds as though the king's statue was speaking.

Bharata. How are my lady mothers now?

Queens. Child, as you see. [*Remove their veils.*]

Sumantra. Ladies, restrain your emotion.

Bharata. [*Looking at Sumantra.*] So intimate on all occasions,[1] that tells me something. Tell me, old man, are you Sumantra?

Sumantra. Yes, Prince. I am.

Pursued by the evils of longevity, disgraced by my ingratitude, I still live on, though that king has passed away. The driver of an empty chariot. **(15)**

Bharata. Alas, poor old man. [*Getting up.*)

I want you to tell me, old gentleman, which lady should I first address.

Sumantra. Certainly. This is Prince Rāma's mother, Queen Kausalyā.

Bharata. Mother, I that am innocent salute you.

Kausalyā. My child, I wish you freedom from distress.

Bharata. [*Aside.*] That implies a reproach. [*Aloud.*] I thank you. And then—

Sumantra. This is Prince Lakshmana's mother, Queen Sumitrā.

Bharata. Mother, I that am forestalled by Lakshmaṇa salute you.

Sumantra. My child, I wish you glory.

Bharata. Why, mother, I shall strive for it. I thank you. And so—

Sumantra. This is your own mother.

Bharata. (*Rising angrily.*) Oh, wicked woman!

Betwixt this my mother and that one thou lookest not well, like a foul stream slipping between the Ganges and the Jamnā. **(16)**

Kaikeyī. My child! What have I done?

Bharata. What have you done, you say?

Thou hast covered me with infamy, and my elder brother with bark. Thou has brought the king to his death too soon,[2] and all Ayodhyā to endless lamentation. Thou hast sent Lakshmaṇa to dwell with beasts, and mothers doting on their sons to dwell with sorrow. Thou hast laden thy daughter-in-law with the toils of travel, and thyself with harsh words of reproach. **(17)**

Kausalyā. My child, you are versed in all the rules of etiquette, why don't you salute your mother?

Bharata. 'Mother', say you? Nay, lady, you are my mother, and you do I salute.

Kausalyā. No, no, she is your mother.

Bharata. She used to be, but not now. Look you, lady,

Sons cease to be sons when they cease to love, with virtue

[1] Lit. 'your proximity (on the occasion) of all their behaviour', i. e. even when the ladies remove their veils.

[2] *gṛha-mṛtyu*, 'house-death', i. e. death while still a householder and not arrived at the later stages.

turned to sin. I will establish a new law in the world that a mother be no mother for perfidy to her lord. **(18)**

Kaikeyī. I said what I said, my child, to make the king keep his word.

Bharata. What did you say?

Kaikeyī. 'Let my son be king.'

Bharata. And what else but a son is my elder brother to you?

Is he not the son legitimate of my sire? Is he not the heir in succession? Did he not adore his brothers? Did the people disapprove? **(19)**

Kaikeyī. Shall a woman be questioned for wanting her bridal fee?

Bharata. Thou sendest him on foot with his bride, his royal splendour replaced by bark, and biddest him dwell in the forest. Is that too written in the bridal bond? **(20)**

Kaikeyī. I will explain, my child, at the proper time and place.

Bharata. If thou wast greedy of shame, why bring in my name?

What profit from kingship didst thou desire? What would the king not have given? Or didst thou but crave the title 'Mother of the King'? Speak truly, madam, was not my elder brother thy son? **(21)**

The deed was evil, madam.

In thy lust for power thou hadst no thought for the king or his life. His eldest son didst thou send away to wander in the forest. Alas! the Creator has made thy heart as hard as adamant, that it was not broken at the sight of Sītā dressed in bark. **(22)**

Sumantra. Prince, here are Vasishṭha and Vāmadeva and the people. They approach your Highness with preparation for your consecration and would have you know:—

As cattle without a herdsman are unprotected and soon destroyed, so perishes a people that has no king. **(23)**

Bharata. Let the people follow me.

Sumantra. Whither away, your Highness, without waiting for the consecration?

Bharata. 'Consecration', say you? Bestow it on her ladyship here.

Sumantra. Where is your Highness going?

Bharata. Where Lakshmaṇa's friend abides. Without him Ayodhyā is not Ayodhyā. For Ayodhyā can only be where the scion of Raghu dwells. **(24)**

[*Exeunt omnes.*]

END OF THE THIRD ACT.

ACT IV

[*In Ayodhyā.*]

INTERLUDE

[*Enter two Maids.*]

Vijayā. Nandanikā, my dear, do tell me: Is it true that when Queen Kausalyā and all the other ladies went to see the gallery of statues, they saw Prince Bharata in that very place? I, unluckily, had to remain at the door.

Nandanikā. Yes, my dear, we were so curious, and we saw the king's son Bharata.

Vijayā. What did the prince say to the queen his mother?

Nandanikā. Say to her? He won't so much as look at her.

Vijayā. Dear, dear, it's a bad business. By doing prince Rāma out of the succession through greed of power she decreed her own widowhood. The people are going to rack and ruin. She is cruel indeed. 'Twas a wicked thing to do.

Nandanikā. Besides, my dear, the prince wouldn't wait for the consecration the people had all ready, but went off to Rāma's penance-grove.

Vijayā. [*Disappointed.*] Oh! So the prince has gone. Come Nandanikā, let us find the queen.

[*Exeunt ambo.*]

END OF THE INTERLUDE.

[*Enter Bharata in a chariot with Sumantra and a charioteer.*]

Bharata. Now that the king has gone to heaven with his virtuous deeds behind him, I set forth, followed by the streaming tears of citizens, to find in the wide penance-groves that second moon in the world that we call Rāma. (1)

Sumantra. Here is Prince Bharata.

Son of the king who crushed the pride of Indra and the demons, grandson of the king who devoted his wealth to ritual, brother of Rāma so loving to his father and the darling of the world, he fares forth by the selfsame road as Rāma. (2)

Bharata. Old gentleman!

Sumantra. Prince, I am here.

Bharata. Where is his highness, my elder brother Rāma? Where is that image[1] of the king? that shining example of the steadfast? that reproach to Kaikeyī with her lust for power? Where is that vessel of glory, true son of the king and devoted to the truth?

Him do I long to see that gave up his fortune to please my mother, he is my greatest deity. (3)

Sumantra. Here, prince, in this hermitage.

Here dwell the glorious Rāma, Sītā, and Lakshmaṇa, embodiments of truth, virtue, and devotion. (4)

Bharata. Then stop the chariot.

Charioteer. As the prince commands. [*Does so.*]

Bharata. [*Alighting from the chariot.*] Driver, rest the horses in a quiet place.

Charioteer. As the prince commands. [*Exit.*]

Bharata. Old sir, make the announcement, do!

Sumantra. What announcement, prince?

Bharata. The arrival of Bharata, son of greedy Kaikeyī.

Sumantra. Nay, prince, do not reproach your elders.

Bharata. Very good, it is not right to mention the faults of others. Then say that Bharata wishes to see them, he that has become the disgrace of the royal clan.

Sumantra. Nay, prince, I cannot say that. Rather I will simply say, 'Bharata has arrived'.

Bharata. No, no. Merely to mention my name would suggest I made no expiation. But are brahman-murderers announced by others? So stay, old gentleman. I will announce myself. Ho, there! make known to his Highness Rāghava, maintainer of his father's word,

There has arrived a cruel and ungrateful man, unrefined and violent, but full of devotion. Is he to stay or to go away? (5)

[*Enter Rāma with Lakshmaṇa and Sītā.*]

Rāma. [*Listening with delight.*] Lakshmaṇa, do you hear? And you, Princess of Videha, do you hear?

Whose voice is that, so like my sire's? Its tone is deeper than the thunder in the clouds. Making my heart surmise a kinsman, it is doubly welcome to my ears. (6)

Lakshmaṇa. Noble brother, the sound of this voice affects me too with a feeling of great respect as for a kinsman. For

This is a powerful voice, clear and steady, soft and mellow like that of an amorous bull. Melodious in tone and rapid with

[1] L. S. 'representative'.

easy breathing and with clear articulation of every sound, this voice rings out to free the world from fear.[1] (7)

Rāma. In any case it is not a stranger's voice. It seems to move my heart. Dear Lakshmaṇa, do find out whose it is.

Lakshmaṇa. As my brother bids. [*Steps around.*]

Bharata. Ah! Why does no one answer? Have they discovered that Bharata, Kaikeyī's son, has come?

Lakshmaṇa. [*Gazing at him.*] Why this is Rāma! No, no, it's only similarity.

His peerless countenance, lovely as the moon, is like my elder brother's. That broad chest that the god's foes have scarred with arrows resembles father's.

Circled with lustre, all splendour, a delight for the world to see, is he a king or the lord of gods, Madhusūdana himself? (8)

[*Catching sight of Sumantra.*] Oho, old gentleman!

Sumantra. Ha! Prince Lakshmaṇa.

Bharata. Yes, he is my elder brother. Noble sir, I salute you.

Lakshmaṇa. Welcome, welcome! Long may you live. [*Looking at Sumantra.*] Tell me good sir, who is this gentleman?

Sumantra. Prince,

Fourth from Raghu, from Aja third and second from thy illustrious sire, he is Prince Bharata, younger brother of that standard of the clan, that is thine own elder brother. (9)

Lakshmaṇa. Welcome, royal prince! Good health be yours, dear boy and long may you live.

May your valour equal that of kinsmen unsurpassed in might and courage, whose bows, so skilled in battles with fiends, were matched with thunderbolts. Like that king Raghu who spent his treasure on sacrifice, be thou a vessel of the most glorious qualities in the world. (10)

Bharata. I thank you.

Lakshmaṇa. Prince, stay here a moment. I will tell my brother you have come.

Bharata. Please tell him quickly, noble brother. For I am longing to salute him without delay.

Lakshmaṇa. Very well. [*Goes up to Rāma.*]

Noble brother, greeting!

[1] Lit. 'Melodious in the throat and forceful with the passages unobstructed in the chest, with clearness of articulation of the several sounds, as it comes to each organ it issues to give, as it were, security to the four castes.'

This is your well-beloved brother Bharata, so affectionate to his brethren. In him your own form stands reflected as in a mirror. (11)

Rāma. Dear Lakshmaṇa, has Bharata arrived ?

Lakshmaṇa. Why, yes.

Rāma. Lady of Mithilā, open wide your eyes to look at Bharata.

Sītā. What, my lord, is Bharata here ?

Rāma. Yes, Princess,

To-day I am to learn how hard a thing my father did. However great a man's affection for his son, a brother's love is no less. (12)

Lakshmaṇa. Shall the prince enter, sir ?

Rāma. My dear Lakshmaṇa, do you want my order even for this, your heart's desire ? Go bring in the prince at once with honour.

Lakshmaṇa. As my brother bids.

Rāma. Nay, stay.

Let the princess go herself to show him honour, like a mother, whose heart is melting for her son, her eyes shedding a shower of joyful tears like a blue-lotus leaf wet with dew. (13)

Sītā. As my lord commands. [*Rises, steps round and sees Bharata.*] So then, my lord has just come out himself ! No, no. It is only a similarity.

Sumantra. Ah, the bride !

Bharata. Ah, this is her Highness, King Janaka's daughter.

This is that glory in woman's form gotten on a field by the plough as a manifestation of King Janaka's austerities. (14)

Lady, Bharata salutes you.

Sītā. [*Aside.*] Not only his looks, his voice, too, is the same. [*Aloud.*] Dear brother, long life to you.

Bharata. I thank you.

Sītā. Come, dear, and delight your brother's heart.

Sumantra. Let the prince go in.

Bharata. What wilt thou do now, old sir ?

Sumantra. Later I shall see. Since the king went to heaven this is my first glimpse of Rāma now he knows the truth. (15)

Bharata. So be it. [*Approaching Rāma.*] Noble brother, Bharata greets you.

Rāma. [*Joyfully.*] Welcome, welcome ! royal prince. Long life and health be thine,

Spread out thy breast as wide as the panel of a door and embrace me in thy two stalwart arms. Lift up this face lovely as the autumn moon, bring delight to this my body burnt by calamity. (16)

Bharata. I thank you.

Sumantra. [*Approaching.*] Long live the prince!

Rāma. Alas, old gentleman,

Erstwhile there was a king that with his armies mounted to the sky at the moment of assault in the battle of Gods and Demons with aerial cars as swift as theirs. He was renowned for it and pointed out by many: 'There goes the hero.' But now that the glorious king has left the body to dwell in heaven with the shades of his royal ancestors, what comfort can he find therein deprived of you, so devoted and so beloved? (17)

Sumantra. [*Sorrowfully.*]

For living through this varied dreadful woe, the king's demise, your own exile, Bharata's distress, and the helpless state of the royal house, my old age seems guilty of a string of crimes. (18)

Sītā. Oh, my lord, ere your tears are dry, this old man is making you weep again.

Rāma. Lady of Mithilā, lo, I control myself. Dear Lakshmaṇa, bring water.

Lakshmaṇa. As my brother bids.

Bharata. Nay, brother, it is not proper. It is my turn to serve and I will go. [*Takes the pitcher. Exit and re-enters.*] Here is water.

Rāma. [*Sipping.*] Lady of Mithilā, Lakshmaṇa has lost his occupation.

Sītā. My lord, he also should attend on you.

Rāma. True, let Lakshmaṇa serve me here and Bharata in Ayodhyā.

Bharata. Oh, please, my noble brother,

I will stay here in the body and over there in action. Your very name will protect the realm. (19)

Rāma. My dear Bharata, say not so.

I came to the forest at my sire's behest, not from pride, dear lad, or fear or confusion. Our house, I tell thee, keeps its word. Wilt thou then start on a lower path? (20)

Sumantra. Where now is the consecration water to rest?

Rāma. Where my mother has directed.

Bharata. May it please my noble brother, do not strike me on the raw.

My lineage, worthy brother, is the same as thine. Thy father so resolute and wise was my father too. A man cannot be blamed for his mother's fault, great hero. See, kindly one, how Bharata is distressed. (21)

Sītā. My lord, the words of Bharata are piteous. What think you?

Rāma. Lady of Mithilā,

I am thinking of the king that passed to the world of the gods and never saw the splendid qualities of this son of his. Ah, fie upon fate if it can overcome the best of men after getting such a son, a treasure-house of virtues! (22)

Dear Bharata,

'Tis sooth I am content with thee, and thy soul is clear of stain. Thy qualities so manifest have won me and incline my will to what you say. But it is not fitting thou shouldst make that great king's word prove false. Having obtained a son like thee should thy father be dubbed a liar? (23)

Bharata. I will abide at thy feet, O king, until thy vow has been fulfilled.

Rāma. Nay, a king must gain success by his own good deeds. My curse is on thee if thou dost not protect thy realm. (24)

Bharata. Alas, to that there is no answer. So be it. On one condition will I maintain the kingdom.

Rāma. What is the condition?

Bharata. I want you to resume thy kingdom, given in trust to me, at the end of the fourteen years.

Rāma. Agreed.

Bharata. Bear witness all of you, you brother, you, lady, and you, old gentleman.

All. Yes, we are witnesses.

Bharata. Noble brother, I crave another boon.

Rāma. What would you have, dear boy? What can I give? What can I do for you?

Bharata. Vouchsafe to me who bow my head, those two sandals thou dost wear. I shall be their vassal till thou comest to fulfil thy duty. (25)

Rāma. [*Aside.*] Ah! What little glory I had attained at length, Bharata has acquired it all to-day in no time at all. (26)

Sītā. My lord. Please grant Bharata his first request.

Rāma. So be it. Dear brother, take them.

Bharata. I thank you. [*Takes them.*] Noble brother, let me pour on them the consecration water.

Rāma. Old gentleman, let all be done as Bharata desires.

Sumantra. As the prince commands.

Bharata. [*Aside.*] Ah,

Now my kin can trust me, now can the people love me, and I can hold my head up in the world. Now am I the virtuous beloved son of the deceased monarch. I am honoured by my excellent brothers, a vessel of great glory, talked of in the conversation of good men, an object of affection to all who obtain what they desire. **(27)**

Rāma. Dear Bharata, a kingdom should not be neglected even for a moment. So for success you should return this very day.

Sītā. Oh, must Prince Bharata go this very day?

Rāma. Affection must be restrained. This very day must the prince return to power.

Bharata. Noble brother, I shall depart this very day.

The burghers will be waiting in the city hoping to see thee: I shall content them by showing them thy favour. **(28)**

Sumantra. Great prince, what am I to do now?

Rāma. Look after the prince, old gentleman, like the king himself.

Sumantra. If I live, I shall do my best.

Rāma. Dear Bharata, mount the chariot in my presence.

Bharata. As my brother bids. [*Gets into the chariot.*]

Rāma. Come, Maithilī, and you, dear Lakshmana. We will see Bharata to the gate of the hermitage.

[*Exeunt omnes.*]

END OF THE FOURTH ACT.

ACT V

[*Enter Sītā and a female ascetic.*]

Sītā. Lady, I have swept up the votive blossoms scattered through the hermitage. The gods have been honoured with such means as a grove affords. Now, until my husband returns, I will tend these young trees, giving them some water.

Ascetic. Be there no let or hindrance therein.

[*Enter Rāma.*]

Rāma. [*Sorrowfully.*] Deserting fair Ayodhyā forsaken by the king and me, Bharata, that treasure-house of virtues, came here to me presenting all the gear for my coronation: but I have sent him back, to guard the realm. All alone, alas, he has to bear the heavy burden of a king. **(1)**

[*Reflecting.*] It must be so. To soothe so keen a grief I must see the princess of Mithilā, my true mate in every situation. Where now has she gone? [*Stepping and looking around.*] Ah, the roots of these trees have just been watered. That shows she has not gone far. For

The water is still swirling with its bubbles in the trench; the thirsty birds alighting are not yet drinking the muddy stream; as their holes are flooded out, draggled insects are crawling to dry ground. The trees appear to have new girdles with the wet rings where the water sinks at their roots. (2)

(*Looking round.*] Ah, here is the lady of Videha—alas!

That hand of hers that erstwhile was wearied by a mirror, now feels no fatigue in carrying a water jar. Alas, the forest makes delicate ladies as hard as creepers. (3)

[*Approaching.*] Maithilī, how goes it with your task?

Sītā. Oh, it is my lord! Greeting, my lord.

Rāma. If your duty will allow, please sit down.

Sītā. As my lord commands. [*Sits down.*]

Rāma. You look to me as if you wished to say something, Maithilī. What is it?

Sītā. My lord's face is pale as if his heart was troubled by some sorrow. Why is that?

Rāma. There is ground for my grief, Maithilī.

My body is smitten by the shafts of Fate, the wound in my heart remains the same. Thereon beat the blows of sorrow's darts of manifold result again and again. (4)

Sītā. What is the trouble, my lord?

Rāma. To-morrow is the anniversary of my reverend father and the memorial rites[1] must be performed. The shades require oblations to be made exactly as ordained by the sacred law. I am sad to think I cannot conform. Yet,

As they know my present state they will be content with anything, and yet I wish I could perform this worship in a manner worthy of Rāma and his sire. (5)

Sītā. But Bharata, my lord, will perform the rite in royal style, and you in your present state will do it with water and with fruits. That will father esteem the more.

Rāma. Ah Maithilī,

When father sees the fruits placed on the sacrificial grass with

[1] Lit. Śrāddha ceremonies, offerings to the shades of the departed at certain intervals.

our own hands, 'twill remind him of our exile in the forest, and he will weep even in the other world. (6)

[*Enter Rāvaṇa disguised as an ascetic.*]

Rāvaṇa. Ha, here am I,

Of a spirit uncontrolled, I adopt this virtuous guise to cheat the son of Raghu, whom I hate for killing Khara. I have set out with full intent to carry off the daughter of king Janaka, like a stream of oblations deficient in fitting word and accent.[1] (7)

[*Turning round and looking down.*]

This is the entrance to Rāma's hermitage. I will descend. [*Descends.*] I shall behave like a guest. I am a guest. Holla! Who is there?

Rāma. [*Listening.*] Welcome to a guest.

Rāvaṇa. His good looks are well matched by his voice.

Rāma. [*Catching sight of him.*] Ah! a holy man. Reverend sir, I salute you.

Rāvaṇa. Good health to you.

Rāma. Pray be seated here, sir.

Rāvaṇa. [*Aside.*] I feel as if he were ordering me about. [*Aloud.*] Very well. [*Sits down.*]

Rāma. Maithilī, bring water for the feet of this holy man.

Sītā. As my lord commands. [*Exit and re-enters.*] Here is water.

Rāma. Wait upon this holy man.

Sītā. As my lord commands.

Rāvaṇa. [*Apprehensive lest his disguise be revealed.*] Let be, let be.

She alone is an Arundhatī[2] among the women of the world, for they name thee with respect as her spouse. (8)

Rāma. Then bring the water here, I will wait on him myself.

Rāvaṇa. So, I may avoid the shadow and not escape the thing itself. Speech suffices to entertain a guest. I am honoured. Pray be seated.

Rāma. Very well. [*Sits down.*]

Rāvaṇa. [*Aside.*] Now I must behave like a brahman.

[*Aloud.*] I belong to the Kāśyapa clan. I have studied the Veda with all its branches, the code of Manu, the Yogaśāstra of Maheśvara, Bṛihaspati's Science of Politics, the Logic of Medhātithi and Pracetas' scripture on memorial rites.

Rāma. What do you say? 'Scripture on memorial rites'?

Rāvaṇa. Without a word of the other scriptures you show an interest in that of the memorial rites. Why so?

[1] And therefore liable to be stolen by evil spirits.

[2] Arundhatī wife of Vasishṭha and small star in the Great Bear.

Rāma. Reverend sir, now that I have lost my father that is the text for me.

Rāvaṇa. Do not hesitate. Ask me what you will.

Rāma. With what can I satisfy the shades at the time of oblations?

Rāvaṇa. Everything given gladly expresses homage.[1]

Rāma. Ay, sir, and what is given without respect is rejected. But I am asking you for particulars.

Rāvaṇa. Hearken. For humans are prescribed, *darbha* grass among the plants, sesamum among the medicines, of vegetables pulse, of fish the carp, of birds the crane, of beasts the cow, the rhinoceros, or . . .

Rāma. 'Or' you say, sir, so there is an alternative.

Rāvaṇa. There is, but it can only be obtained by might.

Rāma. Reverend sir, that is my intention.

Both are at hand that shall accomplish it, the bow when penance flags and penance when the bow is slack. (9)

Rāvaṇa. They exist. They live in the Himālayas.

Rāma. In the Himālayas? Proceed—

Rāvaṇa. They are deer called golden-sides. They live on the seventh summit of Himālaya. They are swift as the wind and their backs as dark as beryl.[2] They drink the water of the Ganges where it falls on the head of Śiva before them. With these it was the great seers like Vaikhānasa, Vālakhilya, and Naimiṣīya performed their memorial rites, killing them and bringing them in by the power of thought.

Appeased by these, the shades obtain full profit of their sons. Leaving old-age behind they mount resplendent up to heaven. Like gods they come to dwell in aerial cars and are drawn no longer by transient objects. (10)

Rāma. Lady of Mithilā,

Bid farewell to thy adopted children, the deer, the trees, the Vindhya forest, and thy friends thy beloved creepers. I am to dwell in the Himālayan groves coloured by the brilliant growth of healing herbs. (11)

Sītā. As my lord commands.

Rāvaṇa. Son of Kausalyā, do not expect too much. They are not visible to mortal eyes.

Rāma. Do they dwell, sir, in the Himālaya?

Rāvaṇa. Why, yes.

Rāma. Then look you, sir,

Either the Himālaya will show me the golden deer or split by

[1] What is given with *Śraddhā* (faith, desire) is *Śrāddham*.

[2] Cats-eye.

the force of my shaft, 'twill share the fate of the Krauñca mountain.[1] (12)

Rāvaṇa. [*Aside.*] Oh, his pride is intolerable. [*Aloud.*] Aha! Here comes something like a flash of lightning, O Son of Kausalyā; the Himālaya honours you even here. This is the Deer with Golden Sides.

Rāma. This good fortune is due to you, holy man.

Sītā. Happily my lord is fortunate.

Rāma. Nay,

This is my father's luck, it comes of its own accord. He is worthy of the offering. Speak to Lakshmaṇa, Maithilī. (13)

Sītā. My lord, you sent him to meet the chief of the hermitage returning from a pilgrimage.

Rāma. Then I will go myself.

Sītā. What shall I do, my lord?

Rāma. Attend upon this reverend gentleman.

Sītā. As my lord commands. [*Exit Rāma.*]

Rāvaṇa. Ah, there is Rāma running to obtain a proper offering. And now intent upon his worship, he sees the running deer and draws his bow.

How strong he is, how brave! How great his spirit and his speed! Well may the world be pervaded by that one little word of 'Rāma'. (14)

The deer in a single bound has passed beyond the range of his arrows and entered a thicket in the forest.

Sītā. [*Aside.*] I am parted from my lord and now I am afraid.

Rāvaṇa. [*Aside.*]

Rāma removed by guile, I shall carry off from the hermitage the weeping damsel Sītā left lonely like an offering devoid of sacred stanzas. (15)

Sītā. I will just go into the hut. [*Begins to go.*]

Rāvaṇa. [*Taking his own form.*] Sītā, stay.

Sītā. [*Fearfully.*] Oh! Who is this?

Rāvaṇa. Dost thou not know me?

I conquered in the battle Indra and the other gods with hosts of demons. When I saw my sister's[2] mutilation and heard of both my brothers slain I beguiled Rāma with my ruses; he is matchless in his strength, but his wits are dulled by pride; and I have come to carry thee off, large-eyed lady—and I am Rāvaṇa. (16)

Sīta. Oh! Rāvaṇa! [*Moves away.*]

[1] Split by the God of War.

[2] Śūrpaṇakhā 'With nails like winnowing fans', Rāvaṇa's sister who was mutilated by Lakshmaṇa.

Rāvaṇa. Ah, once in Rāvaṇa's view, whither will you go?

Sītā. My lord! Save, save me. Lakshmaṇa, help! help!

Rāvaṇa. Sītā, listen to my heroic deeds.

Indra did I smash and made Kubera tremble. Soma dragged I in the dust and thrashed the child of the Sun. Ho! a fig for them. They're frightened gods that live in heaven. Blessed is the earth where Sītā dwells. (17)

Sītā. My lord, protect me! Lakshmaṇa, save me, save me!

Rāvaṇa. Run to Rāma for protection or to Lakshmaṇa, or, if thou wilt, to Daśaratha the king in heaven. What boot these coward's words? Can fawns assail a tiger? (18)

Sītā. Save me, my lord! Help! Lakshmaṇa, help!

Rāvaṇa. Why this lament, large-eyed lady? Count me as thy lord. This Rāma with all his mighty strength and a host of gods to help him is no match for me. (19)

Sītā. [*Angrily.*] Thou art accursed.

Rāvaṇa. Ha, ha, ha! See the fire in the virtuous wife.

When I sped rapidly aloft the sun's rays could not burn me. Now her few words, 'Thou art accursed', make me burn. (20)

Sītā. Save me, my lord, save me!

Rāvaṇa. [*Seizing Sītā.*] Ho there! ye hermits that dwell in Janasthāna, hearken to my words.

Ten-necks is making off perforce with Sītā. If Rāma cares ought for a warrior's role let him show his powers. (21)

Sītā. Save me, my lord, save me!

Rāvaṇa. [*Stepping and looking around.*] Oho! here is the Vulture King[1] rushing at me, with his savage beak, uprooting the forest thickets with the hurricane raised by his wings. Ha! stop now!

Drawing my blade I slice off both thy wings. From the wounds spouts out the gore to drench thy body. So send I thee to the abode of Death.

[*Exeunt ambo.*]

END OF THE FIFTH ACT.

[1] Jaṭāyu.

ACT VI

[*In the Forest.*]

INTERLUDE

[*Enter two old ascetics.*]

Both. Help! help!

First Old Man. Here is Sītā being overpowered and haled away by one who is dark in hue as a garland of blue lotus, who laughs with teeth gleaming white like lotus stalks. She is like a gazelle taken by the lord of nocturnal roamers wandering at dead of night. (1)

Second Old Man. Here is the Princess of Videha,

Struggling like a serpent maiden, shaken like a flowering creeper she is borne away perforce by the wicked Rāvaṇa, away as it were perfection from the penance grove. (2)

Both. Help! help!

First Old Man. [*Looking upwards.*] Ah! at the very moment of my cry the Vulture King has soared into the air to pay his debt to Daśaratha and challenge Rāvaṇa, 'Whither away while I remain'?

Second Old Man. Here is Rāvaṇa returning, his eyes bulging with rage

First Old Man. That is Rāvaṇa.

Second Old Man. That's Jaṭāyu.

Both. Oh, the duel in the sky begins.

First Old Man. Kāśyapa, Kāśyapa, see how powerful is this lord of carrion eaters.

With his wings he flies around manœuvring for the valorous duel, with his mandibles well worn and sharp[1] he strikes unmoving to enclose his foe. With talons sharp as iron hooks he tears the horrid entrails from his breast, as a rock is torn from a crag roughly split by the facets of a thunderbolt. (3)

Second Old Man. Alas! the enraged Rāvaṇa has wounded the carrion king on the right pinion.

Both. Alack! The noble vulture falls.

First Old Man. Woe, woe, this noble Jaṭāyu,

After an effort supreme worthy of his valour, recking no more of his foe than of a pet peacock and shaking the bright glory of the Goblin King, he has come to grief like a forest tree crushed by a lordly tusker. (4)

[1] Epithet transferred to *saṃveṣṭanam*.

Both. May he go to heaven!

First Old Man. Come, Kāśyapa, let us report this news to the Rāghava Prince.

Second Man. Yes, that were best.

[*Exeunt ambo.*]

END OF THE INTERLUDE.

[*In Ayodhyā.*]

[*Enter the Chamberlain.*]

Chamberlain. Who 's here? Who guards the Golden Gate?

[*Enter Portress.*]

Portress. I, sir, Vijayā. What 's to do?

Chamberlain. Take word at once, Vijayā, to Prince Bharata, that the venerable Sumantra, who was sent to Janasthāna to see Rāma, has returned.

Portress. Was he successful, sir?

Chamberlain. Madam, I do not know.

My mind misgave me straight when I saw him returned with a face all wilted by the fire of grief within his breast. **(5)**

Portress. I am disturbed to hear it, sir.

Chamberlain. What are you standing here for, madam. Tell him quickly.

Portress. I am off to tell him, sir. [*Exit.*]

Chamberlain. [*Looking round.*] Ah, there is his Highness the Prince Bharata. He is coming this way, clad in bark dress, with his forehead tawny with a varied mass of matted locks, moved no doubt with curiosity at Sumantra's return. He is

The sum of famous qualities, death to his opponents, ornament of the Solar race, peer of the chief of gods. Glorious protector by command of all the earth, he stalks along like a magnificent young elephant. **(6)**

[*Enter Bharata and the Portress.*]

Bharata. So, Vijayā, the venerable Sumantra has returned.

A former time I went myself to see my elder brother and I returned with a favour and a promise, and now has the venerable Sumantra come after seeing Rāma, delight of the people's eyes, their hearts and minds. **(7)**

Chamberlain. [*Approaching.*] Greeting, prince!

Bharata. Where is the venerable Sumantra?

Chamberlain. At the Golden Gate.

Bharata. Then bring him in at once.

Chamberlain. As the prince commands. [*Exit.*]

[*Enter Sumantra and the Portress.*]

Sumantra. [*Sorrowfully.*] Alas! Alas!

I have seen the king's demise and the ruin of his son, and now I hear of the disappearance of the princess. Calamities fall on my old age as in a string. (8)

Portress. [*To Sumantra.*] Come this way, sir. There is the prince. Go up to him.

Sumantra. [*Approaching.*] Greeting, prince!

Bharata. Well, old gentleman, have you seen that revelation to the world of filial affection? Have you seen the double of Arundhatī's good character? Have you seen that model brother a voluntary exile in the forest?

[*Sumantra remains deep in thought.*]

Portress. The prince is speaking to you.

Sumantra. What, to me, madam?

Bharata. [*Aside.*] His fatigue is great indeed. His mind is wandering in his distress. [*Aloud.*] Have you returned without completing the journey?

Sumantra. Oh, prince, I set out for Janasthāna at your bidding to see Rāma. How could I return while on the way?

Bharata. Are they hiding then from anger or from shame?

Sumantra. Oh, prince!

Whence anger in the well-controlled? Or shame for those whose hearts are pure? Yet I saw the hermitage empty, bereft of them. (9)

Bharata. Did you learn where they had gone?

Sumantra. There is a colony of forest-dwellers[1] at a place called Kishkindha. That's where I heard they had gone.

Bharata. Alas, apes know nothing of human distinctions. They must be living in great difficulty.

Sumantra. Prince, animals also recognize their obligations.

Bharata. How so, old gentleman?

Sumantra. When Sugrīva was thrust from his kingdom by his elder brother Vāli, and dwelt on a mountain robbed of his wife, Rāma relieved him of trouble like his own. (10)

Bharata. Trouble like his own? What do you mean by that, old man?

Sumantra. [*Aside.*] I have given it all away. [*Aloud.*] Oh, nothing, prince. I meant they both had lost their sovereignty.

[1] Meaning 'monkeys'.

Bharata. What are you hiding? By the feet of his late Majesty be you accursed if you do not speak the truth.

Sumantra. No way out. Listen then,

In guarding the saints there was a feud with a powerful demon.
Then resorting to a ruse Rāvaṇa abducted Sītā. (11)

Bharata. Abducted Sītā? [*Goes off in a swoon.*]

Sumantra. Oh, prince, take heart.

Bharata. [*Coming to himself.*] Alas! alas!

Bereft of sire and kin, enduring great affliction in the forest,
my noble brother is now parted from his spouse as in the sky
a clouded moon is robbed of its light. (12)

Oh! What shall I do now? I have it. Follow me, old gentleman.

Sumantra. As the prince commands.

[*Both step round.*]

Sumantra. Nay, prince, not this way. Here are the chambers of the queens.

Bharata. My business is even here. Ho there! Who keeps the door?

[*Enter Portress.*]

Portress. Hail, prince! I am Vijayā.

Bharata. Inform her Majesty that I am here.

Portress. Which queen shall I tell?

Bharata. She that wished me king.

Portress. [*Aside.*] Hullo! What? Can it be? [*Aloud.*] Very well, master. [*Exit.*]

[*Re-enters with Kaikeyī.*]

Kaikeyī. Has Bharata come to see me, Vijayā?

Portress. Yes, mistress. Old Sumantra has come back from Prince Rāma. Prince Bharata wants to see you with him.

Kaikeyī. [*Aside.*] With what wounding words will Bharata reproach me?

Portress. Mistress, shall the prince come in?

Kaikeyī. Go, bring him in.

Portress. Very well, mistress. [*Stepping round to Bharata.*] Greeting, prince! Pray enter.

Bharata. Have you announced us, Vijayā?

Portress. Yes.

Bharata. Then let us go in.

[*They enter.*]

Kaikeyī. My child, Vijayā tells me Sumantra has come back from Rāma.

Bharata. And I have other pleasant news to tell your Majesty.

Kaikeyī. Then, child, we should send for Kausalyā and Sumitrā.

Bharata. No, it is not for them to hear.

Kaikeyī. [*Aside.*] What can it be? [*Aloud.*] Speak out, my son.

Bharata. Hearken.

There was one that yielded up the sovereignty and went at thy behest into the forest. His wife Sītā has been stolen. Are thy wishes now fulfilled? **(13)**

Kaikeyī. Eh?

Bharata. Alack, since thou camest as a bride to this house of brave high-minded warriors, it comes to pass that their women are molested. **(14)**

Kaikeyī. [*Aside.*] So be it, the time has come to tell him. [*Aloud.*] My son, you do not know of the curse upon the king.

Bharata. What? A curse upon the king?

Kaikeyī. Tell him the whole story, Sumantra.

Sumantra. As you wish. Listen, prince. Some time ago the king went out a-hunting. Now there was a blind sage who had a son that served the holy man like a pair of eyes. And the boy was filling his pitcher at a pond. And the king misled by the sound as of an elephant's trunk thought it was an elephant, and aiming an arrow at the sound he slew him.

Bharata. Slew him? Forgiveness on the sin! And then?

Sumantra. Then finding him in that plight,

That sooth-speaking sage when he made an end of weeping declared, 'Like me, sir, shalt thou perish through grief for thy son'. **(15)**

Bharata. Ah! This was terrible.

Kaikeyī. That was the cause, my son, that threw me into wrong, so that dear Rāma was exiled to the forest. 'Twas not through lust of power. The sage's curse was inexorable and could only be fulfilled by the exile of a son.

Bharata. But if the exile of one son was like another's, why was not I sent to the forest?

Kaikeyī. My child, you were staying at your uncle's house, you were in exile already.

Bharata. But, fourteen years? What did you mean by that?

Kaikeyī. Oh, my child, it was fourteen *days* I meant to say, but in the confusion of my mind the fourteen years slipped out.

Bharata. True wisdom lies in complete consideration. Is this known to the preceptors?

Sumantra. Yes, prince, known and approved by Vasishṭha, Vāmadeva, and the others.

Bharata. Ah, they indeed are witnesses of three worlds. I am happy that your Majesty has done no wrong. Mother, I spoke hard words to you in anger from affection for my brother, please forgive all that. Mother, I salute you.

Kaikeyī. Ah, child, what mother but forgives a son's offence ? Nay, rise. How are you to blame ?

Bharata. I thank you. Now must I take leave of your Majesty. This very day must I mobilize all the forces of the kingdom to help my noble brother. Now will I

> Darken the coast with raging elephants and cover it with camps of my army's multitudes. With my battalions crossing over will I impose an equal lassitude on the ocean and on Rāvaṇa. **(16)**

Aha, some noise, it seems. Find out quickly what it is.

[*Enter Portress.*]

Portress. Greeting, prince ! On hearing this news the first queen has fainted away.

Kaikeyī. Ah !

Bharata. What, has my mother fainted ?

Kaikeyī. Come, my son, let us comfort the noble lady.

Bharata. As my mother bids.

[*Exeunt omnes.*]

END OF THE SIXTH ACT.

ACT VII

INTERLUDE

[*The Scene is at Janasthāna.*]

[*Enter an Ascetic.*]

Ascetic. Nandilaka ! Nandilaka !

[*Enter Nandilaka.*]

Nandilaka. Here I am, sir.

Ascetic. The chief of the hermitage sends word that his Highness Rāma has arrived, beautiful as the moon shining in the clear autumnal sky. He has slain Rāvaṇa, that put the three worlds to flight and stole away his wife and put on the throne Vibhīshaṇa, adorned with crowds of virtues, the very opposite of crowds of demons. He is bringing the Lady Sītā with him, pure and chaste as the gods, as seers divine and perfected saints ; and around him are the chiefs of the bears, the demons, and the monkeys. So everything that can be thought of must be got ready in our hermitage to-day to the best of our resources.

Nandilaka. Everything is ready, sir, but—

Ascetic. But what?

Nandilaka. There are these demons of Vibhīshaṇa's. About their food—the chief himself knows best.

Ascetic. Why so?

Nandilaka. But they eat . . .

Ascetic. Don't get flurried. Vibhīshaṇa will look after the demons.

Nandilaka. All honour to that excellent demon. [*Exit.*]

Ascetic. [*Looking round.*] Ah here is his Highness Rāma.

The lord of men steps down to the ground from his aerial car.
Numerous kindly sages laud him crying 'Victory, best of men!
Vanquished be any second foe! May all the earth be subject
to thy single rule.' (1)

Greeting, Highness, greeting. [*Exit.*]

END OF THE INTERLUDE.

[*Enter Rāma.*]

Rāma. Rāvaṇa have I slain for all his host and valour, regaining
Sītā ever pure, endowed with all the virtues in the world, and
now fulfilling to the very end my parent's word I have come
once more to the hermitage of the saints. (2)

The Lady of Mithilā went within to greet the ladies of the hermitage and tarries there. [*Catching sight of her.*] Ah, there she is.

King Janaka's daughter moves slowly on while the sage's
wives converse with her and call her 'Sītā', 'Dear', or 'Jānakī'
according to their age, or still more loving 'daughter'. (3)

[*Enter Sītā and a female ascetic.*]

Female Ascetic. Why, here is your husband. Go up to him. I cannot bear to see you alone.

Sītā. Ah! Even to-day it seems too good to be true. [*Going up to Rāma.*] Greeting, my lord!

Rāma. Maithilī, do you remember we used to dwell in Janasthāna? Do you recognize these trees, your fosterlings?

Sītā. Yes, yes, I see. But then every leaf was visible and now one must look up at them.

Rāma. Quite so. Time produces ups and downs. Do you recollect, Maithilī, that under this tree[1] a herd of deer was startled on seeing Bharata dressed in white?

Sītā. Yes, my lord, I remember very well.

Rāma. And here is the great tortoise that witnessed our austerities.

[1] *Sapta-parṇa* = Alstonia scholaris.

We were sitting here, thinking of the oblations to be made for my beloved father, when we saw the golden deer.

Sītā. Oh, my lord, don't speak of it, pray don't. [*Trembles with fear.*]

Rāma. Calm your fears. That time is past. [*Looking at the sky.*] Ah, what is this?

Dust is rising yellow as *lodhra* flowers and, carried along by the breeze, completely veils the sky. The blare of conches reverberating with the deafening din of kettledrums makes this forest as noisy as a city. (4)

[*Enter Lakshmaṇa.*]

Lakshmaṇa My noble brother, greeting!

Here with the queens and a large army comes Bharata, so devoted to his brothers and eager for the sight of you. (5)

Rāma. Dear Lakshmaṇa, has Bharata arrived?

Lakshmaṇa. Yes, my brother.

Rāma. Lady of Mithilā, open wide your eyes to gaze on Bharata in the vanguard of the queens.

Sītā. Bharata, my lord, has come at a happy time.

[*Enter Bharata accompanied by the queens.*]

Bharata. I have come to-day with a contented mind and followed by my people, intent to see my elder brother with his noble spouse, released from calamities dire and prolonged, like the clear autumnal moon released from clouds. (6)

Rāma. Mothers, I salute you.

Queens. My child, long life to you. We are fortunate indeed to see you in good health with your wife at the fulfilment of your vow.

Rāma. I thank you.

Lakshmaṇa. Mothers, I salute you.

Queens. My child, long life to you.

Lakshmaṇa. I thank you.

Sītā. Ladies, respectfully I greet you.

Queens. Long may you be happy, child.

Sītā. Thank you.

Bharata. Noble brother, I salute you. I am Bharata.

Rāma. Come hither, dear prince of the Ikshvāku clan. Long life and health be thine!

Spread out thy breast as wide as the panel of a door and embrace me in thy two stalwart arms. Lift up this face lovely as the autumn moon, bring delight to this my body burnt by calamity. (7)

Bharata. I thank you. Lady, Bharata salutes you.

Sītā. Long may you be the companion of my lord.

Bharata. I thank you. Brother, I salute you.

Lakshmaṇa. Come to me, dear boy, long life be yours. Embrace me tightly. [*Embraces him.*]

Bharata. Thanks. Noble brother, now accept the burden of the State.

Rāma. But why, dear boy?

Kaikeyī. My son, I have long cherished this desire.

[*Enter Śatrughna.*]

Śatrughna. My mind is hurrying to see my elder brother, Rāvaṇa's destroyer, troubled by various misfortunes, while the lustre of his virtues remained untroubled. (8)

[*Approaching.*] Noble brother, I, Śatrughna, salute you!

Rāma. Come, dear boy. Long life and health be thine.

Śatrughna. I thank you. Lady, I salute you.

Sītā. Long life, my dear.

Śatrughna. Thank you. Brother, I salute you.

Lakshmaṇa. Long life and health be thine.

Śatrughna. Thanks. Noble brother, Vasishṭha and Vāmadeva here have come with the people and all preparation for the inauguration. They desire to see you.

Holy water from many a river and stream have the sages brought themselves by thy favour. Hosts of sages wish to see thy face anointed this first time like a lotus with drops of dew. (9)

Kaikeyī. Go, my son, receive the consecration.

Rāma. As my mother bids. [*Exit.*]

[*Voices behind the scene.*]

Victory! Victory to our lord! Victory to our king! Victory to his Majesty! Hail to thee of blessed mien! Hail, noble sir! Hail, destroyer of Rāvaṇa!

Kaikeyī. The priests and chamberlains are raising the cries of victory for my son and honour him with blessings.

Sumitrā. The people, the attendants and his kinsfolk celebrate the triumph of my son.

[*Voice behind the scene.*]

Ho, ye ascetics dwelling in Janasthāna, hearken, hearken, I say!

As the sun smiteth the darkness with his mighty rays, so hath Rāma smitten the murky mass of enemies unparalleled and having rescued Sītā free from every harm, Rāma the delight of all mankind is Victor of the Earth. (10)

Kaikeyī. Ah, good! There rises the paean of my son's victory.

[*Enter Rāma newly consecrated and his retinue.*]

Rāma. [*Looking up into the air.*] Dear Father.

Even in the other world be thou now content and relinquish all thy wretchedness. The thing thou didst desire for me has come to pass. Here am I king of the earth, bearer of a noble burden, and I have assumed the protection of the people in accordance with the Law. (11)

Bharata. I can never tire of gazing at my noble elder brother now entitled king, with the umbrella of state borne above him, with a coruscating diadem. Sprinkled with the holy water, he has attained the royal grace and is adored by myriads of people like the crescent moon. (12)

Śatrughna. By this consecration of my elder brother my house has lost its stain. The world shines bright again, as at the rising of the moon. (13)

Rāma. Dear Lakshmaṇa, I am invested with the sovereignty.

Lakshmaṇa. My felicitations! [*Enter Chamberlain.*]

Chamberlain. Victory to his Majesty! King Vibhīshaṇa sends a message of congratulations, so do Sugrīva, Nīla, Mainda, Jāmbavat, Hanumat and others in their train; 'By good fortune you have won.'

Rāma. Say, rather, by the favour of my comrades.

Chamberlain. As the king commands.

Kaikeyī. Blessed indeed am I! I wish I could see this happiness in Ayodhyā.

Rāma. Your ladyship shall see it soon. [*Looking round.*] Why, all this wood looks as radiant as the sun. [*Reflecting.*] Ah, I have it! This is Pushpaka, the aerial car of Rāvaṇa, arrived in the sky. This time was fixed and it comes at the mere thought of it. Let every one get into the car. [*They all do so.*]

Rāma. To-day shall I go to Ayodhyā city accompanied by friends and kin.

Lakshmaṇa. To-day shall the citizens see thee ascendant like the moon with the stars. (14)

EPILOGUE

As Rāma was united with Janaka's daughter and his kin, so may our king rule the earth in conjunction with the goddess of beauty and prosperity. (15)

Exeunt omnes.

FINIS.

VOLUME TWO

THE EMBASSY

(*Dūtavākyam*)

INTRODUCTION

AFTER the wedding mentioned at the end of *The Five Nights* messages were sent between the Pāṇḍavas and the Kurus. No satisfaction being obtained from the Kurus, Kṛishṇa offers to go himself to make peace, if this be possible. (Mahābhārata LXII, *Bhagavadyāna-parvan* 73.)

After a discussion as to the tone he should adopt, he sets out. The old king Dhṛitarāshṭra advises an honourable reception of Kṛishṇa.

Duryodhana thinks it better to send him no presents. Bhīshma says Kṛishṇa's advice should be followed. Duryodhana says he cannot divide the kingdom with his enemies and wishes to have Kṛishṇa taken prisoner. This intention is disapproved by all. Bhīshma leaves the chamber in disgust. Kṛishṇa is received at Hastināpura by Dhṛitarāshṭra, Bhīshma, &c., and stays with Vidura. Then he enters the palace and is received by Duryodhana and the princes. Duryodhana asks him why he did not partake of viands sent to him. Kṛishṇa replies. It is because Duryodhana is at enmity with his boyhood's friends the Pāṇḍavas. Returns to Vidura's house, where he takes a meal. In the night Vidura tells Kṛishṇa the Kurus are set on war and that his words will be in vain. Kṛishṇa explains that nevertheless he must try. The next day he goes to Dhṛitarāshṭra's council, where he is greeted on all sides. He states that the Pāṇḍavas are ready to obey Dhṛitarāshṭra if they are accorded their rights. Some long stories are narrated by way of precedent or warning. Then (124) the old king says he cannot talk round Duryodhana, and Kṛishṇa had better try himself. Kṛishṇa speaks forcibly to Duryodhana and advises him to divide the realm with the Pāṇḍavas. Bhīshma, Droṇa, Vidura, and the old king try to induce the young prince to follow Kṛishṇa's advice. Duryodhana is determined to fight things out as beseems a warrior. Kṛishṇa answers with reproaches. Duryodhana and his brothers leave the assembly. Kṛishṇa advises that Duryodhana should be imprisoned and so peace could be maintained. Duryodhana is brought back by Vidura and lectured by Queen Gāndhārī, but he leaves the hall again and determines with Śakuni, Karṇa, and Duḥśāsana to capture Kṛishṇa.

Word comes of this, and the rebellious princes are summoned to the assembly and reproached by Dhṛitarāshṭra and Vidura. Kṛishṇa shows himself in his true form (131) and leaves the assembly. Dhṛitarāshṭra begs his pardon. After an interview with Kuntī, mother of the three elder Pāṇḍavas, Kṛishṇa takes leave of Bhīshma and the others, puts Karṇa on his car, and drives back to Upaplavya.

The Embassy compresses the story of Kṛishṇa's visit into a single Act. The wickedness of Duryodhana is emphasized and so is the divine power of Kṛishṇa. The old king appears only at the end to entreat Kṛishṇa's forgiveness. Before that, Duryodhana appears as the actual ruler, and he is represented as threatening to fine the princes if they rise to honour Kṛishṇa. The introduction of the painted scroll as part of the plan to insult the envoy is an invention of the dramatist. In the epic Kṛishṇa reveals his true form. In the play he is definitely identified with Vāsudeva, Nārāyaṇa, and Vishṇu. Moreover, Vishṇu's weapons are introduced, and the discus speaks at length about the others. There is nothing of this in the epic.

It should be noted with regard to these weapons that verses 51 and 52 appear to be alternative to 47, 48, 49. The discus has already dismissed the three weapons individually, and there is no point in their reappearing together.

One may go a step further and hazard the conjecture that all of this passage describing Vishṇu's weapons is by a later hand.

With verse 41 Duryodhana rushes from the assembly uttering threats. Then Vāsudeva converses with his discus, which itself talks to and about the other weapons. When the discus has gone, Vāsudeva says he must go, and the blind old king comes to stop him. The drama would lose nothing if after Duryodhana's exit (verse 41) Vāsudeva said 'I too must leave—for the Pāṇḍavas' camp', and the old king's voice was heard behind the scenes. 'No, no; he must not go.'

An interesting feature of this play is the way in which all the Kuru assembly is played by one actor—at least one man does all the talking; the rest could be imagined or indicated by a few supers.

DRAMATIS PERSONAE

(In order of appearance.)

Stage-manager, in Prologue.
Chamberlain = Bādarāyaṇa.
DURYODHANA = eldest son of Dhṛitarāshṭra, leader of the Kurus.
VĀSUDEVA = Kṛishṇa, Nārāyaṇa, Vishṇu.
Sudarśana = Vishṇu's discus, one of his four weapons.
Dhṛitarāshṭra = the blind old king, father of Duryodhana and his 99 brothers.

PROLOGUE

[*At the end of the Opening*[1] *enter the Stage-Manager.*]

Stage-Manager. May Vishṇu's[2] foot protect you—the foot that brings joy to all the worlds; that with slender dark-red nails sent Namuci[3] whirling through the sky. (1)

With these words, my lords and gentlemen, I have to announce to you—But what is that? I thought I heard a noise, just as I was to make my announcement. Well, I must see what it is.

[*Voice behind the scene.*]

Ho there, guardians of the gate! King Duryodhana commands.

Stage-Manager. Good. I understand.

As hostilities have arisen between the sons of Dhṛitarāshṭra and the Pāṇḍavas, a servitor prepares the council-chamber at Duryodhana's command. (2)

[*Exit.*]

ACT I

[*Palace at Hastināpura.*]

[*Enter a Chamberlain.*]

Chamberlain. Ho there, guardians of the gate. King Duryodhana commands. 'To-day will we take counsel with all the sovereigns. So let all the kings be summoned.' (*Stepping and looking around.*) Oh, here is King Duryodhana coming this very way.

A dusky youth in a white silk robe,[4] with anointed limbs beneath the royal parasol and chowrie. Splendid with limbs lit up by glistening jewellery, a full moon among the constellations. (3)

[1] Nāndī, see note vol. i, p. ix.

[2] Upendra. 'Younger brother of Indra', i.e. Vishṇu or Kṛishṇa.

[3] The demon Namuci is generally supposed to have been destroyed by Indra, or Indra and the Aśvins with the foam of sea.

[4] Sarup takes *dukūla* to mean 'silk'—following Apte's Sanskrit Dictionary. Kālidāsa has *cīnāṃśuka* ('Chinese cloth') for 'silk', but he also speaks of *dukūla*, which does not seem to be identical with *kṣauma* (linen made from flax). There are other kinds of silk in India besides that of the mulberry-eating silkworm introduced from China.

[*Enter Duryodhana as described.*]

Duryodhana. My heart it seems has dispelled its wrath in the joyful thought that this festival of battle has at last arrived.
I long to mar the faces of the champion tuskers in the Pāṇḍava force by hacking out their ivory pestles. (4)

Chamberlain. Victory to the king! The whole body of kings has been assembled at your Majesty's command.

Duryodhana. Well done. You may retire within.

Chamberlain. As your Majesty commands. [*Exit.*]

Duryodhana. My lords Vaikarṇa and Varshadeva,[1] I have a vast army of eleven divisions. Tell me, who is fit to be the Commander-in-Chief? What do you say?—'an important matter'—'opinion after due deliberation.' Quite so. Come, then, let us go into the council-chamber. Preceptor, my salutations; please enter the council-chamber. Grandfather, my respects; please go in. My lords Vaikarṇa and Varshadeva enter. And all ye warriors pray enter freely. Karṇa, my comrade, let us go in.

[*Entering the Council-Chamber.*]

Preceptor, this is the tortoise seat; please sit down. Grandfather, here is the lion seat; do you sit there. Uncle, there is the leather seat for you. Vaikarṇa and Varshadeva, pray sit down. And all you gentlemen take your seats as you will. What's that—the king is still standing? Aha! how loyal are you all. Well, well, I take my seat. Do you sit down also, Karṇa, my friend. (*Sits down.*) Tell me, my lords Vaikarṇa and Varshadeva, who is fit to be Commander-in-Chief of my vast army of eleven divisions?
What do you say?—'His Highness of Gāndhāra should speak first.' Very well, let my uncle have his say. What's that, uncle? 'Who else should be Commander while Ganges' son is there?'[2] Well said, uncle. So let it be. It shall be, grandfather. That is also our desire.
May the hearts of their chieftains sink as the consecrating water falls on Bhīshma's head, to the roar of the host, the rolling of the drums and the conch-shells' blare, loud as the thundering of the sea lashed to fury by a gale. (5)

[*Enter Chamberlain.*]

Chamberlain. Victory to the king! Here is Nārāyaṇa, the best of men, arrived as an ambassador from the Pāṇḍavas' camp.

Duryodhana. Nay, not so, Master Bādarāyaṇa. What? Is Kaṃsa's

[1] There is no stage-direction for the entry of all these people. They do not speak themselves and are evidently to be imagined.

[2] Bhīshma, the son of Gaṅgā.

serving-man Dāmodara[1] your best of men? Is that cowherd thy best of men? Deprived of lands, reputation, and wealth by Bṛihadratha's son, is he thy best of men? What conduct is this for an attendant on the sovereign's person. What insolent words. Ha! to hell with you.

Chamberlain. Forgive me, Majesty, forgive me. In my confusion I forgot the proper etiquette. (*Falls at his feet.*)

Duryodhana. Confusion? Ah! men are liable to confusion. Rise.

Chamberlain. I thank you.

Duryodhana. Now I am satisfied. Who is this envoy that has come?

Chamberlain. An envoy has come, one Keśava.

Duryodhana. 'Keśava'; yes, that's the way to announce him. That's the proper etiquette. Tell me, Princes, what is the proper thing to do with Keśava, who has come as an envoy? What do you say?—'he should be received with honour'? That is not my opinion. Prison, I think, is the best place for him.

> If Kṛishṇa is made captive, the Pāṇḍavas will have lost their eyes. The Pāṇḍavas destitute of resource and counsel, the whole earth will be mine without a rival. (6)

What's more, if anyone rises to meet Keśava, I will fine him twelve gold pieces. So don't you be forgetting it. [*Aside.*] Now, how can I avoid getting up myself? Yes, I see a way. [*Aloud.*] Bādarāyaṇa, fetch me that scroll with the painting of Draupadī dragged by the hair and by her clothes. [*Aside.*] I can fix my eyes on that and need not rise for Keśava.

Chamberlain. As your Majesty commands. [*Exit and re-enters.*] Victory to the king! Here is the scroll.

Duryodhana. Spread it out before me.

Chamberlain. As your Majesty commands. [*Spreads it out.*]

Duryodhana. Oh! what a splendid picture. Here is Duḥśāsana. He has seized Draupadī by the locks of her hair. This is Draupadī—

> Rudely beset by Duḥśāsana, eyes staring wide in fright, she looks like the digit of the moon in the jaws of the demon of eclipse. (7)

Here is the evil-minded Bhīma. Seeing Draupadī insulted in the presence of all the princes, wrath swells within him, and he measures the pillars of the chamber. Here is Yudhishṭhira—

> Truthful, righteous, and compassionate, though his wits be lost in gaming, he tranquillizes Bhīma with sidelong glances. (8)

And here is Arjuna—

[1] *Dāmodara* means 'having a rope round one's waist', i.e. like a thief.

Lips quivering, eyes blurred with rage, he recks but a straw for that ring of foes, and, as if he would annihilate all those kings, softly draws Gāṇḍīva's string. (9)

Here is Yudhishṭhira restraining Arjuna.

[Here are Nakula and Sahadeva—

Girded up, with sword and buckler in their hands, their faces flushed and stern, biting hard their lower lips, they are free from fear of death. Fiercely they attack my brother like two fawns setting on a lion. (10)

Here is Yudhishṭhira approaching the princes and restraining them.][1]

'Tis I that have fallen low, with a mind perverse may be. How then? Do ye now lay aside your wrath, knowing right and wrong. Men too proud to bear defeat at the decision of the dice may find their prowess questioned by the brave. (11)

Here is the king of Gāndhāra—

The master gambler breaks into insolent laughter as he casts the dice, nipping his opponent's happiness in the bud with his own renown. Sprawling as he pleases, he leers at the weeping Draupadī, and skilled at the game scrapes the ground. (12)

Here are the preceptor and grandfather. Ashamed to see her in this plight they hide their faces in the end of their robes. How rich the colours are. What wonderful expression! A perfect scene—The picture is excellently painted. We are pleased. Who is there?

Chamberlain. Victory to the king!

Duryodhana. Ah, Bādarāyaṇa, bring in that envoy, so puffed up just because it is a bird he rides.

Chamberlain. As your Majesty commands. [*Exit.*]

Duryodhana. Karṇa, my comrade—

Black-hearted Kṛishṇa has come here to-day as an envoy, like a hireling at the Pāṇḍavas' behest. Prepare thine ears, friend Karṇa, to hear the words of Yudhishṭhira, gentle as a woman's. (13)

[*Enter Vāsudeva and Chamberlain.*]

Vāsudeva. At the bidding of Yudhishṭhira, and from true friendship with Arjuna, I have taken on to-day the thankless role of envoy to Suyodhana,[2] so overbearing in war and catching at what one has not said.

The forest of the Kurus' family tree will be blasted in battle by the fierce gusts of Arjuna's arrows fanning flames of Bhīma's ire; his wrath is fired by the shaming of Draupadī, and ever

[1] Yudhishṭhira referred to twice. Perhaps v. 10 is a later addition.
[2] Euphemistic name of Duryodhana.

he bears the terrible mace to crush the broad foreheads of elephants in the foeman's host. (**14**)

This is Suyodhana's camp. Here indeed!

The king's pavilions are like celestial cities set up at heart's desire; vast armouries are crammed with weapons of every sort and kind; troops of fine horses are neighing in their stalls; elephants are trumpeting; all this opulent power is doomed to dissolution because of the flaunting of kin. (**15**)

Alas! This evil-speaking, virtue-hating rascal Suyodhana, ruthless to his kinsmen, will not do the thing he ought, even on seeing me. (**16**)

Bādarāyaṇa, am I to enter?

Chamberlain. Why, yes. Vishṇu[1] may be pleased to enter.

Vāsudeva. [*Going in.*] Why, what is this? On seeing me all the warriors are disturbed. Do not disturb yourselves; pray sit at ease.

Duryodhana. What's this? All the warriors are disturbed at the sight of Keśava. Stop moving now. Remember the fine that was proclaimed. I am master here.

Vāsudeva. [*Approaching.*] Ah, Suyodhana, how are you?[2]

Duryodhana. [*Falling off his seat. Aside.*] It's clear enough; Keśava has arrived.

Boldly I made up my mind and firmly I stuck to my seat.
But by Keśava's power I have soon fallen off. (**17**)

Ha! this is a tricksy messenger. [*Aloud.*] Here is a seat, Master Envoy. Pray be seated.

Vāsudeva. Preceptor, take your seat. Bhīshma and other princes, sit down at your ease. We too will sit. (*Sitting down.*) Oh, what a splendid picture! No, no! It is a painting of Draupadī being dragged by the hair and clothes. And here forsooth—

Here is Suyodhana. In his childishness he thinks the shaming of his kin a deed of valour. Who in the world is so lost to the sense of decency as to expose his own crime in an assembly? (**18**)

Oh, let that picture be removed.

Duryodhana. Take the picture away, Bādarāyaṇa.

Chamberlain. As your Majesty commands. (*Takes it away.*)

Duryodhana. Say Master Envoy—

Are they all in health, the son of righteousness, wine-begotten Bhīma, my cousin Arjuna, the son of the lord of gods and the

[1] Padma-nābha, 'lotus-naveled'. [2] Could also be 'Are you seated?'.

modest twins, the Aśvin's sons—are they and their people well? (19)

Vāsudeva. This is worthy of Gāndhārī's son. Yes, yes, all are well. And for the prosperity and health within and without of your realm and person the Pāṇḍavas, led by Yudhishṭhira, make enquiry, adding this message:

Great trouble have we endured; the time decreed is now fulfilled. So let the share be given of whatever inheritance is ours by law. (20)

Duryodhana. What inheritance?

My uncle once, hunting in the forest, did an evil deed. So he incurred the sage's curse. Thenceforth desire for his spouses left him. How shall there be patrimony for the sons of others? (21)

Vāsudeva. To you, so versed in family lore, I put this question.

Vicitravīrya the profligate was destroyed by wasting sickness. Then how did thy father Dhṛitarāshṭra, begotten by Vyāsa on Ambikā, succeed to the kingdom? (22)

Nay, do not make this claim.

In this way, by the waxing of mutual enmity, oh king, the Kuru race will soon be but a name. So restraining wrath, your highness should do what the Pāṇḍavas request with all affection. (23)

Duryodhana. Master Envoy, you know nothing of state affairs.

Kingship belongs to brave princes who defeat their foes. It never goes by begging in this world, nor by charity to the poor. Would they win sovereignty, let them join forthwith in battle, or else go as they will to seek peace in a hermitage inhabited by men of tranquil minds. (24)

Vāsudeva. Oh, Suyodhana! Speak not so harshly to your kin.

Though by store of merit one attains royal glory, yet should one cheat a kinsman or a friend all one's efforts are in vain. (25)

Duryodhana. Master Envoy—

Thou hadst no pity for King Kaṃsa, sister's brother of thy sire. Why should we feel pity for these our constant enemies? (26)

Vāsudeva. Do not think that was my fault.

Many a time had he brought sorrow on my mother by the loss of her sons, and imprisoned his own old father, so was he slain by death himself. (27)

Duryodhana. You cheated Kaṃsa in every way.

No self-praises now. That was no brave act. Look you,

when the Lord of Magadha blazed with wrath at the slaughter of his son-in-law—and thou didst flee sick with fear—where was thy bravery then? (28)

Vāsudeva. Suyodhana, the bravery of the politic regards the place, the time, the situation. So much then for our own pleasantry. Come now to my errand.

Show affection to thy cousins; forget their faults. An alliance made with kin is good for both the worlds. (29)

Duryodhana. How can there be kinship twixt mortal man and sons of gods? This is grinding what is ground. Enough, cut short the tale. (30)

Vāsudeva. [*Aside.*] Propitiated for peace he bates nothing of his haughty nature. Well, I must probe him with harsh and bitter words. (31)

[*Aloud.*] Suyodhana. Do you not know the might and prowess of Arjuna?

Duryodhana. Not I.

Vāsudeva. Hearken then—

To the Lord of Beasts in hunter's guise he gave his fill of fighting. When Fire consumed the Khāṇḍava wood a deluge of rain was held off by his arrows. The fiends in mail impenetrable, that harassed the Lord of Gods, he destroyed as if in sport. Single-handed he put Bhīshma and the rest to flight in the city of Virāṭa.[1] (32)

Again I will tell you something you witnessed yourself.

Visiting the herdsmen's stations thou wast carried off screaming to the sky by Citrasena and set free by Arjuna.[2] (33)

In short,

O son of Dhṛitarāshṭra, give half the kingdom at my demand, or else the Pāṇḍavas will seize the earth from sea to sea. (34)

Duryodhana. What's that? The Pāṇḍavas will seize it?

Though the Wind-God himself in Bhīma's form be smiting in the battle and Indra manifest in the shape of Arjuna, not a blade of grass will I give of my realm. My father held it, and with valour will we guard it for all thy words, thou champion in bitter speech. (35)

Vāsudeva. Disgrace of the Kuru house; seeker after shame. Are we talking of grass?

[1] As related in *The Five Nights*.

[2] Refers to Mahābhārata iii. liii. 236-57. *Ghoshayātrāparvan*. Citrasena was a king of the Gandharvas.

Duryodhana. Why, cowherd, grass is the stuff for you.

Having slain an innocent[1] maid, a horse and even a bull, and wrestlers too, oh shameless one, thou wouldst fain converse with the good. (36)

Vāsudeva. What, Suyodhana, are you mocking me?

Duryodhana. Nay, but that is true.

Vāsudeva. I shall withdraw at once.

Duryodhana. Go! Go to your stall with limbs white with the dust from the hooves of your cattle. Your time has been wasted.

Vāsudeva. So be it then. But we will not go without delivering the message. Hearken then to the message of Yudhishṭhira.

Duryodhana. Bah! You are not worthy to be spoken to.

Over me is borne the royal white umbrella, my head is sprinkled with holy water from the hands of the highest priests. I do not speak, I say, with men like thee, attendants of my vassal kings. (37)

Vāsudeva. Suyodhana, forsooth, holds no converse with me. Ha!

Thou cheat, ruthless to thy kin. Thou crow, thou squint-eyed yellow man.[2] The Kuru house shall come swiftly to destruction on account of thee. (38)

Princes, let us depart.

Duryodhana. How now? Keśava would be off. He has abused an envoy's privilege. Bind him, Duḥśāsana; and you, Durmarshaṇa, Durmukha, Durbuddhi, and Dushṭeśvara. What, are you weaklings? Duḥśāsana, are you helpless?

This Kṛishṇa murdered Kaṃsa, slew a horse and elephant. Bred in a family of cowherds, he is ignorant of etiquette. Devoid of strength and valour, he is guilty by his own mouth in the presence of princes. Straightway let him be bound. (39)

This man is a weakling. Uncle, do you bind this Keśava. What, he turns his face and falls down! Well, I myself will bind him with a noose. [*Advances with uplifted noose.*]

Vāsudeva. What! Suyodhana, forsooth, wishes to fetter me. Very well; I shall test his strength. [*Assumes his universal form.*]

Duryodhana. Master Envoy—

To-day am I going to bind thee, amid the host of kings, though thou makest thine own magic or magic divine all around, even though thou smitest with celestial weapons hard to parry—proud as thou art of the felling of elephant, horse and bull. (40)

[1] avadhyām, 'not to be killed'.

[2] Or *piṅgala* separately in the sense of 'ape' or 'snake', as L. S. would prefer.

Ah, stay now. How is it I cannot see Keśava? Here he is. How small he looks. Stay now. Why can't I see him? Oh, here he is. How tall he looks. He's gone again. No, here he is. There are Keśavas all round the council-chamber. What shall I do? Yes, I have it. Princes, do each of you bind one Keśava. How now, they are falling down bound in their own bonds. Bravo, sorcerer, bravo!

The Pāṇḍavas will be sighing deeply, with eyes bedimmed with tears, when they see thee carried to their camp, wounded with a network of arrows sped by my bowstring, with every limb dyed with running gore. **(41)** [*Exit.*]

Vāsudeva. [Well, I shall accomplish the Pāṇḍavas' business myself. Come hither my discus Sudarśana.[1]

[*Enter the discus Sudarśana.*]

Sudarśana. Lo!

Hearing the voice of the Blessed One, by his bountiful favour forth do I rush, dispersing masses of clouds. With whom is he wroth, the Lotus-eyed. On whose head must I be manifest? **(42)**

Now, where is the blessed Nārāyaṇa?

Source of the subtle unseen transcending thought, the Majestic One of many forms, destroyer of enemies' power, he has risen to protect the world. **(43)**

[*Looking around.*] Ah, here is the Blessed One at the gate of Hastināpura acting as ambassador. Water now; where to find water. Blessed Ganges in the sky vouchsafe some water. Ah, it flows. [*Sips water and approaches.*] Hail, blessed Nārāyaṇa! [*Makes obeisance.*]

Vāsudeva. Sudarśana, matchless be your power.

Sudarśana. I thank you.

Vāsudeva. You have arrived luckily in the nick of time.

Sudarśana. What, in the nick of time? Command me. Blessed One, command me.

Shall I overturn all the Meru and Mandara mountains? Shall I convulse the whole ocean? Or hurl down to earth all the brood of stars? There is nothing I cannot do, O Blessed One, by thy favour. **(44)**

Vāsudeva. Ha, Sudarśana, come hither. And thou, Suyodhana, though thou hidest in the briny sea, or in the mountain cave, or in the track of winds traversed by starry hosts, to-day shall my disk, thou wanton, be the disk of thy death swiftly sped by the force of my arm. **(45)**

[1] See remarks in Introduction about these weapons.

Sudarśana. Ha, stay thou miserable Suyodhana.

[*Reflects.*] Pardon, blessed Nārāyaṇa.

Thou didst descend upon the earth, O God, to ease its burdens; if now this man should pass like this, thy trouble would be in vain. **(46)**

Vāsudeva. Sudarśana, in anger I forgot my duty. Return to your abode.

Sudarśana. As the blessed Nārāyaṇa commands. Who now calls him cowherd? He is indeed the Majestic Nārāyaṇa who covered the triple universe in three strides. Take refuge with him, O men. I shall go. Why, here is Śārṅga, the Blessed One's excellent bow.

Endowed with womanish qualities—lovely, soft, and slender—it is an unfailing death to hosts of foes, with its middle grasped by Vishṇu's hand. It gleams with its back set with gold at Kṛishṇa's side like a lovely streak of lightning on the edge of a darkling cloud. **(47)**

Ho, Śārṅga! The blessed Nārāyaṇa's wrath is appeased. Return to your own abode. Ah, he has gone. Now let me go too. Oh, here is the Club Kaumodakī.

Studded with gold and gems, wrapped in beautiful garlands, it yearns to crush the limbs of crowds of foemen to the gods. Shaped like a mountain peak, with prowess irresistible, it comes rushing swiftly through the sky, followed by a mass of clouds. **(48)**

Ho, Kaumodakī! The blessed Nārāyaṇa's wrath is appeased. Ah, she has gone. Now let me go. Why, here comes the conch-shell Pāñcajanya.

Deliciously white as the rounded moon, as jasmine blossom or the centre of a lotus flower, graced by Kṛishṇa's lotus face,[1] its murmuring recalls the roaring of the ocean when the world returns to chaos. At the sound of it the demon dames miscarry. **(49)**

Ho, Pāñcajanya! My master's wrath has passed away. So back to your abode. Away he goes. Now there is the sword Nandaka.

Slender as a woman but in battle dreadful as a mighty demon, it flashes through the sky gleaming like a meteor. **(50)**

The master's wrath is appeased, O Nandaka. Away with you. He has gone; now I must go.**]**

[Why, here are the divine weapons of the Blessed One.

[1] When he blows it.

Here is the sword named Nandaka mocking the burning sun with its rays, and here Kaumodakī, so skilled in smashing the gnarled bosoms of the gods' enemies. And that is Śārṅga the long bow, whose string twangs with the thunder of clouds at the ęnd of the world. This is Pāñcajanya, king of conch shells, deep-toned and moonbeam-bright. (51)

Ho Śārṅga, Kaumodakī, Pāñcajanya, and thou Nandaka, the death of demons, a fire to burn thine enemies? The anger of the Blessed One has been appeased, so go ye now each to thine own abode. (52)

Ah, they have gone. Now I must go.

Why, what a violent wind; how fiercely the sun is burning. The mountains rock, the seas are agitated. Trees are uprooted and clouds are scurrying. Mighty serpents like Vāsuki hide away. What does it all mean? Ah, here comes Garuḍa, my master's steed divine.

The nectar which the gods and demons gained by toil he snatched from his foe to set his mother free, and bestowed this boon on Kṛishṇa to serve him as his mount. (53)

O Garuḍa, the darling son of Kāśyapa, the wrath of the blessed Lord of Gods is appeased. Return to your abode. Ah, he has gone. Now must I go too.

Here are the gods and other folk divine [1] crowding the sky with crowns falling from their heads in their haste. With Vishṇu wroth they lost their beauty and their power, but hearing he is pacified they return to their abodes relieved from anguish. (54)

Now I too will return to my favourite recess in Mount Meru. [*Exit.*]]

Vāsudeva. I too must leave—for the Pāṇḍavas' camp.

[*Voice behind the scene.*]

No, no, he must not go.

Vāsudeva. That sounds like the old king's voice. I am still here, O King.

[*Enter Dhṛitarāshṭra.*]

Dhṛitarāshṭra. Where now is the blessed Nārāyaṇa? Where is the benefactor of the Pāṇḍavas? the friend of brahmans? the delight of Devakī? [2]

By reason of my son's offence, O Wielder of the Śārṅga bow, do I lay my head at thy feet, Ruler of the Gods. (55)

[*Falls at his feet.*]

[1] Lit. according to the restored reading, 'Siddhas, Yakshas, and Kinnaras'.

[2] Mother of Krishṇa.

Vāsudeva. Alas, your Majesty prostrate! Pray rise.

Dhṛitarāshṭra. I thank you. Blessed One, pray accept these tokens of our welcome.[1]

Vāsudeva. I accept everything. What further favour can I bestow?

Dhṛitarāshṭra. If the Blessed One is pleased, what more can I desire?

Vāsudeva. Farewell till we meet again.

Dhṛitarāshṭra. As the Blessed Nārāyaṇa commands. [*Exit.*]

[*Epilogue.*]

This earth, that extends to the ocean with the Himālaya and Vindhya mountains as ear-drops, may our Lion King rule over her, marked with the symbol of a single sovereign sway.[2] (**56**)

[*Exeunt omnes.*]

FINIS.

[1] Lit. 'this (water) for respectful reception and for the feet'.

[2] Identical with the Epilogue in *The Vision of Vāsavadattā*.

POTSHERD AS AN ENVOY

(*Dūta-Ghaṭotkacam*)

INTRODUCTION

ABHIMANYU, the son of Arjuna, was married to Uttarā, the daughter of Virāṭā. That was the conclusion of *The Five Nights*. Later on, in the course of the great battle, Abhimanyu ventured into the fray alone, was set on by a number of his enemies, and slain.

This was a tragic moment of horror. A mere youth had been overpowered and killed by a number of experienced warriors. That youth was the Pāṇḍava heir, and kinsman of the Kurus. A terrible vengeance by Arjuna became absolutely inevitable.

In this play we see the old blind king, Dhṛitarāshṭra, protesting against the wickedness of Abhimanyu's death. The story of his undoing is revealed by the soldier. Then come the wicked prince Duryodhana and his associates Duḥśāsana and the gambler Śakuni. They are delighted at the slaying of Abhimanyu, and Duryodhana argues the matter with his old father. An envoy comes from Kṛishṇa. This is Potsherd (Ghaṭotkaca), Bhīma's son by a demon mother, Hiḍimbā, whom we saw in *The Middle One*.

Courteously received by the old king, he is taunted by Duryodhana. They quarrel, and Potsherd is ready to fight. Pacified by the old king, Potsherd delivers his message, which is a threat of vengeance by Arjuna, and departs.

Abhimanyu's death is described in the seventh book of the Mahābhārata (vii. 48, 49), Section lxxiii being called *Abhimanyuvadha-parvan*. Karṇa deprives Abhimanyu of his car and bow. All the Kurus fight with him at once. Abhimanyu flies into the air, but is followed by his enemies' arrows. He comes to earth again and attacks Droṇa with a wheel. When the wheel also is destroyed he seizes a mace and kills many of his foes. Finally, Duḥśāsana's son kills him with a blow of a mace on his head.

Later on (vii. 73, in lxxiv *Pratijñā-parvan*) Arjuna takes an oath that he will kill Jayadratha next day or burn himself. (Jayadratha was a son-in-law of the old king, husband of Duḥśalā, and King of Sindhu-Sauvīra.)

Section lxxv, *Jayadrathavadha-parvan*, describes how Arjuna fulfilled his oath, assisted by Kṛishṇa's magic. There is no embassy at this stage and nothing about Ghaṭotkaca. Nor was Dhṛitarāshṭra on the scene of the battle. This has been noted in the Introduction to *The Broken Thighs*.

In this play, as in *The Embassy*, there is no action but the taunting of an envoy and his departure in indignation. The dialogue brings out the tragic situation and the doom impending for the Kurus. The piquancy of the scene depends partly on Duryodhana's defiance of Kṛishṇa, who is Nārāyaṇa, that is already, as in *The Embassy*, the god Vishṇu himself.

On the whole this is rather a sketch than a drama.

DRAMATIS PERSONAE

(In the order of their appearance.)

Stage-manager, in the Prologue.
Soldier, on the Kuru side.
DHṚITARĀSHṬRA, the blind old king, father of Duryodhana, and the other Kurus.
Gāndhārī, his wife, who bandaged her eyes.
Duḥśalā, his daughter, wife of Jayadratha, the king of Sindhu-Sauvīra.
Portress.
DURYODHANA, eldest son of Dhṛitarāshṭra, leader of the Kurus.
Duḥśāsana, one of Duryodhana's 99 brothers.
Śakuni, the gambling king of Gāndhāra.
POTSHERD, GHAṬOTKACA, son of Bhīma and Hiḍimbā, sent as an envoy by Krishṇa.

PROLOGUE

[*After the Opening enter the Stage-manager.*]

Stage-manager. May Nārāyaṇa protect you.

Nārāyaṇa, the sole refuge of the three worlds, who determines what expedients are proper for the gods; stage-manager[1] of the main plot, prologue,[2] and epilogue of the ceaseless drama of the triple world. (1)

With these words, my lords and gentlemen, I have to announce to you. But what is that? I thought I heard a noise, just as I was to make my announcement. Well, I must see what it is.

[*Voice behind the scene.*]

Ho there, take word, take word, I say!

Stage-manager. Good, I understand. A band of confederates enticed Arjuna[3] away with Kṛishṇa.[4] Forthwith, on that, the sons of Dhṛitarāshṭra, enraged at the slaying of Bhīshma, surrounded Abhimanyu and killed him. So—

The kings afeared of Arjuna's return, watching the quarter whence he'd come, fly to their own leaguers, distracted by the wounds inflicted by arrows of Subhadrā's son. (2)

[*Exit.*]

END OF PROLOGUE.

[*Enter a Soldier.*]

Soldier. Take word, take word, I say to his Majesty Dhṛitarāshṭra, that hath worthy kin and a hundred sons, far-sighted with his virtue and piety, amplified by knowledge.

Though but a boy playing in the battlefield, Abhimanyu displayed his father's prowess and dismayed the royal forces by slaying warriors, chariot steeds, and elephants; then hundreds of princes rushed swiftly upon him from all sides, and he has been sent straightway to his grandsire's bosom in the sky.[5] (3)

[*Enter Dhṛitarāshṭra, Gāndhārī, Duḥśalā, and Portress.*]

[1] *Sūtradhāra*: originally one who 'held the strings' and made the puppets dance.

[2] *Prastāvanā*, not *sthāpanā*, the term used in these plays for prologue.

[3] Dhanañjaya.

[4] Janārdana.

[5] Reading with editor *sarvataḥ khe yātasya*. Lit. 'has been, as it were, suddenly caused to mount the lap of his grandfather gone (already) in the sky'.

Dhṛitarāshṭra. Oh, what is this I hear?

Who is it offends mine ears? Who utters hateful news thinking it would please me? Who is it dares proclaim the ruin of our house, stained by the crime of killing a child? (4)

Gāndhārī. There it is again, your Majesty. It is absolutely clear this fratricidal war can only end in the destruction of our children.

Dhṛitarāshṭra. Now it will be clear, Gāndhārī.

Gāndhārī. When, my lord?

Dhṛitarāshṭra. To-day, Gāndhārī. Listen,

Arjuna[1] will be at work to-day, furious at Abhimanyu's death, with his dread bow beside him, while angry Kṛishṇa holds the reins and whip. There will be peace when all the world is dead. (5)

Gāndhārī. Alas! Abhimanyu, my grandson, whither hast thou gone now, plunging thy childhood to our misfortune in such a fratricidal war that destroys the best of warriors?

Duḥśalā. The man that inflicted widowhood on our son's wife Uttarā has ordained widowhood for his own young wife.

Dhṛitarāshṭra. But who has built this bridge to a flood of woe?

Soldier. Sire, 'twas I.

Dhṛitarāshṭra. Who are you?

Soldier. Sire, I am Jayatrāta.

Dhṛitarāshṭra. Jayatrāta—

Who has slaughtered Abhimanyu? To whom is life no longer dear? Who has made himself the fuel for the fivefold fire of the Pāṇḍavas? (6)

Soldier. Sire, several kings rushed on him at once and slew Prince Abhimanyu. It may be Jayadratha did the actual deed.

Dhṛitarāshṭra. What? Jayadratha did the deed?

Soldier. Even so.

Dhṛitarāshṭra. Alas! Jayadratha is as good as slain.

[*Hearing this Duḥśalā begins to cry.*]

Dhṛitarāshṭra. Who is that crying?

Portress. Sire, it is the princess Duḥśalā.

Dhṛitarāshṭra. Do not weep, my child. Look you—

Your constant freedom from a widow's state no longer satisfies your lord, so he needs must make himself the mark for Arjuna's[2] arrows. (7)

Duḥśalā. Then permit me, father, I'll go to my daughter-in-law Uttarā.

[1] Pārtha. [2] Gāṇḍīvī, the owner of the bow Gaṇḍīva.

Dhṛitarāshṭra. What will you say to her, my child?

Duḥśalā. I shall tell her, father, that for to-day and for ever I too will don widow's weeds like her.

Gāndhārī Dear daughter, don't say such unlucky things. Your husband is still alive.

Duḥśalā. Oh, mother, no such luck for me. Who can live that has offended Arjuna and Kṛishṇa?

Dhṛitarāshṭra. Poor[1] Duḥśalā is right. For—

Who in the world can long survive his own misdeeds if he has slain the child that grew up in Kṛishṇa's lap, pillowed on his eight arms—the darling of the Pāṇḍavas—brave as the gods, while the love of him was a second intoxication for the excited Wielder of the Plough? (8)

Jayatrāta, when Arjuna saw his son brought to that pass, what did he take on him to do?

Soldier. What, sire? You think this happened in Arjuna's presence?

Dhṛitarāshṭra. Why, was Arjuna not there?

Soldier. Oh, no.

Dhṛitarāshṭra. How did it happen?

Soldier. Hearken, sire. A band of confederates enticed away Arjuna with Kṛishṇa. Then Prince Abhimanyu, in his youthfulness, seeing no harm in it, joined in the battle.

Dhṛitarāshṭra. Alas, naturally he was killed. Who can venture into a cave frequented by a tiger? But what are the other Pāṇḍavas doing?

Soldier. Hearken, sire—

They do not place the body on the pyre themselves, that Arjuna may see it, but repeat the names of the kings that dealt blows thereon. (9)

Dhṛitarāshṭra. Come along, Gāndhārī. We will go to the bank of the Ganges.

Gāndhārī. Why, Majesty, to bathe therein?

Dhṛitarāshṭra. Gāndhārī, listen—

Even to-day will I make oblation for thy sons slain by their own offences. Yet have I no power by my gifts of water to check the princes in their camp. (10)

[*Enter Duryodhana, Duḥśāsana, and Śakuni.*]

Duryodhana. My dear Duḥśāsana—

By the death of Abhimanyu enmity is established firmly, victory attained, our foes bewildered and driven off. Madhu-

[1] Reading *tapasvinī*.

sūdana's[1] arrogance is uprooted. To-day have I won both success and fame. (11)

Duḥśāsana. Yes, indeed.

The sons of Pāṇḍu were held back. Jayadratha's force overcame the enemy and slew Subhadrā's son,[2] a second Arjuna, with a flight of a hundred shafts. We were in straits through Bhīshma's fall, but in this battle we have planted sharp darts of sorrow in their hearts by the slaughter of their son. (12)

Śakuni. In the fight to-day Jayadratha did mighty deeds. The princes found his valour past belief. By his prowess in the battle he robbed them at once of their son and matchless fame. (13)

Duryodhana. Uncle.

Śakuni. Yes, my boy?

Duryodhana. Come hither, uncle; and you, my dear Duḥśāsana. Let us salute his Majesty, my father.

Śakuni. Nay, not so, my dear Duryodhana.

This war in the clan does not suit his liking. His fondness for the Pāṇḍavas will make him reproach us. Indeed is it seemly for us fresh from victory in the battle to approach him thus with jubilant faces? (14)

Duryodhana. Nay, uncle. Come what may, we shall salute his Majesty, our father. (*Steps around.*)

Duryodhana. Father, I salute you; 'tis I, Duryodhana.

Duḥśāsana. Father, I am Duḥśāsana. I salute you.

Śakuni. I am Śakuni. I salute you.

All three. What! is not a word of blessing vouchsafed to us?

Dhṛitarāshṭra. How can there be a blessing, my son—

When Abhimanyu, but a boy, the very heart of Arjuna and Kṛishṇa, has been slain? How may one pronounce a blessing on the lives of those past hope. (15)

Duryodhana. Oh, father, what has caused this agitation?

Dhṛitarāshṭra. What has caused this agitation?

In this house, rich in many sons, there was but one daughter, dearer to me than a hundred sons. She, thanks to you, her kinsmen, will gain inglorious widowhood. (16)

Duryodhana. What's wrong with Jayadratha?

Dhṛitarāshṭra. That gallant warrior held back the Pāṇḍavas.

Duryodhana. Oh! he held them back? So did many others.

[1] Kṛishṇa. [2] Abhimanyu.

Dhṛitarāshṭra. Alas!

When so many rushed together ruthlessly and fell upon one, a child, my grandson, why were their arms not paralysed? (17)

Duryodhana. Father—

Why were their arms not paralysed when they slew old Bhīshma with their tricks? And why should ours for slaying one that was no stripling in his prowess? (18)

Dhṛitarāshṭra. My son, can you compare the fall of Bhīshma to the slaying of Abhimanyu?

Duryodhana. Why not, father?

Dhṛitarāshṭra. Listen, my son.

Bhīshma's death depended on his own will. He was cut down in accordance with his own advice, well content. But this was a child, and in him is cut off the lord to be of the Kuru house and Arjuna's first-born. (19)

Duḥśāsana. Father, that child of yours was no child, Abhimanyu.

Dhṛitarāshṭra. Is that Duḥśāsana speaking?

Duḥśāsana. Why, yes.

While all of us were looking on and fighting he grasped a bow as hot as Indra's thunderbolt[1] and wounded all the kings with arrows, like the sun discharging a network of rays. (20)

Dhṛitarāshṭra. Alas!

If that child, Subhadrā's son,[2] has worked such havoc all alone, what, think you, will Pārtha[3] do, enflamed by the destruction of his son? (21)

Duryodhana. What will he do?

Dhṛitarāshṭra. Those of you that survive will see what he will do.

Duryodhana. But, father, what after all is this Arjuna?

Dhṛitarāshṭra. Do you not know Arjuna, my son?

Duryodhana. Not I.

Dhṛitarāshṭra. So then, nor do I. But there are many that do know the strength and valour of Arjuna. Ask them.

Duryodhana. Who are these people, father, who know Arjuna's strength and valour, that I should ask?

Dhṛitarāshṭra. Hearken, my son—

Do thou ask Indra,[4] honoured aforetime by gifts of demon[5] mail and demon lives. Ask Śiva, in his Kirāta guise, pro-

[1] Reading *vyādhāmoṣmaṁ* with editor. Or perhaps, as he suggests, *vyādhāmoṣmāgṛhya*?

[2] Abhimanyu.

[3] Arjuna.

[4] Śakra.

[5] Nivāta—usually 'impenetrable'—also a class of demons.

pitiated with every kind of weapon. Ask Agni, who longed for serpent offerings and was surfeited in the Khāṇḍava wood. And the divine magician that defeated you to-day—ask Citrāṅgada. (22)

Duryodhana. If that is all it comes to, the valour of Arjuna, are no warriors in our army a match for him?

Dhṛitarāshṭra. If so, who?

Duryodhana. Well, there's Karṇa.

Dhṛitarāshṭra. Ah! Poor Karṇa is ridiculous.

Duryodhana. Why so?

Dhṛitarāshṭra. Listen—

Careless and soft-hearted, he shares a chariot, though Indra has removed his armour;[1] his weapons have lost their power, as he got them by fraud. Karṇa, forsooth, will be equal to Arjuna, if Fire, Indra, and Rudra teach him the gift of weapons. (23)

Śakuni. You have the right to belittle us.

Dhṛitarāshṭra. Is that Śakuni speaking? Ah! Śakuni—

That work of yours, inveterate gambler, was a consuming fire of enmity for this house, that spares not even saplings.[2] (24)

Duryodhana. Oho!

Whence comes it that the earth is trembling all at once with a rumbling roar and the sky seems all ablaze with falling meteors? (25)

Dhṛitarāshṭra. I think, my son,

'Tis clear. These meteors that fall are the teardrops of mighty Indra, distressed to see his grandson slain. (26)

Duryodhana. Jayatrāta, go and find out the reason of this noise in the Pāṇḍava camp with all the din of war-cries, conchs, and kettledrums.

Soldier. As your Majesty commands. [*Exit and re-enters.*] When Arjuna returned from his encounter with the confederate warriors he placed his dead son on his lap and bathed him in tears. Then egged on by Krishṇa's taunts he made a vow . . .

Duryodhana. What is this?

Soldier. With hearts content with his resolve, elated by his prowess, the princes looked at him with beaming faces and suddenly broke forth into a roar of 'Victory'; and the earth, bestrid by kings, like heavy mountains piled together, trembled at that moment like a maiden in confusion. (27)

[1] Described in *Karṇa's Task*.

[2] Lit. 'that is not quenched in the case of children (or young plants)'.

Dhṛitarāshṭra. The earth trembled at the mere sound of his oath. 'Tis clear that when he touches his bow the triple world will totter. **(28)**

Duryodhana. What was the oath?

Soldier. The man that slew my son and those that rejoiced at his death—them will I slay to-morrow ere the sun goes down.[1] **(29)**

Duryodhana. I shall make an effort to thwart his oath.

Dhṛitarāshṭra. What will you do, my son?

Duryodhana. I shall cover Jayadratha with all the mass of my armies. Moreover—

In accord with Droṇa's rules I shall draw up a battle array in a form that none can penetrate. With broken hopes and desires ungained let them enter funeral flames with warriors, elephants, and all. **(30)**

Dhṛitarāshṭra. Though he burrow in the earth, though he climb the firmament, everywhere will those arrows follow him, the arrows of Kṛishṇa's comrade.[2] **(31)**

Soldier. Had any other spoken thus to our ruthless king, ever ready in command, he would not be living now. **(32)**

[*Enter Potsherd* (*Ghaṭotkaca*).]

Potsherd. Here I am—

Faring forth to see that ignoble-minded foe that urged the death of Abhimanyu; obeying the command of the discus-wielder like a lordly elephant urged by the goad to its food. **(33)**

[*Looking down.*] This is the entrance to the enemies' camp. I will get down. [*Gets down.*]

I will announce myself.

Hiḍimbā's son am I, Ghaṭotkaca, come with a message from the Yadu king. I am to see that aged prince involved in hostility by the faults committed by his kin.

Duryodhana. Come, come, enter your enemies' camp. My curiosity is great. Let me hear Kṛishṇa's audacious words. I, Duryodhana, am waiting. **(34)**

Potsherd. [*Entering.*] Ah! here is his Majesty King Dhṛitarāshṭra. He has a fine appearance, gentle and grave.

Wonderful, wonderful!

Old though he is, there are no marked wrinkles, and his shoulders are compact.[3] His fortitude seems to lend his form

[1] Reading *svara* with editor.

[2] Lit. 'of him that has Kṛishṇa as his eye'.

[3] Reading doubtful. For *śutrasaṃhatâṃsaḥ* the editor reads *śata*—'a hundredfold'.

the confidence of his five score sons. The gods, I think, were apprehensive of the protection of the triple world, and through their fear his Majesty was created blind.[1] (35)

Grandfather. Ghaṭotkaca salutes you. Nay, rather, it is my elders, Yudhishṭhira and the rest, salute you, then afterwards I, Ghaṭotkaca.

Dhṛitarāshṭra. Come hither, my son.

This is no pleasant tale[2] for me, for my heart too is wrung by thy brother's fate. And thus this thy message does not suit. I am brought to misery by the misdeeds of my sons. (36)

Potsherd. Oh! Your Majesty is a noble soul. The Blessed One, the Wielder of the Discus, sends word to my grandfather, offspring of a noble stock . . .

Dhṛitarāshṭra. [*Rising from his seat.*] What are the commands of the blessed Wielder of the Discus?

Potsherd. No, no. Take your seat to hear the message of Janārdana.[3]

Dhṛitarāshṭra. As the blessed Discus-wielder commands. [*Sits down.*]

Potsherd. Grandfather, listen—'Oh, my child Abhimanyu, the light of the Kuru clan, alas! my child, my child, the scion of the Yadu house! Thou has left Janārdana, thy mother's brother, and even me and gone to heaven with the hope of seeing thy grandsire.' 'If such is the plight of Arjuna at the loss of one son, what will be yours, grandfather? So, quickly now, muster all your strength lest the fire rising from grief for your sons burn your life as an oblation.' Thus he spake.

Dhṛitarāshṭra. So spake Kṛishṇa[4] with an angry purpose. I seem to see Arjuna enduring when all other warriors have been slain. (37)

Duryodhana. Oh! What a ridiculous speech.

Dhṛitarāshṭra. Do you find it so?

Duryodhana. Ridiculous indeed.

That jealous Kṛishṇa must be plotting with the gods if he believes a host of kings will be slain by Arjuna single-handed. (38)

Potsherd. Thou mockest. I am an envoy sent by Kṛishṇa. But 'twas meet to let thee hear what Arjuna had done. (39)

Besides, you must hear Janārdana's message.

Duḥśāsana. Not so, you despiser of the warrior caste. No other message shall be heard in the presence of this commander, whose orders are obeyed by all the princes on the earth. (40)

[1] The idea reoccurs in *The Broken Thighs*, v. 36.

[2] Reading *priyākhyānam*, suggested by editor.

[3] Krishṇa or Vishṇu.

[4] Cakrāyudha, 'whose weapon is the discus'.

Potsherd. What's that? Is Kṛishṇa then no king for you? Ho!

Kṛishṇa set free the kings with humbled pride from Jarāsandha's city [1]; Kṛishṇa won the prize [2] from Bhīshma's hand while all the ring of princes gazed in envy; Kṛishṇa has Fortune herself as mistress in his chamber,[3] radiant to serve him. Is this wonderful king of kings no king to thee? **(41)**

Duryodhana. Duḥśāsana, no more discussion.

Be he king or no king, be he strong or weak, what's the need of many words? What has your master said? **(42)**

Potsherd. Why, yes. August Nārāyaṇa is indeed the master, the lord of the universe, and especially our master. Besides—

Understand the destruction of thy warriors is determined—may the earth be the lighter for the piled-up corpses [4] of a hundred kings. For in the forefront of the fray nothing will be too hard for Arjuna, made eager by the loss of his son, to discharge his terrible bolts. **(43)**

Śakuni. Could it be done by words alone, the world were won!

Were it by words and nothing but words, the killing of the warriors were done! **(44)**

Potsherd. Bah! Here is Śakuni having his say. Ho! Śakuni—

Abandon dice, and in the fighting be thou a chequer board, so suitable for thee and a ready mark for arrows. For here are no women to steal, no throne to usurp. Here the stake is life, and enjoyment means arrows with their dreadful winnings. **(45)**

Duḥśāsana. If you say 'Bah!' to us,

Thou tauntest us, and speakest rough words beyond all limit. Long in the arm, thou reekest nothing of what thou sayest. If thou art proud and hast a dreadful form from thy mother's side, we too are grim with natures fierce as demons. **(46)**

Potsherd. Heaven forbid! You are much worse than demons.

The spirits of the night do not burn their brothers asleep in a house of lac; the spirits of the night do not touch that way the head of a brother's wife, and the spirits of the night do not

[1] Reading *jarāpurān nṛpatayaḥ*, as suggested by editor. Jarāsandha was king of Magadha and Cedī, an enemy of Kṛishṇa. Gaya was his city. For the freeing of the kings by Krishṇa see M.Bh. ii. 24, in *Jarāsandhavadha-parvan.*

[2] Reading *yenārghaṃ* for *yenāghaṃ*, referring to M.Bh. ii. 36, *Arghāharaṇa-parvan.* Editor suggests *yenārdham*—'half', i.e. 'wife', Rukmiṇī.

[3] Reading *srīr yasya* for *śrīvṛkṣa.* (Ed. śrīvatsa.)

[4] *viniciti.*

celebrate the slaughter of a child in the battlefield. Though they be strange in form and fierce in manner they are not devoid of pity. (47)

Duryodhana. As an envoy hast thou come, not to fight. Take thy message and go. We are not of those that slay an envoy. (48)

Potsherd. What, would you throw it in my teeth that I am an envoy? Nay, then, I am no envoy.

A truce to your trickery. Fall on me all together. I am not Abhimanyu, made helpless by the cutting of a bowstring. (49)

This has been my great wish from boyhood.

Further—

Here stands Ghaṭotkaca, biting his lips with fists upraised; let any man stand up to me that wishes to go to the abode of Death. (50)

Dhṛitarāshṭra. Ghaṭotkaca, my grandson, pardon, pardon. Respect my words.

Potsherd. I cannot restrain my anger. Yet, at grandfather's word, I am again an envoy. What am I to announce to the august Nārāyaṇa?

Duryodhana. Announce from whom? From me you may tell him,

Why so many useless words? We are not to be vanquished by harsh words.[1] No word goes far when a man must fight. I am coming out, surrounded ever by the umbrellas in line of a hundred kings. Wait there with the Pāṇḍavas. I'll give you an answer with my arrows. (51)

Potsherd. Grandfather, I am going.

Dhṛitarāshṭra. Go, my grandson, go.

Potsherd. Hearken, ye kings, to the final message of Janārdana—

Do what is right. Have regard for thine own kin. Fulfil upon this earth whatever thy heart desires. For in the guise of Pāṇḍavas, as if to teach your clan the truth, Death will come upon you with the rays of to-morrow's sun. (52)

[*Exeunt omnes.*]

FINIS.

[1] Reading *pāruṣya* for *pauruṣya*.

KARṆA'S TASK

(*Karṇa-bhāram*)

INTRODUCTION

THIS one-act play has a tragic note. It might almost be called 'Karṇa's Tragedy' or 'How Karṇa drove to his death', for that seems to be what is meant.

Karṇa, the king of Aṅga, was a son of Kuntī, and therefore a half-brother of the elder Pāṇḍavas. During the great battle he was sent out specially to fight with Arjuna. He feels that against his half-brothers he cannot do himself justice, that his weapons have lost their force.

Sūrya (the sun) was Karṇa's father, and Karṇa was born with armour and golden ear-rings. In the third book of the Mahābhārata (*Sections 300–310 Kuṇḍalā-haraṇa-parvan*) we are told that Sūrya appeared to Karṇa in a dream and warned him not to give away his armour and ear-rings, which made him invincible, if Indra should come in the guise of a brahman and ask for them. Karṇa says he will give them; better to die than to injure his reputation by a refusal. Then Sūrya warns him he should at least get the unfailing lance in return. Indra (310) appears and demands the armour and ear-rings. Karṇa agrees if he gets the magic lance. This will kill only one enemy.[1] He hacks the armour off his body. The eighth book of the Great Epic is called the *Karṇaparvan*. Karṇa takes over the chief command of the Kuru army. He undertakes to fight with Arjuna, if Śalya will drive his car.

Śalya dislikes this subordinate position, but agrees provided he may say what he likes to Karṇa.

Śalya and Karṇa mount the car and drive against the foe (**36**). They have a long quarrel.

Śalya points out evil omens, and shows him Arjuna and Kṛishṇa in the fight. Karṇa fights with the Pāñcālas and kills five of them. Yudhishṭhira stuns Karṇa, but Karṇa disarms him, captures him, and lets him go with scornful words. The battle rages with varied fortunes. Finally (**86** onwards) Karṇa and Arjuna come together for their duel, and Arjuna (**91**) shoots his head off.

[1] In vii. 179, Karṇa uses up the lance to Kṛishṇa's glee in killing Ghaṭotkaca.

Our dramatist simplifies the story. Karṇa sets out with Śalya for the fight with Arjuna. Three times he tells Śalya to drive his car where Arjuna is, and the play ends abruptly on that command. All the while he is oppressed by impending disaster. 'There falls on my heart black misery.' He is held back by his mother's word. He tells Śalya the story of a curse upon his weapons, that they will fail him in time of need. But he is resigned, for in battle 'Slain one goes to heaven, victorious one wins glory'. 'Good luck to me whose time has come.'

After this colloquy they mount again, but Indra comes disguised as a brahman and obtains the magic armour. Instead of demanding the invincible spear in exchange, Karṇa receives it with reluctance. (This Karṇa is throughout more saintly than the epic Karṇa.) Then for the third time they mount the car and drive where Arjuna's conch is sounding.

DRAMATIS PERSONAE

(In order of appearance.)

Stage-manager, in the Prologue.
Soldier, on the Kuru side.
KARṆA, King of the Aṅgas, son of Sūrya by Pṛithā (or Kuntī before her marriage to Pāṇḍu), and so an elder half-brother of the Pāṇḍavas, but fights on the Kuru side.
ŚALYA, King of the Madras, brother of Mādrī, the second wife of Pāṇḍu, fights on the Kuru side and drives Karṇa's chariot.
INDRA, disguised as a brahman. Speaks Prākrit like a mendicant of an unorthodox order, e.g. Buddhist or Jain.
Angel, disguised as a brahman: a messenger from Indra.

PROLOGUE

[*After the Opening enter the Stage-manager.*]

Stage-manager. May the Fortunate [1] bring you good fortune—he that smites the hosts hostile to the gods. The sight of him in his man-lion form scared the world and underworld, with all the multitudes of men and women, gods,[2] and fiends. 'Twas he that burst the breast of the demon-king with the axe-edge of his nails. (1)

With these words, my lords and gentlemen, I have to announce to you—But what is that? I thought I heard a noise just as I was to make my announcement. Well, I must see what it is.

[*Voice behind the scene.*]

Ho there, take word to his Highness the King of the Aṅgas.

Stage-manager. Good, I understand.

A flurried servitor with folded hands brings word to Karṇa at Duryodhana's behest that the battle grows tumultuous. (2)

[*Exit.*]

END OF THE PROLOGUE.

[*Enter a Soldier.*]

Soldier. Ho there, take word to his Highness the King of the Aṅgas—'it is time for battle'.

Princes, brave as lions, on elephants, chargers, or chariots, are roaring lion-like before the Pāṇḍu [3] standard. Perceiving what is at stake, the serpent-bannered champion of the world has set out hurriedly for the battlefield, unbearable with the enemies' yells. (3)

[*Stepping round and looking off.*]

Ah! here is the Aṅga king accoutred for the battle, coming hither from his house with King Śalya. But, oh! what means this unwonted anxiety in one that is foremost in the joys of battle and of proven valour? For he—

Counted first in battle, manifest with the fiercest majesty, goes now a wise man sadly to the fray. Karṇa now is like the sun,

[1] *Śrīdhara*—possessing fortune, name of Vishṇu.

[2] Reading *suparva* with the editor for *suparṇa*.

[3] *Pārtha*, matronymic from *Pṛithā*.

when summer comes, obscured by lines of clouds but shining with its innate splendour. (4)

Well, I must be off. [*Exit.*]

[*Enter Karṇa with Śalya as described.*]

Karṇa. Nay, then, have the kings that came as targets within my arrow's range ever returned alive? In the van of the fight to-day I should please the Kurus if I could meet with Arjuna.[1] (5)

King Śalya,[2] drive my car where Arjuna may be.

Śalya. Very well. [*Drives the car.*]

Karṇa. My prowess is a match for cruel death, and yet in the hour of battle, in mighty fights, with charging warriors, elephants, steeds, and cars, with limbs lopped off in the ruin dealt by blades on either side, there falls on my heart black misery. (6)

Alas!

In days gone by I was born of Kuntī,[3] though now I'm known as the son of the charioteer.[4] So Yudhishṭhira and the other Pāṇḍavas are my younger brothers. (7)

This is the glorious hour come at last; this is the excellent day of days, but my weapons and all that I have learnt of war are all in vain as I am held back by my mother's word. (8)

O Madra King, hear the story how I learned the art of war.

Śalya. I am very curious to hear it.

Karṇa. First I went to Jāmadagni.[5]

Śalya. Yes?

Karṇa. To that excellent sage I went, that standard of the Bhṛigu race, that destroyer of the warrior class, with a mass of matted locks long and tawny as streaks of lightning, wielding an axe flashing rings of lustre—humbly I saluted him and stood resolute at his side. (9)

Śalya. What then?

Karṇa. Then Jāmadagni blessed me, and asked me who I was, and why I had come.

Śalya. And then?

Karṇa. Your Reverence, I said, I wish to learn the use of every kind of weapon.

1 *Dhanañjaya*, the great archer.

2 *Śalya-rāja*; but Śalya was king of the Madras.

3 Kuntī, the mother of the three elder Pāṇḍavas.

4 Rādheya, i.e. the son of Rādhā, the wife of Adhiratha, the charioteer and foster-mother of Karṇa.

5 Son of the Ṛishi Jamadagni.

Śalya. What did he say?

Karṇa. The holy man said he would teach brahmans only, not warriors.

Śalya. Yes, he has an ancient feud against the warrior clans. What then?

Karṇa. Then I told him I did not belong to the warrior class and began to receive instruction in the art of weapons.

Śalya. And after that?

Karṇa. A few days later I went with my teacher to fetch some fruit and roots, and some fuel, with grass and flowers. Then wandering in the wood my teacher was tired and fell asleep with his head in my lap.

Śalya. Proceed.

Karṇa. By ill chance an insect called 'steely-teeth'[1] bored through both my thighs. Afraid of disturbing my teacher's slumber I endured the pain with fortitude. Awaking in a stream of blood, he found me out and straightway blazed into fiery wrath and cursed me, saying, 'Useless be thy weapons in the time of need'. **(10)**

Śalya. Oh! That was a dreadful thing for the sage to say.

Karṇa. Now let us examine the condition of our arms. (*Does so.*) These weapons all seem to lack power. Moreover—

These horses stumbling helplessly along blinded by misery, these elephants reeking like the Seven-leaf tree with excitement, they are all heralds of disaster in the battle. **(11)**

Conchs and kettledrums are silent.

Śalya. Oh, this is frightful!

Karṇa. Be not dismayed, King Śalya.

Slain, one goes to heaven, victorious one wins glory. The world thinks much of either, so one must win something in a battle. **(12)**

Besides—

These steeds as swift as Garuḍa, born of splendid Kāmboja stock, though they have no hope of returning from the war, shall protect me, albeit past protection.[2] **(13)**

Endless prosperity to kine and brahmans.

Good fortune to faithful wives. Good luck to warriors that do not turn their backs in battle. Good luck to me whcse time has come. Well, I am glad.

I shall penetrate the Pāṇḍava van, so intolerable, capture

[1] *Vajramukha*, 'of adamantine mouth'.

[2] Reading *rakṣantu mā yadyapyarakṣitavyam.*

Yudhishṭhira, far-famed for wealth of virtue, and overthrow Arjuna by the force of my mighty shafts. So that all may enter as in a wood where the lions have been slain. (14)

Come, Śalya, let us mount the car.

Śalya. Very well. [*They gesticulate mounting the chariots.*]

Karṇa. Now, Śalya, drive me where Arjuna may be.

[*Voice behind the scene.*]

O Karṇa, I beg for a mighty boon.

Karṇa. [*Listening.*] Oh, what a powerful voice!

Not merely a good brahman he, but a noble gentleman, and hence this great impression. These galloping horses of mine stop suddenly, their slender frames out of control, when they hear his deep sweet voice, as if painted in a picture. They prick their ears, and slightly arch their necks, strung with beads, and rub them with their muzzles. (15)

Call up the sage. No, no, I will call him myself. Reverend sir, come hither.

[*Enter Indra, disguised as a brahman.*]

Indra. Back, ye clouds, return with the sun. [*Going up to Karṇa.*] O Karṇa, I beg for a mighty boon.

Karṇa. I am very glad, holy man.

To-day I shall be counted among those that have gained their end. This is Karṇa that salutes you, his lotus feet illumined by the diadems of mighty monarchs, but his own head purified by the dust from the feet of a great sage. (16)

Indra. (*Aside.*] Nay, what am I to say? If I say 'Long life to you' he will live long. If I say nothing he will despise me as a fool. So I must avoid both extremes, but what shall I say? Good, I have it. [*Aloud.*][1] O Karṇa, eternal as the sun, the moon, the Himālayas, and the ocean be your fame.

Karṇa. Should you not say, sir, 'Long life to you!'? However, that is an auspicious wish. For—

Virtue should a man attain by trying, a king's fortune flickers like a serpent's tongue. So if he fix his thoughts on protecting his people, good qualities endure, though bodies be slain. (17)

What would you have, holy man? What can I give you?

Indra. I beg for a mighty boon.

Karṇa. A mighty boon will I bestow. Hear what wealth I have.

If it please thee, worthy priest, I will give thee a thousand kine.

[1] In his own person, i.e. to himself, Indra speaks Sanskrit. In his assumed character of a religious he speaks Prākrit.

Young kine right fit for supplication and to purify, with horns tipped with gold—kine that after contenting all their calves give streams of excellent milk like nectar. **(18)**

Indra. A thousand cows? I drink but little milk. I don't want them, Karṇa.

Karṇa. You do not want them? Well, listen again.

I will give thee straightway several thousand chargers of fine Kāmboja stock, equal to the horses of the sun; bringers of luck to kings, esteemed by all princes; horses as swift as the wind, with no vice, and seen at their best in battle. **(19)**

Indra. Horses? I ride but little. No, I don't want them.

Karṇa. No? Then listen to this.

I will give thee that countless herd of elephants, with white nails and tusks, with black bees all round the ichor streaming down their temples—elephants that resemble a range of lofty hills, roaring deep like thunderclouds. **(20)**

Indra. Elephants? I ride but little. I don't want them, Karṇa.

Karṇa. You don't? Well, listen. I will give you countless gold.

Indra. I'll take that and go. [*Goes a few steps.*] No! I don't want it, Karṇa.

Karṇa. Then I will conquer the earth and give you that.

Indra. What should I do with the earth?

Karṇa. Then I will give you the fruits of a burnt sacrifice.

Indra. What's the good of a burnt sacrifice to me?

Karṇa. Then take my head.

Indra. Ugh! Ugh!

Karṇa. Don't be alarmed. Forgive me, holy man. Listen again.

My body armour was borne with my limbs, nor god nor fiend can pierce it with their weapons. Yet will I gladly give it thee, with both the ear-rings, if it please thee. **(21)**

Indra. [*Joyfully.*] Yes, give me that.

Karṇa. [*Aside.*] So that's what he wants. Now, could this be a trick of wily Kṛishṇa's? If it be, so be it. Fie, it is unbecoming to think so. There is no reason for suspicion. [*Aloud.*] Take it.

Śalya. O King of the Aṅgas, do not part with it.

Karṇa. King Śalya, do not prevent me. Look you—

Learning comes to nought in course of time. Firmly-rooted trees are thrown down. Even in reservoirs water is dried up. But gifts and oblations last for ever. **(22)**

So take it. [*Cuts off the armour and gives it to the sage.*]

Indra. [*Taking the armour. Aside.*] I have them. Now have I done what the gods decreed aforetime for Arjuna's victory. So shall I mount Airāvata[1] and witness the mighty combat between Arjuna and Karṇa. [*Exit.*]

Śalya. King of Aṅga, you have been cheated.

Karṇa. By whom?

Śalya. By Indra.

Karṇa. Not at all; I have cheated Indra. For—

I have contented Indra, that punished Pāka,[2] and destroyed hosts of Dānavas—Indra, who possesses Arjuna, whose hands are rough from patting the celestial elephant, while the twice-born have to propitiate him with the oblations of innumerable sacrifices. (**23**)

[*Enter an Angel disguised as a brahman.*]

Angel. Karṇa, Indra is grateful to you and regrets taking your armour and ear-rings. So he sends this spear, named Vimalā, an unfailing weapon to slay one of the Pāṇḍavas. Pray accept it.

Karṇa. O fie! I do not take a return for a gift.

Angel. Nay, take it at a brahman's bidding.

Karṇa. At a brahman's bidding? That have I never disregarded. When shall I get it?

Angel. When you bring it to mind.

Karṇa. Very well. I thank you. You may return.

Angel. So be it. [*Exit.*]

Karṇa. King Śalya, let us mount the car.

Śalya. Very well. [*They gesticulate getting into the chariot.*]

Karṇa. Ah! I hear some noise. What can it be?

'Tis the sound of a conch like the roar of the ocean at the end of the world. Can it be Kṛishṇa's? No, it is Arjuna's. With his heart enraged by Yudhishṭhira's defeat, he will fight to-day with all his strength. (**24**)

King of the Śalyas, drive my car where Arjuna may be.

Śalya. Very well.

EPILOGUE.

Be there good fortune everywhere, may misfortune disappear for ever. May our King alone, endowed with royal virtues, rule the earth! (**25**)

[*Exeunt ambo.*]

FINIS.

[1] Airāvata, name of Indra's elephant. [2] A demon.

THE BROKEN THIGHS

(*Ūrubhaṅgam*)

INTRODUCTION

THE great battle of the Kurus and the Pāṇḍavas culminated in the duel between the gigantic Bhīma and Duryodhana, the champion of the Kurus. They fought with maces. Bhīma was all but defeated when with a mighty effort he struck a foul blow and broke Duryodhana's thighs. This play is the tragedy of Duryodhana's defeat and death.

In the Mahābhārata there is a section called *Gadāyuddha-parvan* (LXXXII in the IXth Book). Duryodhana (32) challenges the Pāṇḍavas to a single combat. Yudhishṭhira agrees, but Kṛishṇa says he has made a mistake. Nobody can defeat Duryodhana in an honest fight. Bhīma defies Duryodhana. Baladeva comes to see the fight and the two champions fall upon each other (34).

After a digression the story goes on (55). All repair to Samanta-pañcaka. Bhīma and Duryodhana face each other; the princes make a circle round them. The champions abuse each other and fall to with their maces (57). Duryodhana breaks Bhīma's coat-of-mail. Krishṇa tells Arjuna that Bhīma cannot win by honest fighting. Then Arjuna slaps his left thigh, so that Bhīma sees him. Bhīma smashes Duryodhana's thighs (58). Bhīma scorns the fallen warrior and mishandles him. Yudhishṭhira restrains Bhīma and speaks solicitous words to Duryodhana. Baladeva blames Bhīma for breaking the law of fighting. Kṛishṇa holds him back and argues the point. Baladeva is not convinced; he praises Duryodhana and promises Bhīma a bad reputation. He takes himself off.

Kṛishṇa approves what has happened and congratulates the king on regaining the realm. Warriors praise Bhīma. Kṛishṇa advises them to go home and reviles Duryodhana. Duryodhana raises himself half-way up and abuses Kṛishṇa for his cunning. Kṛishṇa answers with repeated reproaches. Duryodhana congratulates himself that he has had the greatest loss on earth and will now go to heaven. Heaven indicates its concurrence. All are depressed at this, but Kṛishṇa assures them that their powerful opponents could not have been killed in lawful warfare, and dismisses them to their homes (61). They go to the Kuru camp. Kṛishṇa is sent to Hastināpura to conciliate Gāndhārī. He endeavours to console Dhṛitarāshṭra and Gāndhārī and then returns. When the remaining Kurus hear what has happened they seek out Duryodhana. Aśvatthāmā swears he will destroy the Pāñcālas. At Duryodhana's command Kṛipa brings a vessel of water and Aśvatthāmā is consecrated to the command of the army. The three Kurus leave Duryodhana and depart. The next section is called *Sauptikaparvan* (X. LXXIII) and describes the night attack on the Pāṇḍava camp. At the end of it Duryodhana expresses his satisfaction and goes to heaven.

It will be obvious on reading this play that our dramatist represents the story in a very different way from that in the epic.

First we may note a feature of the construction of the play. There is only one act with as many as sixty-six verses, but this is introduced by an Interlude or Introductory Scene (*Vishkambhaka*), in which three soldiers (*bhaṭa*), reciting verses in turn, give us a description of battle, of the battle-ground, and of innumerable corpses. Then they tell us of the fight with maces between Bhīma and Duryodhana, that Bhīma is struck down, and Duryodhana taunts him. Then that Kṛishṇa makes a secret sign, striking his own thigh; that Bhīma with a mighty effort and with both his arms hurls the mace on his opponent's thighs. Bhīma is led away by the Pāṇḍavas and Balarāma is very angry.

This long description of what is happening reminds us of the three priests describing the sacrifice in *The Five Nights*, and, to a lesser degree, of the descriptions of the fight in the same play.

Baladeva opens the next scene, and Duryodhana crawls in with both thighs broken. Baladeva threatens vengeance, but Duryodhana, the wicked prince, shows a saintly resignation.

Then the dramatist brings on to the field of battle the old blind king Dhṛitarāshṭra and his devoted wife Gāndhārī, who, according to the epic story, were miles away at Hastināpura. With them come two queens of the fallen prince and his little son.[1] There is a poignant passage, with the boy attempting to climb on his father's knees. All this has been invented. Duryodhana preaches reconciliation to his son and looks for death.

Aśvatthāmā, the son of the old preceptor Droṇa, enters and declares he will slay the Pāṇḍavas. Duryodhana attempts to dissuade him, but he swears he will do it by a raid at night. Baladeva bears witness to the oath. Aśvatthāmā declares Durjaya the heir to the kingdom. (By the compact the realm should go to the Pāṇḍavas and Aśvatthāmā was made commander in the epic.) Then Duryodhana is satisfied. He has

[1] There is nothing about a son of Duryodhana in the epic. Another Duryodhana was the son of a Durjaya.

a vision of his ancestors, which recalls the old king's death in *The Statue Play*,[1] and he dies. They cover him with a cloth.

As we have seen, Duryodhana in the epic died after the night raid, and between his wounding and his death showed a much fiercer spirit.

This death on the stage is remarkable—it has been introduced deliberately, though not in place according to the story, to round off the tragedy. It is against the canons of orthodox Sanskrit dramaturgy. Whoever be the author, we have here a tragedy written for the Indian stage.

Does it date from a time before the convention was fixed, or does it represent a defiance of that convention at a later date? If the play were ancient, it might be expected that later editors would try their hands in adding descriptive verses of their own. This might account for minor inconsistencies.

[1] Compare also the death of Vālin in *The Consecration*.

DRAMATIS PERSONAE

(In order of appearance.)

Stage-manager
Assistant of the Manager } in the Prologue.

Three Soldiers of Duryodhana's army, who describe the battlefield and then the duel with maces.

Baladeva or Balarāma, the wielder of the Plough (Halāyudha), elder brother of Kṛishṇa.

DURYODHANA, eldest of the hundred sons of the blind king Dhṛitarāshṭra, leader of the Kurus.

Dhṛitarāshṭra, the old blind king.

Gāndhārī, his wife, who wore a bandage on her eyes.

Mālavī, one of Duryodhana's Queens.

Pauravī, another of Duryodhana's Queens.

Durjaya, Duryodhana's young son.

Aśvatthāmā, son of the old preceptor Droṇa.

PROLOGUE

[*After the Opening enter the Stage-manager.*]

Stage-manager. May the Lord Keśava ferry you over a flood of enemies, as he ferried Arjuna over the torrent of his foes—a torrent gravelly with blades and shafts, with Bhīshma and Droṇa as the guiding banks; wherein the King of Sindh presents the river-water, Gāndhāra's king a whirlpool, and Aṅgas' king a wave; a stream with Droṇa's son as alligator, with Kṛipa as a crocodile, and with Duryodhana as the tearing current. (1)

With these words, my lords and gentlemen, I have to announce to you—But what is that? I thought I heard a noise just as I was to make my announcement. Well, I must see what it is.

[*Voices behind the scene.*]

Oh! Here we are, here we are!

Manager. Good. I understand.

[*Enter an Assistant.*]

Assistant. Where do these people come from, Master?

Officers are rushing to and fro, touchstones of each other's valour, ready to sacrifice their persons in the van of battle for the sake of heaven. Their limbs are jagged with a hundred arrows and javelins, their bodies chiselled by the tusks of raging elephants. (2)

Manager. Don't you understand, my lad? Duryodhana is the sole survivor on the side of Dhṛitarāshṭra bereft of a hundred sons and wisdom. On Yudhishṭhira's side only the Pāṇḍavas and Janārdana remain. Kurukshetra's plain [1] is strewn with the corpses of kings.

Here is a picture crammed with soldiers and kings, horses and elephants slain in battle; the drawing seems confused. The combat of Bhīma and Suyodhana begins. Their warriors have entered the one house of death for lords of men. (3)

[*Exeunt ambo.*]

END OF THE PROLOGUE.

[1] Sāmantapañcaka, the place in Kurukshetra where Paraśu-Rāma (Rāma with the axe) is said to have slain the Kshatriya race.

INTERLUDE

[*Enter three Soldiers.*]

All together. Oh! here we are, here we are!

First Soldier. We have arrived at the hermitage called battle, the home[1] of hostility and touchstone of valour. This is the abode of pride and glory. This is where warriors assemble to be chosen as bridegrooms by the nymphs of heaven. This is the place of manly prowess, a hero's couch for the death of kings, a burnt sacrifice of lives, a prince's bridge to heaven. (4)

Second Soldier. You speak truly.

The ground is rugged with heaps of elephants' corpses like huge boulders. On every side are vultures' nests. Chariots are empty of their champions. Kings of the earth have gone to heaven; yet such deeds have they done face to face in the battle, where all are busy with death, that they are not killed, though slain long since. (5)

Third Soldier. It is even so.

The battle rite proceeds; a sacrifice, where warriors fall as victims, and roars, as of lions, supply the sacred chanting. In that rite, lit with the fire of hostility, sacrificial posts are seen in the trunks of elephants, sacrificial grass in the litter of arrows, the woodstack in the pile of slaughtered tuskers and in the floating banners, the celestial cars. (6)

First Soldier. Look you on this other side.

Kings lie heaped upon the battleground bereft of life by each other's shafts, and these birds with blood-stained beaks loosen the ornaments from their bodies. (7)

Second Soldier. An elephant arrayed and ready for battle is overthrown by the force of a shower of arrows and sinks down with armour broken, like a royal arsenal, with bows and arrows. (8)

Third Soldier. Here's another thing, look you.

As women-folk help a daughter's husband down from the car, so do eager jackals drag down the dead warrior from the front of the chariot with his jewelled quiver, and a necklace of skulls made of garlands fallen from the top of banner poles. (9)

All together. Oh! How frightful is this battleground, Sāmantapañcaka. The ground is soaked with the blood of horses, men, and elephants,

[1] Reading *Āyatanam*.

wounded and slain. There is a confused mass of torn mail, skins, umbrellas, chowries, javelins, arrows, spears, and armour mixed with headless trunks, and a litter of every sort of weapon—pikes and darts, spears [1] and cross-bolts,[2] spikes and maces, hammers, boars' ears,[3] lances, arrows, swords, and clubs.

First Soldier. Here, indeed.

Rivers of blood are crossed by bridges of elephants' corpses. Steeds draw chariots devoid of princes, whence the charioteers have fallen. When heads are severed, trunks rush on by force of habit. Maddened elephants without a rider are wandering everywhere. **(10)**

Second Soldier. Again, see this.

Vultures, with tawny eyes as big as arrac seeds, with beaks as sharp as goads,[4] and huge long wings outspread, gleam in the sky like fans, with bits of flesh for coral. **(11)**

Third Soldier. The earth shows clearly all around in the pitiless rays of the sun slaughtered warriors and kings, elephants and chargers; it seems to support a host of fallen stars, covered as it is with darts and lances, arrows, javelins, and swords. **(12)**

First Soldier. Even in such a plight warriors do not lose their splendour but look magnificent. For here—

Kings' faces, free from fear, represent a still lotus of the land; their eyes turned up once for ever are the swarming bees, their dark red lips supply a multitude of shoots; their knitted brows pourtray the curving filaments; raised aloft on arrow stalks in the van of battle they sleep unstirred by the sun of valour. **(13)**

Second Soldier. Death prevails over even such warriors as these. It is impossible for less fortunate men to support the power of a king.

Third Soldier. What, then—does death prevail over warriors?

First Soldier. No doubt of it.

Second Soldier. Nay, say not so.

'Twas Arjuna to-day that perforce did introduce to Death those proud and insolent kings with arrows remaining from his fierce fight with Śiva, Arjuna twanging his bow in the van of battle, with the string blackened by the smoke of the Khāṇḍava forest, that bow that destroyed the sworn

[1] *Hāṭaka*, 'a golden spear'.

[2] *Bhiṇḍipāla* (also *bhindipāla* and other spellings), a missile shaped like a pestle and tipped with iron.

[3] Omitting *kaṇaya*, meaning unknown. (? shot).

[4] Lit. 'With beaks as sharp as the bent goad of the elephant of the Demon King'.

confederates,[1] sacrificed the life of demons in impenetrable armour, and removed the distress of heaven. **(14)**

All Together. Aha! a sound.

Is it thunder in the clouds? Are mountains being powdered by a flight of thunderbolts? Or is the earth being torn asunder by convulsions reverberating with tumultuous roar? Or is it the roaring of the sea, seething with a multitude of billows lashed into wild fury by the wind and breaking against the caves in the cliff of Mandara? **(15)**

Well, let us see. [*All step round.*]

First Soldier. Ah! here has begun the duel with maces between the middle Pāṇḍava, Bhīmasena, furious at the dragging of Draupadī by the hair, and the emperor Duryodhana enraged at the slaughter of a hundred brothers. Dvaipāyana, Halāyudha, Kṛishṇa, Vidura, and the other worshipful chiefs of the Kuru and Yadu races are looking on.

Second Soldier. Bhīma's chest, broad as a slab of burnished gold, is struck a violent blow. Duryodhana's muscular shoulders, hard as the trunk of Indra's elephant, are torn open. Weapons cling betwixt and beside their two arms. And with it all there goes up the din made by the violent strokes of the maces. **(16)**

Third Soldier. Here is the Emperor.

His crest is quivering with a skilful shake, his face and eyes are swollen with rage, his body dwarfed as he approaches crouching, and his hands held high aloft. The mace uplifted in his right hand and soaked with his enemy's blood shines like Indra's thunderbolt resting on the highest peaks of Mount Kailāśa.[2] **(17)**

First Soldier. Behold the Pāṇḍava with limbs besmeared with blood from mighty blows.

The blood gushes from his broken forehead, the points of each shoulder are shattered; his huge chest is drenched in gore running in streams from his wounds. Sorely wounded and bleeding from strokes of the mace, Bhīma shines like the mountain Meru with its boulders dyed by streams red with minerals. **(18)**

Second Soldier. He hurls the dreadful mace. He roars as he leaps aside; he quickly lifts his arm and parries the other's stroke.

[1] Trigarta and his brothers who took an oath to slay Arjuna but perished themselves.
[2] Reading doubtful.

He takes a forward step[1] and strikes without remission. The king is well trained, but Bhīma is the stronger. (19)

Third Soldier. Bhīma[2] now,

Matchless in battles, huge as a mountain, with a deep cut on his head drenching his limbs with blood, sinks on the earth like Golden Peak, the king of mountains, struck by a thunderbolt, and running with ruddy ores dislodged. **(20)**

Seeing Bhīma falling, his limbs loosened by a blow of the mace,

Vyāsa stands amazed, his face upturned resting on a single finger.

Second Soldier. Yudhishṭhira is dismayed, Vidura is blinded with tears.

Third Soldier. Arjuna is fingering the Gāṇḍīva bow, Kṛishṇa is gazing at the sky.

All Together. Bala-rāma,[3] a spectator of the battle, from love of his pupil brandishes his plough. **(21)**

First Soldier. Here the Emperor,

Abiding place of valour, his crest flashing with many a jewel, endowed with pride and dignity with majesty and fortitude, speaks a word in mockery. 'Fear not, Bhīma, no hero smites a foe prostrate in battle.' **(22)**

Second Soldier. Now seeing Bhīmasena ridiculed, Kṛishṇa makes a secret sign striking his own thigh.

Third Soldier. That sign has comforted the Wind God's son.[4]

Knitting a frown[5] on his forehead, wiping away the sweat, then grasping his mace 'Citrāṅgadā' with both hands, with strength renewed by the Wind God,[6] who saw his son prostrate, he rises once more from the ground roaring like a lion-bull. **(23)**

First Soldier. Oh! the duel with maces has begun again.

The son of Pāṇḍu rubs his palms upon the ground, bites his lips with intense force, roars with furious rage and with a swift long sweep of both his arms—forgetting love of righteousness, forsaking rules of war, but following Kṛishṇa's sign—he hurls the mace on Duryodhana's thighs. **(24)**

All Together. Alas! the Emperor has fallen.

Third Soldier. Seeing the Kuru king falling with limbs bled white, the Blessed Vyāsa[7] has risen to the sky.

[1] Cārī, 'a step in dancing , M. W.

[2] Vṛikodara 'Wolf-belly'.

[3] Rāma here equals Balarāma, also called Halāyudha, having a plough as a weapon, the elder brother of Kṛishṇa, also called Baladeva.

[4] Bhīma was said to be the son of Vāyu.

[5] Reading *bhrūkuṭīm*.

[6] *Sarvagati*.

[7] Dvaipāyana. According to the Epic he was not present.

Lightly covering his eyes Balarāma shuts out the view. Bhīma sees the Wielder of the Plough has shut his eyes in anger on Duryodhana's behalf, and at Vyāsa's bidding is led away by the startled Pāṇḍavas in their hands enlaced, while Kṛishṇa supports his steps. **(25)**

First Soldier. Why Balarāma with eyes closed in anger, has perceived the flight of Bhīmasena and comes this very way. Here he is,

His lovely crest in disarray, his eyes dilated red with rage, he draws up a little way the garland bitten by bees. Dragging the garments hanging loose on his dark[1] body he looks like a moon with a halo descended to the ground. **(26)**

Second Soldier. Come let us attend on the Emperor.

The other two. Very well, a good suggestion.

[*Exeunt omnes.*]

END OF INTERLUDE.

[*Enter Baladeva.*]

Baladeva. Ho, ye kings! this is not right.

Unmindful of my plough—that is death to the force of foes, recking nothing, in his pride, of me or the violation of the law of battle, he hurled that mace on Duryodhana's thighs in the forefront of the fight, bringing him low with the fortune of his house. **(27)**

Duryodhana, live on a little while,

Till to-day on the broad chest of Bhīma, ripely wet with sweat and blood, I make my plough groan as it furrows heavily through that field. To that ploughshare still cling remains of Saubha.[2] It was a hook for the high rampart of the great Asura city, a guide to Yamunā's waters, appeased by the oblations of countless foemens' lives. **(28)**

[*Voice behind the scene.*]

Be merciful, blessed Wielder of the Plough, be merciful.

Baladeva. Even in this plight the wretched Duryodhana follows me.

He is glorious, his lustre smeared wet with blood, the sandal-paste of battle. Arms dusty white from crawling on the ground, he has taken an infant's role. He is like Vāsuki[3] set loose from the mountain by gods and demons, when the nectar-

[1] *Asita*. But Balarāma is said to have been fair. Sarup thinks *pāriveṣī* means 'wrapped in clouds'.

[2] Saubha, aerial city.

[3] Vāsuki, the serpent twisted round the mountain Mandara at the churning of the ocean.

churning was complete; abandoned and exhausted it drags its coils in the ocean waters. **(29)**

[*Enter Duryodhana with both thighs broken.*]

Duryodhana. Here, alas, am I,

Both thighs crushed with a mace-blow by Bhīma, who has broken the law of fighting, crawling on the ground with my two arms I drag along my body half extinct. **(30)**

Be merciful, blessed Wielder of the Plough, be merciful.

For the first time to-day my head falls at thy feet, myself fallen on the earth. Quench thy wrath. Victory to the funeral clouds[1] of the Kuru race. An end has come to our hostility, to the reason of the war, and to ourselves. **(31)**

Baladeva. O Duryodhana, live on a little while.

Duryodhana. What are you going to do?

Baladeva. Listen,

To thy warriors slain in battle with chariots, elephants, and horses and faring to heaven, I will give the sons of Pāṇḍu, their bodies furrowed by my ploughshare hurled upon them, their hearts and shoulders torn asunder by pestle blows. **(32)**

Duryodhana. Nay, say not so,

Bhīma has fulfilled his vow, my hundred brothers have gone to heaven, myself have come to such a pass, Balarāma. What can war do now? **(33)**

Baladeva. He tricked you before my eyes. That has made me angry.

Duryodhana. You think that I was tricked?

Baladeva. No doubt of it.

Duryodhana. Alas! My life it seems is the price I pay.

Bhīma had the wit to extricate himself from the dreadful house of lac all ablaze. In the battle in Kubera's abode he matched the onrush of mountain rocks. He it was that took the life of Hiḍimba, the lord of giants. If you think that Bhīma has vanquished me to-day by a trick, why, Balarāma, he has not beaten me. **(34)**

[**Baladeva.** Having tricked you in the fight is Bhīmasena to survive?

Duryodhana. What, was I tricked by Bhīmasena?

Baladeva. Why, what brought you to this plight?

Duryodhana. Hearken—

He that defied Indra and likewise stole his coral tree, he that for a whim slept a thousand celestial years in the ocean waters, 'twas he, Hari, the darling of the world, with his innate love of

[1] *nivāpa-meghāḥ.*

battle, that suddenly entered into Bhīmas sharp mace and gave me over to death. (35)][1]

[*Voice behind the scene.*]

Out of the way, sirs, out of the way.

Baladeva. (*Looking off.*) Ah! here comes his majesty Dhṛitarāshṭra led by Gāndhārī and Durjaya, and the ladies of the palace are with him. His heart is overcome with grief.

He is a mine of fortitude, the sight of his eyes distributed among a hundred sons. Upstanding in his dignity, his long arms are like the golden pillars of the sacrifice. At his birth the gods misdoubted them of protecting heaven and smote his eyes with a handful of malignant darkness. (36)

[*Enter Dhṛitarāshṭra with Gāndhārī, two Queens and Durjaya.*]

Dhṛitarāshṭra. My son, where are you?

Gāndhārī. My child, where are you?

Queens. Where are you, my lord?

Dhṛitarāshṭra. Alas!

To-day when I heard of my son struck down in the battle by a trick, my blind face was made still blinder by the tears streaming in my eyes. (37)

Gāndhārī, are you still there?

Gāndhārī. Still bound to life, unhappy that I am.

Queens. Oh! Majesty, alas!

Duryodhana. Woe is me, even my queens are wailing.

Before that I hardly felt the pain of the mace's blow, but now I have it fully, when my women folk come into the field with their tresses exposed to view. (38)

Dhṛitarāshṭra. Gāndhārī, can you see that champion of our house, Duryodhana?

Gāndhārī. Majesty, I do not see him.

Dhṛitarāshṭra. What, not see him? Now am I cursed by fate[2] that I cannot see my son at the time of need.

Proud of begetting a hundred sons, wise and brave, splendid in pride and valour, destruction to the enemies' ranks, does Dhṛitarāshṭra not deserve to have a funeral oblation scattered on the ground by one of his sons at least? (39)

Gāndhārī. Suyodhana, my child, answer me, and his unhappy majesty bereaved of a hundred sons.

[1] Seems to be a later addition.

[2] Reading the nominative for *kṛtānta-ataka*, but perhaps a word is omitted after *adyāsmi*. 'Now am I (unfortunate) that... Oh, wretched fate.'

Baladeva. Ah! Queen Gāndhārī!

Her eyes never yearned to see the faces of her sons and grandsons, but now her fortitude is exhausted by grief at Duryodhana's downfall. She wears the bandage on her eyes—symbol of devotion to her lord, but now it is ceaselessly wetted with her tears. **(40)**

Dhṛitarāshṭra. Duryodhana, my son, sovereign commander of eighteen divisions—where are you?

Duryodhana. A fine sovereign to-day!

Dhṛitarāshṭra. Eldest of five score brothers—answer me.

Duryodhana. I'll tell you another story! How this business shames me!

Dhṛitarāshṭra. Come, my son, and greet me.

Duryodhama. Here I come. [*Makes as if to rise but falls again.*]

Alas! this is a second blow. Alack! To-day when Bhīmasena seized me by the hair [1] and hurled his mace, he did not rob me of my thighs alone, but also of the salutation to my father's feet. **(41)**

Gāndhārī. Here, my daughters.

Queens. We are here, lady.

Gāndhārī. Seek out your husband.

Queens. I go, unhappy.

Dhṛitarāshṭra. Who is it leading me, pulling the hem of my robe?

Durjaya. 'Tis I, grandpa, Durjaya.

Dhṛitarāshṭra. Go and look for your father, Durjaya.

Durjaya. I am so tired.

Dhṛitarāshṭra. Run along, you can rest on your father's knees.

Durjaya. I am off, grandpa. [*Approaching.*] Daddy where are you?

Duryodhana. Oh, he has come too. Come what may, my love for my boy is close to my heart, and now it burns me? For,

Innocent of sorrows, eager to rest on my knees, what will Durjaya say when he sees me vanquished? **(42)**

Durjaya. Here is the king, sitting on the ground.

Duryodhana. Why have you come, my son?

Durjaya. You were away so long.

Duryodhana. Ah me! even in this plight my heart burns with love of my boy.

Durjaya. I'll sit on your lap. [*Tries to climb on to his knees.*]

Duryodhana. [*Preventing him.*] O Durjaya, Durjaya, alas!

This crescent moon, delight of my eyes and heart's delight, by change of circumstance becomes a burning fire. **(43)**

[1] Not consistent with verses 23 and 24.

Durjaya. Why won't you let me sit on your lap?

Duryodhana. My son, give up thy wonted seat. Sit anywhere, but from to-day, thou canst sit no more where thou wast wont to sit. **(44)**

Durjaya. Why, where are you going?

Duryodhana. I'll follow my hundred brothers.

Durjaya. Take me with you.

Duryodhana. Go, my son, and talk to Bhīma.

Durjaya. Come, father, they are looking for you.

Duryodhana. Who are?

Durjaya. Granny and grandpa and all the ladies.

Duryodhana. Go, my son, I cannot come.

Durjaya. I'll take you.

Duryodhana. You are too young, my son.

Durjaya. [*Stepping round.*] Ladies, the king is here.

Queens. Woe, woe, the king.

Dhṛitarāshṭra. Where is the king?

Gāndhārī. Where is my child?

Durjaya. He's here sitting on the ground.

Dhṛitarāshṭra. Alas, is this the king?

In stature he was like a golden pillar, the sole overlord of kings in the world, and now my miserable son lies on the ground no better than the broken bolt of a door. **(45)**

Gāndhārī. Suyodhana, my child, are you tired?

Duryodhana. I am your ladyship's son.

Dhṛitarāshṭra. Who is that?

Gāndhārī. 'Tis I, great king, that gave thee fearless sons.

Duryodhana. Now to-day I feel that I am born indeed. Come, father, there is now no need of anxiety.

Dhṛitarāshṭra. Why should I be anxious, son?

Thy hundred brothers puffed up with strength and courage, consecrated for the sacrifice of battle, were already slain; with thy single death all 's dead. **(46)**

[*Falls.*]

Duryodhana. Alas, the king has fallen. Oh, father, do you console the queen.

Dhṛitarāshṭra. What consolation can I give, my son?

Duryodhana. Why, say that I was slain facing the foe. For my sake, father restrain your grief.

At thy feet alone I bow my crest, without thought of the

blazing fire within I depart for heaven, as proudly as I was born. (**47**)

Dhṛitarāshṭra. I am an old man, blind from birth, with no desire for life. Bitter grief for my sons curbs my will, overspreads my soul and overwhelms me. (**48**)

Baladeva. Alas! He has lost all hope for Duryodhana, his eyes are ever closed. I have no heart to announce myself in his exalted presence. (**49**)

Duryodhana. I would ask a favour from your ladyship.

Gāndhārī. Speak out, my son.

Duryodhana. With folded hands I ask, if I have earned any merit, be thou my mother in another life. (**50**)

Gāndharī. 'Tis my own wish you have expressed.

Duryodhana. Mālavī, listen.

My forehead was shattered by blows of a mace inflicted during a duel. On my breast there is no space for a necklace, such streams of blood are gushing forth. My two arms, look, are well adorned with wounds as golden bracelets. Thy husband fell in battle facing the foe. Why doest thou weep, warrior-lady? (**51**)

Mālavī. I'm but a girl, your wedded wife, and so I weep.

Duryodhana. Pauravī, listen.

We have performed the desired sacrifices enjoined by scripture, and supported our kinsmen. The beloved five score brothers vanquished the foe. Our dependents were never deceived in us. The kings of eighteen armies were sore pressed in the battle. Think of my glory with pride. Wives of such men do not weep. (**52**)

Pauravī. My mind is all made up where I shall go,[1] and so I weep no more.

Duryodhana. Durjaya, you listen too.

Dhṛitarāshṭra. Gāndhārī, what is he going to say?

Gāndhārī. My own very thought.

Duryodhana. You must obey the Pāṇḍavas like myself. Follow the directions of the lady mother Kuntī, Abhimanyu's mother and Draupadī you must honour like your own mother. Look you, my son,

Grieve no more, but remember your father Duryodhana, of glorious splendour and a heart fired with pride, fell in battle face to face with an equal foe. Then you must touch Yudhishṭhira's mighty arm, the right arm in its linen, and join

[1] *pavesa*, 'entering', i.e. the funeral pyre.

the sons of Pāṇḍu to give me the last oblation uttering my name. **(53)**

Baladeva. Ah! hostility has melted to remorse. What, some noise it seems.

All is still, with never a roll of the battle drums; arrows and mail are cast aside with the chowries and umbrellas of state. Charioteers and warriors lie dead. Who is this then twanging his bow and filling the sky with flocks of frightened crows? **(54)**

[*Voice behind the scenes.*]

As a priest selects a great Horse-sacrifice, so do I come to this crowded battle rite, that first I entered with Duryodhana spanning his bow. **(55)**

Baladeva. Ah! hither comes Aśvatthāmā, the preceptor's son.

Large eyes as clear as lotus petals fully blown, long arms outstretched as fair as posts of gold—as he eagerly draws his dread bow, he is like Mount Meru all ablaze with a rainbow resting on its peak. **(56)**

[*Enter Aśvatthāmā.*]

Aśvatthāmā. [*Repeats the verse,* 'As a priest,' &c., 55.] Oh, hearken to me, ye kings renowned in war, though few survive and life is slowly ebbing with every breath, though your bodies be mutilated by those crocodiles, the weapons upraised when the two oceans of opposing forces flowed together in the battle-storm, hearken, I say, to me.

'Twas the Kuru king had his thighs shattered by fraud, not I. 'Twas the son of the charioteer[1] had a sword that broke and failed, not I. Here to-day I stand alone. Droṇa's son, on the field of victory, with sword drawn in eagerness. **(57)**

But to me too what boots the glory of battle without the praise of victory? [*Steps round.*] Nay not so. The Kuru King, ornament of the Kuru race, was tricked when I was busy with funeral oblations to my father. Who will believe it? For,

Waiting on his word stood the sovereigns of eleven armies, with folded hands held high, mounted on cars and elephants, with bows as other hands; fighting in the fray was Bhīshma, with his mail coat licked by Paraśurāma's arrows and my father; 'tis manifest the hero Duryodhana was defeated by destiny. **(58)**

Now where is Gāndhārī's son? [*Steps and looks around.*] Ah here is the king of the Kurus, he has crossed the ocean of war and lies amid

[1] Karṇa reputed son of Adhiratha.

a rampart of broken chariots and the corpses of men, elephants, and horses. Here he is,

> With the netted beams of his hair fallen dishevelled from his crest, with limbs bleeding from blows of the mace, he sits on the stony seat of his last home [1] and sinks like the westering sun plunging into twilight. (59)

[*Going up to him.*] O king of the Kurus, what is this?

Duryodhana. O son of my preceptor, the result of insatiable ambition.

Aśvatthāmā. King of the Kurus, I am about to abandon the root of righteousness.

Duryodhana. What will you do?

Aśvatthāmā. Listen.

> Kṛishṇa is ready for the fight, riding on Garuḍa's back, with his four [2] dread arms, with his disc and bow aloft—him will I wipe out with a network of shafts, and the sons of Pāṇḍu with him, like a picture where the drawing is confused. (60)

Duryodhana. Nay, say not so.

> The whole host of anointed kings now lies in the lap of mother-earth. Karṇa has gone to heaven. Santanu's son has fallen. My five score brethren have been slain in the van of battle facing the foe and I am brought to this plight. Preceptor's son, unstring thy bow. (61)

Aśvatthāmā. O king of the Kurus,

> When the Pāṇḍava in the fight to-day seized thy hair and cast his mace he broke thy spirit along with thy two thighs. (62)

Duryodhana. Say not so. Kings have pride incarnate. For pride's sake I accepted war. Look you, my preceptor's son,

> How Draupadī aforetime was dragged at the gambling match by tresses grasped and twisted in my hand; how young Abhimanyu, still a boy, was slain in battle, how the Pāṇḍavas on the pretext of the dicing had to dwell in the forest with wild beasts; reflect on this, it is little that those chiefs have done to break my spirit. (63)

Aśvatthāmā. I take an oath by everything.

> By your Highness and by my own soul I swear, and by the heaven of the brave, I will make a raid by night and destroy the Pāṇḍavas in the fight. (64)

Baladeva. Uttered by the preceptor's son, that should come to pass.

Aśvatthāmā. The worshipful Balarāma.

[1] Astaka.

[2] Reading *ashṭārdha*, suggested by the editor of the text.

Dhṛitarāshṭra. Alas, there was a witness to these crooked words.

Aśvatthāmā. Durjaya come here.

Be thou king, though unanointed, at the bidding of a priest, of a kingdom inherited through the valour of thy sire, a conqueror by the might of his arms. (65)

Duryodhana. Ah my heart's desire is now fulfilled. My life is slipping away. Here are my revered ancestors Śantanu and the others. There rise my hundred brothers with Karṇa at their head. Here too is angry Abhimanyu seated on Indra's elephant, scolding me. See his side-locks and how Mahendra supports him in his palm. Urvaśī and these other nymphs have come for me. Here are the great oceans manifest. There are the great rivers, Ganges and the rest. Death has sent an aerial car, the wain of heroes, drawn by a thousand swans to fetch me. Here I come. [*Expires.*]

[*They cover him with a cloth.*]

Dhṛitarāshṭra. I'll depart for the penance groves so rich in pious folk. Out on a realm made valueless by the loss of my sons!

Aśvatthāmā. Now do I depart, my bowman's hand uplifted for the slaughter of the sleepers.

May the King destroy all enemies and protect the earth. (66)

[*Exeunt omnes.*]

FINIS.

AVIMĀRAKA

(*Sheep-killer*)

INTRODUCTION

To call this play *The Magic Ring* would lay rather too much emphasis on the ring that caused invisibility. That familiar motif is subordinate to the main story of the Hero which is based on an ancient fairy tale[1]—and which is alluded to by the name Sheep-killer. Nevertheless the ring is an important element in the play. It saves the Hero from suicide and enables him to find his way back to his beloved in the palace he has left as a fugitive. Such a title as *The Magic Ring* would at once suggest some such incident. *Avimāraka*, 'Sheep-killer,' needs some explanation. It is the name of the Hero, who has rescued the Heroine from an elephant just before the play begins. In spite of his gallant conduct it appears he is an outcaste. This seems incredible and we soon suspect that he is a prince in disguise. But outcaste or prince why should he be named 'Sheep-killer'? The explanation comes in the last act, which reveals his history.

Once upon a time there were two sisters, Sudarśanā and Sucetanā. The elder married the king of Benares, but her firstborn was really the son of Agni, the God of Fire. Sucetanā, who married the king of the Sauvīras, secretly adopted her sister's child and brought him up as the Sauvīra prince with the name of Vishṇusena. Semi-divine he grew up with amazing beauty and, while still a child, slew a demon disguised in the form of a sheep. So the people gave him the nickname of 'Sheep-killer'.

Now the king of the Sauvīras, the Hero's reputed father, was cursed by a sage. Out hunting he happened to come upon the holy man, just when his pupil had been mauled by a tiger. The angry ascetic blamed the king and would not listen to his explanation. The king lost his temper and abused the sage.

> 'Unworthy vessel of penance thou by reason of thine anger—
> in form a sage divine, in fact a savage fed on dogs.' (VI. 5.)

[1] Actually traced so far to the eleventh century as in Somadeva's *Kathāsaritsāgara*, B. K. 16, but doubtless much older.

This last word *Śvapāka*—a dog-cooking outcaste—is unforgivable. The sage blazes with anger and curses him.

> 'Whereas a great sage divine like me has been styled an outcaste, so shall thou with wife and son sink to the level of outcastes.' (VI. 6.)

However, the ban was limited to a year, which comes to an end before the play finishes. During the year the king of the Sauvīras, his queen Sucetanā, and Avimāraka were living as outcastes in Kuntibhoja's city, and Avimāraka rescued the princess Kuraṅgī, Kuntibhoja's daughter.

In the play it is clearly indicated that the outcaste youth must be other than he seems. Indeed the audience might well know the outline of the story of Avimāraka. But the full explanation is kept for the last act.

The king and queen are discussing the question of Kuraṅgī's marriage when a minister brings in tidings of the princess being attacked by an elephant. He describes her rescue by a handsome youth, who professed to be low-born. Another minister, Bhūtika, confirms the news. He has made inquiries, but refuses to believe in the youth's ignoble birth. The king orders further investigations to be made and resumes the question of Kuraṅgī's marriage. The King of the Sauvīras had sent an envoy, but now it is learnt that both the king and the prince of that country have disappeared. In the meantime the king of Benares has sent an ambassador to sue for Kuraṅgī's hand, that is for his son Jayavarman. Decision is postponed. (ACT I.)

An Interlude introduces us to the Jester, Avimāraka's companion, who is fooled by a maid from the *palace*. It seems odd that a man living as an outcaste should have a brahman companion. He has to get back to his master's place on the quiet. Yet the maid tricks him by saying 'There's the prince', and the Jester intends to report her conduct to the prince. Evidently she belongs to the household of the king of the Sauvīras.[1]

Avimāraka is sitting at home brooding over the beauty of the princess he has rescued. Kuraṅgī's Nurse and Little Lotus come to look for him. This is a dangerous errand, but the little princess is pining away, longing for a sight of her heroic rescuer. The invitation is conveyed and Avimāraka is to climb into the palace at midnight. He tells the Jester, but refuses to take him with him. (ACT II.)

In the Third Act we see Kuraṅgī with her maidens. Little Lotus tells her that Avimāraka will come.

[1] Not as the Editor suggests to Kuraṅgī's household.

Avimāraka appears disguised as a burglar with a rope and sword. He is supposed to be in the street, and in a long monologue acts the climbing of the wall and finding his way to the princess's apartments. (ACT III.)

In the Interlude introducing the Fourth Act we learn that all has been discovered, the prince has fled, and the princess is broken-hearted.

Avimāraka attempts to throw himself into a forest fire. But the God of Fire is his real father and will not hurt him. Then he determines to throw himself from a precipice. He is diverted from this by the Fairy who gives him the magic ring. He finds his friend the Jester, who is searching for him, and, made invisible by the ring, they enter Kuraṅgī's palace together. (ACT IV.)

Kuraṅgī in the meantime is disconsolate and tries to hang herself. Avimāraka arrives in time to stop her. An amusing scene with the Jester and Little Lotus saves us from an excess of sentiment. The Hero describes the beauty of the rain-clouds and the lovers retire. (ACT V.)

Arrangements are being made for the marriage of Kuraṅgī to the prince of Benares. The king of the Sauvīras, now free from the curse that had reduced him to the status of an outcaste, comes to see Kuntibhoja, Kuraṅgī's father. He tells the story of the curse and how Vishṇusena came to be called Avimāraka.

Nārada the celestial busybody arrives to put things right, and explains the divine origin of Vishṇusena, and his marriage with Kuraṅgī—a love marriage by mutual consent. The prince of Benares is promised Kuraṅgī's younger sister and all is well that ends well. (ACT VI.)

As we do not know what version of the Avimāraka story was familiar to our dramatist, it is not possible to determine how much is original in the plot of this play. It is clear that the Avimāraka story has been combined with another of a magic ring.[1] The subject of the Gāndharva marriage by mutual consent is handled with admirable discretion and delicacy.

The First Act with the discussion about Kuraṅgī's marriage and the obvious hint to the audience recalls the Second Act of *The Minister's Vows*.

The scenes with the Jester are as lively as others in this series, and the dialogue of the Hero with the Nurse is amusing. The most characteristic passages in the play are the monologues of Avimāraka, his brooding, his sentimental burglary, and his attempts at suicide. The

[1] See Introd. to Weller's Translation, p. 13.

descriptions of darkness (III. 3, 4) and of a city at night are striking. The passage about the Fairy's sword (IV. 15) appears to be spurious, and the text of the Sixth Act seems to be badly preserved. The explanations of this Act are necessary, but the ending with mutual complements seems rather feeble.

The final benedictory verse is identical with that of *The Minister's Vows.*

DRAMATIS PERSONAE

(In order of appearance.)

Stage-manager } in Prologue.
Actress }

KING, i. e. Kuntibhoja of Vairantya, father of Kuraṅgī.

Portress, Ketumālī.

Queen, wife of Kuntibhoja.

Attendant in Kuntibhoja's palace. (Jayasena.)

Kauñjāyana, Minister of Kuntibhoja.

Bhūtika, Minister in charge of the princess's palace.

JESTER, Santushṭa, companion of Avimāraka.

Maid, Candrikā of Avimāraka's household.

AVIMĀRAKA, the Hero, really Vishṇusena, elder son of Sudarśanā, Queen of Benares and the God of Fire, adopted by Sucetanā, her sister, Queen of the Sauvīras.

Nurse of Princess Kuraṅgī. (Jayadā.)

Little Lotus, maid in attendance on Princess Kuraṅgī.

Maid in Avimāraka's house.

KURAṄGĪ, the Heroine, daughter of Kuntibhoja.

Māgadhikā } Maids in attendance on Princess Kuraṅgī.
Vilāsinī }

Fairy, Vidyādhara.

Saudāminī, the Fairy's ladylove.

Hariṇikā } Serving woman in Kuraṅgī's household.
Vasumitrā }

King of the Sauvīras, husband of Sucetanā and reputed father of Avimāraka.

Nārada, the sage and busybody.

Sudarśanā, Queen of Benares, real mother of Avimāraka. Also of Jayavarman, betrothed to Kuraṅgī, but in the end married to her sister Sumitrā.

PROLOGUE

[At the end of the Opening enter the Stage-manager.]

Stage-Manager. May glorious Nārāyaṇa direct this [1] earth beneath one royal umbrella ; this earth that, poised on the tip of a single tusk,[2] was gently raised from the ocean brine ; this earth that was bestridden by a single foot [3] and shaken in the combat where Diti's son [4] was slain : this earth that, shielded as one realm, Rāma [5] had his joy of, lovingly grasped in his powerful arms. **(1)**

[Looking towards the curtain.]

Madam, come here.

[Enter an Actress.]

Actress. Here I am, sir.

Manager. Your smile, madam, and that eager look reveal something of the thought within. Clearly you have something to say.

Actress. No wonder, sir, they say you are a thought-reader.

Manager. Then speak out freely.

Actress. I want you to take me to the park, I have a pious duty to perform there, a rite for women.

[Voice behind the scene.]

Bhūtika! Do you go to the park to guard the Princess Kuraṅgī. For the elephant, Añjanagiri [6] is in an excited mood.

Manager. Did you hear, madam? The princess has gone to the park. So just now the gardens will have sentries at every entrance. As soon as the princess has returned, we will go with pleasure.

Actress. As you please, sir.

[Exeunt ambo.]

END OF PROLOGUE.

[1] Reading *tām* for *te*.

[2] Of Vishṇu, in the form of the Boar.

[3] Of Vishṇu, in the form of Vāmana, the dwarf, in which form he took the three strides.

[4] Hiraṇya Kaśipu. A Daitya king killed by Vishṇu in the form of the Man Lion.

[5] Vishṇu, in the form of Rāma, slew Rāvaṇa and regained his wife Sītā and the sovereignty of the earth.

[6] 'Mount Antimony.'

ACT I

[*Enter the King with his retinue.*]

King. The sacrifices are performed and the good priests are content with me. Proud monarchs have been taught the taste of fear. Yet, for it all my mind has no delight. For ever is there anxious care for the father of a maid. (**2**)

Ketumatī, go and fetch the queen.

Portress. As my master bids. [*Exit.*]

[*Enter the Queen with her retinue.*]

Queen. Greeting to your Majesty.

King. You always do look pleased, my queen, but to-day you seem more pleased than ever. What is the reason of this delight?

Queen. Why, your Majesty said an ambassador had come for Kuraṅgī's hand. So I shall soon see my son-in-law.

King. Quite so. But we have not yet made up our mind. Come and sit down.

Queen. As your Majesty commands. [*Sits down.*]

King. My queen, marriages should be made after the greatest circumspection. For—

If a girl is given at her father's whim without a thought of the bridegroom's excellence, the woman's passion destroys both houses, as a stream with swollen waters destroys both banks. (**3**)

Ah! some noise. It might be many things. For—

It is distant but seems near; it is so loud. There may be a thousand reasons, but my mind is troubled for Kuraṅgī. (**4**)

Queen. Oh! my little girl has gone to the park.

King. Who is there?

[*Enter an Attendant.*]

Attendant. Greeting to your Majesty. The noble Kauñjāyana has come to make a report.

King. Bring him in at once.

Attendant. As your Majesty commands. [*Exit.*]

[*Enter Kauñjāyana.*]

Kauñjāyana. [*Despondent.*] Hard indeed is a minister's lot. For—

If things go well, folk say it is the royal power, but when they go wrong, then clearly the minister's advice is to blame. It is fine and pleasing to the ear to be dubbed a 'minister', but the wretched men, for all their clever, powerful minds, are subtly punished by their kings. (5)

Jayasena. Where is our lord? What do you say—in the Audience Hall? That place is free of access. [*Steps round hurriedly.*] Pardon, pardon, my lord.

King. Don't be excited. Sit down at your ease and tell your news.

Kauñjāyana. Listen, my lord. You told me to go to the park with the princess.

King. So I did. What then?

Kauñjāyana. The princess went to the park and played about as she pleased. Then on her return an elephant appeared on the scene, blind with rut, dripping with excitement, made all the worse by hearing the merry stories of the menials, men and women. Its face was wet with a shower of ichor. It had thrown its driver and killed him. Its dreadful form was indistinct and cloaked in dust raised from the ground. Like an incarnation of the wind, its swift movements were visible for a moment and gone the next. It seemed to wish to bring censure on your Majesty's ministers, or to display unique courage.

King. The detail may wait. Tell me, is Kuraṅgī all right?

Kauñjāyana. How could she be otherwise while fortune smiles upon your Majesty?

King. Thank heaven! Now you may tell the tale as you like.

Kauñjāyana. Then the common people took to their heels; women could do nothing but scream. Brave men who approached it were knocked down. Then just at the moment when Nītigupta and I were busy inspecting all the accessories in the park, the elephant made a sudden rush at the princess's carriage.

Queen. Oh, dear, what next?

King. Then who rescued the princess?

Kauñjāyana. A handsome youth. [*Breaks off.*]

King. Speak out now freely. Accidents cannot be controlled.

Kauñjāyana. It was a handsome youth, but not conceited; young but modest, brave but courteous, delicate but strong. When the princess was attacked by the elephant he came to the rescue, a hard thing to do at the moment, and without concern he faced the beast.

King. He has paid his debt to chivalry. Proceed.

Kauñjāyana. Then the brute left the princess and, enraged by the playful but vigorous slaps of his hand, suddenly turned on him to kill him.

Queen. I hope he's all right.

King. What then?

Kauñjāyana. Meanwhile Bhūtika and I appeared on the scene. We put the princess into her carriage again and bringing her quickly back sent her into the inner rooms.

King. Aha! this is great negligence. Then why has Bhūtika not presented himself?

Kauñjāyana. Bhūtika asked me to come and tell your Majesty the news. He himself would come directly after finding out tidings of that youth and his connexions.

King. So Bhūtika will come when he has made all inquiries. Tell me, Kauñjāyana, of what family is this youth who aids others in distress?

Kauñjāyana. Sire, he contradicts himself by saying he is low-born.

Queen. Majesty, how could a low-born man be so chivalrous?

King. What can it mean?

[*Enter Bhūtika.*]

Bhūtika. [*Perplexed.*] Ah! What jewels are hidden in the earth. This man's patent heroism puts in the shade some wise peoples' notions of valour. Only one thing troubles me. Why does he conceal his identity and connexions? Rather, who can conceal the sun with his hand? For, in this world—

> Good men at times remain hidden on this earth for private cause or directed by their elders. Then finding others in trouble and wishing to rescue them, they forget their former resolution and stand revealed. (6)

Jayasena, where is our lord? What do you say—'In the Audience Hall'? That place is free of access. I shall enter. [*Enters.*] Ah! here is his Majesty sitting with the Queen. [*Approaches.*] Greeting to your Majesty.

King. My queen, please go within and comfort Kuraṅgī. I shall follow you directly.

Queen. As your Majesty bids. [*Exit.*]

King. What news of the man who risked his life for the sake of others?

Bhūtika. Hearken, my lord. For a while he played with that elephant carelessly and at his ease, as if amusing himself with a pet, turning it this way and that way in zigzags till it was quite bewildered. Then, as if ashamed of his deed and annoyed at the praise of the crowd, he went slowly away to his house with his head bent towards the ground.

King. Ah, I am glad. This is my second piece of luck to-day.

Bhūtika. In the meantime some female elephants were brought up, and by means of these the rogue elephant was captured and put in his stable, and I went off on some pretext to find out tidings of that youth and his connexions.

King. And what is the result? We hear he is low-born.

Bhūtika. Heaven forfend! He could not be. For some reason he is concealing his identity and connexions.

King. Did you question him?

Bhūtika. What need to question him?

His form divine, his speech saintly, with the brilliance of a warrior, tenderness and strength. If he be all that and yet truly of ignoble birth, then fruitless is our toil in studying the Scriptures. (7)

King. [Has he a wife?[1]

Bhūtika. Very probably. I was not interested in that.

King. But, though you avoided seeing his womenfolk], why didn't you question his father?

Bhūtika. I saw the gentleman, a worthy father of a virtuous son—

His shoulders broad and lofty, huge and firm with exercise; his powerful wrist bears the familiar mark of rubbing on a bowstring. Though in concealment, his appearance proclaims his royal birth. He is like the sun hidden behind a cloud but revealed by its radiance. (8)

King. Enough, all that is merely a possibility. You must inquire into this again.

Bhūtika. As my lord commands.

King. But what now is to be done about the ambassador from the king of Benares?

Bhūtika. Sire, hundreds of ambassadors have come and hundreds more will come.

There's nothing in the world to do with them. Great honour comes to the father of a maid. For all kings regard the daughter of a king as wrestlers do the flag. (9)

King. What do you mean?

Bhūtika. I mean that all should not receive the same consideration. One should bear in mind the greater virtue, the present and the future, avoiding haste and procrastination. So the business should be accomplished as befits both time and place.

King. Bhūtika has spoken well. Kauñjāyana, why are you silent?

[1] *Kalatram* ordinarily means 'a wife'. Weller takes it in the sense of 'harem', and so *kalatraṃ svayam aniviṣṭaḥ* ('but I did not enter the harem'). Sarup takes *aniviṣṭaḥ* in the sense of 'unmarried', *svayam* referring to Avimāraka; compare *nirviṣṭaḥ* ('married') in Act vi. 12. So he would translate:

'**King.** Are there any women in his family?

Bhūtika. Yes, he has everything, but he himself is unmarried.'

Weller quotes the authority of Jacobi for regarding these two lines and the next as spurious.

Kauñjāyana. Sire, of all the princes there are two distinguished by a previous connexion—the king of Sauvīra and the king of Benares; both alike in being married to one of your Majesty's sisters, these two your Majesty thought worthy of this alliance. The king of Sauvīra sent an envoy on a previous occasion on behalf of his son. We sent him back, with all honour, under the pretext that the girl was too young. But now the king of Benares has sent an envoy on behalf of his son. Your Majesty is the best authority as to the relative merit of these two.

King. Well said, Kauñjāyana. Bhūtika, leaving all the other kings out of account and taking these two, which has the superiority?

Bhūtika. Kings should not be criticized by servants, for they are masters of the ministers, your Majesty.

King. Enough of your civility. Tell me, what is your opinion?

Bhūtika. Now, I cannot decline to speak. Sire, the kings of Sauvīra and Benares are equal as being husbands of your Majesty's sisters. But the king of Sauvīra has the further advantage of being a brother of the queen.

King. You certainly say nothing contrary to our intention.

Bhūtika. I thank you on both accounts.

King. Why, sir, has not the king of Sauvīra sent another ambassador?

Bhūtika. I have my own suspicions. I said nothing as I thought I would make a thorough inquiry before I spoke.

King. Isn't his Majesty well?

Bhūtika. Spies declare—

> His Majesty and his son have disappeared; the ministers carry on the government. No one can tell the reason and nobody is admitted to the palace. **(10)**

King. Well, what can it mean?

> Is he smitten by passion? Or seized by treacherous ministers? Is he struck by some disease? Or is he putting the loyalty of his people to the test? Has he been cursed by the priests that he takes to penance and is making expiation? Or what is the reason of closing his palace? **(11)**

You must investigate this matter at once.

Bhūtika. As your Majesty commands.

King. Kauñjāyana, what shall we do now about this envoy from Benares?

Kauñjāyana. Under the circumstances he should be shown all honour. Marriages are best arranged with many doorways open.

King. Ah, a minister's mind ever looks to business, not to sentiment.

[*Voice behind the scene.*]

Greeting to our lord and king. Four hours have gone.[1]

Bhūtika. Sire, we can consider the rest within. The time for your bath is passing, and the princess must be comforted. The queen has been expecting you for some time. Also the populace wish to see their lord after this accident.

King. Aho! sovereignty is a heavy burden. For—

First of all there is the law to be observed, then the king himself must probe the workings of ministers' minds. Love and rage must be concealed. He must show himself gentle and stern at the proper moments. He must know what the people are doing and study the kings around him through the eyes of spies. He must take pains to guard his life, yet disregard it in the van of battle. **(12)**

[*Exeunt omnes.*]

END OF THE FIRST ACT.

ACT II

INTERLUDE

[*Enter the Jester.*]

Jester. Ah! These young bloods can't understand distinctions of position. So his highness Avimāraka doesn't think anything of his loss of caste through the curse of a seer or of living in a low-born family. He cares nothing about his parents or his own right judgement. Ever since the day of that dust-up with the elephant, when he saw Kuraṅgī, Kuntibhoja's daughter, he has been like a different man. Tut, tut, to cut it short, he doesn't want to talk even to me. He spends his whole time in a brown study. It is a true proverb that 'Troubles come in shoals'. How can there be an alliance? She a princess and he low-born? Well, I must avoid the censure of the brahmans and must visit some of their houses and so get to my master's place on the quiet.

[*Enter a Maid.*]

Maid. With all this fuss going on in the palace, there isn't much to

[1] Ten *nālikās* of 24 minutes each. Neither four hours after daybreak nor four hours after midday seem suitable for the king's bath. Weller makes it eight hours. Perhaps after counting up to ten *nālikās* one began again. Sarup takes *nālikā* here to be a vessel for bathing. 'Ten vessels are full of water for the king to bathe.' The phrase reoccurs in the Abhisheka-nāṭaka ii. 18.

do; so I've come out to have a look at the town. [*Stepping and looking around.*] Hullo, there goes Master Satisfied. Good, I will liven up the dullness for a while by joking with him. [*Goes towards him and looks up.*] Oh, Kaumudikā, have you found a brahman? What do you say? 'Not yet'?

Jester. What is it, Candrikā?

Maid. I am looking, sir, for a brahman.

Jester. What do you want a brahman for?

Maid. What do you think? Why, to ask him to dinner.

Jester. But what am I, lady, a Buddhist monk?

Maid. Oh, but you don't know the Scriptures.

Jester. How can you say I don't know the Scriptures? Just listen. There's a treatise on drama called Rāmāyaṇa. I learnt up five verses of that in less than a year.

Maid. I know, I know. You are wonderfully learned by heredity.

Jester. Not only learnt the verses, mind you, but know the meaning too. Besides, I have another distinction. It's hard to find a brahman who can read as well as understand.

Maid. Well, then, read this word for me. [*Shows him a signet ring.*]

Jester. [*Aside.*] I don't know what it is; what am I to say?

[*Pondering.*] Yes, that's the thing. [*Aloud.*]

This word is not in my book, lady.

Maid. If you can't read it, you must dine without a fee.

Jester. Oh, very well.

Maid. May I just have a look at your own ring?

Jester. Yes, look at mine; it's a beauty.

Maid. [*Taking the ring.*] Oh, there's the prince coming this way.

Jester. [*Turning round and looking.*] Where's his highness? Where?

Maid. I've hoodwinked the silly brahman. Now I'll mix with the crowd, give him the slip in the square, and get away. [*Exit.*]

Jester. [*Looking all round.*] Candrikā, Candrikā! Where has she gone? Oh, I have been robbed. I knew what she was, the pickpocket's slut, and then I let myself be diddled by relying on that dinner. [*Stepping round.*] Come to think of it, I believe the dinner was a fake. [*Looking in front.*] Ho! there she is, running away. Stop, stop, you wicked hussy! Stop, I say. Run, will she? Well, I will run too. [*Runs.*] My feet stick to the same spot like those of a man pursued by an elephant in a dream. Dash it, I'll report this minx's conduct to the prince. [*Exit.*]

END OF INTERLUDE.

[*Avimāraka discovered seated.*]

Avimāraka. I see her even now, the maid with sad eyes[1] quivering, all confused with fear, her limbs cooled by the spray of the elephant's trunk; finding her constantly in my dreams, when I wake I remember her again, like one that recalls a former birth. (1)

How powerful is the God of Love, for—

From that day on my eyes desire no other form. My heart delights in the thought of her and then despairs. My face grows pale, my body thin. I pass my days in sorrow and my nights in delusion. (2)

But lack of fortitude is unmanly. Brooding over it makes love wax greater. So now I'll brood no more. [*Recollecting.*] How perfectly beautiful she was. Her youth in keeping with her beauty, as dainty as she is young. In her—

Either the Creator has fashioned an image of a damsel's charms, or the brilliance of the Lord of Stars has somehow taken a woman's form. Or else the Goddess of Beauty has abandoned Kṛishṇa, sleeping on his watery couch, and being afraid is dwelling in this monarch's palace in another woman's form. (3)

How now? I have started thinking about her again. Now, what can I do?

My mind will not answer to my will. For—

Firmly forbidden, it regards not that for a single moment, but gallops along the old accustomed track, like the gabbled repetition of a sacred text. (4)

Nay, then, I cannot overcome my mind. I shall think about her. Ah! All the charms of women are collected in one person. [*Sits down absorbed in thought.*]

[*Enter the Nurse and Little Lotus (Nalinikā).*]

Nurse. [*Reflecting.*] It's a risky business. If I do it, it means the disgrace of the royal house. If I don't, it means she perishes. I have considered a lot of different ways. Even now she hides it even from me. Well, hides it, I say, but how can she? Ever since that day she cares nothing for jasmine paste,[2] has no appetite for food, no pleasure in conversing with her friends. She sighs deeply, talks disconnectedly, doesn't know what is said, laughs to herself, weeps in solitude. She pretends she is ill and grows thinner and paler. There is only one

[1] Reading *viṣādi* with editor. [2] *Sumana-varṇaka*, or 'flower ointment'.

thing strange about it all. In all these varied moods, she doesn't let on a word to a single soul, be it from bashfulness, timidity, family pride, or childishness.

Little Lotus. Not a word to any one? Why, she tells me all about it.

Nurse. I know what you mean to say, my dear. Find out what he is, and in any case unite him with the lady.

Little Lotus. How could such a man with such qualities be low-born?

Nurse. There is some doubt about it. I heard the minister say before the queen: 'He's not what he makes out. For some reason he conceals who he is, saying he's of a low caste.'

Little Lotus. Who could he be?

Nurse. But for this doubt, none but this paragon would be the son-in-law.

[*Voice behind the scene.*]

> If there be wealth and beauty, knowledge and valour, how then? Purity of conduct is not found among the ignobly born. Of his family thou shalt hear in sooth when the time comes. Cease doubting of his family and bring this matter to a happy end. (5)

Nurse. My dear, who was it spoke?

Little Lotus. There's nobody to be seen.

Nurse. My body's all of a thrill with hairs bristling. It must have been a god that spoke. And I am sure he is no ordinary mortal.

Little Lotus. There is no doubt left about his family, but I am wondering whether he will do what we tell him. [*Reflects.*] Happy the man who can infatuate her so. In a word, if Love himself had seen the princess's beauty he would be tormented. And so I reckon he too must be in torment.

Nurse. Here's his house, my dear. We came here from curiosity on the day of the fuss with the elephant.

Little Lotus. Look, dear, what a beautiful doorway, and there's been oblations made. Come, let us go in.

Nurse. [*Speaking to a maid behind the scene.*] My good girl, where is your master's son? What do you say—'In the outer hall'?[1] [*Stepping around and looking.*] Here is our young man sitting alone thinking about something.

Little Lotus. Well, dear, let's go in.

Nurse. Yes, let's. [*Goes in.*] Howdido, sir?

[1] *Caüssāle.*

Avimāraka. Ah, how perfectly beautiful she is.

Nurse. [*Puzzled.*] Eh, what's that? Howdido, sir?

Avimāraka. Her bosom languid with her pouting breasts; her slender form overburdened by her hips.

Nurse. Gracious; he's babbling!

Avimāraka. Her face so delightful to the eye, her lips like the *bimba* pith, nature's hue.

Nurse. Happy the person who can infatuate him so.

Avimāraka. If even in danger she has such beauty for eyes to feast on.[1]

Nurse. Our business will be easy.

Avimāraka. What a wealth of graces would there be twixt dalliance? (6)

Nurse. It's herself has turned his head.

Little Lotus. You may well say—'he too must be in torment'.

Nurse. You're about right. Howdido, sir?

Avimāraka. [*Looking round, bashfully.*] Welcome, ladies.

Both Ladies. Are you well, sir?

Avimāraka. On seeing you I must be.

Nurse. Sir, what were you thinking about?

Avimāraka. Science, madam.

Nurse. What's the name of this delightful science you think about all alone?

Avimāraka. Why, madam, the science of union.

Nurse. [*Smiling.*] There we have the lucky word. Science of union may it be.

Avimāraka. [*Aside.*] Now, what is she driving at? Forced by my heart's desires I imagine something very different. [*Aloud.*] Madam, what do you mean?

Nurse. It is to promote a union that we have come. You, sir, speak of union with approval. So our task is all but done. In the palace, in a lonely spot—there's someone there thinking even more of—union. With that person there your honour may well think out the means of union.

Avimāraka. What, is there still some happiness left to me? [*Rising from his seat.*] Madam, you have restored me to life. For—

When I saw her lovely face, her eyes dilated with alarm were a deadly drug to me, exceeding pungent for all their[2] tenderness, and I completely lost my wits. Now, at last, good

[1] Lit. 'to be quaffed in the goblet of eyes'. [2] Properly, of the face.

ladies, your message is the antidote that has made me once more conscious. (7)

Nurse. I am happy, sir, to be so honoured. There's no need to beat about the bush. This very day you must make your way into the princess's palace. The honourable Bhūtika, the minister in charge of the princess's quarters, has gone out with the ambassador from Benares with all honours from our king.

Avimāraka. Good. It is an excellent suggestion. What sick man, madam, that finds a remedy will hesitate to use it?

Nurse. Getting in 's the only difficulty. Once inside you could stay for ages.

Avimāraka. You may reckon on my being in. But the whole suite [1] should be kept open with nothing bolted.

Nurse. We shall do that. We shall get everything ready inside. Only, do be careful about getting in.

Avimāraka. Madam, explain to me once for all the plan of the palace.

Nurse. It 's like this. [*Explains the plan to him.*]

Avimāraka. Splendid.

Now that I have heard how the king's palace is planned, my mind is certain of my entry. Anyway, my manhood shall not be disgraced by opponents unless destiny is set on disappointment. (8)

[*Reflecting.*] But, madam, what assurance have I in this business?

Both Women. This is the assurance. 'Victory to the Prince.'

Avimāraka. Ah, well. You may go now. Expect me at midnight.

Both Women. As the Prince commands. [*Exeunt ambo.*]

[*Enter the Jester.*]

Jester. How beautiful the city looks at this hour. The blessed sun is setting. On the promenades and the upper terraces of the market, as white as lumps of curd, the sunlight seems like a layer of treacle spread over them.[2] Up and down on the promenades walk the courtesan and city blood with their wanton airs, anxious to show themselves off, and rivalling each other in their finery. I had a look at it all, but now I have left the town as I have to pass the night in the company of His Infatuated Highness. And he, to our misfortune, has become a changed man through some futile preoccupation. Here is his abode. I heard on the market terrace to-day that the princess's nurse and one of her companions came out of his house. Now, what were they after here? Verily, human happiness is as restless as an elephant's trunk. May our

[1] ? *Kriyantām.* [2] Reading?

misfortune pass! I must enter this place well-suited to our condition. [*Goes in.*] Oho! here comes his highness, very pale, as if smeared with the cosmetic that lovers use. Well, any thing serves to adorn the beautiful. [*Going up to him.*] Greeting!

Avimāraka. Ah, comrade, you have been a very long time in the city.

Jester. You spend the day and night dreaming like a brahman that has been taken in by an invitation while I wander about the town by day and come here at night to sleep at your side, like a common strumpet getting no fees.

Avimāraka. My friend, I'll tell you some good news.

Jester. What! Has the sage's curse come to an end?

Avimāraka. Idiot. What joy is there in what's bound to happen?

Jester. What else then?

Avimāraka. Didn't you see Kuraṅgī's nurse and Little Lotus?

Jester. Yes, indeed. I saw the ladies. What did they bring you?

Avimāraka. The remedy for my trouble.

Jester. Let me see it.

Avimāraka. You shall in good time. To-day you must simply listen.

Jester. Go on, speak out.

Avimāraka. The fact is, the lady says I am to enter the princess's quarters this very night.

Jester. [*Laughing.*] How are you going to get in? Do you want to be taken prisoner? Kuntibhoja's ministers are frightful fellows.

Avimāraka. How can you have misgivings? Look you—

All alone I defeated my opponents with their armies. To this day there is no trace of them. Why speak of men? With my two arms I slew the lord of demons that took the form of a sheep. (9)

Jester. Yes, I know your superhuman deeds. All the same, getting into another man's house under the cover of darkness is a risky business.

Avimāraka. The long and short of it is this. Whatever happens I must get into the apartments of Kuntibhoja's daughter. So please agree, great brahman.

Jester. What! Would you leave me behind? I will never, never let you go. Even in abuse you need one other.

Avimāraka. You don't know how the Scripture goes.

One should go alone to another's house, take counsel with a second, and take the field with many. Such is the ruling in Scripture. (10)

So I must go into Kuntibhoja's palace all by myself. You need not worry about me. Look you—

Kuntibhoja's troops have little mettle. Money easily finds the way into a palace. And I am skilled in wrestling. Then why, my friend, should you have misgivings? (11)

Jester. If you are so determined let us go now into the town. I have a friend there. We will wait there till the time comes.

Avimāraka. That is a good idea. I shall go in now, perform my devotions, bid the King good night, and go to bed in my room. Then I'll slip off to the town and wait in your friend's house.

[*Enter a Maid.*]

Maid. To the prince, greeting! The bath water is ready.

Avimāraka. Here I come; lead the way.

Maid. As the prince orders. [*Exit.*]

Avimāraka. Comrade, the sun has set. For now—

The eastern quarter is tinged with black while the west gleams with the evening red. The sky between is divided into two and attains the beauty of Śiva in his form half goddess. (12)

Jester. You are quite right. The day is past, the dusk has come.

Avimāraka. Ah, what a wonderful thing the world is! For—

This world of ours would seem to don another guise—wiping from its brow the red circle [1] of the sun, and flinging far a wreath of stars. Its burning heat has gone, cooled in a soft delicious breeze. With lovers interlaced and robbers [2] scattered here and there it seems another world. (13)

[*Exeunt.*]

END OF THE SECOND ACT.

ACT III

[*Enter Kuraṅgī and two maidens.*]

Kuraṅgī. Well, what did he say?

Maid. Who, Princess?

Kuraṅgī. [*Aside.*] Ah! I'm giving myself away, unlucky that I am. [*Aloud.*] Why, the attendant.[3]

Magadhikā. I saw the attendant and spoke to him; but he said nothing.

[1] *Tilaka.* [2] Reading *-coro* with editor. [3] Lit. harem servant.

Kuraṅgī. Ha! I shall report him to the queen for not making me a parrot's cage.

Māgadhikā. But your highness's parrot cage is finished.

Kuraṅgī. Chatterbox! Is there a second cage?

Māgadhikā. There may be.

Kuraṅgī. Well, what time is it?

Māgadhikā. The evening is passing.

Kuraṅgī. Then let's go up on the roof.

Māgadhikā. Do you go first, Vilāsinī; get the divan ready and the seats.

Vilāsinī. You must be asleep. They've been ready ages.

Māgadhikā. Ho, I know you, you lazy thing. Ready for the siesta; I suppose you call that ready.

Vilāsinī. Don't talk like that, my dear. They have all been rearranged according to the princess's wishes.

Māgadhikā. Well, I shall go and see.

[*All step round.*]

Māgadhikā. Here is the terrace.

Kuraṅgī. Lead the way. [*Indicates mounting steps.*]

Māgadhikā. Well done, Vilāsinī; your work is equal to your name.[1] Here is the divan spread on the stone bench.

Vilāsinī. There's a bed laid inside the pavilion. See, Māgadhikā, how lazy I am.

Māgadhikā. You're getting too clever for words. So you'd better marry a learned chamberlain.

Kuraṅgī. My dears, I'll sit awhile on this stone bench.

Māgadhikā. As the princess pleases. Come.

[*They all sit down.*]

Māgadhikā. Princess, shall I tell you a story?

Kuraṅgī. Oh, I know your absurd rigmaroles.

Māgadhikā. Oh, Princess, it's quite a new story.

Kuraṅgī. I beg you, don't disturb me. I'll sleep awhile.

Vilāsinī. Sleep well, Princess. [*To Māgadhikā.*] Tell me the story.

Kuraṅgī. [*To herself.*] What's it about, I wonder.

Māgadhikā. Well, listen. It's about our princess.

Kuraṅgī. [*To herself.*] Oh, dear, they know my secret. I am undone.

Vilāsinī. Where did you hear it, my dear?

Māgadhikā. Vasumitrā, the queen's attendant, told me.

Vilāsinī. The queen herself must have told her.

Māgadhikā. There's a son of the king of Benares named Jayavarman.

[1] *Vilāsinī*—'charming'.

The princess is betrothed to him. His envoy has arrived and has been honourably received by the king. The wedding paint has been accepted.

Kuraṅgī. [*Aside.*] That 's not true. I can dispose of myself.

Māgadhikā. Then the queen said her daughter was only a child, and she couldn't live a single day without seeing her. If his Majesty agreed they could send for the bridegroom here.

Vilāsinī. What then?

Māgadhikā. Then his Majesty agreed to that. As the stars were said to be favourable to-day, the minister Bhūtika has set out with the envoy.

Kuraṅgī. [*Aside.*] Well, that will take some time.

Vilāsinī. I am glad the youth and beauty of our princess will now bear fruit.

[*Enter Little Lotus.*]

Little Lotus. My mother told me to come here and tell this news to the princess. 'Pleasant news,' she said, 'told in a pleasant way becomes the more delightful. She doesn't look me in the face and tell me everything, but in course of time I shall get at it indirectly.' So now I must tell the good news to the princess. [*Steps around.*]

Kuraṅgī. This is some malady I never had before. The more I think of it the more it drives me silly. I[1] care nothing for jasmine paste. I've no pleasure in conversation. It's dreadful and yet delightful. [*Sighing.*] What is that, Little Lotus?

Māgadhikā. Princess, it is I, Māgadhikā.

Vilāsinī. And I, Vilāsinī.

Little Lotus. [*Approaching.*] Princess, it is I, Little Lotus. Your highness knew me by my footsteps on the stairs. Princess, the queen says . . .

Kuraṅgī. Yes, what?

Little Lotus. [*Whispering.*] This—

Kuraṅgī. Oh, my character is gone.

Little Lotus. Nay, he is worthy of honour. He is indeed the same man.

Kuraṅgī. Massage me, Little Lotus.

Little Lotus. As the princess bids.

Vilāsinī. When will the wedding take place, Little Lotus?

[*Voice behind the scene.*]

To-day.

Little Lotus. Long life to you!

[*Voice behind the scene.*]

Good watchmen, they say the minister has gone away, and he has sent

[1] Reading the first person.

nobody to look after the princess's palace. Well, never mind. I shall report the matter to the king to-morrow.

Vilāsinī. Oh, what did he say, Little Lotus?

Little Lotus. He says the wedding will take place as soon as the prince arrives.

Vilāsinī. May he come without hindrance.

Little Lotus. Amen to that.

Māgadhikā. Come, dear, let's sit in the room.

Vilāsinī. Yes, let's. The dusk is nearly gone; the moon is up.

Little Lotus. Spread a place for me too, dears.

Māgadhikā. But are you free? Wait on the princess till she goes to sleep.

Little Lotus. Very well.

[*Exeunt the two maidens.*]

[*Enter*[1] *Avimāraka carrying a rope disguised as a burglar and with a sword in his hand.*]

Avimāraka. [*Thoughtfully.*] Ah! Youth is a terrible thing. For—

Youth manifests passion and resorts to recklessness; takes no heed of difficulties but goes straight for rashness; goes its self-willed way caring nothing for the path of law, and overwhelms the clear intellect of those who know much better. (1)

How now? Shall I loiter in a matter that depends on me alone? For here—

I am familiar with the town and know the watchmen's strength.
'Tis nigh midnight, grim with darkness nought can pierce.
I have my sword as trusted friend. My mind's made up.
What need of long reflection? What could be difficult for me? (2)

Ah, how fearsome is the middle of the night! For now, all creatures are unconscious in their slumber, like babes in the womb. The palaces with people silent, fast asleep, seem sunk in meditation. Swallowed up by the encircling gloom the trees can be detected only by the touch. With its outlines blurred the whole world becomes invisible. (3)

'Tis now forsooth the night of doom.[2]

The streets are streams that bear along the darkness, the lines of houses look like shoals; the ten quarters are merged in gloom. This darkness one could swim across. (4)

[*Stepping round and listening.*] Ah! that sounds like strains of

[1] He appears to the audience, but he is still in the street.

[2] *Kāla-rātrī.* Night of the dissolution of the universe.

music. Who, I wonder, is that man so happy at every hour, enjoying music with his beloved? Clearly he plays the lute himself. For—

The mansion is lofty and the lattices are closed, yet the sound of the strings resounds. To make it sound so clearly out of doors were past the power of a woman's finger-tips. (5)

But that is a woman singing. For—

The tone is soft but clear, the sound from mouth and nose. While the beat[1] is strong, the sound of clapping hands is mingled with the jingling of bracelets. (6)

[*Stepping and looking around.*] Ha! ha! Who is this other trying to appease his lady-love? His offence must be great if she is not appeased at such an hour as this. Or is she really content but wants an excuse? For—

With stammering tongue and a sob in her throat as if choked with tears, 'What am I to thee?' she asks, too lovingly. Her good nature makes her yield to her lover's will, but her woman's nature makes her say the most contrary things. (7)

What is this bird with a dreadful note? Ah, it is an owl. The man laughs. The lady is scared at the hoot of the owl and the poor fellow gets his embrace. This befits their age, but why should I be witness to other folks' affairs? Let's get about our business.

[*Steps around.*] But whom have we here on the market terrace talking so softly in tremulous whispers? The poor fellow is like me, chaste against his will.[2]

His attendants urge him to speak low, and he is alarmed at the jingle of a jewel. Overcome by passion, he complains that desire brings no joy. He desires an assignation but hesitates to keep it. (8)

[*Steps around.*] Ah, moonlight. No, it's not moonlight; it's lamplight from the windows of houses on both sides of the street. It's difficult here to hide oneself. Oh, here's a robber. For—

Glad to feel his loins well girt, his glances follow the sounds from others' houses. He moves at a run, but with an eye on the lamps and trembles at the sound of a step. (9)

Ho, I must avoid him. [*Stands on one side.*] The rascal has gone. Now we can get on.

[*Steps round.*] Oh, here are the guards! What am I to do now? Good, I have it! I'll go into that rogue's hall at the crossways. [*Crosses over and waits.*]

[1] Sarup takes *hetu* in the sense of 'impulse, passion'.

[2] Sarup. 'He is that poor student of ours.'

This sword of mine mocks at me running from timid watchmen. Nay, it is not the guards that trouble me. I came in here intent on achieving my design. (10)

The guards have gone. Who can guard against the man who guards himself?

Those who roam at night, be it from love, or greed, or passion, rely on courage, not the aid of many men. This wandering at night, witness of the cream of manly deeds, is full of danger, but delightful. (11)

Here is the royal palace. The wall is very strong and very high. This is where men use their girdle string. If the coping[1] holds, I am as good as in. I'll stand here and throw the rope. Obeisance to Prajāpati. Honour to all magic sprites! May Śiva, Śambara, and Bali smile on me. Darker be the night, and deeper sleep. May fortune favour me. May all obstructions disappear. Death to all that hinder. Victory to the Queen of Magic.

[*Throws the rope.*] Ha! the noose[2] has caught in the coping. See the power of destiny. The rope has stuck at the very first throw. This looks like success.

The blessed Prajāpati is almighty. For—

If an effort be made, what is the blame for not succeeding? And who ever succeeds that thinks the task beyond him? Heroes show their mettle by goodly efforts. Success depends on the dictates of destiny. (12)

Good, I will climb up by the rope. [*Climbs up and looks over.*] Oh, what a fine palace.

Huge as this palace is, its parts are arranged in symmetry. It appears compact, rising tier above tier, and with its series of mansions seems eager to pass from the earth into the clouds. (13)

But I must not stop here. Obstructions all come from watch-towers, gate-houses,[3] and the paths along the walls.[4] Well, I will get down with the same rope. [*Descends.*] Now, where shall I hide the rope? [*Reflects.*] Good, I have it. I'll cut it off and throw it in this elephants' stable.

[*Throws it in and steps around.*]

[1] Lit. 'Monkey-heads', alluding to the merlons on the crenellated wall.

[2] Lit. 'Crab-rope'. *Karkaṭaka* is applied to different objects. Could it mean a piece of wood fastened at the end of the rope? Cf. Daśa-Kumāra-Caritam, p. 77, l. 7.

[3] *Pratolī.* For the meaning see Vogel, *J. R. A. S.* 1906, p. 539.

[4] *Indrapatha.* 'Indra paths'—probably the paths for sentries along the walls, between turrets. Editor suggests 'Indramaha = dog', which is pointless. On the top of the wall he would be safe from dogs.

Hark, that is a lute with the soft melody of a damsel singing.
I'll go elsewhere.

Ha! a perfume made more pungent by the ichor of the royal elephants.

I'll wait a moment and then go on.

Lo, the light of lamps. The guards are spread out this way.

What's to do?

The palace has long been hushed in nocturnal slumber like the lotus beds. **(14)**

I'll go on. Here is the path she told me of. Here is the water-course.[1] This is the mound with trees. And this the audience hall. Ah, here is the palace of the princess. There is plenty of woodwork and the lattices are near the ground, so it will be easy to climb. Nay, but were it hard to climb—

How should I hesitate, intent on climbing up now that my longing has brought me nigh to my beloved? Who that is tortured with thirst would shun a lotus pool through fear of the thorns on the stalks? **(15)**

Well, I must get up. [*Climbs up.*] Here's the lattice window the nurse described. [*Unbolts the window, steps in, and looks round.*] Bravo, Kuntibhoja, bravo! This palace makes heaven look ridiculous. For—

Swans are sleeping on jewelled slabs, gravel paths[2] are made of pearls and beryl, pillars branch with coral. What need of words? The lamps grow dim in the flashing of the gems. **(16)**

Away with this dreadful disguise. [*Takes off his burglar's dress and removes the cord round his waist.*]

Little Lotus. I wonder what has happened to the prince. When the princess heard her sweetheart would come to-night she actually fell asleep. She was too troubled to sleep before.

Avimāraka. [*Overhears and approaches quickly.*] Lady, see what has happened to me.

Little Lotus. [*Looking up joyfully.*] Welcome, Prince.

Avimāraka. [*Gazing in delight.*] This is she. At this sight—

Mine eyes are not content though caressing every limb; my heart is racing as though it would waken her from slumber. Love drives me on as if he would crush her in his arms. My inner soul is tranquil but faints with joy. **(17)**

Little Lotus. [*Aside.*] This is the Lord God of Love tormenting them

[1] *Mandākinī.*

[2] *-pratānaḥ* (?) *v. l. pradhānāḥ.*

as a flood sweeps away the banks on either side. [*Aloud.*] Prince, pray grace this couch.

Avimāraka. Very well. [*Sits down.*]

Little Lotus. Shall I wake the princess?

Avimāraka. Good lady, restrain your youthful impetuosity. Look you—

I have but two eyes, not a thousand. My mind is in a maze from long-deferred desire. But to-day, when the shore is glimpsed across the flood of passion, let my two eyes enjoy this game over and over again. (18)

Little Lotus. Yes, I know your highness's solicitude for the princess.

Avimāraka. To-day my solicitude finds its reward.

Kuraṅgī. [*Waking.*] My dear, what did the cruel fellow say?

Little Lotus. I told you before, princess.

Avimāraka. Now have I gained the crown [1] of my life; that her mind is so confused.

Kuraṅgī. [*Aside.*] My wits are wandering. [*Aloud.*] What did I say, dear?

Little Lotus. You didn't say anything, princess.

Avimāraka. This intensity of her distraction distracts me once again.

Kuraṅgī. You've been sitting here a long time, Little Lotus. What's the time?

Little Lotus. It is now midnight.

Kuraṅgī. Then you must be tired. Come and clasp me in your arms.

Little Lotus. [*Aside to Avimāraka.*] Prince, I am busy rubbing her feet. Do you clasp the princess in your arms.

Avimāraka. [*Joyfully.*] Delighted, and may you too hear hundreds of words as sweet.

Kuraṅgī. Don't be too devoted. Come along.

Little Lotus. Princess, here I am.

Kuraṅgī. [*Catches hold of Avimāraka, pulls him towards her, and embraces him.*] Oh, but who is rubbing my feet?

Little Lotus. [*Whispering.*] It's like this.

Kuraṅgī. [*In confusion.*] Alas, my reputation is ruined, I am afraid.

Avimāraka. Thou art no stranger, love, to me because our hearts have met. Why tremblest thou like a creeper smitten by the force of the wind? Banish fear, good lady, and be merciful to me. Why make a lengthy story? I come to thee a suppliant. (19)

[*Kuraṅgī looks bashfully at Little Lotus.*]

Little Lotus. Rise, your highness, rise. The princess begs you; rise.

[1] *Phalam*—'Fruit'.

Avimāraka. Very well. [*Gets up.*]

[*Enter the Nurse.*]

Nurse. Greeting, Prince.

Avimāraka. How are you, madam?

Nurse. Little Lotus, there's a couch prepared in the inner bower. Take them in there.

Little Lotus. Just so.

[*Exit Nurse.*]

Little Lotus. Prince, there's a couch prepared in the inner bower. Please take the princess there.

Avimāraka. May you too listen to hundreds of words as sweet.

[*Takes her hand in his. Gets up.*]

Little Lotus. Come, Prince, this way.

Avimāraka. Lo, here I come.

[*They both step round.*]

Avimāraka. [*Joyfully.*] Now have I discharged the debt of youth. For—

> Her eyes are swimming with happy tears; her bosom throbs beneath her hand. Though her hips are not too weighty, her dainty feet are tottering from bashfulness. Lo, here is the warrant of the seven steps, so is our union complete. Could this night endure a hundred æons, what man more fortunate than I?

[*Exeunt omnes.*]

END OF THE THIRD ACT.

ACT IV

INTERLUDE

[*Enter Māgadhikā with a basket in her hand.*]

Māgadhikā. How careless the maids are! Past sunrise and the terrace not yet done. I can't hear them chattering together. What can it mean? Ah, they must have been awake all night and have dropped off to sleep at dawn. I will just waken the princess. [*Steps around.*]

[*Enter Vilāsinī with a fan.*]

Vilāsinī. Stop, Māgadhikā, stop.

Māgadhikā. Don't stop me, my good girl. I have brought flower paste for the princess.

Vilāsinī. What does she want with flower paste or any kind of ornament?

Māgadhikā. Impudent girl! Don't say such unlucky things. Ever may the princess need her ornaments.

Vilāsinī. Nay, I meant to say her beauty is its own adornment.

Māgadhikā. Idiot! Even a flower has fragrance.

Vilāsinī. That's right. What's lovely in itself becomes still more lovely when adorned.

Māgadhikā. Ah, my dear, the prince is well matched with a beautiful mate.

Vilāsinī. Now, don't be partial. Before the prince she looks like a lotus in the sun.

Māgadhikā. You're right. I really think the God of Love incarnate looks like him.

Vilāsinī. That's why she can't do without him for a moment.

[*Enter Little Lotus in tears.*]

Little Lotus. It's a true word what people say—that joys are beset with troubles. Here's a year gone that the princess has found delight in unbroken joy. And, of course, we girls were in paradise. Now to-day I hear the king knows all about it, and my whole body has gone limp. And the princess, tormented by shame and fear and love, stupefied [1] by her trouble, is like someone in a faint. This palace seems to me as dismal as a lamp with the light blown out. Since the prince left [2] I haven't found a scrap of comfort. However, I am glad to hear he got away without difficulty. Now the princess's apartments are guarded all round. [*Steps round.*] Hullo, two of the girls. What is it, Māgadhikā?

Māgadhikā. Oh, how can you ask? You know it's the hour of the princess's toilet.

Little Lotus. The festival is over. [*Weeps.*]

The Two Maids. What, was it only a dream? Speak out; let us share your sorrow.

Little Lotus. The prince has gone—for ever.

Two Maids. Oh!

Little Lotus. I came out here because I couldn't bear to see the princess's trouble any longer.

[1] *Muddhā.* Sarup takes it in the more usual sense,—'simple girl'.

[2] Sarup thinks *virahidāe* refers to the princess. 'Since the prince left her, I haven't found her any comfort.'

Māgadhikā. One couldn't bear to see her present plight. So let us go and cheer her up.

Two Maids. Yes, let us do so.

[*Exeunt omnes.*]

END OF INTERLUDE.

[*Enter Avimāraka.*]

Avimāraka. [*Sadly.*] With the last remnant of my luck I have managed to escape from the princess's palace. That is, my body has, for even now my heart has not come back to me, but held prisoner by that darling girl, leaves me in the lurch. (1)

In what plight can Kuraṅgī be?

Put to shame by the servants' chatter and closely guarded by the king, she will be afraid. At night, when she cannot find me, blinded by tears she will swoon away. Alas, what can I do? (2)

Ha, I see a way. In her regard for me she took no thought for herself. And so for her sake I must sacrifice my life. [*Steps round.*] I have been in exile only the last few days, and yet the torture of my body and my mind seems past bearing. For—

If I should leave that beautiful maid, so exquisite in the glory of fresh youth, whose artless love grew greater with familiarity, and be cheated into living even for a moment, what ingratitude in the world could be baser? (3)

And now the blessed sun with a thousand rays begins to corrode the body of a man whose heart is consumed by love. [*Looking all round.*] Ah, how dreadful is this heat. For now—

The earth is burning hot, as if in a high fever, all its moisture drawn off by the rays of the sun. The trees, through harbouring forest fires, have been robbed of their shade, and seem stricken with a wasting sickness. The mountains, gaping with their lofty caverns, cry helplessly for water, while the whole world, losing its senses in the baking rays of the sun, falls into a swoon. (4)

What shall I do now? I can go no farther. For—

Arid winds cover all with fiery sand. The trees are dropping down[1] discoloured leaves. The sun streams along melted by forest fires, and baked by the heat of the sun the world is cracking. (5)

[1] *Saṃsvedayanti*—lit. 'are all in a sweat with'. *Nagāḥ* may be 'mountains' as in verse 12.

Oh, my darling, beautiful maid, answer me.

[*Acts a swoon. Then revives and looks upward.*]

Why, the blessed sun with a thousand rays is obscured. Nay—

What wonder if the spreading clouds carried in the wind obscure the sun? The wonder would be if they could assuage the flame in my heart. (6)

What is the use of this living death? I shall abandon life. [*Rises, and steps round.*] Now what shall I do? Good, I see. I will drown myself in this forest pool. Nay, for shame this death of mine were ignoble. In a moment of pride I forgot the right path. I must try another way. [*Looking off.*] Good, I have it. Yonder forest fire seems fairly near. I will offer up my life in that. [*Approaching and saluting.*] Blessed Fire—

If Agni will bring to pass the wish of those devoted to one thing, in the next world, too, let her be my love, bringing fame to me alone. (7)

[*Enters the fire. In surprise.*] Why, what is this?

Burnt trees are falling with showers of sparks, but to me the flames are as cool as Malaya sandal paste. For as if fire took pity on a lovesick wight, it embraces me as a father hugs his son with joy. (8)

Can there be a greater miracle? The fire does not burn me. Now has this some natural cause?[1]

I must try in another way.

[*Steps round.*] Here is a lofty mountain.

Its summit merges in the masses of black clouds that cover it, and it forms a resting-place for troops of heaven's denizens. With all the varied charm a poet could conceive, ideal for friends to meet on, its riches all seem useless like those of a low-born king. (9)

So be it. On this rock will I abandon life. For a precipice brings all one can desire. I will climb up. [*Ascends and looks down.*] Here is a mountain pool. I will bathe therein, and, sipping it, recite a prayer. [*Does so.*]

[*Enter a Fairy[2] with his lady-love.*]

Fairy. Last night I passed in northern Kuru-land, and then I bathed in Mānasa. Then we frolicked[3] on the inner slopes of Mandara's glens, played hide and seek in Himalaya's caves, and

[1] *astikāraṇam.* [2] *Vidyādhara*—a semi-divine being of magic power.
[3] *āmoditaṃ yauvanam.*

feasted our eyes on the view. Now we shall go to sandal trees of Malabar, delightful for a midday slumber. **(10)**

[*Gesticulates flying through the air.*]

Saudāminī, look. How beautiful is the distant earth. For now—

Mighty mountains look like little elephants and seas like swimming tanks. Trees resemble duckweed. All the hollows on the surface of the earth have disappeared. Streams are boundary lines, sumptuous mansions glistening drops. The whole world in its contracted form seems to be seen awry. **(11)**

Take heed, my love. We will go to Malaya, the home of cool sandal-wood trees.

Saudāminī. Very well, my lord.

[*They both gesticulate flying through the air.*]

Saudāminī. I can't go any further without a rest.

Fairy. Then we'll rest awhile on some mountain before we go on.

Saudāminī. I'd love to. [*Both descend.*]

Fairy. Look. Saudāminī, look—

Our swift descent makes it seem that the mass of clouds is flying from us while the sea-girt earth rushes up to meet us. These mountains coming into view are very bright, like clouds in the rainy season. **(12)**

Lady mine, this mountain seems suitable to entertain us for a while. So let us rest before we go on.

Saudāminī. Let us do so, my lord.

Fairy. Saudāminī, we have a right to take a sixth part of the flowers of these trees. So let us help them to pay their debt.

Sāudaminī. Very well, my lord.

[*They gesticulate picking flowers.*]

Fairy. [*Catching sight of Avimāraka.*] But who is this? I know. It must be some fairy that has lost his magic.[1] And why? Because no others have such beauty. I am glad I saw him. Come, I'll ask him what 's forgotten.

Avimāraka. Well, I've done my duty by the gods. I'll throw myself down. [*Looking sideways sees the fairy.*] Hullo, who is this? Nay, it must be a dream. But I am not asleep. Ah, but a man sees many things at the time of death. That must be it. Yet that happens to the stupidest people, and I know everything. Well, I'll ask him. Sir, of what lineage are you the ornament?

Fairy. Hearken. I am a fairy, Meghanāda by name, and this is my

[1] *mantra-bhraṣṭa.*

wife Saudāminī. The fairies hold a festival to-day on the Malaya mountain in honour of the holy sage Agastya. We are invited there. We have alighted here to rest awhile before going farther. That is all about us. But now how is it that you are turning this earth into paradise?

Avimāraka. [*Aside.*] Now, what shall I say? At the hour of death I must not tell a lie. [*Aloud.*] My name, sir, is Avimāraka, the son of the king of Sauvīra.

Fairy. [*Aside.*] That is untrue. This is no human form. [*Aloud.*] Then why have you come here all alone?

Avimāraka. [*Aside.*] What shall I say? [*Remains with his eyes downcast.*]

Fairy. [*Aside.*] Well, I must find out for myself. [*Applies his magical science.*] Alas! He is the son of the divine Agni, but does not know it. He fell in love with Kuraṅgī, Kuntibhoja's daughter, was enjoying her company when it was found out and he escaped. Finding no way of returning to her, he was bent on suicide, and climbed up here to throw himself down a precipice. She, too, in her place is suffering a living death. I must help him in this affair. [*Aloud.*] Avimāraka, friendship should be free from guile. You cannot conceal from me what I know already.

Avimāraka. Continue.

Fairy. From now on let us be friends. I know all about the state you are in. You climbed up here in order to abandon life. Now, didn't you?

Avimāraka. Yes, my friend, that is so.

Fairy. Good, I am delighted at your confidence. Now, if you had the means of getting back unbeknown, what would you do?

Avimāraka. [*Delighted.*] What do you think? Why, I should go straight in. That's the reason of my distraction.

Fairy. Well, my friend, look at this ring. [*Shows him a ring.*]

Avimāraka. Yes, comrade, what is the good of that?

Fairy. By wearing this ring on a finger of the right hand one becomes invisible; on the left hand as one was before.

Avimāraka. Oh, comrade, is it possible?

Fairy. Come, I will convince you. Say now, can you see me?

Avimāraka. Of course.

Fairy. Now pay attention.

Avimāraka. I'm all attention.

Fairy. [*Putting the ring on right hand.*] Can you see me, comrade?

Avimāraka. Even your shadow is invisible, not to speak of your body. How happy these people are—

That roam through the sky attended by their darlings, and sport on mountain slopes for all to follow. All things they know by magic powers, and wander at their ease, seen or unseen, as they please. **(13)**

Why, with that I were as good as in already.

Fairy. [*Putting the ring on his left hand.*] Then pray accept this ring.

Avimāraka. I am much obliged to you.

Fairy. No, no; 'tis I that am obliged. For—

The satisfaction that a good man feels on gaining a jewel is less than the joy of giving it to one that stands in need thereof. **(14)**

Avimāraka. I have only one doubt. It seems ungracious to say it, but if I might try it on myself.

Fairy. Then put it on a finger of your right hand.

Avimāraka. Very good. [*Does so.*]

Fairy. Comrade, take this sword.

Avimāraka. Very good. [*Takes the sword. In surprise.*] Oh, what a splendid sword!

It is a thunderbolt with its form invisible, or by some magic flashes of lightning have been welded into a sword. Eclipsing the brilliance of the sun it moves with a rush like a forest fire. **(15)**

Fairy. See the prowess of Agni's son. How few among the fairies even could endure the brilliance of this sword. Truly the God of Fire protects him.

Avimāraka. [*Looking at the sword.*] How powerful is the sacred lore.

I have attained to superhuman power. I am the same, distinguished with my proper qualities; and this is my body, while hosts of mortals less fortunate know nought thereof. **(16)**

Comrade, my task is done. Take the sword.

Fairy. As you wish.[1] It is certain that the man himself is invisible, and so is any one he touches and a third man touched by him.

Avimāraka. My friend, I am delighted. This is luck upon luck. But I am afraid I have delayed you. Do not let me detain you further.

Fairy. As I take leave of you, I'll be straightway there.

Avimāraka. What is the use of many words?

What return can be made by a man like me to those like you that have your magic powers? By restoring life to me thou hast made me thy chattel. Command me. What shall thy servant do? **(17)**

[1] This passage with the sword, which is returned, seems superfluous.

Fairy. I recognize your sincerity. And if you would fulfil my request—

Speak of me and of my lady to thy lady-love. Nor do thou forget me, friend, but watch for my coming. With merry sport beguile the princess, and at need I shall again be at thy side. **(18)**

Oh, he is the cream of manliness. My heart is loth to leave him. Comrade, we must go.

Avimāraka. Fare thee well. We shall meet again.

Fairy. Oh, yes.

[*Fairy rises in the air with his lady.*]

Avimāraka. [*Looking upwards.*] There goes the noble Meghanāda plunged in the ocean of the sky.

The breeze is tossing the locks on his brow. The unguent is swept from his limbs by the pressure of clefts in the clouds. Well girt with a sword in his girdle, his waist is hidden by the clinging hands of his youthful bride. His robe is tossed by the wind, and the stars are obliterated by jewels crowded on his diadem. And now the majestic magician grows smaller and smaller so fast in his flight through the air. **(19)**

And she, too, follows her beloved by magic power.

Side curls have worked loose with the speed. Her slender waist is wearied by the heaving of her bosom. With her lover's arm around her[1] she flashes in the sky and disappears like lightning in the clouds. **(20)**

The noble Meghanāda has gone. I must set out for the city this very day. I will climb down at once. [*Descends.*] I feel tired. I will rest awhile on this stone slab before I go on. [*Sits down.*]

[*Enter the Jester.*]

Jester. Alas, how unlucky is Sugṛihīta, the Sauvīra King. For a long time he had no son. Then by divine favour and his own observance he obtained a fine son, such as mortals rarely get. Now he is no better off than before. For by the bad luck of his relatives and to the certain conclusion of my life, the prince has disappeared. [*Steps around.*] Only to-day her ladyship said that the prince departed safely. But who knows whether he is all right? He is very delicate, and has gone off alone tormented by love. Anyhow, I must find him, alive or dead, if I have to wander over the whole earth. If I don't find him in this world, I shall accompany his highness in the next. I am dead beat. I'll rest a bit in the shade of this tree before I go on. [*Sleeps.*]

[1] Lit. 'with the upper part of her body given to her beloved'.

Avimāraka. In what plight, I wonder, is Santushṭa? If he has heard of my escape, all will be well. Otherwise the poor old brahman will perish. Without him all my plans will be in vain. For he is—

Droll to converse with, but a warrior in battle. A preceptor in sorrow and stout-hearted to face the foe, the great delight of my heart. In short, he is my other half. **(21)**

[*Looking all round.*] Hullo, who is this traveller asleep in the shade? [*Approaching.*] All at once it seems a load is lifted from my heart,[1] and I am all eager to embrace him.

Jester. [*Waking.*] I've had a long sleep. I must be going. What good is rest to the broken-hearted? [*Steps round and catches sight of Avimāraka.*] What! Prince Avimāraka?

Avimāraka. My dear Santushṭa! [*They embrace.*]

Jester. [*Laughing loudly.*] Tell me, comrade, what have you been up to all this time?

Avimāraka. My friend, just this. [*Puts the ring on his right hand and becomes invisible.*]

Jester. Hullo! Where's his highness got to? He is nowhere to be seen. Ah, my thoughts are always fixed upon him, and so I must have thought I could see him. Nay, but I will clear this up. Comrade, if you hide yourself I'll curse you.

Avimāraka. Here I am, comrade.

Jester. Where? Where?

Avimāraka. [*Changing the ring to his left hand.*] Why, here I am.

Jester. It used to be simple Avimāraka, but now it's magic Avimāraka. Well then, magician, why don't you go invisible to the princess's palace?

Avimāraka. I have only just got it.

Jester. Wonderful! wonderful! Where did it come from?

Avimāraka. I will tell you all about it in the ladies' chambers.

Jester. Now you are the greedy one.[2]

Avimāraka. Vaidheya, come at once to enter the arena.[3] Don't you let go of my hand.

Jester. Wonderful! wonderful! I, too, am invisible. Does my body exist or not? I'll spit. [*Does so.*]

Avimāraka. Idiot, don't delay. My heart runs forward to see my beloved. [*Drags him along.*]

Jester. I feel no confidence.

Avimāraka. What, must I wait till dinner-time?

Jester. Let's rest awhile before we go.

[1] Lit. 'the sunrise of my heart has come'.
[2] Or reading *mhi* for *si*—'I am ravenous now.' [3] *prakṣepa-bhūmi*?

Avimāraka. Do you think Kuraṅgī has forgotten me?
Jester. Is she still alive—that ragged and blind old nun?
Avimāraka. Seriously, comrade, I request you. Pray, come at once.
Jester. Why are you in such a hurry, like a student going home at the end of his course?
Avimāraka. Idiot! Come along.
Jester. Don't drag me. I am running after you.
Avimāraka. [*Stepping around.*] Here is the city.
Jester. Yes, I can see what a beautiful city it is.
Avimāraka. Here is the king's palace.

Here stands the royal mansion. Erstwhile I entered it at night, mustering my daring, but full of apprehension. But now with magic's kindly aid I enter it by day without a tremor, as a clever rogue enters a group of worthy men. **(22)**

[*Stepping round.*] At this hour Kuraṅgī must have bathed and will be in her palace within.
Jester. Go here, go there. Dinner-time is passing.[1]
Avimāraka. Come, let us go into the inner rooms. [*Enters.*]

When the high-minded men have dwelt happily before in house or town, though anxious for an aim hard to attain, what happiness to return with hearts satisfied by their object gained and with something yet to be achieved. **(23)**

[*Exeunt ambo.*]

END OF THE FOURTH ACT.

ACT V

[*Enter Kuraṅgī and Little Lotus.*]

Little Lotus. Come, princess, don't torment yourself for ever. Let's go up to the terrace on the roof and admire the view.
Kuraṅgī. Ah, my dear, can you read my heart? For my servants don't understand, and, just to please me, bring the most fragrant flowers—*bakula, sarala, kadamba* [2]—and all the favourites of the rainy season.[3] They drive me mad. And these peacocks by our royal lake are much too keen on their bowing and scraping.[4] I've always petted them, yet they

[1] Lit. 'begging time'.
[2] Bakula (*Mimusops Elengi*), Sarala (*Pinus Longifolia*), Sarja (*Vatica Robusta*), Arjuna (*Terminalia*), Kadamba (*Nauclea Cadamba*), Nīpa (*Idem?*). Nicula (*Barringtonia acutangula*), &c.
[3] The rains being the happy season of lovers.
[4] 'Overdo the sycophantic business.'

show no sense of time or place, but needs must show off their superior art. The parrot-starling has started telling stories. This *maina*, knowing nothing of my trouble, comes to tell me the news of all the world. My retinue comes to ask about my health and is persistent in its gossip. So I should like to go on the terrace for awhile.

Little Lotus. As the princess pleases. Let us go.

[*They both go up.*]

Kuraṅgī. Oh, my dear, even here there's a great disadvantage—a black cloud coming up with its lightning lamp.

Little Lotus. Oh, princess, do not torture yourself. Look at that sky. The sun is shut in by dark clouds and the sky is made beautiful by a light shower of rain.

Kuraṅgī. Yes, it is a lovely sky.

[*Enter Avimāraka and the Jester.*]

Avimāraka. Comrade, I can see Kuraṅgī there—

Wet with aloe and sandal, out of season, by reason of her malady, her ornaments laid aside, every playful gesture gone. She shines with natural charm, like a sacred text without the application. (1)

Jester. Ho, I am content. You used to think yourself the most beautiful person in all the world. Now you are surpassed by that lady's inherently delightful beauty. Separation from you, I think, has made her thinner. Even so she delights the eye like a digit of the new moon.

Avimāraka. Too bookish for words, my friend. How is that?

Jester. Ah, you're used to me and so you mock me. People who haven't seen me before and know nothing of my intelligence praise me highly. And I know that so well that I won't chum up with anybody in town.

Avimāraka. How can you be so indifferent? With so many people round my beloved I have had no opportunity to let her know. But now she has gone on to the roof. We will speak to her there.

Jester. Right you are. Let's go up on the roof.

Avimāraka. My friend, we must go up very carefully so as not to make a sound.

Jester. Oh, but it can't be done. Who can eat without spoiling what's left.[1] I'll stay here. You go up alone.

Avimāraka. If you let go, you will become visible.

[1] Anything left, when one person has helped himself, is *ucchiṣṭa*, a remnant, impure for any one else.

Jester. Oh, I had forgotten that. Tell me again and again.

Avimāraka. This way. [*Ascends and looks round.*] My friend, here is my beloved seated on a stone slab with Little Lotus.

> Leaning her unhappy face on her left hand, she cannot endure this season with its passionate associations. Absorbed in thought she gazes upwards with eyes almost still and seeks to restrain her tears. (2)

Kuraṅgī. [*Aside.*] What's the good of this living death? [*Aloud.*] Little Lotus, go and fetch Māgadhikā with the bathing things.

Little Lotus. How can I leave your highness alone? There is nobody here.

[*Enter Hariṇikā.*]

Hariṇikā. To the princess, greeting. The queen asks, how is your headache now, and sends this medicine to rub on.

Kuraṅgī. Little Lotus, now you can go. I think it's just going to rain. I want to bathe in the fresh rainwater. So hurry up these things.

Little Lotus. As the princess bids.

Avimāraka. Now what is she up to?

Kuraṅgī. Come here, my dear.

Little Lotus. Here I am, princess.

Kuraṅgī. Is your body cool?

Little Lotus. I don't know.

Kuraṅgī. Come here and embrace me.

Little Lotus. So, princess. [*Embraces her.*]

Kuraṅgī. Yes, my dear, your body is very cool and delightful.

Little Lotus. Thank you, princess.

Kuraṅgī. Now the burning pain in my body seems to be vanishing. [*Aside.*] Alas, a loving farewell.[1] This is the last time that I shall clasp her in my arms. [*Aloud.*] Now, you can go.

Little Lotus. As the princess bids. [*Exit.*]

Hariṇikā. Princess, what shall I tell the queen?

Kuraṅgī. Tell her the pain is gone and I am well to-day.

Hariṇikā. And what shall I say if she questions me as to how I know?

Kuraṅgī. You know very well. Say it was through her excellent medicine.

Hariṇikā. As the princess bids. [*Exit.*]

Avimāraka. Now what has she in mind?

> With burning sighs the slender maid keeps gazing all around.
> Her eyes are full of tears. What does she mean to do? (3)

[1] Lit. I have shown my affection for my friend.

Kuraṅgī. Good, I'll hang myself with this robe. [*Gets up, and is about to do so when she hears a clap of thunder.*] Oh, save me, save me!

Avimāraka. My friend, I cannot bear it any longer. [*Changes the ring to his left hand.*] Beloved, have no fear. [*Lifts up Kuraṅgī.*]

Kuraṅgī. [*Joyfully.*] Can it be true? I am all in a maze.

Avimāraka. Beloved, put all doubt away. [*Embraces her.*]

Kuraṅgī. Wonderful! My burning pain has gone in a moment.

Avimāraka. Thus to clasp her in my arms,

Though constantly familiar through the union of our hearts, is even more delicious than our first meeting. To-day I'm like a king enjoying victory that he has won[1] by prowess in the van of battle. (4)

Jester. What, are they beginning to cry? Don't you worry too much or I shall cry too. No, not a single precious tear comes out of my eye. When my old dad died I began mighty hard to cry. But not a tear. What chance for somebody else's trouble? And yet, though I am not excited, I am weeping.

Avimāraka. Enough of your mockery. For true love has no guile.

No blame to me and none to thee if I should make thee laugh. A wise man and a fool are much the same for any task in body not in mind. (5)

[*Enter Little Lotus.*]

Little Lotus. Hariṇikā, Hariṇikā! Why is the door locked? Alas, I am afraid she has fastened the door to free herself from pain. Hariṇikā, Hariṇikā! Oh, dear, that's what's happened.

Avimāraka. That sounds like the voice of Little Lotus. Comrade, unbolt the door.

Jester. As you command. [*Undoes the door.*] Come in, lady.

Little Lotus. Oh, who is this man?

Jester. How discerning you are! There is something queer about the palace. Nobody else takes me for a man. I'm an old woman.

Avimāraka. Come in, Little Lotus.

Little Lotus. What, the prince? Your highness, greeting! But who is this man?

Jester. I am a maidservant called Lily.[2]

Avimāraka. He is the brahman Santushṭa I have often told you about.

Little Lotus. Ah, I have seen this brahman before on the terrace of the city market.

[1] Reading *sāhasāptaḥ*, suggested by editor. [2] *Pukkhariṇī*; lit. 'Lotus Pool'.

Jester. Yes, lady. With my sacred thread I am a brahman; with my rags I am a friar.[1] If I take off my clothes I am a monk.[2] What have you there, lady?

Little Lotus. Things for the princess's bath.

Jester. What does she want with bathing things when she's crying with hunger? Go at once and fetch something to eat. I'll take the head of the table.

Little Lotus. Wretched brahman! Always thinking about something to eat. That can all wait. But how did the prince come in by day with the highroad crowded with men?

Avimāraka. Santushṭa will tell you all about it.

Little Lotus. With these courteous words I'm dismissed. Very well. I'll take him to the hall and hear his story with all my gossips. Come along, brahman. [*Drags him away.*]

Jester. Help! An outrage on a brahman!

Kuraṅgī. What a ridiculous old brahman he is!

Avimāraka. Do you hear that, old fellow? You're ridiculous.

Jester. Now who can say anything so incredible about me. I am not ridiculous, but her ladyship. Finding her situation so bad, she determined to do something desperate. Then she heard a clap of thunder, forgot all about her purpose, and fell in a heap.

Kuraṅgī. Oh, so they saw that too.

Little Lotus. I beg you, brahman, come this way.

Jester. I'll go if you'll promise to feed me. Very welcome is the food given to a new arrival.

Little Lotus. Come along. I'll give you all my ornaments.

Jester. Fine words butter no parsnips.[3] Give them into my hands.

Little Lotus. Very well. [*Takes off her jewels and gives them to him.*]

Jester. Listen, lady.

Little Lotus. Idiot of a brahman! I'll sit in the hall with the other girls and hear it there.

Jester. I'll take leave of the princess and then I'll come.

Little Lotus. Who do you think you are? You've taken all my jewellery, so now you're my fancy man. Come along at once. [*Seizes him.*]

Jester. Don't do that, lady. I am very tender.

Little Lotus. I know all about your tenderness. If you are, come along, quick.

Jester. Oh, lady, here I come.

[1] A *raktapaṭa* (red cloth) mendicant.

[2] Presumably a Jain monk.

[3] Lit. 'The word "butter" does not remove bile.'

Avimāraka. Darling, look at those dark clouds, so welcome at the beginning of the rains and exquisitely beautiful. For—

Beauteous are these dark blue clouds, like dancers acting many parts to the drumming of the thunder in the rains. The kine of Him that wields the thunderbolt—curtains of the host of stars—Anthill homes of those she-snakes the lightning flashes—Bushes growing on the celestial road—Hones for the Love God's arrows—They guarantee the favours of the sulkiest of damsels. Water-jars to bathe the mountains, they bring us alms, water from the sea—Bars to hold the sun and moon —and cisterns of heaven's shower-bath. (6)

Kuraṅgī. Yes, my lord, they are beautiful now.

Avimāraka. The showers are heavy and then light. So—

The clouds resound like waves of heaven's ocean. Showers drop down as if they grew out from the clouds. Lightning flashes like the frowns of demon ladies. The season has come when lovers press the rounded breasts of early youth. (7)

Kuraṅgī. My lord, it's beginning now to rain.

Avimāraka. Come, darling, we will go within.

Kuraṅgī. [*Joyfully.*] As my lord commands.

[*Exeunt ambo.*]

END OF THE FIFTH ACT.

ACT VI

INTERLUDE

[*Enter the Nurse.*]

Nurse. Oh, what a fickle thing is fate! First of all the princess was selected by his majesty the king of the Sauvīras for his son Vishṇusena. And now she is united with somebody of unknown descent, though indeed his remarkable qualities and appearance are rare in this mortal world. And then, if you please, comes Jayavarman, prince of Benares, brought here by the minister Bhūtika, with Queen Sudarśanā as well, to stay in the palace. The king of Benares couldn't come because he was busy with a sacrifice. Now what on earth is going to happen next?

[*Enter Vasumitrā.*]

Vasumitrā. Drat these crotchety astrologers! They only think of some particular constellation and don't understand what's really important. The prince has only arrived to-day, and they have gone and fixed to-day for the wedding. [*Steps round.*] Now, what's wrong with Jayadā here? What's she thinking about that she looks so cross and worried? Jayadā, the queen wants you to go to her.

Nurse. Do you know what for?

Vasumitrā. What could it be but to consider what's to be done about this business?

Nurse. What is the queen's present inclination?

Vasumitrā. She doesn't want to marry the princess to Jayavarman until we get some news of Vishṇusena, who is a relation of hers. And the king too is very troubled at hearing nothing about the Sauvīra prince.

[*Enter Little Lotus.*]

Little Lotus. It seems as if all our difficulties had conspired to come together this very day. [*Stepping and looking round.*] Why, there is my mother discussing something with Vasumitrā. I'll go up and hear the bad news.

Vasumitrā. Oh, come here, Little Lotus. You're thick with the chamberlain, so you know all the news of the palace.

Little Lotus. The very latest. That's what I've come to tell you.

Vasumitrā. Speak out, my child.

Little Lotus. The ministers of the king of the Sauvīras have sent a messenger to inform our king that their secret agents have found out that their king is living in disguise with his wife and son in our city.

Nurse and Vasumitrā. What, living in disguise? Go on.

Little Lotus. When the king heard all this and had looked at the end of the letter he went out with the noble Bhūtika to search for him.

Nurse. I wonder what will happen.

Vasumitrā. Little Lotus, you'd better go inside.

Little Lotus. As madam says. [*Exit.*]

Vasumitrā. Come along. Let us see the queen.

Nurse. Yes, let us do so.

[*Exeunt ambo.*]

END OF THE INTERLUDE.

[*Enter Kuntibhoja with the king of the Sauvīras and Bhūtika.*]

Kuntibhoja. My friend—

Meeting again after so long, why doest thou gaze at my face?
Bring to mind our childhood's days and embrace me closely.
With my delight in gazing intently at thee affection seems
to-day to have renewed our friendship. (1)

King of the Sauvīras. As you will. [*They embrace.*]

Kuntibhoja. Thy mind would seem oppressed by trouble. Thy speech is faltering and choked with tears. Thine eyes are wet; thy face is sad. Why this agitation at a time of joy? (2)

Sauvīra. Do not think I am not delighted to see you again. But my love for my son is so strong.

My sorrow for my son hidden in my heart now shows itself, and gaining thee to aid, bubbles forth in tears. (3)

Kuntibhoja. How do you mean? Sorrow for your son?

Bhūtika. Be it known to your Majesty—the prince has not been seen for a whole year.

Sauvīra. My love for my son is so strong. Look you—

It is for my boy I grieve to-day, for Avimāraka, matchless in strength, in courage, and in beauty. Were he but here, his locks anointed[1] with the dust from thy feet, who were happier than I? (4)

Bhūtika. [*Aside.*] His great sorrow about the prince grows greater. I will put an end to it. [*Aloud.*] How did this misfortune befall your Highness?

Kuntibhoja. In my distraction I quite forgot to ask you that.

Sauvīra. Listen. Nay, Bhūtika knows all about it. Or do you wish to hear it from my mouth?

Kuntibhoja. We are all attention.

Sauvīra. There is a divine sage known as Caṇḍabhārgava—a very irascible person.

Kuntibhoja. We have heard of him—a treasure-house of penance.

Sauvīra. He came to my kingdom. In the forest a tiger attacked and killed his pupil.

Kuntibhoja. And then?

Sauvīra. I was hunting at the time and happened to come to the place that very moment.

Kuntibhoja. Go on.

Sauvīra. When he saw me he flew into a rage, blazing with the fire of wrath, his face distorted by his scowling brows, his long matted locks hanging loose, and his hand upon the boy. He wouldn't listen to a word I said but, stuttering with rage, began to abuse me in every way.

Kuntibhoja. What did you do?

Sauvīra. Then by the predominance of what is destined to take place I became impatient and lost my temper and said, 'You say nothing of the facts and abuse me without cause'.

[1] Reading *añjita* for *añcita* ('curled').

Thou doest not say what's happened but fliest into a rage. Without cause doest thou abuse me as thou wilt. Unworthy vessel of penance thou, by reason of thine anger, in form a sage divine; in fact, a savage fed on dogs.[1] (5)

Kuntibhoja. You shouldn't have said that.

Sauvīra. When he heard that, his eyes blazed out like the fire when they pour the butter in. 'What, what!' he cried, shaking his head several times, and then he began to lay a curse upon me.

Whereas a great sage divine like me has been styled an outcast, so shalt thou with wife and son sink to the level of outcasts. (6)

Kuntibhoja. Ah, how a little thing may lead to the misfortune of the great.

Bhūtika. There is good fortune for the Sauvīra's royal house. For—

The wrathful sage converted you into an outcast, and yet by that form all was not burnt to ashes. (7)

Kuntibhoja. Well said. Pray proceed.

Sauvīra. Then I was disturbed in my mind by that imprecation, and after I besought him for a long time he gradually regained his normal composure and granted a favour.

While thou livest in disguise a year shall pass. When the year is over thou shalt be free of the ban. (8)

With those words he became cheerful and shouted 'Come along, Kāśyapa', and the lad who had been mauled by a tiger got up and followed him. A whole year I have lived as an outcast. To-day I am freed from the curse.

Kuntibhoja. What a rise and fall of trouble! I congratulate you.

Bhūtika. Victory to your Highness!

Kuntibhoja. Have Vishṇusena's mother and her retinue gone to the ladies' court?

Bhūtika. Her ladyship has gone within and revives the affection so long asleep.

Kuntibhoja. But tell me now how did Vishṇusena become Avimāraka?

Bhūtika. Hearken, my lord; there was a demon called Smoke-banner.[2] Roaming about to slaughter the whole world he once began to destroy the Sauvīras' kingdom.

Kuntibhoja. What a strange story. Proceed.

Bhūtika. When the king saw the distress of all his subjects and was unable to find a remedy against the demon he was sorely troubled.

[1] *Śvapāka*—a dog-cooking outcast. [2] Dhūmaketu.

Kuntibhoja. Go on.

Bhūtika. Now Prince Vishṇusena—who knew all about it—was romping with children of his own age, his side curls hanging loose, and his limbs all white with dust from the ground. And suddenly by the power of fate, while his guards were not looking, he came to the place where that demon happened to be.

Kuntibhoja. How wonderful! What happened then?

Bhūtika. The demon was delighted to see the prince, regarding him as a dainty morsel, and began to set about his business.

Kuntibhoja. Oh, the cruel demon! What then?

Bhūtika. The prince gave a little laugh—

Then the prince unarmed, fighting as in play, slew that ogre even as a flying thunderbolt smites a mighty mountain or a forest fire destroys a woodland region. (9)

Kuntibhoja. At the very first in the confusion about the elephant I said he was of divine descent and could not be a mortal.

Sauvīra. With your spies, sir, you have a thousand eyes. What do you think about Avimāraka?

Bhūtika. My lord—

Every accessible country have I had thoroughly explored, and nowhere have my agents seen the prince. There remains the power of the mind to find him out, and doubtless he resorts to magic. (10)

[*Enter Nārada.*[1]]

Nārada. With verses from the Veda I propitiate the grandsire, Brahmā, with songs make Hari thrill with joy. Day by day with various devices I produce melodies for strings and quarrels in the world. (11)

Duryodhana, the father of Kuntibhoja, honoured us for many years. Since he passed to the common lot of mortals Kuntibhoja acts as our attendant. To-day Kuntibhoja and the king of the Sauvīras are in great difficulty owing to the disappearance of Avimāraka. So now I have descended on the earth to remove their anguish by revealing Avimāraka. [*Stands in front of Kuntibhoja and the king of the Sauvīras.*]

Kuntibhoja. Oh, here is the divine sage Nārada. I salute your reverence.

Nārada. May all go well with you.

Kuntibhoja. I thank you.

[1] The celestial busybody who so often set people by the ears but sometimes puts things right.

Sauvīra. Reverend sir, I salute you.

Nārada. Peace be with you.

Sauvīra. I thank you.

Kuntibhoja. [*Whispering.*] Bhūtika, will you please . . .

Bhūtika. As my lord commands. [*Exit and returns.*] Here is refreshment and water for the feet.

Kuntibhoja. Reverend sir, do us the favour.

Nārada. Very well.

Kuntibhoja. [*With a gesture of adoration.*] Reverend sir, your visit has purified our house.

Sauvīra. Now am I indeed freed from the curse at the sight of the divine sage.

Nārada. I have not come here at this moment merely to see you. I came down because I knew of the trouble that has come to you through the disappearance of Avimāraka.

Both Kings. If that is so, our sorrow is removed.

Nārada. Bhūtika, bring Sudarśanā here.

Bhūtika. As your reverence commands. [*Exit and re-enter with Sudarśanā.*]

Sudarśanā. Has the divine sage arrived?

Bhūtika. That is so.

Sudarśanā. Now my son's marriage is under good protection. [*Approaching.*] Your reverence, my greeting.

Nārada. Even so, fortunate lady, may you ever attain happiness.
And may king Kuntibhoja ever be overwhelmed with joy. (**12**)

Sudarśanā. I thank you.

Nārada. Now you two may ask me questions.

Both Kings. We thank you.

Kuntibhoja. Sir, is the Sauvīra prince alive?

Nārada. Yes.

Sauvīra. Why is he nowhere to be seen?

Nārada. Because of the distractions of marriage.

Sauvīra. What, is the prince married?

Kuntibhoja. In what place?

Nārada. In the city Vairantya.

Kuntibhoja. Is there another town called Vairantya? Well, whose son-in-law is he?

Nārada. Kuntibhoja's.

Kuntibhoja. Who is he?

Nārada. Kuraṅgī's father, lord of Vairantya city, Duryodhana's son, thyself Kuntibhoja. (**13**)

Kuntibhoja. No need of many questions. You say the prince has married my daughter Kuraṅgī.

Nārada. Quite so.

Kuntibhoja. I feel ashamed. Who gave her in marriage and how? How did he enter the princess's palace?

Nārada. Destiny gave her in marriage. He saw her first in the
confusion about the elephant. He entered first by daring,
afterwards by magic. (14)

Kuntibhoja. Be it so. There is no answer to the dictum of a sage. Reverend sir, is it now an auspicious time for the prince and Kuraṅgī? First of all, their wedding should be celebrated.

Nārada. The wedding has taken place—a love marriage by mutual consent. Now—

Kuntibhoja. I want the ceremony with fire as witness.

Nārada. It has fire as an eternal witness. Still, to satisfy your relations, you may have the ceremony performed by the priest in accordance with the family tradition. Then at once bring the prince here with his bride.

Kuntibhoja. Sir, I'll go at once.

Nārada. Nay, stay. Do you go, Bhūtika.

Bhūtika. As your reverence commands. [*Exit.*]

Kuntibhoja. Sir, I have something to tell.

Nārada. This way then. Speak out freely.

Kuntibhoja. I have already promised Kuraṅgī's hand to Jayavarman, the son of Queen Sudarśanā, and invited the queen here with her retinue. Tell me, what am I to do now?

Nārada. I will see to it. Stand aside a moment.

Kuntibhoja. Very well. [*Does so.*]

Nārada. Sudarśanā, come here.

Sudarśanā. Here I am, your reverence.

Nārada. Did you hear what we were saying?

Sudarśanā. I heard the praises of the Sauvīra prince.

Nārada. Nay, say not so. Have you forgotten your first-born, the Fire-God's son?

Sudarśanā. Oh, do you know that too?

Nārada. Attend to what I say.

Sudarśanā. I will do so. Tell me.

Nārada. This is your son by the Fire-God. The son of your sister Sucetanā died at birth. You gave your own son to your sister. The king of the Sauvīras was delighted, performed ceremonies in keeping with his affection, and named the boy Vishṇusena. He grew up with superhuman beauty, strength, courage, and energy; and because he killed a demon in the form of a sheep the people called him Avimāraka ('Sheepkiller'). Then he was degraded by the sage's curse. He saw Kuraṅgī on the day of the excitement about the elephant, fell in love with her, and married her with remarkable daring. Kuraṅgī's appearance made the palace guards suspicious, but while they were searching for Avimāraka, he was concealed by the God of Fire and escaped. In great sorrow he threw himself into a fire, but his father Agni embraced him tenderly. So as fire did not burn him, he climbed a mountain in order to throw himself down a precipice.

Sudarśanā. Oh, how dreadful!

Nārada. There some fairy, charmed by the very sight of him, gave him out of affection a ring of invisibility. If he wears it on his right hand he becomes invisible; if on his left hand he resumes his natural form.

Sudarśanā. How marvellous!

Nārada. Then, wearing the ring on his right hand and accompanied by a brahman named Santushṭa, he entered Kuntibhoja's daughter's palace as if it was his own house, and lived at his ease, enjoying Kuraṅgī's company to his heart's content—that's the story. Now, what is to be done?

Sudarśanā. My mind is agitated about the lady who has been deceived, but I find it delightfully interesting. Kuraṅgī, you know, sir, has been spoken of the last few days as the wife-to-be of Jayavarman. From to-day on she is entitled to his respect.[1]

Nārada. Your words are worthy of you. How indeed can an elder's bride be given to a younger brother? Sudarśanā, tell the king of Benares that Kuraṅgī is too old for Jayavarman. Kuraṅgī has a younger sister, Sumitrā. She shall be Jayavarman's wife.

Sudarśanā. The sage's word is accepted.

Nārada. Now go over to Kuntibhoja.

Sudarśanā. As your reverence commands.

[*Enter Avimāraka in wedding robes, Kuraṅgī, and Bhūtika.*]

Avimāraka. This affair makes me rather ashamed.

Those who saw me then in the business with the elephant and
praised my powers, will they not accuse me of misbehaviour
when they hear this story? **(15)**

[*Steps round and sees Nārada.*]

Why, here is the blessed Nārada.

His mind is set on praise and imprecation; his voice melodious

[1] As his elder brother's wife.

in Vedic texts and songs. He toils to sow discord among the closest friends and sets things right when all seems lost. (16)

Kuntibhoja. This way, Prince. Salute the divine sage, guardian of our house.

Avimāraka. Reverend sir, I salute you.

Nārada. May you and your wife be prosperous.

Avimāraka. I thank you. [Uncle, I salute you.

Kuntibhoja. Come here, my child.

With kindness conquer holy brahmans; with compassion conquer your retainers; with knowledge of the truth conquer thyself, and with courage conquer kings.[1]] (17)

Avimāraka. I thank you.

Kuntibhoja. Come, boy, salute your father.

Avimāraka. Oh, father dear, I salute you.

Sauvīra. Come here, my child—

Splendid in thy bridegroom's dress, thy bright face intent on saluting thy elders. Like us, mayest thou some day gaze upon thy son with eyes full of tears of joy. (18)

My son, salute your uncle.

Avimāraka. Uncle, I salute you.

Kuntibhoja. Come here, my child.

With constant auspicious sacrifices be thou like Hari. With truth inflexible be thou Daśaratha's equal. And be thou like thy father with unending[2] charity in thy self and worthy prowess. (19)

Sauvīra. My son, salute Queen Sudarśanā.

Kuntibhoja. Nay, that is not right. He should first salute Sucetanā.

Nārada. There is a reason why it should be Sudarśanā.

Both Kings. Agreed.

Avimāraka. Lady, I salute you.

Sudarśanā. My son, long may you live with this your bride. [*Embraces him.*] 'Tis so long since I saw you that I feel to-day once more the joy of having a son. [*Weeps.*]

[**Kuntibhoja**. This lady with eyes full of wonder and wet with tears and bosoms swelling with affection[3] appears to me the real mother, though this was not revealed by Sucetanā, who now ranks but as his foster-mother. (20)]

[1] He salutes his uncle further on. Spurious, as Weller notes.

[2] Reading *nityārpitaiḥ* with editor.

[3] Lit. 'With her two breasts streaming with milk.' Weller, following Jacobi, omits the verse as spurious.

Nārada. A truce to sentiment. Now let them go within, Sucetanā the wise and Sudarśanā the beautiful,[1] with her son and his bride.

Kuntibhoja. As your reverence commands.

Sudarśanā. As his reverence bids.

Nārada. The king of the Sauvīras should soon depart and go to his own country. Let Sumitrā be given to Jayavarman, prince of Benares.[2] And, Kuntibhoja, do you be ever at my right hand.

Kuntibhoja. I thank you.

Nārada. Kuntibhoja, what other favour can I show to you?

Kuntibhoja. If your reverence is pleased with me, what else can I desire?

> Ever prosperous be priests and kine. And all subjects in the world be happy.

Nārada. Sauvīra, what further favour can I offer you?

Sauvīra. If your reverence is pleased with me, what else can I desire?

> May our king rule this earth clad in blue robes of the mighty oceans. **(21)**

EPILOGUE

May the kine be without blemish, and, subduing the sovereignty of his foes, may our Lion King rule over this earth in its entirety.[3]

[1] *Sucetanā sucetanā sudarśanā sudarśanā ca.* A poor pun, probably spurious. Sucetanā is not on the stage.

[2] Lit. King of Benares, but his father is still alive.

[3] Identical with the epilogue of *The Minister's Vow*, vol. i, p. 35. Perhaps verse 21 was the original epilogue here.

THE ADVENTURES OF THE BOY KṚISHṆA

(*Bāla-caritam*)

INTRODUCTION

THIS play is based on a number of incidents in the early life of Kṛishṇa, leading up to the death of the wicked king Kaṃsa. Modern works on this subject are mainly based on the versions found in the Harivaṃśa, the Vishṇupurāṇa, and the Bhāgavata-purāṇa. The main story is of course much older than these works. When our dramatist differs from the usual version it is a question how far the difference is due to his own originality and how far it is due to an earlier and more popular form of the story.

This much is common to all versions. Some demon was born as the wicked Kaṃsa, who imprisoned the old king of Mathurā. Kṛishṇa, an incarnation of Vishṇu, was born to overthrow the wicked Kaṃsa. Kṛishṇa was the son of Devakī, sister or cousin of Kaṃsa. The wicked king knew there was a prophecy that he would be killed by a child of Devakī. So he had Devakī's children destroyed. At last the eighth (or seventh) child was hidden and brought up unknown to Kaṃsa, among the herdsmen. This child was Kṛishṇa, Vasudeva's son whom the herdsmen called Dāmodara. The divine child performed many marvels, slew Kaṃsa, and set free the old king of Mathurā.

In this play there are features not found in the late epic and purānic stories. For instance, the portents after Kṛishṇa's birth, the great weight of the baby, the brilliant light and the gushing of water from the sand; the introduction of Cāṇḍāla maidens, the bad king's Fortune, of Kārtyāyanī and Vishṇu's weapons. It has been urged [1] that the absence of the erotic element, so familiar in later descriptions of Rādhā and the Gōpīs, indicates an older version. On the other hand it might be suspected that Vishṇu's weapons have been introduced by the later hand of a pious Vaishnavite.[2]

In the First Act Nārada, the lover of music and strife, is brought on as a sort of chorus to introduce Devakī with her baby and her husband Vasudeva. Vasudeva carries the baby out of Mathurā by night.

[1] H. Weller, Introduction to German translation, p. 13.

[2] Compare the Weapons scene in *The Embassy*.

Describing the darkness he recites the famous verse I. 15 *Limpatīva* ... which recurs in *Cārudatta in Poverty*, I. 19. The child produces light to show the way. The Jamna is in flood, but the waters divide for them to pass. Vasudeva comes across the herdsman Nandagopa carrying a dead girl-baby, daughter of his wife Yaśodā. Nandagopa is persuaded to substitute the boy Kṛishṇa, but finds him too heavy to lift. Then the action is interrupted by the incursion of Garuḍa and the weapons, who recite verses about their prowess, and announce their intention of going to the herdsmen's station disguised as cowherd boys. The Discus asks Kṛishṇa to make himself lighter, and the weapons and Garuḍa disappear. The passage is clumsy, and the Act reads better without it.

Nandagopa goes off with the boy, and Vasudeva finds the little girl is alive, and determines to take her to Devakī, the better to deceive Kaṃsa. (ACT I.) The wicked king Kaṃsa has strange visions. Young outcaste women plague him. Then comes the Seer's curse to warn him, and disputes the ground with the king's Good Fortune, who leaves him, at Vishṇu's command, to the tender mercies of Curse, Bald-head, Yellow-eye, and other spectres. The king thinks he has been dreaming, but is troubled by bad omens. He sends for Vasudeva, who tells a lie, that Devakī has been delivered of a daughter. The king determines to kill the girl, and dashes her upon 'Kaṃsa's stone'. The child is transformed into a goddess of destruction. As Kārtyāyanī, she enters with a Serpent, Spear, and other figures. They recite verses, and decide to disguise themselves as cowherds. The king goes out to make an offering of expiation. (ACT II.)

In an Interlude the Old Herdsman tells us of many of the Boy's pranks and exploits. Then Dāmodara, as they call him, comes on to lead a rustic dance. He is interrupted by the Dreadnought Bull, really a demon, whom he slays. Then he gets news of the serpent Kāliya. (ACT III.)

The Fourth Act is devoted to the struggle with the serpent Kāliya, while the girls and herdsmen look on from a distance. At the end they are invited by the king to a great festival, the Consecration of the Bow. Dāmodara announces his intention of killing Kaṃsa. (ACT IV.)

The wicked king has heard disturbing tales of Dāmodara's prowess, and determines to have him smashed by a wrestler in the ring. News is brought of Dāmodara's entry into Mathurā, how he robbed the *dhobis*, killed an elephant that was set upon him, cured the humpbacked maiden, killed the guardian of the archery hall, and broke the Bow in two. The king's two prize-fighters boast of their strength, but are defeated by Dāmodara and his elder brother Saṅkarshaṇa.[1] Then Dāmodara leaps into the king's balcony, seizes Kaṃsa by his hair, and throws him down, smashed to pieces.

Vasudeva addresses the citizens, and the old king Ugrasena is restored to the throne. Nārada comes in to worship Vishṇu in the form of Dāmodara. (ACT V.)

There is in this play a curious blend of ferocity and mildness. The Bull is slain on the stage, but he has guessed the identity of his victor and says, 'If I am slain by Vishṇu I shall go to heaven'. (III. 13.) The frightful Serpent is hauled out of his pool, but he departs penitent, promising to take the poison out of the water he has defiled. (IV. 12.) A dead child is left on the ground, but comes to life again. (ACT I.) Then the girl is dashed upon the stone before our eyes, but arises as a goddess. (II. 17.) The two prize-fighters and the wicked king are ruthlessly slaughtered, but rapidly in two verses. (V. 10, 11.) The consequent excitement is soon quieted, and the herdsmen restore the old king to the throne.

King Kaṃsa himself is driven by the curse, and has to summon all his courage to kill the child (II. 17), and goes out to make a great offering of expiation. (II. 25.) He meant to have Dāmodara put out of the way by his pugilists, but he is by no means represented as a complete demon like Rāvaṇa.

[1] Born of Rohiṇī, Vasudeva's other wife. In the Harivaṃśa Saṅkarshaṇa-Balarāma is the seventh son of Devakī, transferred to Rohiṇī's body to deceive Kaṃsa. In this play Kṛishṇa is the seventh son of Devakī. This is simpler and more artistic.

DRAMATIS PERSONAE

(In the order of their appearance.)

Stage-manager. In Prologue.
Nārada, divine sage and busybody.
Devakī, wife of Vasudeva, mother of Kṛishṇa.
Vasudeva, father of Kṛishṇa.
Nandagopa, headman of the cattle station, foster-father of Kṛishṇa.
Garuḍa, the fabulous bird, the vehicle of Vishṇu (or Kṛishṇa).
Discus, one of Vishṇu's weapons. Cakra.
Bow, Śārañga, another of Vishṇu's weapons.
Club, Kaumodakī, another of Vishṇu's weapons.
Conch, Śañkha.
Sword, Nandaka.
Cāṇḍāla women.
King of Mathurā, Kaṃsa the wicked usurper, brother or cousin of Devakī.
Curse of the seer Madhuka. 'Arms of Thunderbolt.'
Fortune, Śrī, the king's good fortune.
(Other spectres—Ill-luck, Baldhead, Midnight, Deep-sleep, and Yellow-eye do not speak.)
Portress, Yāśodharā.
Chamberlain, Bālāki.
Nurse.
Kārtyāyanī, the goddess Dūrgā, arising from the body of the daughter of Nandagopa and Yaśodā.
Pot-belly, Kuṇḍodara, the serpent in the goddess's train.
Spear, the goddess's weapon.
Speed of Thought, another figure in the goddess's train.
Nīla, Dark-blue.
Old Herdsman.
Dāmaka, a herdsman.
Girls—*gopīs* of the cattle station.
Belle of the station, Ghoshasundarī.
Wood garland, Vanamālā.
Crescent, Candralekhā.
Gazelle, Mṛigākshī.
Dāmodara, Kṛishṇa.

Saṅkarshaṇa, 'Plougher'. Halāyudha or Balarāma. Kṛishṇa's elder brother, born of Rohiṇī.

Meghanāda, a herdsman.

(Other herdsmen—Meghadatta, Bull, Pott, and Herder—do not speak separately.)

Dreadnought Bull, Arishṭa-vṛishabha.

Kāliya, a Nāga or Serpent.

Servant of King Kaṃsa, Dhruvasena.

Another Portress in Kaṃsa's palace, Madhurikā.

Cāṇūra, a pugilist.

Boxer, a pugilist, Mushṭika.

Ugrasena, the former king of Mathurā, imprisoned by Kaṃsa.

PROLOGUE

[*At the end of the Opening enter the Stage-Manager.*]

Stage-Manager. For ever and ever may that God protect you—who, with a body white as milk or conch, of old was named Nārāyaṇa in the golden age; who shone like gold and measured the triple world, entitled Vishṇu in the silver age; who dark as *dūrvā* grass slew Rāvaṇa, and was called Rāma in the copper age; who now is black like collyrium, Dāmodara in the age of iron.[1] (1)

With these words, my lords and gentlemen, I have to announce to you . . . But what is that? I thought I heard a noise, just as I was to make my announcement. Well, I must see what it is.

[*Voice behind the scene.*]

I, that roam in the sky . . .

Stage-Manager. So be it—I understand.

There falls a shower of blossom. The celestials' instruments resound. Here comes Nārada swiftly to see Hari born in the Vṛishṇi clan. (2) [*Exit.*]

END OF THE PROLOGUE.

ACT I

[*Enter Nārada.*]

Nārada. I, that roam in the sky, renowned in all three worlds have come from highest heaven, Nārada, lover of strife. (3)

Ha! Now that the battles of the gods and the demons have come to an end, I find no enjoyment in a sky that is always calm. For in my leisure from study of scripture I strike the strings and stir up strife. (4)

Moreover, I have great faith in my grandsire's words and respect for all the penance groves. Sooth to say, I love the lute touched by finger tips, and enmity and dreadful bitter quarrels. (5)

So I have come here to see the Lord Nārāyaṇa, who has been born in the Vṛishṇi clan in order to help the world by slaying Kaṃsa. Nārāyaṇa,

[1] The four ages *yugāni*, Kṛita, Tretā, Dvāpara and Kali, the names of which are connected with those of throws of dice, i. e. nothing, three, two, or one over, when divided by four. Dāmodara is a name of Kṛishṇa.

the beginning of the Universe, unceasing and imperishable. Ah, here is the lady Devakī. In her arms she holds the lord of the triple world transformed by magic power into a child. She is coming slowly from her house with Vasudeva.

Here she comes by night with her pale face,[1] oppressed by sorrow but resigned, carrying in her arms as it were a mighty mountain,[2] the Lord of Gods, Refuge of worlds, the Wielder of the Discus and Destroyer of Demons. (6)

Here is the blessed Nārāyaṇa—

He is the Ancient that supports all living things, the Banner of the Triple Word, Creator of the Universe. His large eyes are lovely as the lotus, but his strength is limitless. Master of the mighty gods he strikes down the power of demons. (7)

Ha, here we have the very root of strife. I will circumambulate the blessed Nārāyaṇa and then return to highest heaven. Salutation to the Blessed One, Cause of all the Universe—

Obeisance to Nārāyaṇa, the Supreme Protection of the world of men. Obeisance to Him with the white lotus eyes, Mask of all the World, a Rāma to put out the light of Rāvaṇa, the warrior that is the source of valour, the Best of All. (8)

[*Exit.*]

[*Enter Devakī with a child in her arms.*]

Devakī. Ah me! When my child was born I beheld the wondrous signs that will proclaim his greatness. Yet when I think of the accursed Kaṃsa's[3] cruelty, I cannot believe them, so unfortunate am I. Where's my husband gone?

[*Stepping round and looking before her.*]

Ah, here he is coming this very way, his eyes full of joy and wonder.

[*Enter Vasudeva.*]

Vasudeva. [*Reflecting.*] Ah, what can this mean?

The sky reels and the earth trembles with the thundering of dark clouds pierced by lightning and fierce gusts of wind. Has Vishṇu descended secretly, the smiter of demon clans for the protection of the people? (9)

[*Looking up.*] Here is Devakī.

After woes innumerable she goes to save her seventh and avoid the loss that befell six sons. She is made eager by his many

[1] 'Moon-faced'.

[2] Mt. Mandara, used for churning the ocean.

[3] Her cousin (or brother) king of Mathurā who had her children killed because of a prophecy that he himself would be slain by a son of Devakī.

qualities revealed by signs at birth, and carries the death of Kaṃsa, calling it her son. (10)

Devakī. [*Approaching.*] Greeting, my lord.

Vasudeva. It is midnight, Devakī. Everybody in Mathurā is asleep. So, while no one is looking, I will take the boy away.

Devakī. Where will you take him?

Vasudeva. Well may you ask. I do not know. The wicked Kaṃsa rules over the whole earth with a single sway. So where should I take this child, long life to him? Nay, I will take the boy where destiny decides.

Devakī. My lord, I want a long look at him.

Vasudeva. Ah, mother, all too fond,

Wouldst thou gaze at this infant moon in the dragon's[1] maw? While thou hast thy long, long look, Kaṃsa will be the death of him. (11)

Devakī. That shall he never be.

Vasudeva. May all the gods say the same. Bring him here.

Devakī. Take him, my lord.

Vasudeva. Oh, how heavy the child is.

With eyes of lotus petal this child is weighty as the Vindhya and Mandara mountains. How wonderful the endurance of the woman that carried him in her womb. (12)

Devakī, go within.

Devakī. I am going, unhappy that I am. [*Exit.*]

Vasudeva. Poor Devakī,

Her heart is here, her body there. So is she cut in two, as the crescent moon is seen at once in the water and in the sky. (13)

Devakī has gone in. Come, I must hasten to the city gate.

Full of wrath at the slaughter of my first-born but fearful of the King, I must take the child, and race along the road, swifter than the swift, though my arms seem to lift a mountain. (14)

[*Stepping round.*] Here is the city gate. I'll slip through. [*Does so.*] Everybody in Mathurā is asleep. I'll be off. [*Stepping round.*] Now I'm away from Mathurā. How thick this darkness is. For now—

Darkness anoints my limbs, the sky, it seems, is raining lamp black; my sight is useless, like service rendered to a rascal.[2] (15)

How great the power of darkness.

[1] Rāhu the demon that swallows the moon and causes its eclipse.

[2] Stanza recurs in *Cārudatta in Poverty*, i. 19.

The quarters are invisible, the trees one solid mass. The familiar world is utterly transformed. (16)

I can go no farther. Hullo! the light of a lamp. Can the wicked Kaṃsa have learnt of my departure and have come with lights to seize me? If so, I shall teach him a lesson. [*Draws his sword, turns, and looks back.*] No, there is no one to be seen. Ah!

When my sight was overcome with darkness and I could not see my way, the child produced this brightness to assist our flight. (17)

This is the way. I must be off again. Hullo! this is the sacred Jamna that I've come to, swollen with the rains. Alas, all my efforts are in vain. What am I to do now? Good, I have it.

Though this stream is alive with snakes and crocodiles, and tumultuous with mighty waves, difficult to pass even in imagination, timidity is useless, and I must win through and swiftly swim across, if fate allows. (18)

[*Proceeds to do so. In amazement.*] Why, the water is cut in two; on this side it stands still, on the other runs away. The holy river makes a way for me. I must hurry on. [*Goes down into the river.*] Now I have crossed the Jamna. Hist! that sounds like voices.[1] I am unlucky. Obviously I must be close to a herdsmen's station. Yes, my old friend Nandagopa lives in a station near here. Once I flogged him at Kaṃsa's orders and put him in fetters. I will go in. Nay, but the herdsmen will be suspicious, if they see me coming here by night. So I'll pass the night under this banyan tree and wait for dawn. O spirit of this banyan tree, if this child has been born in the Vrishṇi clan to slay Kaṃsa for the good of all the world, let some one come from the cattle station. No, no, let my old friend Nandagopa come.

[*Enter Nandagopa carrying a girl-baby.*]

Nandagopa. [*Sorrowfully.*] Little lass, little lass, wilt go away and leave us with never a taste of the luck of the house? And now how dark it is, with hundreds of buffaloes all in a heap.

The night's so dark with the welkin all obscured and the moonlight hidden by the dirty weather, 'tis like a shepherdess arrayed in black and fallen asleep in her clothes. (19)

This midnight my wife Yaśodā had a daughter, but the poor child died as soon as she was born. To-morrow our station is to hold a festival in Indra's honour. So lest the herdsmen should be downcast by this trouble, I took this little girl in my arms and came out alone, with my feet encumbered by my chains. Poor Yaśodā fainted away not even know-

[1] *huṃkāra*, grunting, &c.

ing whether the baby was a boy or a girl. Oh, little lass, poor little lass!

Vasudeva. Now, who is this lamenting in the night? This poor fellow must be a companion in misfortune.

Nandagopa. Wilt go away and leave us with no taste of the luck of the house?

Vasudeva. I recognize him by his voice. It must be my old friend Nandagopa. I'll call him. Nandagopa, my friend, come here.

Nandagopa. [*Alarmed.*] Now who the deuce is this calling me by name? 'Nandagopa, Nandagopa'; I've heard the voice before. Is it a demon or a goblin sprite?[1] Such a frightful night and the little girl in my arms, what am I to do?

Vasudeva. My dear Nandagopa, don't be alarmed. Come here.

Nandagopa. [*Listening attentively.*] Bless me, by the voice I think it's Master Vasudeva. I will go up to him. Nay, what have I to do with him? He listened to the word of Kaṃsa the king, and had me thrashed, he did, and put fetters on my feet. I'll not go near him. Nay now, out on this hard heart o' mine. He's done me a thousand kindnesses, he has, sorrowed in my sorrow, was glad when I was glad, besides I mind 'twas by the king's order he put me into jail. I'll go up to him. But here's the lass. What'll I do? Ay, good! that's the thing.

[*Approaches and looks round in surprise.*]

Why, it's getting light! Here's Master Vasudeva with a child in his arms. [*Coming up.*] How d'ye do, master, how d'ye do?

Vasudeva. Ah, good Nandagopa, and how are the royal kine?

Nandagopa. Ay, master, they're all right.

Vasudeva. And all your people?

Nandagopa. 'People', say you? Ay, they're fine.

Vasudeva. Come, good fellow. What are you hiding?

Nandagopa. Nay, master, naught at all.

Vasudeva. By my life I charge you, tell the truth.

Nandagopa. No help for 't. Well listen, master. This midnight my wife, nay, nay, I mean your honour's humble servant Yaśodā, had a daughter, but the poor child died as soon as she was born. To-morrow our station is to hold a festival in Indra's honour. So lest the herdsmen should be downcast by this trouble, I took this little girl in my arms and came out alone with my feet encumbered by chains. Poor Yaśodā fainted away not even knowing whether the babe was a boy or a girl.

Vasudeva. Alas, good fellow, one cannot cozen Death that commands the world. Come, friend, the corpse is stiff and stark,[2] abandon it.

[1] A Rākshasa or a Piśāca. [2] *Lit.* 'become wooden'.

Nandagopa. Nay, master, I can't do that.

Vasudeva. Such is the way of the world. Abandon it.

Nandagopa. As you order, master. Oh, little lass, little lass! [*Weeps.*]

Vasudeva. Do not grieve too much, my friend. Now rise, I say.

Nandagopa. [*Rises and comes near.*] Greeting, master, what orders for your humble servant?

Vasudeva. You know, good fellow, that the wicked Kaṃsa has had my six sons done to death.

Nandagopa. Yes, master, I know.

Vasudeva. Well, this is the seventh, long life to him. I have no luck with my sons. Do you take him, that he may live by your luck.

Nandagopa. I'm scared, master, wholly scared. If Kaṃsa should hear of it, a son of yours in my hands, why it 'll be all up with my head.

Vasudeva. [*Aside.*] My scheme miscarries. Remorseless men know what to say. That 's how I must speak. [*Aloud.*] My dear Nandagopa,

> If ever I have done thee any kindness, the time has come for thee to make some return thereof. **(20)**

Nandagopa. Some return, you say. Then I care nought for Kaṃsa or his father Ugrasena. Bring along the boy.

Vasudeva. Good fellow, take him.

Nandagopa. Nay, master. I am polluted by carrying the dead lassie. Wait a moment, master, while I purify myself in a pool of the Jamna.

Vasudeva. My good fellow, you're pure by nature from living in a cattle station.

Nandagopa. Then I'll purify myself with dust as the herdsmen do.

Vasudeva. No harm in that. Do so if you will.

Nandagopa. As my master orders. [*Does so. In surprise.*] Wonderful, master, wonderful. As I was picking up some dust, a stream of water two yards wide broke out of the ground.

Vasudeva. 'Tis the power of the child. Well, wash yourself.

Nandagopa. All right, master. [*Does so and returns.*] Master, here I am.

Vasudeva. Take him.

Nandagopa. Master, my arms are too weak to carry a child as heavy as a mountain.

Vasudeva. Come, old fellow, I know your strength and courage.

Nandagopa. Strength and courage? I'll tell you, master—when a bull 's tearing mad I can catch him by the horns and make him leave go. I can lift out a goods cart stuck in the mire. All the same I can't carry this child.

[*Enter the Five Weapons and Garuḍa.*]

Garuḍa. Garuḍa am I of beauteous wings and mighty speed. The chariot and pennon of the wielder of the Śārṅga bow. For of old in the battles of gods and demons it was I that carried Vishṇu with his force. (21)

Discus. I am Kṛishṇa's discus gleaming in his fingers. Dazzling is my lustre like the noon-day sun. At the three steps and the churning of the ocean I slew hordes of demons and evil sprites. (22)

Bow. I am the Bow. On my slender waist lies Vishṇu's hand. Female in form I boast the strength and courage of a man. For Vishṇu's sake in the van of battle have I smashed the serried lines of foes, destroying men and horses, elephants and cars. (23)

Club. I'm Hari's Club Kaumodakī. At his command I churned up Sarayū, slew the demons, and sported [1] in the torrents of their gore. (24)

Conch. The Conch I am, picked up by Vishṇu himself from the ocean. At the noise of me in battle these foes of the gods perish. (25)

Sword. I am Nandaka the sword. None can avoid me in battle. The moment mighty Vishṇu brings me to mind, out I come. (26)

Discus. We the discus, the bow, the club, the conch, and the sword, manglers of monsters, have come to serve the son of Vasudeva. (27)

So come. The holy Vishṇu has descended to the mortal world. We, too, will go down to the herdsmen's station disguised as cowherd boys to join the adventures of the Boy.

All the Weapons. So be it. [*They approach Vishṇu.*]

Vasudeva. My friend, pay homage to the child.

Nandagopa. Very well, master. O prince, my homage. Do thou make thyself much lighter, as easy to carry as hay. Otherwise how can a poor herdsman carry thee? [2]

Discus. Hail, divine Nārāyaṇa, Lord Vishṇu the Almighty.

The deeds of all immortals, good deeds and bad, will be forces in the world through thee. So do a favour to this man, O Banner of Yadu's House, by becoming light. (28)

Vasudeva. Take the child.

Nandagopa. As you order, master.

[1] Reading *prakrīḍitam* as suggested by the Editor.

[2] Adopting the Editor's ingenious emendation of a corrupt line.

Vasudeva. There is the dawn. Go back home, my friend.

Nandagopa. Wonderful! Oh master, a miracle! My fetters have fallen off.

Vasudeva. That's all through the prince's power. Go home.

Nandagopa. As you order, master.

Vasudeva. Nay, come here a moment.

Nandagopa. Here I am, master.

Vasudeva. I know thou art ever affectionate by nature, yet for this
child I demand thy love in the widest sense. At this time the
seed of the Yādavas, the last remnant of what is burnt, is
entrusted to thy keeping. (29)

How will you bring him up?

Nandagopa. Listen, master. He'll go to one hut and drink milk; in the second he'll drink curd. Then he'll go to another hut and swallow fresh butter; in another he'll eat rice pudding; in yet another he'll spy a jar of buttermilk. In short, he'll be the lord of our station.

Vasudeva. Very good. Now go.

Nandagopa. As you order, master. [*Exit.*]

Vasudeva. Well, Nandagopa is gone. I, too, must go back to Mathurā. [*Stepping around.*] It sounds as if some one were crying. Can Nandagopa have returned through fear of Kaṃsa? [*Stepping around.*] Why this little girl has come to life again. I'll take her and put her in Devakī's arms, so shall I deceive the wicked Kaṃsa. [*Takes up the girl.*] Oh, how heavy she is. This, too, is another wonder caused by the prince. I must away. Hullo, here is the Jamna, the same as it was before. I must get along. Now I've passed the Jamna. Here is the city gate. Everybody in Mathurā is still asleep. I'll go in. [*Enters.*] Here's the house of wicked Kaṃsa, looking like the abode of Ill-luck. And here is my own house, like the home of Fortune. I'll go inside and comfort Devakī.

May the gods be kind to us. [*Exit.*]

END OF THE FIRST ACT.

ACT II

[*Enter some young Cāṇḍāla*[1] *women.*]

All. Come, master, come along. Make a marriage with our girls.

[*Enter the King.*]

King. Ha! What is this?

[1] Outcastes.

The palace pinnacles are fallen. The earth is rocking like a ferry boat, cleaving a line of mighty billows. Such omens are of moment with the consequence of great qualities and deeds. Do they mean my fortune in the future—or calamity? (1)

All. Come, master, come along. Make a marriage with our girls.

King. No watchmen are on duty here, no maids with torches, and so my house is all invaded by these fearsome outcaste wenches, as dusky as blue lotus or collyrium. (2)

All. Come, master, come along. Make a marriage with our girls.

King. Oh, how impudent are these outcaste sluts?[1]

All my enemies perish before my wrath. Sun, moon, and fire, are in my control. I am death to the god of death, inspiring terror in the heart of fear, yet even me they harass with their insolence. (3)

All. Come, master, come along.

King. Despicable creatures. Why, they have suddenly disappeared! I'll go within.

[*Enter Curse.*]

Curse. Ho, there, where are you going? This house belongs to me.

King. Who is this appearing suddenly from inside? He's black as a mass of collyrium with a firebrand in his hand. His face is dreadful with projecting teeth, his eyes are yellow like a snake's. He has come to the earth, like wrath incarnate, from the mouth of Śiva. (4)

Who are you?

Curse. Don't you know me? I am the seer Madhuka's Curse, named Arms of Thunderbolts.

From the cremating ground I come, ugly and fierce, in a pariah's dress, adorned by a fine chaplet of skulls. I am here to enter the heart of King Kaṃsa. (5)

King. You seek the impossible.

The mountain Meru with its lovely golden bowers, its summits and its caves is not shaken by the wind of a crow's wings flapping. How ludicrous you are, desiring to drink up the ocean with its lines of tumultuous waves and all its monsters in your hollowed hands. (6)

Curse. In good time you will know. [*Vanishes.*]

King. Ho, vanished all of a sudden! I'll go to bed and rest my weary eyes. [*Sleeps.*]

Curse. [*Reappearing.*] Ah, he is asleep.—Poverty, Bald-head, Mid-

[1] Reading *dhṛṣṭāḥ* for *sṛṣṭāḥ*.

night, Deep-sleep, and Yellow-eye. Come here. Let us all go in.

All. Be it so.

[*Enter Fortune.*]

Fortune. You must not enter.

Curse. Who are you, lady?

Fortune. Don't you know me? I am his good fortune.

Curse. So? The king's fortune are you? Then you may leave at once. This house now belongs to me.

Fortune. Oh, indeed!

Thou fool, dost thou forget this house as rich as Laṅkā belongs to me? Who gave thee the right to come in here by night and drive me away? No need of many words. Thou canst not enter, or even gaze upon this house still possessed by me. (7)

Curse. Sweet Goddess, resting on the lotus, please leave this Kaṃsa's body. Such is Vishṇu's command.

Fortune. Vishṇu's command? Alas!

I have dwelt with the king so long, I am unable to desert him. This powerful chief, ever grasping his bow,[1] fills me with sore remorse. (8)

Still, the command of Vishṇu must not be disobeyed. So I must go to Vishṇu. [*Exit.*]

Curse. The king's fortune has gone. Now, indeed, this abode is ours. Come in Ill-luck, Baldhead, Midnight, Deep-sleep, and Yellow-eye; let us play the game that befits our breed.

All. From to-day be thou devoid of virtue and good deeds.

Curse. I clasp thee close ever on the path of wrong. The sage's curse am I, and now, I have thee fast. Ere long shalt thou come to destruction. (9)

[*Disappears.*]

[*Enter Portress.*]

Portress. Greeting, my lord.

King. Ha!

Portress. It's Yaśodharā, my lord.

King. Yaśodharā, didn't you see those outcaste women come in?

Portress. Outcaste women? Why, even the people who wait daily on my lord's lotus feet, find it hard to enter, let alone outcaste women.

King. Have I been dreaming then? Go, Yaśodharā and call the chamberlain, Bālāki.

Portress. As my lord commands. [*Exit.*]

[1] *Guṇa-saṅgrāhe*, H. Weller takes as 'with his fist on the bowstring'. Sarup takes it as 'collection of qualities'.

[*Enter the Chamberlain.*]

Chamberlain. Greeting to your Majesty!

King. My good Bālāki, put this question to the household priest and the astrologer. What portend to-night's storm of wind, earthquake, and shower of meteors, that are clearly signs of destiny?[1]

Chamberlain. Your Majesty, the priest and the astrologer declare—

King. Yes? What?

Chamberlain. Hearken—

The Eternal One, that dwells above the sky, has descended to the mortal world with some mysterious purpose. This tumult with the rolling of heaven's drums, and the earthquakes proclaim his birth. (10)

King. At whose birth has this earth with its mighty hills been shaken? Find out whose son it is, and the purpose of this incarnation. (11)

Chamberlain. As your Majesty commands. [*Exit and returns.*] Greeting, your Majesty! (The Princess Devakī has been delivered of a daughter.[2]

King. Is this true?)

Chamberlain. I have never told your Majesty a lie. She was seen in the nurse's arms with all your servants round.

King. Well, a brahman's word I hold as true, though it be false. Go summon Vasudeva.

Chamberlain. As your Majesty commands. [*Exit.*]

King. Vasudeva is virtuous and truthful. He will not tell me a lie. Good, we shall hear the truth.

[*Enter Vasudeva.*]

Vasudeva. Six of my sons have perished. Yet summoned by the cruel king, I drag this body wasted by sorrow to his presence like a helpless slave. (12)

Alas, such is the way of the world.

Whether one heeds the danger[3] or heeds it not, both ways, one must go to the king, from fear or from want of fear. (13)

[*Approaches the king.*] Oh, son of Śaurasenī, I am here.

King. Son of Yādavī, sit down.

Vasudeva. Very well. [*Sits down.*] Tell me, son of Śaurasenī, why have you summoned me?

[1] Reading doubtful. Weller, 'mysterious spirits appear'. Before the Chamberlain's statement one would expect him to 'Exit and re-enter' as the Editor points out.

[2] Following the Editor's suggested connexion of the text where there is clearly a lacuna.

[3] Sarup takes *bhayam* as nominative. 'Source of fear'. 'A king is a terror—heed him or heed him not'.

King. Devakī, I understand, has been delivered of a child.

Vasudeva. Why, yes, she has.

King. A boy or a girl.

Vasudeva. [*Aside.*] Shall even I have to tell a falsehood? Nay, to save the prince, I regard even a falsehood as truth. What am I to do? Good, I have it.

[*Aloud.*] She was delivered of a daughter.

King. Be it girl or prince I must have it slain in any case. With human effort I am sure to cozen fate. **(14)**

[*Enter Portress.*]

Portress. Greeting, my lord! The princess says, it is only a daughter, a little girl, let your majesty be merciful.

Vasudeva. O, son of Śaurasenī, grant Devakī's prayer. Women love their daughters more dearly than their sons.

King. Do you remember the compact?

The compact made with me, when thou didst hear the curse of the Seer Madhuka, that thou would'st give me all the babes born of Devakī? **(15)**

Vasudeva. Ay, the compact; I have nothing to say.

Portress. My lord, what am I to tell the princess?

King. Yaśodharā, you may tell the princess, it is not seemly now to make this appeal. I will show her some other greater kindness.

Portress. As my lord commands.

King. Yaśodharā, it should be done like this. [*Whispers.*]

Portress. May your lordship be content.

Vasudeva. My wishes have been pure, and shall I now bring another's child to death? Shall I not rather go and fetch the prince? Nay,

This maid was dead before and came to life again. That boy's power will save her from slaughter. **(16)**

Now I must go and comfort Devakī. [*Exit.*]

King. Yaśodharā, go and fetch that girl.

Portress. As my lord commands. [*Exit.*]

[*Enter a nurse with a girl-baby in her arms and guards.*]

All. Gently, lady, gently. Here is the middle door. Enter.

Nurse. Greeting, my lord. Here is the girl. I've looked after her all the time.

King. Ah, the child has a royal look. Must even I put a girl to death?

Nurse. Forbear, my lord, forbear.

King. Here is Kaṃsa's stone. I must summon all my courage.

This is the seventh child born by the power of the sage's curse.
When that has perished I shall be at peace. **(17)**

[*Seizes the child and dashes it on the stone.*]

Oh, one part has fallen on the ground, another risen to the sky. It's mounted up with hands agleam with weapons to destroy me. **(18)**

And now, oh, woe is me,
This dreadful form reveals herself, grasping a keen-edged lance, and looms up like the night of death at the destruction of the world. **(19)**

[*Enter Kārtyāyanī*[1] *with her retinue.*]

Kārtyāyanī. The demons Sumbha and Nisumbha and the Buffalo I slew, smiting the ranks of the celestials' foes. Now am I Kārtyāyanī born in Vasudeva's house[2] to destroy the Kaṃsa brood. **(20)**

Pot-belly. Pot-belly[3] am I, invincible, of fierce deeds in battle. Dreadful in my mighty hissing issued at the Goddess's wish. Swiftly I glide from the sky to the wide earth, eager to slaughter the haughty demons vainglorious of their powers. **(21)**

Spear. I am the Spear, a spirit brought down to this earth and given a beautiful gleaming form by the favour of the Goddess. Kaṃsa will I strike down and drag him hither and thither on the battle-field as the God of War dragged Tāraka rooted in the ocean.[4] **(22)**

Nīla. And I am Nīla,[5] stirrer up of strife, a hero of the battle, who never turns his back. I shall slay the wicked Kaṃsa as the great Spear-wielder[6] split the Krauñca rock. **(23)**

Speed of Thought. I am Speed of Thought, swift as the wind. Hither I come to fulfil the Goddess's purpose. I do away with demons in the forefront of the fight just as fire goes through a house of reeds. **(24)**

Kārtyāyanī. Pot-belly, Pointed-ears, Big Blue, and Speed of Thought, come here. We'll disguise ourselves as cowherds and go down to the herdsmens' station to observe the Blessed Vishṇu's exploits as a child.

All. As the Goddess bids. [*Exit Kārtyāyanī with her train.*]

King. Ah, here comes the dawn,

[1] The terrific goddess Dūrgā.

[2] But the girl was born in the herdsman's family.

[3] Kuṇḍodara a serpent.

[4] *Pādapaṃ jalanidher*, 'tree of the ocean'.

[5] Dark-blue.

[6] Skanda the God of War.

To find peace, I'll go straightway to the house of peaceful rites and make a great offering of expiation. So peace shall come to me. **(25)**

[*Exeunt omnes.*]

END OF THE SECOND ACT.

ACT III

INTERLUDE

[*Enter the Old Herdsman.*]

Old Herdsman. Ho, Meghadatta, and you there, Bull, and Pott, and Herder[1] drive along the cattle. Let 'em drink their fill and come along lowing in the woods of Brindaban.[2] That bull there, straying from the herd,[3] has been rootling in the anthills. With the black snakes sticking to his horns he looks as if he was dressed up with strings of blue lotus. And here's another bull with its tail in the air and its fore-legs bent tossing up the earth with its sharp horns. He's white all over like the moon. I'll just call Dāmaka. Dāmaka, hullo there! Take the blessed cattle and their calves to dry ground and then come here.

[*Enter Dāmaka.*]

Dāmaka. Ha, Master Nandagopa's got a powerful crop of grass. Since the day that son of his was born everything has gone wonderfully well. So let the cattle graze on here and I'll step across to uncle. [*Approaches.*] Hullo, uncle, good day to you!

Old Herdsman. Peace be on us and on the cattle.

Dāmaka. Uncle, ever since Nandagopa's son was born, our cattle has been free from sickness. All the herdsmen are very happy, and besides, anywhere you dig there's roots, and on every bush there's fruits. And however much you milk, the milk still comes in streams.[4]

Old Herdsman. And I'll tell you another wonder. When Nandagopa's son was but ten days old, a witch named Pūtanā took the form of Nandagopa's wife and came to the house with her dugs full of poison. Then she took up the boy and put her breast to his mouth. But he knew her for what she was and threw her down. Then she went back to her witch's form and straightway died. Then, when the boy was no more than a month old a goblin called Śakaṭa came in the form of

[1] Vrishabha-datta, Kumbhadatta, and Ghoshadatta.

[2] Reading *vundāvaṇe.*

[3] Reading doubtful.

[4] Reading doubtful.

a cart. But the boy knew him and with one kick knocked him to pieces. And he turned back into a goblin and died. Then just over a month old he was, when he ran into one house to drink milk, into another to eat curd, in another swallowed the butter, in another devoured rice pudding—and in yet another went for the pot of butter-milk. The angry dairy-maids told Nandagopa's wife. And she was furious and took a cord and tied it round his middle and fastened him up to a large mortar. And what did he do? Why he pulled up the mortar and cast it at two demons he caught sight of, Yamala and Arjuna disguised as trees. And the two of them were squashed into one, for he went in between them dragging the mortar and felled them root and branch, and they turned into demons and expired. Then the herdsmen said—his strength and courage were so great—from that day on, he should be called Master Dāmodara.

And the boy had hardly learnt to run about, when a demon called Pralamba came disguised as Nandagopa. He threw Saṅkarshaṇa across his shoulder, but as he went Master Saṅkarshaṇa knew him and gave that demon a blow on the head with his fist. The blow brought the demon's eyes out, so he too turned back into a demon and gave up the ghost.

Then with cowherds round him he went to the palm wood to gather fruit. And the demon Dhenuka came there disguised as a donkey. But Master Dāmodara saw through him and seizing his left foot threw him to the ground and upset the fruit. And he too changed back into a demon and died. Then there was another demon called Keśī that came in the form of a horse. Master Dāmodara spotted him and put some camphor in his mouth. Then he split him in two, and there was another demon dead.

That 's what Master Dāmodara has done and more besides.

Dāmaka. Ay, uncle; but let all that be. To-day he 's coming here to lead a round dance with the girls.

Old Herdsman. Then we must go with all the herdsmen to see Master Dāmodara's dancing in a ring.

Dāmaka. As you say, uncle.

[*Exeunt ambo.*]

END OF THE INTERLUDE.

[*Enter Old Herdsman.*]

Ere the sun has fully risen bow the head in homage to the kine, the mothers of the world, ever full of nectar. (1)

How prosperous our hamlets are. Now we 'll go and call the girls proud as punch and dressed up with tabors. Ho there, Belle of the station, Wood Garland, Crescent, and Gazelle,[1] come along and come along quickly.

[*Enter all the girls.*]

Girls. Good day to you, uncle.

Old Herdsman. Lassies, here's Master Dāmodara with Master Saṅkarshaṇa as white as milk. Here he comes with all the lads around him looking like a lion in a cave.[2]

[*Enter Dāmodara accompanied by cowherds and Saṅkarshaṇa.*]

Dāmodara. [*In surprise.*] Ah, these cowherd girls are naturally charming, but how delightful when dressed up.

Their faces are like full-blown lilies and their eyes like lotuses. Fair as golden champak flowers, in garments of varied hues, they romp around sweetly prattling, with their hands and tresses laden with woodland blossom. (2)

Saṅkarshaṇa. Here come all the young herdsmen.

Here are some stand shouting in delight with coloured drums, and there are others with eyes and cheeks of lotus petal playing divers games. Others have been awake with glee in the hamlet at Brindaban echoing with the lowing of the kine, and are singing as merrily as ever. (3)

Old Herdsman. Yes, master, they 're all along.

Dāmaka. Greeting, master.

Saṅkarshaṇa. Have all the lads come in, Dāmaka?

Dāmaka. Yes, master, they 're all along.

Dāmodara. Come now, Belle of the station, Wood Garland, Crescent, and Gazelle, we must do this round dance made for herdsmen folk.

Girls. As you tell us, master.

Saṅkarshaṇa. Dāmaka and Meghanāda, let them beat the drums.

Both. Right, master.

Old Herdsman. Master, you 're all to foot it in the dance—what am I to do?

Dāmodara. Why, you are the spectator.

Old Herdsman. Very well, master.

[*All dance.*]

Old Herdsman. Bravo, that 's good.[3] Well sung. Well danced. I'll dance a bit myself. Now I'm tired out.

[1] Ghoshasundarī, Vanamālā, Candralekhā, and Mṛigākshī.

[2] *guhānikshipta*.

[3] Reading *idam*.

[*Enter Herdsman.*]

Herdsman. Oh, master, master, get away from here.

Dāmodara. Why are you so excited, Dāmaka?

Herdsman. Here 's that demon Dreadnought Bull[1] made of destruction in a lump—tearing up the ground with his sharp hoofs, and his bellowing sounds like thunder. That 's why I 'm scared.

Dāmodara. So Dreadnought Bull has come. [*To Saṅkarshaṇa.*] Well, sir, take these lads and lasses to the hill top and watch me fight this wicked creature. I 'll cure his pride for him.

[*Exit Saṅkarshaṇa with the others.*]

Dāmodara. Here comes the wicked Dreadnought.

His hoofs are cleaving the surface of the earth, his horns tear away the banks. While terror-stricken herdsmen only gaze at him, he rushes bellowing along. (4)

[*Enter Dreadnought Bull.*]

Dreadnought. Ho, here am I.

To slay mine enemy I have taken the form of a bull, slitting the sky, as it were, with a million rays from the points of my horns.[2] I shall feel happy to-day, when I have easily overcome my vainglorious foe in the wood of Brindaban. (5)

At the sound of my bellow the women in this hamlet miscarry. The earth with its forests of trees trembles, stamped with crescents by the blows of my hoofs. (6)

Now where is Nandagopa's son? Ho there, son of Nandagopa, where are you?

Dāmodara. Vilest of bulls, this way. I am here.

Dreadnought. [*Looking at him.*] Oho,

There must be mettle in this boy, for at the sight of me the mighty one, of terrible form and terrific roar, he is neither daunted nor amazed. (7)

Dāmodara. What 's that, sirrah? I hear of fear only to-day from thee, I am born on the earth to grant safety to those that are alarmed. (8)

Dreadnought. Pooh! You are only a boy. That 's why you know no fear.

[1] Arishṭavṛishabha—a bull unscathed or immune from injury.

[2] Taking *koṭi* in the sense of a *crore*. Otherwise *śṛṅgāgrakoṭi*—could be '*points* at the end of my horns'. *ālikhan* either 'painting' or 'scratching'. If *kiraṇa* could be taken in the sense of 'particle of dust' we could translate 'flecking the sky with dust from the points of my horns' which is somewhat less extravagant, and in keeping with the action of the bull's horns in the previous verse. But this is not the most natural meaning of the words.

Dāmodara. Vilest of bulls, will you taunt me, that I am a boy?

If a man is bitten by a black snake does he not perish though the snake be young? So of old the infant Skanda destroyed the Krauñca mountain. (9)

Dreadnought. That may be.

Dāmodara. And hearken again to this, thou fool. Is not a rock of the hardest stone compact cast down by a thunderbolt as slender as a twig? (10)

Dreadnought. Ho, son of Nandagopa, what do you mean to do?

Dāmodara. To destroy you.

Dreadnought. Do you think you can?

Dāmodara. No doubt of it.

Dreadnought. Then take the weapon suited to your breed.

Dāmodara. 'Weapon' say you, sirrah?

I have these two arms of mine with shoulders hard as mountain boulders. Weaklings like thee may need some other weapon. And if thou doest not fall quickly on the ground clubbed to death by these same arms, my name is not Dāmodara. (11)

Dreadnought. Come then, begin the fight.

Dāmodara. Vile bull, I'll stand upon one leg. Knock me over, if you can.

Dreadnought. No doubt of that. [*Tries to do so, but falls down senseless.*]

Dāmodara. Take heart now, bull. Is this the strength you boasted of?

Dreadnought. [*Recovering. Aside.*]

Ha, this boy is not easy to subdue.

He may be Rudra, Indra or Vishṇu himself. Nay, my guess is near the mark, he must be the Almighty. (12)

Ah, wherever we are born, there is the Supporter of the Triple World, incarnate as Madhusūdana for the destruction of demons. (13)

So be it then. If I am slain by Vishṇu I shall go to heaven. So I shall fight. [*Aloud.*] O Son of Nandagopa, now am I as proud as ever.

Dāmodara. Ho ho, stay now.

Why dost thou bellow, lord of bulls, pressed in my arms, like a monsoon cloud swollen before it falls?[1] Come now, I will cast thee on the earth like the cliff of Mount Añjana smitten by the thunderbolt. (14)

[1] So Jacobi (quoted by Weller) *pāta-pravṛddhaḥ* meaning *pātāya pravṛddhaḥ*. Reading *vāta-pravṛddha* 'swollen by the wind' Sarup.

[*Does so.*] There lies the wicked Dreadnought Bull.

Eyes, mouth, and nose are bathed in streams of flowing blood, the hair of his hump stands erect. With twitching feet and ears this bull, the lord of demons, falls lifeless to the ground, like a mountain with its topmost pinnacles cleft by a thunderbolt. (15)

[*Enter Dāmaka.*]

Dāmaka. Greeting, Master. Saṅkarshaṇa has just heard of a great serpent called Kāliya coming up in a pool of the Jamna, and has gone there from the hill. Stop him, master, stop him.

Dāmodara. I have heard of Kāliya, a haughty serpent king. Very well, I 'll break his pride.

He battens on the people, cows and brahmans. From to-day he will lose his power and lie in peace. (16)

[*Exeunt ambo.*]

END OF THE THIRD ACT.

ACT IV

[*Enter Dāmodara.*]

Dāmodara. These cowherd maidens follow me, frightened at the sight of the serpent king, confused and incoherent in their terror. How lovely they are! They have the eyes of young *cakoras* drunk with joy, their delicate breasts are swelling into prominence. Charming, with quivering lower lips, in their excitement they let the wreath fall from their locks and their upper robes slip down. (1)

[*Enter the Cowherd Girls.*]

Girls. Oh, master, don't! Don't go into that pool! It 's the home of a great and wicked serpent.

Dāmodara. Do not be anxious, maidens. Look you,

All the birds and troops of beasts avoid this ocean pool, the herds of elephants regard its depths with fear and trembling; but I will enter it and agitate its oily water. Though timid cowherd maidens would restrain me with charmingly tender words of warning, I shall drag forth the mighty serpent Kāliya so fond of his Jamna home. (2)

Girls. Master Saṅkarshaṇa, don't let him go.

[*Enter Saṅkarshaṇa.*]

Saṅkarshaṇa. No need for terror or anxiety. You girls show your devotion, but look you,

The circle of the quarters is ruddy with the baneful burning poison flames, that issue from that furious dragon's maw. Yet one glance at Kṛishṇa's impetuous onset alarms him, and he lowers his head among his coils. (3)

Girls. But Dāmodara hasn't turned a hair.

Dāmodara. For the good of all people I shall straightway subdue this dragon.

[*Enters the pool.*]

Girls. Oh, see the clouds of smoke.

Dāmodara. How deep this pool is. And now,

This Jamna, seething with poison fire within, gray with the dragon's smoky breath, will I make ripple as with liquid sapphires and the sheen of dark blue silk [1] in folds. (4) [*Exit.*]

[*Enter the Old Herdsman.*]

Old Herdsman. Oh, master, has he gone into the Jamna pool, though the lasses tried to stop him? Hi there! don't be rash in going in. There 's tigers and boars and elephants that drunk water at that there pool and dropped down dead. What? I can't see him. What 'll I do? I'll climb this pot *palāśa* tree [2] and get a view. Ho, there 's smoke rising.

Saṅkarshaṇa. Look, my dears,

Dāmodara has seized the dragon, stirring up the water from the bottom. Standing on the hood of the dark blue serpent he looks like Indra riding a storm cloud. (5)

Old Herdsman. Ha, ha! bravo, master, bravo!

[*Enter Dāmodara dragging the serpent.*]

Dāmodara. Here you are.

To make a mock of Kāliya, quivering with rage, I set one foot upon his head, and, waving my arms like pennons, lightly dance the lovely herdsman's reel [3] on the great snake's hood distended with venom. (6)

Girls. Wonderful, master, wonderful! He 's doing the reel as he steps on Kāliya's five hoods.

Dāmodara. Now I, too, will pluck some flowers.

Kāliya. Ah,

The world's expanse is girt by the mountain chain 'twixt light

[1] *dukūla*. See note *The Embassy*, I. 3.

[2] *kumbha-palāśa*. *Palāśa* = *Butea frondosa*.

[3] *Hallīśaka*.

and dark,[1] the mountain Mandara in the ocean[2] was squeezed by the Serpent,[3] Śiva's bowstring. So now in a moment will I roll thee up in my coils, for I 'm as hard as the massive trunk of the Destroyer's[4] elephant, and dispatch thee to the gods' abode. (7)

Old Herdsman. Oh, master, master, here 's Dāmodara with his two feet like flowers kicking along the great snake, like an incarnation of a Jamna pool, while he 's picking flowers. [*Coming down.*] Bravo, master, bravo. Pick away, pick away. I 'll come and help. Nay, I 'm scared, master. I 'll just go and tell Nandagopa all about it. [*Exit.*]

Dāmodara. From within this Jamna pool, with its fish and crocodiles destroyed, I 'll drag perforce the dirty venomous snake. He 's breathing hard with his round hood expanded in the height of swelling insolence, but I'll cast him on the ground. (8)

Kāliya. Here am I,

By whose wrath the human body is set on fire and the earth consumed. I'll burn thee up with lines of flames; let the worlds and hosts of Maruts protect thee. (9)

Dāmodara. Kāliya, if you can, burn this single arm of mine.

Kāliya. Ha, ha,

I could burn the entire earth, with its seven mighty mountains, bounded by the four oceans. Why not burn thy arm? (10)

Come, wait a moment. Herewith I reduce you to ashes. [*Emits venomous flames.*]

Dāmodara. Ho, have you shown your strength?

Kāliya. Have mercy, blessed Nārāyaṇa.

Dāmodara. Is this the strength you boasted of?

Kāliya. Mercy, Lord,

Thine arm of matchless might as powerful as Mount Mandara lifted up the hill Govardhana.[5] What strength have I, Lord of the Gods and Triple World, to burn that heroic arm, on which all the world depends. (11)

[1] Sarup thinks there is only one simile intended by *yathā, yadvacca*, identifying 'the world's expanse' with Mandara and *Lokālokamahīdhara* with the serpent bowstring. *Lokālokamahīdhara*, he translates, 'supporter of the visible and the invisible world'. It seems more natural to take *mahīdhara* as 'mountain' and the whole as 'the mythical mountainous belt (light on the one side and dark on the other) which separates the visible world from the world of darkness' (Macdonell, *Sanskrit-English Dictionary*).

[2] 'Receptacle of sea-monsters.'

[3] Śesha.

[4] Indra.

[5] Krishṇa held it up for seven days to protect the cattle.

Blessed One, I erred in ignorance. With all my household I seek thy protection.

Dāmodara. Kāliya, why did you enter this Jamna pool?

Kāliya. Because I was afraid of Garuḍa your exalted mount. That is what I seek by your blessed favour—safety from Garuḍa.

Dāmodara. It shall be so.

> When he sees my footprint on thy head, great serpent, Garuḍa himself will grant thee that security. (12)

Kāliya. I thank you.

Dāmodara. You may go home.

Kāliya. As the blessed Nārāyaṇa commands.

Dāmodara. Nay, come here a moment.

Kāliya. Here I am, Blessed One.

Dāmodara. From to-day on you must leave my folk alone, cows, brahmans, and all.

Kāliya. Blessed One, this water is poisoned with my venom. I will take out the poison and leave this pool.

Dāmodara. Go your ways.

Kāliya. As the Blessed Nārāyaṇa commands.

[*Exit with his household.*]

Dāmodara. Now I will offer the girls these flowers gathered in the pool.

Girls. Here comes our master to delight our hearts, and not a scratch upon him. Greeting, master.

Saṅkarshaṇa. Well done. That 's a service done to cows and brahmans.

Dāmodara. Take these flowers.

Girls. Our folk have never plucked these flowers before. They have not been touched by the rays of the sun or moon or damaged in the slightest. We're afraid of them, master.

Dāmodara. The poor things are frightened by what they have not seen before. Don't be afraid, don't be afraid. The touch of my hand has made them lucky. So take them.

Girls. As our master bids.

[*Enter a Servant.*]

Servant. Ho, cowherd. Where is the son of Nandagopa?

Cowherd. There he is with the cowherd girls all round him. He has just subdued the great serpent Kāliya.

Servant. [*Approaching.*] Son of Nandagopa, King Kaṃsa, son of the Great King, fitly called Ugrasena, orders you—

Dāmodara. What? Orders me?

Servant. To come with your brother and all your people, to attend a great festival called the Consecration of the Bow that is to take place at Mathurā.

Dāmodara. Noble brother, now is the time for the secret purpose of the gods.

Saṅkarshaṇa. Let us go quickly.

Dāmodara. Yes, that 's the thing.

To-day will I drag out Kaṃsa—his locks dishevelled, his jewelled crown knocked off, necklace broken, bracelets fallen, and sacred thread dangling loose—ruthlessly I'll slay him as a lion slays an elephant that has long insulted him. (13)

[*Exeunt omnes.*]

END OF THE FOURTH ACT.

ACT V

[*Enter the King.*]

King. They tell me that Dāmodara in the herdsmen's station with his brother[1] is exhibiting great prowess and heroic valour. I will bring him here, with the pretext of the Bow, and have him smashed by a wrestler in the ring. (1)

Dhruvasena!

[*Enter a Servant.*]

Servant. Victory to your Majesty.

King. Dhruvasena, has Nandagopa's son arrived?

Servant. Deign to listen, Majesty. No sooner had he entered the city, with Saṅkarshaṇa and the herdsmen, than he robbed the washermen of their clothes. When the Chief Minister heard of it he had the mad elephant 'Lotus Crusher' driven against him to trample on him. But,

When the boy, amid the troop of cowherds gathered round him, suddenly saw the lordly elephant bearing down upon him like a mountain, violently he tore out its tusks and slew it straight away. (2)

King. 'Slew it', you say? Go and bring further news.

Servant. As your Majesty commands. [*Exit and returns.*] Victory to your Majesty! Now I hear this son of Nandagopa's got into the High Street, with flags and banners flying to celebrate the festival, decorated with hanging wreaths and garlands thick with fumes of aloe-wood and incense. Well, when he came to the palace gate he saw the hump-

[1] Bala, i. e. Balarāma or Saṅkarshaṇa.

backed girl Madanikā carrying a casket of scented unguents. So he took the unguents out of her hands and anointed his own limbs. Then he rubbed her hump with his hand and made her straight. Then he snatched some flowers from the garland maker and put them on. And now he is going towards the archery hall.

King. What does he mean to do? Go, quickly, and find out more?

Servant. As your Majesty commands. [*Exit and returns.*] Victory, Majesty, Siṃhala, the guardian of the archery hall, tried to stop him, but he hit him under the ear and killed him. Then he took the bow and broke it in two. And at present he is making his way towards the audience hall.

Here he comes, black as a line of rain clouds, in yellow robes, brightly adorned with garlands and peacocks' feathers. Here he comes with Balarāma, his great eyes rolling with rage, like an incarnation of Death. (3)

King. My heart it seems is fluttering. Go, bring in those wrestlers as directed, Cāṇūra and Boxer, and bid the Yādava youths prepare.

Servant. As your Majesty commands. [*Exit.*]

King. Now I will go up to the balcony to see Cāṇūra and Boxer fight. [*Goes up.*] Madhurikā, unbolt the door.

Portress. As my master bids.

[*King enters above and sits down.*]

[*Enter Cāṇūra and Boxer.*]

Cāṇūra. Here am I ready for the fray, as full of pride as an elephant in rut. To-day I smash the boy Dāmodara in the middle of the ring. (4)

Boxer. My name is Boxer, and my fist is made of iron. To-day in fury will I throw down Balarāma, as a thunderbolt throws down the summit of a lofty mountain. (5)

Servant. There is the king. Pay your respects.

Both Wrestlers. [*Approaching.*] Victory, my lord!

King. Cāṇūra and Boxer, you two must do your utmost, so as to repay me.

Wrestlers. Ay, be sure, my lord. We'll succeed with various tricks of fighting, with the half-moon grip[1] and binding blows. You'll see, my lord.

King. Good, do you so. Dhruvasena, bring in the cowherd boys.

Servant. As your Majesty commands. [*Exit.*]

[*Enter Dāmodara and Saṅkarshaṇa with Dhruvasena.*]

[1] Accepting Weller's emendation *aḍḍhindu-karasandhāna.*

Dāmodara. Noble brother.

My birth in the mortal world is of no avail, nor can I find any satisfaction in my deeds at the cattle-station or in the town to-day, till in combat I have vanquished this wretched Kaṃsa, a devil in a former birth, and drag him round the ring. (6)

Saṅkarshaṇa. Entering the ring to-day, that angry Boxer, with his iron fist, with my fist will I slay, rushing like a raging gale that smites a cloud hanging in the sky. (7)

Servant. The Great King is here. Approach.

Both. Great King? Of what?

Servant. Of all the world, and us.

Dāmodara. Not after to-day.

Servant. Victory, Majesty! Here is that pair!

King. [*Looking at them.*] So this is Dāmodara. Ah—

Dark in hue, arms and shoulders strong, his breast is broad and muscular; splendidly made, he stalks along with the firm grace of a tusker blind with rut. No wonder he has done these deeds I've heard of, for he is fit to overturn the universe. (8)

And this other, looking so artless but inscrutable, is, I hear, Balarāma his elder brother.

His great eyes are white as new-blown lotuses. His body gleams like the moon in lovely dark-blue raiment. His long arms are rounded like silver bars. He is brightly garlanded with quivering petals of blue water-lilies. (9)

Dāmodara. Brother, I think these two are ready to fight with us.

Saṅkarshaṇa. Very likely.

King. Dhruvasena, let the fight begin.

Servant. As your Majesty commands. [*Throws down a garland.*]

Wrestlers. Fi-fo-fum, beat the battle drum.

Cāṇūra. Come now, Dāmodara, try your luck with my two arms.

Dāmodara. Here I come. Stand thou, and resist my charge.

Boxer. Yah, you Balarāma, to-day you'll lose your life, drowned in a pool of blood, running from all your limbs smashed up by my fists.

Saṅkarshaṇa. To-day, thou Boxer, I'll send thee off to hell.

[*Both pairs start wrestling.*]

Dāmodara. [*Laying out Cāṇūra.*] This one's dead with broken ribs.

Saṅkarshaṇa. So is mine.

Dāmodara. Now I'll send that devil Kaṃsa down to hell. (10)

[*Mounts the balcony, seizes Kaṃsa by the head, and throws him down.*]

There lies the wicked Kaṃsa,

His visage thick with gore, with goggling eyes, with broken neck and thighs, with shattered shoulders, loins, and legs, with fractured hands and knees, with necklace broken, bracelets fallen, and sacred thread dangling loose.[1] He has fallen like a mountain whose peak is crushed by a thunderbolt. (11)

[*Voice behind the scene.*]

Alas, alas, the king!

[*Another voice behind the scene.*]

Warriors of the Yādava race,[2] now is the time to repay our master's salt. Come quickly, come.

Dāmodara. Brother, do you hold off the army.

Saṅkarshaṇa. See how I keep it back.

This army, with its dreadful roar of warriors whirling round with swift steeds, elephants, and chariots, flashing with bright swords, javelins, spears, lances, and pikes—this army will I throw into confusion with my two arms, like an ocean with lines of billows in a lattice of foam driven by the fury of the gale. (12)

[*Enter Vasudeva.*]

Vasudeva. Citizens of Mathurā, no violence, I pray you.

This is my eldest son, born of Rohiṇī, and do you not know this son of Devakī? A truce to this excitement. What 's to do with weapons? Vishṇu himself has come down to us to slay Kaṃsa. (13)

Saṅkarshaṇa. [*Looking across.*] Oh, there 's father. Father, I salute you.

Dāmodara. Father, my salutations, too.

Vasudeva. May you both be invincible in victory. As the father of goodly sons I gain to-day the noblest fruit.

Both. We thank you.

Vasudeva. Who 's without there?

[*Enter Servant.*]

Servant. Greeting, your honour.

Vasudeva. Throw out these corpses.

Servant. As your honour orders.

All the Herdsmen. Hurrah! The kingdom now belongs to herdsmen.

Vasudeva. Ho, without there.

Servant. Your honour.

Vasudeva. Go quickly and give this order to Anāvṛishṭi in Dāmodara's

[1] Identical with iv. 13*b*.

[2] Text enumerates 'Anāvṛishṭi, Śivaka, Hṛidika, Pṛithuka, Somadatta, Akrūra, &c.'

name. Release the Great King Ugrasena from his fetters, renew his consecration, and bring him here.

Servant. As your honour orders. [*Exit.*]

Vasudeva. Ah,

The celestial instruments are sounding, it is raining flowers.
All the gods have come to honour the destroyer of Kaṃsa. **(14)**

[*Voice behind the scene.*]

The best of deities guard Mathurā, this city with its rows of mansions adorned with gold, with its spacious palaces and markets, its gates and towers—ever may he guard it, glorious with large lotus eyes, lord and leader of the gods, the conqueror of the triple world. **(15)**

Vasudeva. Citizens of Mathurā, hearken to my words. By favour of Vasudeva here, the son of Vasudeva, who looks down with scorn on all earthly champions, who is skilled in bursting the bolts of the lord of demon's city, Ugrasena has recovered his kingdom, and his rule is now proclaimed.

All. The Yādava kingdom is now confirmed.

Vasudeva. Bring in his Majesty.

Servant. As your honour orders. [*Exit.*]

[*Enter Ugrasena.*]

Ugrasena. Kṛishṇa[1] has removed my misery endured in long incarceration, as by his might Vishṇu aided Indra. **(16)**

By your kindness I am rescued from a flood of troubles.

[*Enter Nārada.*]

Nārada. Now that Kaṃsa is destroyed, I have come down from heaven at the gods' command with nymphs and celestial musicians to worship Vishṇu. **(17)**

Dāmodara. Ah, here is the divine sage, Nārada. Welcome, sage. Here is water for thy feet and all hospitality.

Nārada. I accept it all. The nymphs and celestial musicians are singing.

Obeisance be to thee, Nārāyaṇa. Deities bow low before thee.
By the slaughter of this demon the earth is well protected. **(18)**

Dāmodara. Divine sage, I am well pleased. What further favour can I show you?

Nārada. If Vishṇu is pleased with me my efforts are well repaid.
I shall now return to heaven with all the greatest gods. **(19)**

Dāmodara. You may go. We shall meet again.

Nārada. As the blessed Nārāyaṇa commands. [*Exit.*]

[1] Keśisūdana—'Slayer of the maned demon'.

Epilogue.

This earth that extends to the ocean with the Himālaya and Vindhya mountains as ear-drops, may our Lion-King rule over her, marked with the symbol of a single sovereign sway.[1] (**20**)

[*Exeunt omnes.*]

FINIS.

[1] Identical with the Epilogue of *The Vision of Vāsavadattā* and of *The Embassy.*

THE CONSECRATION

(*Abhisheka-nāṭakam*)

INTRODUCTION

THE Consecration is another Rāmāyaṇa play, but distinctly different in character and quality from *The Statue Play.*

The latter play begins with the breaking oft of Rāma's consecration by his father and ends with his consecration on his return to Ayodhyā after fourteen years of exile.

The present play ends at the same point, but begins with another consecration, that of the monkey prince Sugrīva, when his elder brother Vālin is slain by Rāma.

We have a picture of Sītā in captivity, an account of the exploits of Hanumān in Laṅkā, and a representation of the arrogance and downfall of the Demon king, Rāvaṇa.

In the First Act Rāma promises Sugrīva that he will kill his brother Vālin. Sugrīva was formerly a king of the monkeys, but Vālin had taken possession of his kingdom and his wife. On arriving at Kishkindhā, the capital of Vālin's kingdom, Sugrīva fights with Vālin. Vālin knocks his brother down. Hanumān reminds Rāma of his promise. Without a word of warning Rāma shoots Vālin with an arrow. Vālin complains that this act is unworthy of a hero. He is told, in an unconvincing argument, that this is punishment for taking his younger brother's wife. Vālin is satisfied, asks forgiveness, and expires. Lakshmaṇa is told to arrange for Sugrīva's consecration. (ACT I.)

The Interlude at the beginning of the next Act tells us that Sītā has been lost and the monkey prince Aṅgada has gone south to look for her.

Hanumān comes to Laṅkā and searches all the town for Sītā. From a roof he spies her, just as Rāvaṇa appears, and listens to the Demon king's efforts to win the affections of the scornful captive. Rāvaṇa goes to take his bath and the monkey introduces himself to Sītā. She hesitates whether to believe him. He goes off to ruin Rāvaṇa's park. (ACT II.)

Rāvaṇa gets news of the damage done by Hanumān, who is eventually brought before him as a prisoner. Hanumān defies the Demon king and delivers Rāma's message. Rāvaṇa is furious but

Vibhīshaṇa restrains him from killing an envoy. Vibhīshaṇa urges Rāvaṇa to restore the stolen bride, but the king banishes him for sympathizing with the enemy. (ACT III.)

In the Fourth Act Rāma's host reaches the sea, and is joined by the banished Vibhīshaṇa. The Ocean enters and provides a passage. Two spies are caught, but sent home with a message to the Demon king. (ACT IV.)

In the Fifth Act Rāvaṇa renews his advances to Sītā, and shows her what appear to be the severed heads of Rāma and Lakshmaṇa. He hears of the death of his son, and then of the defeat of his army. He wishes to kill Sītā, but is dissuaded, and goes out in his chariot to fight Rāma. (ACT V.)

In the Interlude at the beginning of the last act, three fairies describe the battle in the favourite manner of our dramatist.

Rāma refuses to see Sītā, and assents to her wish to burn herself. The God of Fire will not hurt her, but leads her back to her husband. Rāma then receives her, saying that he was aware of her purity, but 'acted thus to bring conviction to the world'. We hear the singing of celestial musicians and the shouts of the people at Rāma's consecration. Rāma re-enters newly anointed as king, and the play ends in mutual congratulation. (ACT VI.)

This play is not equal to *The Statue Play*.[1] There is nothing in it comparable to the scene in the Statue Gallery, nor is there the same delicacy in portraying the characters of Rāma and Sītā. Rāma is simply the ruthless warrior, or should we say, relentless divine force? For he is definitely identified with Vishṇu. His refusal to receive Sītā, until she is declared to be Lakshmī, reads very differently from the passage in the Seventh Act of *The Statue Play*:

> **Female Ascetic.** Why, here is your husband. Go up to him. I cannot bear to see you alone.
>
> **Sītā.** Ah! Even to-day it seems too good to be true. [*Going up to Rāma.*] Greeting, my lord.
>
> **Rāma.** Maithilī, do you remember we used to dwell in Janasthāna? Do you recognize these trees, your fosterlings?
>
> **Sītā.** Yes, yes, I see. But then every leaf was visible and now one must look up at them.
>
> **Rāma.** Quite so. Time produces ups and downs. Do you recollect, Maithilī, that under this tree a herd of deer was startled on seeing Bharata dressed in white?
>
> **Sītā.** Yes, my lord, I remember very well.

[1] Dr. Sarup regards it as an early work of Bhāsa.

Rāma. And here is that great tortoise that witnessed our austerities. We were sitting here, thinking of the oblations to be made for my beloved father, when we saw the golden deer.

Sītā. Oh, my lord, don't speak of it, pray don't.

[*Trembles with fear.*]

Rāma. Calm your fears. That time is past. Vol. i, p. 198.

The most *human* figures in this play are Rāvaṇa, the Demon king, and Vālin, the Monkey chief. A familiar feature in many of these plays is the interest in, one might almost say the sympathy with, kings and warriors on the brink of ruin, whether this be due to a curse or to their own wickedness. Rāvaṇa breaks down at the news of his son's death. He is not all devil incapable of emotion. He is an arrogant powerful king, deceitful in his courting of the captured lady, but not utterly brutal. It is only at the end, when all his realm is falling to pieces and his son is killed, that for a moment he is on the point of slaying the fatal beauty that has brought him to destruction. As the bad news keeps pouring in, he feels the oppression of a curse that seems to be closing in upon him.

The other characters are more conventional and of less interest.

The most striking divergence from the Epic story lies in the manner of crossing the ocean. Instead of the famous bridge built by the monkeys hurling rocks into the sea, we have the miracle of divided waters, as when Vasudeva crossed the Jamna in *The Adventures of the Boy Krishna.*

DRAMATIS PERSONAE

(In order of appearance.)

Stage-manager. } in Prologue.
Assistant. }
RĀMA.
Sugrīva, a monkey prince.
Hanumān.
Lakshmaṇa.
Vālin, elder brother of Sugrīva.
Tārā, his wife.
Aṅgada, a monkey prince.
Kakubha, a monkey officer.
Hollow-face (Bila-mukha), a monkey soldier.
SĪTĀ.
RĀVAṆA.
Spike-ear (Śaṅkukarṇa), a demon attendant of Rāvaṇa.
Portress (Vijayā), of Rāvaṇa's palace.
Vibhīshaṇa, younger brother of Rāvaṇa.
Monkey Chamberlain.
Monkey General.
Ocean.
Indigo (Nīla), a monkey officer.
Parrot and Mate (Śuka and Sāraṇa), two of Rāvaṇa's ministers disguised as monkeys.
Demon Chamberlain.
Demon Porter.
Lightning-tongue, a demon.
Three Fairies.
Agni, the God of Fire.

Other monkeys and demons.

PROLOGUE

[*At the end of the Opening enter the Stage-manager.*]

Stage-manager. May Rāma protect you—he that slew the obstructors of Viśvāmitra's[1] sacrifice, vanquishing in battle the valour of Virādha,[2] he that killed Kabandha and the Monkey King, swelling with overweening pride, and smote the house of the demon chief. (1)

With these words, my lords and gentlemen, I have to announce to you . . . [*Stopping and looking around.*] But what is that? I thought I heard a noise just as I was to make my announcement. Well, I must see what it is.

[*Voice behind the scene.*]

Sugrīva, this way.

[*Enter Assistant.*]

Assistant. Master,

Whence has arisen this mighty noise that pierces our ears? It is like the roar of thundering clouds of dreadful speed raised on high by furious winds. (2)

Manager. Don't you understand, my lad? Rāma, the light of the Raghu house, and a delight to the eyes of all the world is tormented by the rape of Sītā. Sugrīva, with the great bull-neck, king of all the bears and apes, has been deprived of his wife's caresses. So these two are mutually pledged to help each other. Now preparations are being made to slay Vālin of the golden garland, the overlord of all the monkeys. So these two,

Rāma and Lakshmaṇa have arrived to reinstate Sugrīva, who was deprived of his kingdom, as Hari and Hara came to Indra's aid. (3)

[*Exeunt ambo.*]

END OF THE PROLOGUE.

ACT I

[*Enter Rāma, Lakshmaṇa, Sugrīva, and Hanumān.*]

Rāma. Sugrīva, this way,

To-day, in a trice I will throw your enemy on the ground, his body cut down and chopped into mincemeat by my arrows.

[1] 'Son of Gādhi.' [2] Virādha, Khara, and Dūshaṇa.

Abandon fear, O king, and close to me thou shalt see Vālin slain in battle. (4)

Sugrīva. By your favour, sire, I can hope for the kingdom of the gods, let alone the kingdom of monkeys. For,

Thine arrow, sire, will fly to-day, I cannot doubt, to cleave the heart of Vālin, for in the great forest it split seven *sāl* trees like Himālayan peaks and with its impetus clave the earth, O glorious warrior, passed to the serpents' home, sank in the ocean, and has now come back again. (5)

Hanumān. The words that have fallen from thy lips, O king, have removed our fear. So we grieve no more. Best of Raghus come to the mountain like a rainy cloud to vouchsafe victory to the Tawny One.[1] (6)

Lakshmaṇa. Noble brother, we must be nearing Kishkindhā : there is more moisture in the forest.[2]

Sugrīva. The prince is right.

Well-protected by thine arm, O king, we have reached Kishkindhā protected well by the great monkey's arm. Wait here, O best of men, while I roar a challenge, shaking the mountains and stupefying mortals. (7)

Rāma. Very well, do so.

Sugrīva. As my lord commands. [*Stepping round.*] Ho, there—Chieftain, thou didst leave Sugrīva in the lurch through no fault of his, and now he comes eager to wait on thee in battle. (8)

[*Voice behind the scene.*]

What, what? Is it Sugrīva?

[*Enter Vālin with Tārā clinging to his robe.*]

Vālin. What, what? Is it Sugrīva?

Let go my garment, Tārā. Why are thine eyes and cheeks so wet with tears—lady of faultless limbs? To-day shalt thou see Sugrīva struck down in the battlefield with every limb bathed in blood. (9)

Tārā. Oh, please your Majesty, Sugrīva will not come without good reason. So take counsel with your ministers before you go.

Vālin. Ah, Moonface, my foe may resort to Indra, or to Śiva, if he will, with the sharpened axe. Not even Vishṇu with eyes of full-blown lotus can face me and prevail. (10)

[1] Hari, 'the Monkey'.

[2] Compare a similar line in *The Statue Play*, iii. 2.

Tārā. Oh, please, your Majesty. Do, please, do this favour to poor little me.

Vālin. Hearken to my prowess.

Aforetime, Tārā, at the churning of the nectar, I went and laughed at the legions of gods, demons, and ogres. And they were all astounded when they saw me dragging that lengthy [1] lord of serpents with his glaring eyes. **(11)**

Tārā. Oh, please, your Majesty.

Vālin. Come now, be obedient and go within.

Tārā. I am going, unhappy that I am. [*Exit.*]

Vālin. Well, Tārā has gone in. Now I'll break Sugrīva's neck. [*Rushing forward.*] Stay, Sugrīva, stay,

Though Indra should protect thee or Lord Vishṇu, once thou comest to-day within my sight thou shalt not return alive. **(12)**

This way, this way.

Sugrīva. As your Majesty commands.

[*The two fight with their fists.*]

Rāma. Look at Vālin,

Biting his lips with protruding teeth, eyes red with rage, he clenches tight his fists. Roaring dreadfully, the ape shines in the fight, like the fire of dissolution on the point of blazing forth. **(13)**

Lakshmaṇa. And look, noble brother, at Sugrīva,

With eyes as red as a full-blown lotus, his stout arms bound by golden bracelets, he makes for the monkey chief. But being an ape, he neglects the tradition of good men and attacks his elder brother. **(14)**

Vālin has knocked Sugrīva down.

Hanumān. Alas. [*Anxiously approaching Rāma.*] Greeting, sire. This is a bad business,

The monkey chief is strong, my master weak. Pray see the state of things and bear in mind your pledge. **(15)**

Rāma. Do not be anxious, Hanumān. The thing is done. [*Lets fly an arrow.*] Ha, Vālin falls.

Lakshmaṇa. There lies Vālin.

With blood-stained limbs and red eyes bleeding, with long arms stiff, he soon will see the world of the dead. He falls,

[1] Sarup takes *udagra* in the sense 'with hood raised up'. This is quite appropriate of a cobra.

but bravely drags his body, pierced by a goodly dart, and with its strength ebbing away. (16)

Vālin. [*Faints, recovers consciousness, and reads the name on the arrow.*[1] *To Rāma.*]

Oh, Rāma, was it worthy of a hero past all doubt about his duty, upholding the right conduct of kings, to cheat me unfairly in battle? Was it worthy of thee that art come to remove treachery from the world? (17)

Out on it,

Thou art kindly in seeming and a vessel of glory. But attacking me with treachery thou hast done an inglorious deed. (18)

Ho, Rāghava, you wear bark garments, but your heart contradicts your dress. To slay me by stealth while I was engaged in fighting my brother was an unholy deed.

Rāma. What, is slaying by stealth an unholy deed?

Vālin. No doubt of it.

Rāma. Nay, it is not so. Look you,

One may slaughter beasts by snares and guile. Thou art a beast and a guilty beast and so art thou punished by guile. (19)

Vālin. You think that I deserve punishment?

Rāma. No doubt of it.

Vālin. For what reason?

Rāma. Adultery.

Vālin. Adultery? But that is our custom.

Rāma. Nay, sirrah, that won't do.

As lord of the apes thou canst distinguish right and wrong. Thou didst show thyself a beast in possessing thy brother's wife. (20)

Vālin. In possessing a brother's wife our fault is equal. Only I am punished, not Sugrīva.

Rāma. Thou art punished because thou art guilty. The guiltless is not punished.

Vālin. Sugrīva embraced the lawful wife of me, his elder brother.

If I did the same by his, why am I guilty, Rāghava? (21)

Rāma. Why, because an elder brother should never touch a younger brother's wife.

Vālin. Alas, I have no answer. Being punished by you shall I be freed from sin?

Rāma. It shall be so.

Sugrīva. Alas,

[1] Compare *The Five Nights*, iii. 18.

O best of monkeys with the gait of a lordly elephant, my heart sinks within me when I see thy arms, like tuskers' trunks, lying on the ground, with bracelets broken by your enemy's shaft. (22)

Vālin. Do not grieve, Sugrīva. Such is the way of the world.

[*Voice behind the scene.*]

Oh, woe, the king.

Vālin. Sugrīva, keep away the womenfolk. They must not see me in this state.

Sugrīva. As your Majesty commands. See to it, Hanumān.

Hanumān. As the prince commands. [*Exit.*]

[*Enter Aṅgada and Hanumān.*]

Hanumān. This way, Aṅgada.

Aṅgada. I am overwhelmed with grief to hear the monkey lord of troops of bears is in the hands of death, and come with tottering steps. (23)

Hanumān, where is the king?

Hanumān. Here lies the king,

His heart transfixed by an arrow, lying on the ground, he looks like Krauñca, best of mountains, assailed by Guha's[1] spear. (24)

Aṅgada. [*Approaching.*] Alas, great king!

Lord of the apes, thou usedst to sleep in comfort because of thy mighty power. Now thou rollest on the ground, and every limb has lost its movement. Obviously leaving this body pierced by a goodly dart, dost thou desire to go to-day to the heroes' heaven? (25)

[*Falls on the ground.*]

Vālin. Do not grieve, Aṅgada. Well, Sugrīva,

Thou art now the monkeys' ruler. Put completely out of mind the wrong I did thee. Put wrath aside, embrace the right, and protect this scion of our family. (26)

Sugrīva. As your Majesty commands.

Vālin. Rāma, whatever the offence, pray forgive these two their monkeys' tricks.

Rāma. Very well.

Vālin. Sugrīva, accept this golden necklace, the treasure of our house.

Sugrīva. I thank you. [*Accepts it.*]

Vālin. Hanumān, some water.

[1] Son of Śiva.

Hanumān. As your Majesty commands. [*Exit and re-enters.*] Here is water.

Vālin. [*Sipping.*] Life seems to leave me. Here are the great rivers, Ganges and the rest. Urvaśī and those other nymphs have come for me. Death has sent this aerial car to fetch me, the wain of heroes, drawn by a thousand swans. So be it. Here I come.[1] [*Expires.*]

All. Woe, woe, the king.

Rāma. Alas, Vālin is dead. Sugrīva, perform the funeral rites.

Sugrīva. As my lord commands.

Rāma. Lakshmaṇa, arrange for Sugrīva's consecration.

Lakshmaṇa. As my noble brother bids.

[*Exeunt omnes.*]

END OF THE FIRST ACT.

ACT II

INTERLUDE.

[*Enter Kakubha.*]

Kakubha. Our task is almost finished, so all the captains of the monkey troops are busy dining. Then I too shall do a bit of honour to the viands. [*Does so.*]

[*Enter Hollowface.*]

Hollowface. King Sugrīva has sent me out to go and bring news of Prince Aṅgada. He went off south to search for Sītā. But all the other monkeys sent out for this in every direction, as a return for noble Rāma's aid, have come back again. Now where in the world has the prince got to?

[*Stepping round and looking in front.*]

Here is Master Kakubha. I'll just ask him. [*Approaches.*] Howdido, sir.

Kakubha. Hullo, Hollowface. Where did you spring from?

Hollowface. Why sir, I've come by his Majesty's command to look for Prince Aṅgada.

Kakubha. Is the noble Rāma well? And the king?

Hollowface. Ay.

Kakubha. What is the king's intention?

Hollowface. He 's sent me out to go and bring news of Prince Aṅgada. He went off south. . . .

[*And so on as before.*]

[1] Compare the death of Duryodhana in *The Broken Thighs.*

Kakubha. Don't you know that half the task is done?

Hollowface. What do you mean?

Kakubha. Listen.

Gaining tidings of Rāma's consort from the lord of birds, we mounted Mount Tremendous, with its tremendous elephants.[1] And, to-day, to reach Laṅkā quickly, the wind-god's son with his wondrous strength has leapt across the ocean. (1)

Come along then, let us wait upon the prince.

[*Exeunt ambo.*]

END OF THE INTERLUDE.

[*Enter Sītā attended by several she-devils.*]

Sītā. Alack, I'm too enduring, wretched me. Parted from my noble lord, brought to the palace of the demon king, listening to disgusting, wicked, and reckless words, I go on living, wretched me. Still, I get a little consolation trusting in my lord's arrows. How is it that to-day I feel some comfort in my heart, like the water sprinkled when the ring of sacrificial fire is blazing? Can it be my lord is pleased with me?

[*Enter Hanumān with a ring on his finger.*]

Hanumān. [*Arriving in Laṅkā.*] How extensive is Rāvaṇa's palace.

Rich in gateways, gilt and variegated with squares decorated with coral and great gems, with quantities of white palaces, one above the other,[2] Laṅkā is as bright as the city of Mahendra in heaven. (2)

And yet forsooth,

Possessing this most excellent royal fortune, Ten-necks[3] is ready to destroy it by taking the wrong path. (3)

[*Going all round.*] I have traversed nearly all Laṅkā.

Several times have I passed through the ladies' quarters and private gardens,[4] through halls and palaces, through bathing tanks, pavilions, terraces, and mansions of the goblin king. Through taverns, temples, and dungeons, I have searched through every corner, but I have not seen the consort of the king. (4)

Alas, all my efforts are in vain. Well, I'll go up on the roof of this mansion and look round. [*Does so.*] Ah, here is a series of pleasure

[1] A jingle in the original, *agendraṃ sadvipendraṃ mahendraṃ*.

[2] *Vikṛta?*

[3] Rāvaṇa, the demon king of Laṅkā.

[4] *viniṣkuṭeṣu?*

grounds. I will go in and have a look round. [*Goes in and looks about.*] Oh, what a fine park!

With its beauty spots in rows of great trees adorned with coral and sapphires set in gold, with its beautiful mound, it is as lovely as the pleasure ground of the lord of gods in heaven. (5)

Moreover,

I have seen rocks with beautiful waterfalls and golden ore, I have seen ponds full of every kind of waterfowl, and orchards with trees laden with flower and fruit. All that I've seen, but not a sign of Sītā in the house of Rāvaṇa. (6)

Now, who is that I see, something like her, over there. I will go and see. [*Does so.*] Ah, now who is this lady?

Slender in form she is attended by hideous she-devils. She shows up bright like a streak of lightning in the midst of dark-blue clouds. (7)

She wears a single braid of hair that resembles a black snake. Her waist can be spanned by the hand. Her heart is set on her beloved, her body thin with fasting, while her face is bathed in tears. She is like a garland of wild[1] lotuses tossed aside in the heat. (8)

Ha, what is the meaning of this glare of torches? Ah, there is Rāvaṇa.

His diadem is set with gems. With fine large dark red eyes, he stalks along with a lively grace, as sportive as an elephant in rut. The lord of demons in a bevy of young women looks like a lion disporting himself among gazelles. (9)

What shall I do now? Good, I have it. I will climb into this *aśoka* tree and hide in its hollow. In that way I shall learn the news for certain. [*Does so.*]

[*Enter Rāvaṇa with his train.*]

Rāvaṇa. I, Rāvaṇa, with my celestial weapons, put to flight the hosts of gods, devils, and demons; in the fight my broad breast was scarred, as if by thunderbolts, with the tusks of the angry elephant of heaven. Sītā, of the bewitching eyes, shows no discrimination if she likes me not, infatuated with the little warrior ascetic. Assuredly, 'tis fate that makes the obstacle. (10)

[*Looking up.*] There is the moon—

Shining like a silver mirror the moon rises, displaying his beauty in the sky, a beloved friend of lotus beds, but oppresses my heart with his netted beams. (11)

[1] Sarup would read *nava* for *vana*, Sītā being like a fresh garland withered in the sun.

[*Stepping around.*] Here is Sītā at the foot of a tree, absorbed in contemplation. Her face is thin from fasting. She seems to shrink into herself, and sits crouching with her bosom and waist concealed, surrounded by a group of demon women, like a digit of the moon hidden by an eclipse.

She scorns delights, and me, and all this mighty fortune. Devoted to a mortal, she is beyond my power. (12)

Hanumān. Ah, now I understand.

This is that king's daughter of Mithilā, Rāma's bride. She is troubled like a gazelle frightened at the sight of a lion. (13)

Rāvaṇa. [*Approaching.*] Sītā, renounce this terrible ascetic vow. Accept me, beauteous lady, with all thy heart.[1] Put away that mortal, lady, moribund and averse from the ways of love. (14)

Sītā. Little Rāvaṇa is absurd. He knows nothing of a curse's mystic power.

Hanumān. [*Angrily.*] How arrogant this Rāvaṇa is, knowing nought of Rāma's two arms, nought of the great bow or the arrow, he calls him moribund. (15)

I cannot restrain my anger. Well, I will carry out the noble Rāma's task. Either,

If I kill Rāvaṇa, the task will be fulfilled. Or else if the demon overwhelms me, a great attempt will come to nought. (16)

Rāvaṇa. Exquisite lady, of slender form and lovely eyes, unloose that braid like a garland of blue lotuses. Take me to thy heart with my ten necks adorned with all kinds of gems and precious stones. (17)

Sītā. Right will be wrong if this wretched demon remains alive.

Rāvaṇa. Well, queen?

Sītā. Be you accursed.

Rāvaṇa. Ah, the majesty of a chaste wife,

In battle I crushed the gods with Indra at their head as well as demons. But even I seem stupefied by Sītā's three syllables. (18)

[*Voice behind the scene.*]

Victory to the King, Victory to the Lord of Laṅkā, Victory to his Majesty our Master. Four hours have passed.[2] The bathing time is passing. This way, Majesty, this way.

[*Exit Rāvaṇa with his retinue.*]

[1] *Lit.* 'with all your limbs'. [2] See note, p. 70.

Hanumān. Ha, Rāvaṇa has gone and the demon women gone to sleep. Now 's the time to approach the queen.

[*Comes down from the hollow.*]

Greetings, lady of a living lord—

I am sent by King Rāma, his very self, whose heart is saddened by anxiety through love for thee. **(19)**

Sītā. [*Aside.*] Who can this be? It may be some wicked demon pretending to come from my lord and trying to deceive me by disguising himself as a monkey. Well, I shall keep silent.

Hanumān. Do you not believe me? Away with your suspicion. Hearken, lady,

I am the monkey, Hanumān, sent to search for thee, by the Monkey King in alliance with Rāma, the light of Ikshvāku's house. **(20)**

Sītā. [*Aside.*] Be he who he may, he has mentioned my husband's name; so I will speak with him. [*Aloud.*] What, sir, is the news of my noble lord?

Hanumān. Hearken, lady.

His face is pale and thin, drawn by fasting. His charm and grace have gone through brooding on thy perfections. His body grows weaker, his fortitude is gone; burnt by the Love God's arrows, his eyes are full of tears. **(21)**

Sītā. [*Aside.*] Alas, unhappy me, I feel ashamed to hear my lord is so stricken by grief. But I see the pain of separation has its fruits, if indeed this monkey speaks the truth. Hearing of my husband's sympathy and pain on account of my humble self, my heart is swinging between joy and sorrow. [*Aloud.*] How was it, sir, that my husband made an alliance with your people?

Hanumān. Lady, listen,

For thy sake he slew in battle Vālin, the monkey-warrior, Sugrīva's elder brother. Then, princess, he gave Sugrīva the monkey kingdom, and the king sent out his apes to every quarter to search for thee. I am one of them, and have found thee out to-day, O queen, by a vulture's guidance. **(22)**

Besides, as such . . .[1]

Sītā. How cruel are the gods to make my husband so sorrowful!

Hanumān. Do not grieve, lady. For Rāma,

Grasping his great bow and surrounded by a host of monkeys, will assail Laṅkā and overwhelm the ten-headed Rāvaṇa. **(23)**

Sītā. Am I dreaming? Is it true, sir? I am not sure.

[1] Apparently some hiatus.

Hanumān. [*Aside.*] Alas!

She loves her lord and at heart recognizes it must be he, yet in her grief she will not believe it like one born in another body. (**24**)

[*Aloud.*] Lady, now will I,

Bring hither thy lord, O princess, with his mighty bow upraised and arrows in his hand. Set aside thy doubts of me, when thou art at his side with all thy sorrow gone. (**25**)

Sītā. Oh, sir, tell him how I am, in such a way that he may not be seized with grief at hearing of my plight.

Hanumān. As your ladyship bids.

Sītā. Go, I wish you success.

Hanumān. I thank you. [*Stepping around.*] Now how shall I announce my arrival to Rāvaṇa? Good, I have it:

With blows of fists and feet I will pulverize this park, so full of flocks of cuckoos, delightful with its lotus beds and clumps of beautiful trees. With its three mounds like clouds—t shall I rob the demon king of his pride in his estate. (**26**)

[*Exeunt ambo.*]

END OF THE SECOND ACT.

ACT III

[*Enter Spike-ear.*]

Spike-ear. Ho, there! who is on duty at the door of the Golden Gate[1] house? [*Enter Portress.*]

Portress. 'Tis I, Vijayā. What's to do?

Spike-ear. Oh, Vijayā, take a message at once to his Majesty the Lord of Laṅkā—the *Aśoka* Park is nearly all destroyed. For,

The tidings must be told. That *Aśoka* Park, where even the chief queen, Mandodarī, so fond of ornaments, does not gather sprays from kindness, where the Malaya zephyrs are afraid to flutter or to finger the young coral trees, that park of Indra's foe is destroyed. (1)

Portress. You, sir, are always in attendance on the king, and I have never known you so put about? Why is it?

Spike-ear. My good woman, the matter is most urgent. Please take the message at once.

Portress. Very well, sir, I'll take it. [*Exit.*]

Spike-ear. [*Looking in front.*] Why, here is his Majesty, the Lord of Laṅkā, coming this way.

Like pure white lotus are his savage eyes. With bright golden torches before him he rushes swiftly in a fury, like the sun arising at the dissolution of an aeon. (2)

[*Enter Rāvaṇa as described.*]

Rāvaṇa. What, what? Strange words are these thou utterest. I am listening. Speak out at once. What fearless wight intent on death has dared this deed to-day? By rooting up this grove he has done me grievous injury. (3)

Spike-ear. [*Approaching.*] Greeting, Majesty. Some monkey slipped in unnoticed and has thoroughly uprooted the *Aśoka* Park.

Rāvaṇa. [*Contemptuously.*] A monkey, say you? Go at once and catch him and bring him here.

Spike-ear. As your Majesty commands. [*Exit.*]

Rāvaṇa. Well, well,

If the gods have done this hostile thing to me, that terrified the triple world in battle, those nectar-eaters soon shall have the fruit arising from their insolence. (4)

[*Enter Spike-ear.*]

Spike-ear. Greeting, Majesty. That monkey is very powerful. He has snapped *sāl* trees like lotus stalks, and smashed the wood hill with his fist. He has made a clean sweep of the creeper bowers with the flat of his hands. Simply with his roar he has made the guards of the pleasure ground unconscious. Sire, be pleased to order a force sufficient for his capture.

Rāvaṇa. Then order a body of a thousand slaves to capture the ape.

Spike-ear. As the king commands. [*Exit and re-enters.*] Greeting, Majesty,

He uses trees as weapons, and in a trice he has slain our large force of slaves with our own great trees. (5)

Rāvaṇa. What, slain them? Then bid Prince Aksha catch the ape.

Spike-ear. As the king commands. [*Exit.*]

Rāvaṇa. [*Reflecting.*]

The prince is well trained in arms, brave, and strong. He should catch this forest-dweller perforce or slay him. (6)

[*Enter Spike-ear.*]

Spike-ear. Sire, be pleased to order another force.

Rāvaṇa. What for?

Spike-ear. Deign to listen. Seeing the prince going out against the monkey, five generals followed him without waiting for your Majesty's orders.

Rāvaṇa. Well, what then?

Spike-ear. When the monkey saw them rushing on him, he seemed rather scared and went off to the gate-house. Then lifting the golden bar he laid low all five generals.

Rāvaṇa. Go on.

Spike-ear. Then Prince Aksha,

His eyes red with anger, the prince was driving his chariot with the swiftest steeds, letting fly with the greatest ease a network of arrows, like a mass of monsoon clouds. But the monkey shook off the arrows and suddenly jumped on the chariot, seized the prince by the throat, and, grinning with glee, killed him with his fist. (7)

Rāvaṇa. [*Angrily.*] What? Killed him?

Stay thou here. I myself will go for this miserable monkey and in a moment burn him to ashes with the sparks of the fire of my wrath. (8)

Spike-ear. May it please your Majesty, when he heard of the death of Prince Aksha, Prince Indrajit, his heart consumed with anger, went out to attack the monkey.

Rāvaṇa. Then go, and get more news.

Spike-ear. As the king commands. [*Exit.*]

Rāvaṇa. The prince is well trained in arms.

In battle heroes needs must be slain or gain the victory. Yet this creature of mean deeds somewhat [1] disturbs my mind. (9)

[*Enter Spike-ear.*]

Spike-ear. Victory to your Majesty. Victory to the Lord of Laṅkā. Victory to the Blessed One.

A tumultuous battle ensued betwixt the prince and the ape, who has now been quickly bound with snares. (10)

Rāvaṇa. What wonder if Indrajit (Indra's conqueror) has captured a monkey. Who is without there?

[*Enter Demon.*]

Demon. Greeting, Majesty.

Rāvaṇa. Go and summon Vibhīshaṇa.

Demon. As your Majesty commands. [*Exit.*]

Rāvaṇa. And do you bring the ape.

Spike-ear. As the king commands. [*Exit.*]

Rāvaṇa. [*Reflecting.*] Out on it,

[1] Reading *īṣan manojvaraḥ* with Editor.

God and demons in alliance dare not think of Laṅkā. Yet in defiance of Ten-Heads, the king, it has been entered by an ape. (**11**)

Moreover,

I conquered the three worlds in battle and proudly strode over Kailāsa with its deities and demons. Lord Śiva, with his train, together with his queen, I rudely shook and took a boon from him. But Pārvatī and Nandin, because I ignored them, laid a curse upon me. What if this should be that curse of mine, disguised in the form of an ape? (**12**)

[*Enter Vibhīshaṇa.*]

Vibhīshaṇa. [*Thoughtfully.*] Alas, how perverse the king has become. For,

Again and again I have asked him to restore the lady of Mithilā to her Lord. To the sorrow of his friends he will not listen to my words. (**13**)

[*Approaching.*] Greeting, Majesty.

Rāvaṇa. Come here, Vibhīshaṇa. Sit down.

Vibhīshaṇa. Very well, I'll sit down here. [*Sits down.*]

Rāvaṇa. Why are you looking so despondent, Vibhīshaṇa?

Vibhīshaṇa. The servants of an overweening master may well be despondent.

Rāvaṇa. Cut out that tale. You, too, go and fetch the monkey.

Vibhīshaṇa. As the king commands. [*Exit.*]

[*Enter Hanumān held by demons.*]

Demons. Ha, this way.

Hanumān. I was not caught by an evil-minded devil. I made myself a prisoner to see the Demon king. (**14**)

[*Approaching.*] Ho, king, how are you?

Rāvaṇa. [*Disdainfully.*] Did he do all that, Vibhīshaṇa?

Vibhīshaṇa. Yes, sire, and even more.

Rāvaṇa. But how? Do you know?

Vibhīshaṇa. Deign to ask him, sire, who he is.

Rāvaṇa. Who are you, monkey? Why had you the impudence to enter our ladies' quarters?

Hanumān. Hearken.

I am the Wind-God's lawful son born in Añjanā. Hither sent by Rāghava. I am an ape and Hanumān 's my name. (**15**)

Vibhīshaṇa. Sir, did you hear?

Rāvaṇa. What if I did?

Vibhīshaṇa. Hanumān, what was the message of his honour, Rāghava?

Hanumān. Hearken to Rāma's orders.

Rāvaṇa. What, what? Rāma's orders, does he say? Have this monkey put to death.

Vibhīshaṇa. Pardon, your Majesty, but envoys should never be put to death, whatever their offence. First let us hear Rāma's message, afterwards you can do as you please.

Rāvaṇa. Well, monkey, what did that mortal say?

Hanumān. Hearken,

'Seek the best protection that thou canst, go to Śiva, or hide in the nethermost hell; with every limb cleft by my goodly arrows I will send thee to the abode of death.' **(16)**

Rāvaṇa. Ha, ha, ha,

With celestial weapons I defeated the legions of gods. All the demon chieftains bow to my will. Even Kubera is brought to nought with the loss of his aerial car. How can a mortal like Rāma pit himself against me? **(17)**

Hanumān. If you are as wonderful as all that, why did you steal his wife on the sly?

Vibhīshaṇa. Well said, Hanumān.

Thou didst lure Rāma away by magic, demon hero, and in the guise of a mendicant take her away by stealth. **(18)**

Rāvaṇa. Vibhīshaṇa, are you taking the side of my enemies?

Vibhīshaṇa. Pardon, king, my words are wise. Give back the wife of Rāghava. For I'd fain not see this house destroyed through thee, O demon hero. **(19)**

Rāvaṇa. No need to be alarmed, Vibhīshaṇa.

Is a long-maned lion slain by a deer? Or a mighty elephant in rut struck down by a jackal? **(20)**

Hanumān. Do you think it proper, Rāvaṇa, for you whose fate is sealed to speak like that of Rāma? Speak not so, oh Rāvaṇa.

Thou worthless outcaste goblin, hopelessly evil,[1] is it right for thee to breathe such words of Rāma, the peerless paragon of heroes, Indra's equal, the one lord of the worlds? **(21)**

Rāvaṇa. What? He addresses me by name? Put this monkey to death. Nay, we should be blamed for killing an envoy. Spike-ear, set light to his tail and turn him loose.

Spike-ear. As the king commands. This way.

Rāvaṇa. Nay, come here a moment.

[1] *Lit.* 'whose merit is exhausted'.

Hanumān. Here I am.

Rāvaṇa. Take that mortal this message from me.

Rāma, I have humiliated thee by abducting thy wife. If thou hast any name for archery give me a great combat. **(22)**

Hanumān. You will soon see,

Thou shalt see thy Laṅkā with its great ramparts, gateways, and towers demolished, while all around the surrounding pleasure groves are rooted up by troops of apes, and thou art vanquished by the twang of Rāma's bow. **(23)**

Rāvaṇa. Ha, throw this monkey out.

Demons. This way, this way. [*Exit Hanumān with guards.*]

Vibhīshaṇa. May it please your Majesty, I have something I would wish to say all for your Majesty's good.

Rāvaṇa. Speak out; if it is good, we are ready to listen.

Vibhīshaṇa. I fear that utter destruction threatens the Demon race.

Rāvaṇa. But why?

Vibhīshaṇa. Because of your Majesty's indefensible idea.

Rāvaṇa. What do you mean?

Vibhīshaṇa. Why, the abduction of Sītā.

Rāvaṇa. What is wrong about that?

Vibhīshaṇa. It means a breach of the law and . . .

Rāvaṇa. And what? Your sentence is incomplete. Speak out.

Vibhīshaṇa. That is all.

Rāvaṇa. Vibhīshaṇa, what are you hiding? By my life, I'll curse you if you do not speak the truth.

Vibhīshaṇa. Pray promise not to punish me.

Rāvaṇa. I grant you that. Speak out.

Vibhīshaṇa. It means a breach of the law and a dangerous feud.

Rāvaṇa. [*Angrily.*] Dangerous feud? How so?

This base demon sides with my foe. Feeding fat mine ire he speaks harsh words to me without a tremor. **(24)**

Who is without there?

He disregards fraternal love and takes the side of my enemy. I cannot endure to see him before me, so let him be cast into banishment. **(25)**

Vibhīshaṇa. May it please your Majesty, I will go myself.

Forth I go, punished by thee, O king, but free from blame.
Do thou abandon wrath and lust and do as thou shouldst do. **(26)**

[*Stepping round.*] And now,

This very day I'll betake myself to Rāma, of the lotus eyes and dreadful bow, who has made a vow to slaughter Rāvaṇa. That god among men strives ever for his dependents' good. Thus shall I raise again the demon race from annihilation. (27)

[*Exit.*]

Rāvaṇa. Ha, Vibhīshaṇa has gone. I must take measures to protect the town.

[*Exit.*]

END OF THE THIRD ACT.

ACT IV

INTERLUDE.

[*Enter a monkey Chamberlain.*]

Chamberlain. Oh, general, order the monkey army to be in readiness.

[*Enter a General.*]

General. What, sir, is the reason of this preparation?

Chamberlain. The worthy Hanumān has brought news of Sītā the wife of the noble Rāma.

General. What news?

Chamberlain. I will tell you.

The princess bides in Laṅkā utterly cast down by grief. Besides, she's plagued by Rāvaṇa, who defies all moral usage. Our king, on hearing this, and wishing to help Rāma, whose heart is burning with intense grief, gave orders for the formidable monkey army to prepare. (1)

General. Very well. As his Majesty commands.

Chamberlain. I shall report to the king that the army is in readiness

[*Exeunt ambo.*]

END OF THE INTERLUDE.

[*Enter Rāma, Lakshmaṇa, Sugrīva, and Hanumān.*]

Rāma. I have traversed the broad ridges and trackless thickets of mountains, huge as clouds. I have crossed rivers, where lions and tigers and lordly elephants slake their thirst; I have passed through a wonderful great forest, where the trees are rich with flowers and fruit; and now with the host of the monkey chief I have reached the shore of the sea. (2)

Lakshmaṇa. Here is the sacred ocean.[1]

[1] *bhagavān Varuṇaḥ.*

The ocean shines like sleeping Vishṇu, with the blue of sapphires and rainy clouds, with beautiful garlands of billows breaking into foam, and a thousand arms in the merging streams. (3)

Rāma. How now?

All ready to destroy my foe, with an arrow on my bow, the ocean now, to give him life, restrains my hand. (4)

Sugrīva. Lo, in the sky,

Whence comes this demon flying? Brilliant as a rain-cloud, with his limbs blazing with pure gold ornaments, he is like a moth about to rush into a fire. (5)

Hanumān. Ho, monkey warriors, be on your guard.

The monkey chiefs must now stand fast in battle for to slay the fiends with rocks and trees, with bound fists, with teeth and claws and knees, and with dreadful roars, and so protect our king. (6)

Rāma. A demon is it? Don't get excited, Hanumān.

Hanumān. As the prince commands.

[*Enter Vibhīshaṇa.*]

Vibhīshaṇa. Ah, I have come to Rāma's camping place. [*Reflecting.*] Now how will Rāma know who I am? I sent no messenger, and he does not know that I am coming, while I am related to his enemy. For,

My heart is anxious as to what the Lord of the Raghus will say to me. I come to him for shelter, but I am the younger brother of the enemy of the gods. Before him raging in the battle even the Thunder-wielder aided by all the gods was unable to make a stand. (7)

However, He is good, versed in the very essence of the law, kindly to dependents. How can I doubt Rāma, as my own heart is free of guile. (8)

[*Looking down.*] Here are the head-quarters of the hero of the Raghu house. I will descend. [*Descending.*] Ha, I shall stay here and send the prince word of my coming.

Hanumān. [*Looking upwards.*] Hullo. What, is it his Highness Vibhīshaṇa?

Vibhīshaṇa. Why, it is Hanumān. Hanumān, tell the prince that I have come.

Hanumān. Very well. [*Approaching.*] Greeting, prince.

Here is the righteous Vibhīshaṇa seeking thy protection, O king, being banished by his brother on account of thee. (9)

Rāma. What? Vibhīshaṇa seeking my protection? Dear Lakshmaṇa, go and bring him with all honour.

Lakshmaṇa. As my noble brother bids.

Rāma. Sugrīva, I see you wish to say something.

Sugrīva. Prince, these demons are very artful and fight by fraud. So one should think twice about admitting Vibhīshaṇa.

Hanumān. Nay, no need, your Majesty,

Vibhīshaṇa I deem as loyal to the prince as we are. I have seen him before in that city disputing with his brother. **(10)**

Rāma. If that is so, go bring him in with all honour.

Lakshmaṇa. As my noble brother bids. [*Stepping around.*] Ah, there is Vibhīshaṇa. Are you quite well, Vibhīshaṇa?

Vibhīshaṇa. Ah, the prince Lakshmaṇa. Prince, I am well indeed to-day.

Lakshmaṇa. Vibhīshaṇa, let us go to the prince.

Vibhīshaṇa. Certainly.

[*They both approach.*]

Lakshmaṇa. Greeting, noble brother.

Vibhīshaṇa. May it please your Highness, greeting.

Rāma. Ha, Vibhīshaṇa. Are you well, Vibhīshaṇa?

Vibhīshaṇa. Highness, I am well indeed to-day.

Come for protection to thee, the protector with eyes of lotus petals, I am well indeed to-day, O king, purified by the sight of thee. **(11)**

Rāma. From to-day be Lord of Laṅkā by my command.

Vibhīshaṇa. I thank you.

Rāma. Vibhīshaṇa, your very arrival means the accomplishment of our task. We have found no means of crossing the sea.

Vibhīshaṇa. Why, prince, what do you need for that? If the sea does not give a passage let fly your divine shaft upon him.

Rāma. Well said, Vibhīshaṇa. Good, that is what I will do. [*Suddenly standing up angrily.*]

If the sea vouchsafe me not this passage, swiftly will I still the roaring of his waves; my burning arrows will dry up both mud and brine; the shore will be strewn with fish dying by the score. **(12)**

[*Enter Ocean.*[1]]

Ocean. [*In confusion.*]

Against Nārāyaṇa, come here in human form to fulfil his purpose, I am guilty of offence. Fearful of his shaft, that destroys the forms of the celestials' foes, I fly at full speed to seek my lord's protection. **(13)**

[1] Varuṇa.

[*Looking round.*] Ah, here is the Blessed One. Wielder of discus, bow, and mace, he has taken on a human form. Himself the cause of all, he has come to fulfil some purpose. (14)

Salutations to the blessed Nārāyaṇa, the cause of the triple world.

Lakshmaṇa. [*Looking round.*] Why, who is this?

His diadem is set with gems. His body blue as fresh water-lilies, his beautiful great eyes are red like copper. Of rolling gait like an elephant in rut, he has risen from the midst of multitudinous waters. Swiftly his lustre seems to make the mortal world bow down before him. (15)

Vibhīshaṇa. Prince, here is the Ocean just arrived.

Rāma. Is this the Ocean? Holy sir, my salutation.

Ocean. The lord of the gods should not salute me.

Whence thy wrath, O prince? Wilt not forgo thine ire?
Command forthwith, O best of men, what should I do? (16)

Rāma. Pray grant a passage that we may go to Laṅkā.

Ocean. Lo, here is the passage. Pray proceed. [*Disappears.*]

Rāma. What, has the blessed Ocean disappeared? Look, Vibhīshaṇa, by his favour all the ocean's waves are motionless.

Vibhīshaṇa. Prince, the sea seems now to be cut in twain.[1]

Rāma. Where is Hanumān?

Hanumān. Here, your Highness.

Rāma. Hanumān, lead the way.

Hanumān. As the prince commands.

[*All step round.*]

Rāma. [*Looking round in surprise.*] Look, dear Lakshmaṇa, and you, my comrade Vibhīshaṇa. Your Majesty Sugrīva, look, and you, friend Hanumān. How varied is the ocean.

In one place spouting foam, in another the water is alive with fishes. In one place full of shells, in another like a dark blue cloud. Here are rows of billows, and there the peril of crocodiles. Here is a dreadful whirlpool, and there still water. (17)

By the favour of the Blessed One we have crossed the ocean.

Hanumān. Prince, this is Laṅkā.

Rāma. [*Gazing for a long time.*] Ah, the glory of the demon city will soon pass away.

Broken by the buffets of the blasts of my goodly arrows, it will sink, the very ends of it struck down by the waves of the

[1] This is very different from the well-known story of the monkeys building a bridge by dropping rocks in the sea. It reminds us of Vasudevas' passage across the Jamna. *Adventures of the Boy Kṛishṇa*, i. 18.

simian host, like a ship that's lost in the ocean by the helmsman's fault. All through the fault of Rāvaṇa. (18)

Sugrīva, pitch the camp on this hill Suvela. [*Sits down.*]

Sugrīva. As the prince commands. See to it, Indigo.

Indigo. As your Majesty commands. [*Exit and re-enters.*] Greeting, prince. While the armies were being encamped in proper order, and the numbers of the troops were being checked by the registers, two monkeys were caught that had come in from somewhere unnoticed. We don't know what to do with them. So your highness must decide.

Rāma. Bring them in at once.

Indigo. As your highness orders. [*Exit.*]

[*Enter Indigo with Parrot and Mate, with folded hands, disguised as monkeys, and held by monkey guards.*]

Monkeys. Hi, speak, you two, speak!

Parrot and Mate. Master, we are servants of Master Kumuda.

Monkeys. Master, they make out they're servants of Master Kumuda.

Vibhīshaṇa. [*Scrutinizing Parrot and Mate.*]

These two are not our soldiers, they are not even apes. Both are demons sent by Rāvaṇa: their names are Parrot and Mate. (19)

Parrot and Mate. [*Aside.*] Alas, the prince has recognized us. [*Aloud.*] Sir, we saw the demon race was doomed on account of the perversity of the demon king. So finding no place there we came here disguised as monkeys to seek refuge with your honour.

Rāma. What do you think, Vibhīshaṇa?

Vibhīshaṇa. Prince,

These twain are intimate ministers of the demon king; they will not abandon the Lord of Laṅkā even in mortal straits. (20)

So have them punished as they deserve.

Rāma. Nay, Vibhīshaṇa, say not so.

By chastising these my victory is not gained, nor is the demon king destroyed. So set them free. (21)

Lakshmaṇa. If you set them free, your highness might have it done after they have gone and examined all our camp.

Rāma. Lakshmaṇa has made a good suggestion. See to it, Indigo.

Indigo. As the prince commands.

Rāma. Nay, come here a moment.

Parrot and Mate. Here we are.

Rāma. Take this message from me to the demon king.

By abducting my bride thou broughtest this warfare on thyself. I have come as a guest of war eager to see thee, but see thee not. (22)

Parrot and Mate. As your highness orders. [*Exeunt.*]

Rāma. Vibhīshaṇa, we will now inspect the entire force.

Vibhīshaṇa. As your highness wishes.

Rāma. [*Stepping and looking around.*] Ah, the blessed sun has set. For now,

> The sun has gone home, contracting all his rays on the western mountain. His body tinged by the evening glow, he shines like a golden mark[1] on the forehead of an elephant covered with bright red cloth. **(23)**

[*Exeunt omnes.*]

END OF THE FOURTH ACT.

ACT V

INTERLUDE.

[*Enter a demon Chamberlain.*]

Chamberlain. Ho, there! who is on duty at the door of the Coral Gatehouse?

[*Enter another Demon.*]

Demon. Sir, it is I. What am I to do?

Chamberlain. Go, summon Lightning-tongue by order of the king.

Demon. Very well, sir. [*Exit.*]

Chamberlain. Ah me, the prosperity of the Demon house is failing. All means of recovery are cut off. Heroic warriors are dead. The life of the king himself is in danger. But even now his mind has not returned to common sense. For who, indeed,

> Would not make peace by giving him back his wife on seeing him cross the sea?—the deep blue sea, full of monsters rising from the depths, its dreadful shore bounded by the rolling billows? **(1)**

Besides, The heroes have been slain by Rāma from Longhand down to Pot-Ear. Now to-day, Indrajit, has gone out too. **(2)**

In such a state of things,

> He disregards the minister's advice. Driven by desire, but thinking himself a mighty hero, for our misfortune he is keen to fight, and will not give back Janaka's daughter—the queen of the Rāghava bull. **(3)**

[*Enter Lightning-tongue.*]

Lightning-tongue. How are you, sir?

[1] *Jāmbunadena racitaḥ pulako yathaiva.*

Chamberlain. Lightning-tongue, go and bring a likeness of the heads of Rāma and Lakshmaṇa by order of the king.

Lightning-tongue. As the king commands. [*Exit.*]

Chamberlain. Well, I will go and attend on the king. [*Exit.*]

END OF THE INTERLUDE.

[*Enter Sītā attended by a crowd of she-devils.*]

Sītā. My heart was thrilled at the coming of my lord. Why does it seem troubled to-day? Bad omens have appeared. Even so, I am greatly elated. May the gods grant that all is well.

[*Enter Rāvaṇa.*]

Rāvaṇa. Nay, do not go.

This lady with a pure fresh lotus in her hand would go forth and leave my abode for ever. Yet I captured her, when in a trice I defeated Kubera in battle and Laṅkā came into my possession. (4)

Stay, lady, stay.[1] I pray you do not go. What do you say? You will leave me and go to Rāma? Well, be off with you.

I seized thee by force erstwhile in Kubera's house. By force will I seize thee again, slaying Rāma in the fight. (5)

Let her go. Still I'll try to beguile Sītā.

[*Assuming a love-sick manner.*] Ah, none so powerful as the Lord of the Flowery Bow. For,

Beholding Sītā's face, my eyes forget to sleep all night. Yearning for the joy of her embraces my form grows pale and wasted. With his flower-shaft he fixes torment on a lovely target. Alack, poor Rāvaṇa, whose arms subdued the triple world, is now subdued himself. (6)

[*Coming nearer.*]

Sītā, with eyes like lotus leaves, mistress of my heart, give up thy heart set on a mortal man. In the battle-field to-day thou shall see thy heart's beloved, with Lakshmaṇa as well, being slaughtered by my weapon. (7)

Sītā. Oh, what a silly little Rāvaṇa it is, wanting to balance Mount Mandara in his hand.

[*Enter a Demon.*]

Demon. Victory to the king.

Here are the two heads of those two human princes, slain by our prince in battle, and brought here for your pleasure. (8)

[1] He appears to be addressing a personification of his Fortune; compare *The Adventures of the Boy Kṛishṇa.*

Rāvaṇa. See, Sītā, see the heads of these two mortals.

Sītā. Alas! my noble lord. [*Falls down in a faint.*]

Rāvaṇa. Abandon thy affection, Sītā, for this man whose life has fled. This very day, O large-eyed lady, thou mayest gain great fortune. **(9)**

Sītā. [*Coming to herself.*] Alas, my lord, I am too cold-hearted, wretched me, gazing on your face, like a lotus fresh and fragrant, with your eyes so changed. Alack, dear lord, where have you gone, casting me in this sea of troubles? Yet I do not die. Can it be false? Good sir, with the very sword with which you wrought this dreadful deed upon my lord put me too to death.

Rāvaṇa. 'Tis clear. Indrajit has killed the wretched man in battle as well as Lakshmaṇa his brother. Who now will set thee free? **(10)**

[*Voice behind the scene.*]

Rāma, Rāma—

Sītā. Long life to you—

[*Enter a Demon.*]

Demon. [*Excited.*] Rāma, Rāma—

Rāvaṇa. What do you mean by 'Rāma, Rāma—'?

Demon. Pardon, Majesty. In my hurry to report most urgent news I did not notice you were otherwise engaged.[1]

Rāvaṇa. Speak out, fellow. What has the ascetic mortal done?

Demon. Deign to listen, Majesty,

With his high courage and mighty strength Rāghava, with Lakshmaṇa, to-day has humiliated thee, the Lord of Laṅkā; swiftly winning the battle, he has slain thy son. **(11)**

Rāvaṇa. Ah, wretched coward.

Is Indrajit, who vanquished Indra and the gods with all the demons facing him, slain in battle by a man? **(12)**

Demon. Pardon, Majesty. In your Majesty's presence none dare tell a lie about the prince.

Rāvaṇa. Alas, my darling Meghanāda. [*Falls down in a swoon.*]

Demon. Take heart, your Majesty, take heart.

Rāvaṇa. [*Coming to himself.*]

Alas, my child, so skilled in arms, a torment to all the worlds. Alas, my child, that conquered Indra—encircled by submissive foes. Alas, my child, so loving to thy parents—a hero devoted to battle. Alas, my child, why hast thou gone and left me here? **(13)**

[1] *Lit.* 'the altered situation'.

[*Faints away.*]

Demon. Alack, 'tis cursed fate has brought the Lord of Laṅkā to this state, after conquering the three worlds. Majesty, take heart.

Rāvaṇa. [*Coming to himself.*] What good now is Sītā, the cause of this misfortune? What good this fickle Fortune who brings to naught the conquest of the universe. What then, thou cursed Fate? Art thou still tremulous with fear?

> Now devoid of all affection, now darling Indrajit has gone,
> this hard-hearted Ten-heads, O misery, is still alive. **(14)**

[*Falls down overcome with grief.*]

Demon. Ho, there, goblin warriors—the king is in a bad way. So you guards on the inner rampart must be careful.

[*Voice behind the scene.*]

Ho, there, you goblin warriors, are you timidly turning your backs in fear, because the ocean of the army is somewhat lessened by the deaths of Longhand, Nikumbha, Pot-ear, and Indrajit in the van? Time and again you have won battles against the gods. This timorous flight is disgraceful. And, mind you, our master the Lord of Laṅkā is still here, adorned with twenty arms, and famed for his conquest of the universe.

Rāvaṇa. [*Listening. Angrily.*] Go, and get the latest news.

Demon. As your Majesty commands. [*Exit and re-enters.*] Greeting, Majesty.

This Rāma,

> Surrounded by troops of monkeys, his large eyes full of laughter, comes with an arrow fitted to his bow, ignoring thee in his arrogance, and having slain thy son in the forefront of the battle, is rushing on Laṅkā as if he would set it ablaze. **(15)**

Rāvaṇa. [*Getting up suddenly in a rage.*] Where is he? Where is he? [*Draws his sword.*]

> This sword I hold in my hand has its edge hardened by cleaving the temples of Indra's elephants. 'Twill make thee a present to my wrath. Let the gods protect thee now. Whither art thou going, little creature? Stay, thou wicked ascetic, wait for me. **(16)**

Demon. Oh, sire, do not be rash.

Sītā. Rāvaṇa does horrid wicked things without any reason. But now he'll soon be dead.

Rāvaṇa. On account of her, so many of my brothers, sons, and friends have been killed. So I shall cut out her heart, the home of enmity, pull out her entrails and tie them round my neck. Then with a blow of my lightning sword I shall kill the monkey troops and the pair of humans also.

Demon. Pardon, Majesty. The present is no time for endless futile efforts to match the arrogance of the enemy's force. And it 's certainly no good killing a woman.

Rāvaṇa. Well, send for my chariot.

Demon. As your Majesty commands. [*Exit and re-enters.*] Victory to your Majesty. Here is the chariot.

Rāvaṇa. [*Mounting the chariot.*]

Sītā, to-day shalt thou see Rāma, with the gods around him,
bewildered [1] by the sharp arrows streaming from my bow. (17)

[*Exit Rāvaṇa with his train.*]

Sītā. Ye gods, as surely as I am loyal to my lord, as beseems the traditions of our house, so surely may he gain the victory.

[*Exit.*]

END OF THE FIFTH ACT.

ACT VI

INTERLUDE

[*Enter three Fairies.*[2]]

All Three. Here we are, here we are.

First Fairy. Rāma is the standard of the Ikshvāku house, large and blazing bright.

Second Fairy. He girds his loins to slaughter Rāvaṇa.

Third Fairy. Our hearts are all agog with eagerness to view their combat.

All Three. So we have swiftly come from the peaks of the Himalayas. (1)

First Fairy. Citraratha, all the sky is crowded with gods, divine sages, saints, and fairies. So let us avoid those groups and take our stand on any vacant spot to see the wonderful duel between Rāma and Rāvaṇa.

Two Fairies. Very well.

[*They do so.*]

First Fairy. Ah, this battle-field is an appalling sight.

This battle-field is like an ocean with floods of goblin corpses,

[1] *ākrānta-cetasam*, 'his wits beset', but Sarup takes *cetas* to be the physical heart, translating, 'his heart shot'.

[2] Vidyādharas. See note, p. 88.

where mighty monkeys form the waves, sharp swords the crocodiles, where the tide surges with the ray-like arrows of the moon-like Rāma. (2)

Second Fairy. 'Tis so indeed—

These demon troops fall in the battle, heads battered with trees and rocks, hammered by blows of fists. They are hemmed in by mighty monkey captains, in a fury, with tails and ears all erect. With fierce faces and bitten lips, with eyes goggling wide as they are strangled, the demons swiftly fall like mountains struck by thunderbolts. (3)

Third Fairy. And mark you these,

With sharp and shining swords, eyes with ire distended, with hideous white teeth, they look like dark blue clouds. Eager to kill all the leaders of the monkey host, these demons are charging on, their mouths gaping with the speed. (4)

First Fairy. Oh, now again.

The demons are raining arrows on the apes.

Second Fairy. The apes are hurling rocks upon the demons.

Third Fairy. With hefty blows of fists and knees,

They have started smashing each other in a strange and dreadful scrimmage. (5)

First Fairy. Look at Rāvaṇa.

Whirling a spear with a golden shaft, with hideous white teeth, he drives his chariot. When he sees Rāma, enraged, he is like a planet that beholds the full-orbed moon, lord of stars, on a peak of the eastern mountain. (6)

Second Fairy. See Rāma too.

In his left hand holding the bow, and drawing a goodly arrow with his right, the hero stands on the ground and regards his foe in chariot, as the God of War in battle gazed at the mighty Krauñca mountain. (7)

Third Fairy. Ha, ha.

Rāvaṇa let fly his spear resembling Death. But Rāma the archer smiled and split it in two. (8)

First Fairy. Rāvaṇa sees his spear shot down, and with eyes dilated in wrath he rains a shower of arrows on Rāma. (9)

Second Fairy. Oh, how beautiful Rāma looks.

Showers of arrows from the cloud that is Rāvaṇa, sparkle on reaching Rāma like drops of water on a bull. (10)

Third Fairy. There he is,

Swiftly raising his keen golden bow, he throws out the dreadful network of arrows in the van of battle. He advances on foot against Rāvaṇa mounted on a car, as a sharp-toothed tiger rushes on a raging elephant. (11)

All Three. Why, all this place is ablaze with light. What can it be?

First Fairy. Ah, Indra has become anxious because the battle is so even,[1] so he has sent his chariot driven by Mātali.

Second Fairy. Rāma sees Mātali beside him and at his request mounts the car.

Third Fairy. There he goes.

This chariot is the index of the chief god's pride in victory and the destroyer of Diti's devilish brood. Therein he shines as the cause of the demon's downfall, just as Śiva[2] shone aforetime at the massacre of three cities. (12)

First Fairy. Aha, a mighty fight 's toward.

The soldiers of the ape and demon armies have given over hurling divers weapons. They stand at ease to watch the fight 'twixt the Lord of men and the demon, wherein the goodly bolts drink up the sharpest arrows. (13)

Second Fairy. Oh, and now,

These two, wheeling round in military movements, stand in their cars emitting flights of arrows; like two suns wandering in the sky and burning up the earth with their netted rays. (14)

Third Fairy. Look at Rāvaṇa.

With darts of dreadful speed he has slain the steeds. In a trice he furiously attacks the standard. Roaring, he discharges a mighty shower of arrows, trying to frighten the lord of men, who only laughs. (15)

First Fairy. Here is Rāma.

Taking breath a moment, his body is dwarfed as he takes his stance, glancing at a sharp arrow with eyes as red as the noonday sun. Mātali gives him a clear space, and the heroic lord of men angrily aims the weapon of unmeasured power, his grandsire's[3] gift. (16)

Second Fairy. This weapon,

Discharged by the force of Rāma's arm, its sharp edge reflecting the burning sun, smites down the goblin chief and swiftly returns to Rāma. (17)[4]

[1] Reading with Editor *ā yuddha-sāmānya-*. Sarup would read *āyuddhāsāmānya-* 'because the fighting is uneven', i. e. because Rāma is on foot and his opponent in a chariot.

[2] Kapardin with hair wound in the form of a cowrie.

[3] Brahma.

[4] Like a boomerang.

All Three. Ah, Rāvaṇa has fallen.

First Fairy. Beholding Rāvaṇa slain the gods have sent a shower of flowers, and their kettle-drums are roaring loudly. **(18)**

Second Fairy. Well, the gods' task is accomplished.

First Fairy. Come along, then. Let us also honour Rāma, the universal benefactor.

Two Fairies. Yes, an excellent proposal.

[*Exeunt omnes.*]

[END OF THE INTERLUDE.]

[*Enter Rāma.*]

Rāma. Rāvaṇa I killed to-day in battle swiftly beset by the speed of my shafts.

Vibhīshaṇa, the noble-minded, I have now made lord of Laṅkā. Thus, having swum across an ocean of vows, where mighty beings roam,[1] I make my way to Laṅkā with my kinsmen to comfort Sītā. **(19)**

[*Enter Lakshmaṇa.*]

Lakshmaṇa. Greeting, noble brother. Your noble consort is approaching, sir.

Rāma. My dear Lakshmaṇa.

By reason of Sītā's misfortune, and at the sight of her that has dwelt in my enemy's halls, my anger will now prevent my patience. **(20)**

Lakshmaṇa. As my noble brother bids. [*Exit.*]

[*Enter Vibhīshaṇa.*]

Vibhīshaṇa. Greeting, prince!

Here comes thy faithful wife, O king, her misery removed by thy strength of arm. By thy favour she has come, like the goddess of Prosperity erstwhile released from the demon house. **(21)**

Rāma. Let her wait there, Vibhīshaṇa. She is sullied by contact with the demon, and has become a stain on Ikshvāku's house. As king Daśaratha was my father, it is not meet that she should see me, Lord of Laṅkā. Besides,

Who stays a man from sinking in unworthy objects of the senses, he is a friend, O king; if he does not, he is a foe. **(22)**

Vibhīshaṇa. But pardon, prince—

[1] That is of the ocean—inhabited by great sea-monsters, of vows—kept by the great. A tasteless verse that does not fit in with what follows.

Rāma. Pray do not vex me further.

[*Enter Lakshmaṇa.*]

Lakshmaṇa. Greeting, noble brother! Learning of your intention, your wife awaits your permission to mount the funeral pyre.

Rāma. Lakshmaṇa, accede to the wish of this pious lady.

Lakshmaṇa. As my noble brother bids. [*Stepping round.*] Alas!

Convinced of the princess's chastity and hearing of my brother's command, my heart is swung betwixt duty and affection. **(23)**

Who's there?

[*Enter Hanumān.*]

Hanumān. Greeting, prince!

Lakshmaṇa. If you are capable of doing it, Hanumān, such is my brother's order.

Hanumān. But what does your highness think about it?

Lakshmaṇa. What I think is of no consequence. Nay, we have but to carry out my brother's purpose. Let us go.

Hanumān. As your highness bids. [*Exeunt ambo.*]

[*Enter Lakshmaṇa.*]

Lakshmaṇa. If you please, my brother, oh, a miracle. For the noble lady,

Like a wreath of full-blown lotus, giving up all hopes of life, is swiftly entering the fire, making all thy labour fruitless, as a swan enters a field of lilies. **(24)**

Rāma. Marvellous. Oh, prevent her, Lakshmaṇa.

Lakshmaṇa. As my brother bids.

[*Enter Hanumān.*]

Hanumān. Greeting, my lord,

This pure lady in the purifying fire has received no injury, but like a golden necklace has come from the flames with added lustre. **(25)**

Rāma. [*Astonished.*] Oh, what is this?

Lakshmaṇa. Oh, a miracle!

[*Enter Sugrīva.*]

Sugrīva. Greeting, prince,

Who, pray, is this, born of the blazing fire in a worshipful form, that brings Janaka's daughter alive? **(26)**

Lakshmaṇa. Ah, this is the holy God of Fire that comes hither leading the noble lady.

Rāma. Yea, it is the blessed God of Fire. Let us go to meet him.

[*They all do so.*]

[*Enter Agni leading Sītā.*]

Agni. Here is the blessed Nārāyaṇa. Greeting, my lord.

Rāma. Blessed one, I salute you.

Agni. The lord of the gods should not salute me.

Lord of kings and best of men take this lady, Janaka's daughter. She is sinless, pure, unscathed, and honoured of all the world. (**27**)

Besides, Know thou that this child of Janaka is the blessed Lakshmī, come to thee in human form. (**28**)

Rāma. I thank you.

Well, I knew Vaidehī's purity, oh God of the Smoky Banner. Yet I acted thus to bring conviction to the world. (**29**)

[*Celestial musicians sing behind the scene.*]

Salutations to Nārāyaṇa, cause of the triple world.

Brahmā is thy heart, Lord of the Triple World, Rudra is thy wrath. The Sun and Moon are thy two eyes, Lord of Gods, and Eloquence[1] thy tongue. All three worlds with Brahmā, Indra, and the Marut hosts are created by thee alone, oh Lord. Sītā here is She that loves her lotus home,[2] thou art Vishṇu, so do thou receive her. (**30**)

[*Again, other voices sing behind the scenes.*]

When this earth had sunk in the briny deep, thou alone didst raise it in the body of a boar. With thy three strides, oh Lord of Gods, thou didst encompass all three worlds. Of thine own accord thou and thy queen have taken on these forms. Slaying Rāvaṇa in battle thou hast now made the gods feel secure as they never did before. (**31**)

Agni. Blessed sir, these hosts of gods, divine sages, saints, fairies, celestial nymphs, and musicians, congratulate you, all according to their powers.

Rāma. I thank them.

Agni. Come hither, blessed sir, for your consecration.

Rāma. As your holiness commands.

[*Exeunt ambo.*]

[*Voices behind the scene.*]

Victory to the King. Victory to our Lord. Victory to the Blessed One. Victory to his Majesty. Victory to the destroyer of Rāvaṇa. Long live the King.

[1] Bhāratī, goddess of speech.

[2] Lakshmī, called Kamalālayā, the wife of Vishṇu from whose navel the lotus springs. 'Devoted to him whose abode is on the lotus', i.e. to Brahmā, would be impossible mythology.

Vibhīshaṇa. Here is the King.

Crossing the ocean of his vows and winning the queen to-day in battle, free from sin, he is crowned to-day by all the gods and shines like the moon in a clear sky. **(32)**

Lakshmaṇa. Ah, one sees divinity in his Majesty.

Surrounded by Yama, Varuṇa, Kubera, Vāsava, and hosts of other gods, and consecrated by the command of Daśaratha he is as glorious as Indra, when he gained the lordship of the gods. **(33)**

[*Enter Rāma, consecrated, with Sītā.*]

Rāma. Dear Lakshmaṇa,

When the king had placed me on the sacred throne, and the lucky cord was on my arm, he broke off the consecration, intent to please my mother. 'Tis clear that though he now has gone the way of fate, my father has crowned me once again to-day with a happy heart. **(34)**

Agni. Blessed sir, here come your subjects to meet you, led by Bharata and Śatrughna, at the injunction of Mahendra.

Rāma. Blessed One, I rejoice.

Agni. Mahendra here, and the other nectar-loving gods congratulate you.

Rāma. I thank them.

Agni. Blessed sir, what further favour can I bestow on you?

Rāma. If the blessed one is pleased with me, what further favour can I desire?

EPILOGUE.

May the kine be without blemish and, subduing the sovereignty of his foes, may our Lion King rule over this earth in its entirety.[1]

[*Exeunt omnes.*]

[1] Identical with the Epilogue of *The Minister's Vows.*

SELECT INDEX

I and II refer to Volumes, other numbers to pages.

Actress, I. 5, 74, 158 ; II. 64.
adagdhā, I. 45 n.
ākrānta-cetasam, II. 172 n.
anivișța, II. 68 n.
Archery Hall, II. 137.
arjuna, II. 44 n.
Arrow inscribed, I. 138 ; II. 150.
Arthaśāstra, I, 30 n.
asana, I. 53 n.
aśoka, I. 159 ; II. 157.
Audience Hall, II. 67, 83.

bakula, II. 44 n.
Balarāma, I. 40 n.
Balcony, II. 137, 138.
Bark dress, I. 159, 165.
Bhāmaha, I. 1, 11.
bhayam, II. 124.
bhindipāla, II. 47.
Buildings (and parts), *see*: Archery Hall, Audience Hall, Balcony, *Caüssāla*, Concert Hall, Council Hall, Dungeons, Elephant Stable, Fire Shrine, Gambling Hall, Hall, *Indrapatha*, Lattice Window, *maṇibhūmi*, Middle Palace, Monkey-heads, *Pratolī*, Rogues' Hall, *Samudragrha*, *Śāntigrha*, Stage, Terrace, Tiring-room, Watch-towers, Wooden pavilion.
Burglar, I. 91 ; his drone, I. 92.

campaka, I. 96 ; II. 129.
cañgerikā, I. 76, basket.
cārī, II. 44.
caüssāla, II. 73 n.
Chariots' speed, I. 173.
Chequer board, II. 41.
Concert Hall, I. 159, 165.
Coral trees, II. 157.
Council Chamber, II. 4.
Curse, II. 102, 106, 155.
Curtain, I 69 n.

Darkness described, I. 79 ; II. 80, 116, 117.
Death on stage, I. 171 ; II. 138, 152.
Door panel, I. 62, 198.
dukūla, II. 4 n., 133.
Dungeons, II. 153.

Elephant, blue, I. 9 ; counterfeit, I. 10, 33 ; infuriated, I. 26 ; pawned, I. 30 ; excited, I. 88 ; II. 64, 66, 67 ; stable, II. 82.

Fire shrine, I. 24, 28.
Flame of the Forest. I. 112.

Gambling Hall, I. 116.
Gatehouse, II. 18, 168.
gāvaḥ, kine or regions, I. 35 n.
Ghoshavatī, I. 21, 64, 65.
guṇa-sañgrahe, II. 123.

Hall, II. 98.
Hastināpura, II. 12.
hāṭaka, II. 47 n.
hetu, II. 81 n.

indrapatha, II. 82 n.

kadamba, II. 44 n.
kalatram, II. 68 n.

Kāmboja horses, II. 36.
kaṇaya, II. 47 n.
karkaṭaka, II. 82 n.
Kauśāmbī = Kosam, I. 1, 7.
kurarī, I. 34.

Lake (Royal), II. 94.
Lattice window, II. 83.
Lāvāṇaka, I, 44, 59.

mādhavī, I. 54 n.
maṇibhūmi, I. 50 n.
maṇibhūmika, I. 22 n.
Manu, I. 187.
Medhātithi, I. 187.
Middle Palace, I. 21.
Monkey-heads, II. 82 n.
moriṅga, I. 57.
Music, I. 89; II. 81.
Music lesson, I. 4, 18, 52 n., 67.

nālikā, II. 70 n., 155.
Nāndī, I. ix, note, 6, 40, &c.
Narrated fight, I. 10, 11, 126, 127, 136, 137, 191; II. 46-50, 149, 159, 172–74.
nicula, II. 94 n.
Night, I. 79, 89, 90; II. 80, 117.
nimbu, I. 96.
nīpa, II. 94 n.
nivāta, II. 24.

ovajjhai, I. 7.

Painted scroll, II. 6.
Painting on walls, I. 53.
— of Draupadī, II. 6–8.
— portraits, I. 4, 67 n., 68.
pāriveṣī, II. 50.
Park, II. 64, 66, 157–8.
Parrot cage, II. 78.
— starling, II. 95.
Pāṭaliputra, I. 86.
Peacocks' perches, I. 21.
piṅgala, II. 11.
plaintains, I. 112.
Plants and Flowers, *see* *Arjuna*, *Asana*, *Aśoka*, *Bakula*, *Campaka*, Coral tree, Flame of the Forest, *Kadamba*, *Mādhavī*, *Moriṅga*, *Nicula*, *Nimbu*, *Nīpa*, Pot-*palāśa*, *Saptacchada*, (*-parṇa*), *Sarala*, *Sarja*, *Seolī*, *Sāl*.
Portrait gallery, I. 172, 174.
Pot-*palāśa*, II. 133.
Pracetas, I. 187.
Prakrit, spoken by—
  Buddhist monk, I. 24 ff.
  Madman, I. 23 ff.
  Mendicant (Indra), II. 37.
prakṣepabhūmi, II. 93.
prastāvanā, II. 20.
pratāna (?), II. 83 n.
pratisarā, I. 7.
pratolī, II. 82 n.
pratyāśā, I. 8.
pulaka, II. 168.

Rājagṛiha, I. 41, 44.
raktapaṭa, II. 98 n.
Ring inscribed, II. 71.
River divided, II. 117.
Rogues' Hall, II. 81.

sāl trees, I. 10; II. 158.
samudragṛha, I. 58 n., 59, 61.
-gṛhaka, I. 167 n.
śāntigṛha, I. 15.
saptacchada, I. 54 n.
saptaparṇa, I. 197 n.
sarala, II. 94 n.
sarja, II. 94 n.
seolī, I. 51 n., 52 n., 54.
śilā, I. 69.
sopasnehatā, I. 173; II. 148 n.

Split verses:
Same speaker, I. 6 (verse 2); II. 74 (v. 6), 83 (v. 14).
Two speakers, I. 124 (v. 34 and 37), 166 (v. 31), 172 (v. 1), 176 (v. 14), 184 (v. 24), 200 (v. 14); II. 58 (v. 66), 108 (v. 21), 138 (v. 10).
Three speakers, II. 49 (v. 21), 172 (v. 1), 173 (v. 5).
śṛṅgāgrakoṭi, II. 130.
Stage, I. 159.
Statues, I. 174.
Statue gallery, I. 174.
sumana-varṇaka, II. 72.
sūta, I. 103 n.
sūtradhāra, II. 20 n.
śvapāka, II. 102 n.

Terrace (on roof), II. 94.
— market, II. 75, 97.
Tiring-room, I. 159.
Tortoise seat, II. 5.
Triads: Three Brahmans, I. 110–13.
— Three sons of old Brahman, I. 145 ff.
Triads: Three soldiers, II. 46–50.
— Three fairies, II. 172–75.

ucchiṣṭa, II. 95 n.
udagra, II, 149.
Udayana, I. 1 ff.
Ujjain, I. 1 ff., 86.

varaṇḍī, I. 74.
Viniṣkuṭa, II. 153.
Voice described, I. 180.
— singer's, I. 89; II. 81.

Watch towers, II. 82.
Water for vow or solemn act, I. 14, 134; II. 12.
— for purification, II. 119, 152.
— for feet, I. 90, 187; II. 15, 104, 140.
— for tears, I. 57, 116, 161, 183.
Water divided, II. 117, 166.
Wedding paint, II. 79.
Wooden pavilion, I. 53.
Women unveiled, I. 166 (? I. 69); young girl, I. 26.